MW01221655

Gestures of Conciliation

Also by Christopher Mitchell

HANDBOOK OF CONFLICT RESOLUTION (*with Michael Banks*)

INTERNATIONAL RELATIONS THEORY: A Bibliography (*with A. J. R. Groom*)

IN THE AFTERMATH: Anglo-Argentine Relations since the War for the Falklands–Malvinas Islands (*with Walter Little*)

NEW APPROACHES TO MEDIATION (*with Keith Webb*)

PEACEMAKING AND THE CONSULTANT'S ROLE

THE STRUCTURE OF INTERNATIONAL CONFLICT

Gestures of Conciliation

Factors Contributing to Successful Olive Branches

Christopher Mitchell
Drucie French-Cumbie Professor of Conflict Analysis and Resolution
Institute for Conflict Analysis and Resolution
George Mason University
Fairfax
USA

First published in Great Britain 2000 by
MACMILLAN PRESS LTD
Houndmills, Basingstoke, Hampshire RG21 6XS and London
Companies and representatives throughout the world

A catalogue record for this book is available from the British Library.

ISBN 0–333–47433–3

 First published in the United States of America 2000 by
ST. MARTIN'S PRESS, INC.,
Scholarly and Reference Division,
175 Fifth Avenue, New York, N.Y. 10010

ISBN 0–312–23052–4

Library of Congress Cataloging-in-Publication Data
Mitchell, C. R. (Christopher Roger), 1934–
Gestures of conciliation : factors contributing to successful olive branches /
Christopher Mitchell.
     p.   cm.
Includes bibliographical references and index.
ISBN 0–312–23052–4 (cloth)
1. Conflict management. 2. Mediation, International. I. Title.
HM1126 .M57   1999
303.6'9 — dc21
                                                              99–049412

This book is printed on paper suitable for recycling and made from fully managed and sustained
forest sources.

10   9   8   7   6   5   4   3   2   1
09 08 07 06 05 04 03 02 01 00

Printed and bound in Great Britain by
Antony Rowe Ltd, Chippenham, Wiltshire

To Ed and Helen Lynch –
friends, and friends of
conflict resolution

Contents

List of Tables

List of Figures

Acknowledgements

A number of people and institutions have given me the time, space, resources and encouragement to continue to work on this book over the inordinate length of time it has taken me to complete it. John Burton, Ed Azar and their colleagues made me welcome at the Center for International Development and Conflict Management at the University of Maryland, and helped me start the work. Ray Hillam, Ladd Hollist and other friends at the David M. Kennedy Center at Brigham Young University, Utah provided a stimulating context to continue developing initial ideas. All my colleagues at the Institute for Conflict Analysis and Resolution here at George Mason University tolerated my summer absences and escapes from the normal hurly burly while I worked on this or that chapter. Tim Farmiloe, my editor at Macmillan, showed admirable restraint over the non-delivery of the promised manuscript. I am very grateful to all of them.

In addition, I am more than grateful to my in-laws, Bernard and Elaine Brandchaft and to cousins Larry and Joan Jones for allowing Lois and me to spend a peaceful and productive time up at the Hollister Ranch near Gaviota completing the final draft and enjoying the quiet and the views of the Pacific.

More directly, I want to thank a number of people who have helped me with specific parts of the work. It was very kind of my friends Hal Saunders and Taseen Bashir to spend time reading the sections dealing with President Sadat's thoughts, actions and policies and correcting my errors. Similarly, I benefited greatly from Shimon Shamir's knowledge and advice about Israeli reactions to Anwar Sadat and his initiatives. At ICAR, Mohammed Abu Nimir helped with the initial analysis of regional information about events in 1977 and Josh Weiss with producing more comprehensible diagrams and figures. Dan Druckman, Howon Jeong and Susan Allen Nan went through versions of sundry chapters and saved me from error and incoherence – at least as far as they were able. Finally, my wife read through the whole of the final manuscript and helped me make arguments clearer, examples more relevant and the whole work more tightly structured. As Lois had been putting up with me and the book for several years, this was help 'above and beyond', and I am not sure how I will be able to repay her time or tolerance.

Ultimately, the responsibility for the work, warts and all, is mine but I hope that it might serve the purpose of increasing our understanding of how and why some conflicts come to an end and others drag on seemingly without a solution – or, at least, of opening up some avenues of thought about such matters along which other scholars can travel.

Institute for Conflict Analysis and Resolution　　　　CHRISTOPHER MITCHELL
George Mason University
Virginia

The author and publishers are grateful to EMI Publishing Ltd, London WC2H OEA, for permission to reproduce copyright material from 'A Puzzlement', words and music by Richard Rodgers and Oscar Hammerstein II © 1951, Williamson Music International, USA.

CONCILIATE vb. [L. *conciliatus* pp. of *conciliare* to assemble, unite, win over] vt. 1. to gain (as goodwill) by pleasing acts 2. to make compatible; reconcile 3. to gain the good will or favor of.

Webster's 7th New Collegiate Dictionary

CONCILIATE vt. win over from anger or lasting hostility; win good will of; reconcile (disagreeing) parties.

Pocket Oxford Dictionary

CONCILIATION n 1. the action of bringing into harmony; harmonising, reconcilement: 2. The gaining or winning by quiet means: 3. Peaceable or friendly union: 4a. Conversion from a state of hostility or distrust; the promotion of goodwill by kind and considerate measures; the exhibition of a spirit of amity, practice of conciliatory measures ...

Oxford English Dictionary

Prologue: The Sadat Initiatives

Whatever might have been the intermediate effects or the long-term outcome, it was generally agreed at the time that President Sadat's action in visiting Israel on 19 November 1977 marked a major turning point in de-escalating the conflict between Israel, Egypt as leader of the Arab states, and – more indirectly – the Palestinians. Subsequent analysis has tended to date the beginnings of a successful Middle East 'peace process' from that event.

Contemporary reactions to 'the Sadat initiative' clustered about two extremes. On the one hand, it was denounced by Egypt's Arab allies and clients as a surrender to the Israeli adversary which could only set-back Arab and Palestinian causes. Both the Libyan and Iraqi governments were swift in their denunciation of Sadat's move, the former characterising even the proposal of a visit as 'the regretable and dramatic collapse of Arab confrontation against the Zionist enemy',[1] while at a UN debate on the Middle East held the day following the ending of the visit, the Syrian ambassador described the move, almost inevitably, as 'a stab in the back of the Arab people', thus occasioning an unprecedented walk-out by the Egyptian delegation. Both Al Fatah and the PFLP headed the chorus of condemnation, the latter talking about 'a flagrant defiance of Arab popular and official will' and the former rather more passionately of 'an imperialist, Zionist and reactionary conspiracy to liquidate the Palestine people's cause'. Soviet reactions were more muted but equally unenthusiastic.

Elsewhere, Sadat's visit was viewed more positively. President Carter greeted the announcement of the visit with expressions such as 'unprecedented', 'very courageous', 'constructive' and 'a step in the right direction' and later described the visit itself 'as a great occasion', commenting further that 'it was just the reluctance of leaders to take this momentous step that was an obstacle'. The nine members of the European Community (with some reluctance on the part of the French Government) adopted a resolution praising Sadat's visit to Jerusalem as a 'courageous initiative'.

Most importantly, from Sadat's own viewpoint, the offer and the visit were seen in Israel as constituting an undeniable gesture of conciliation and a major breakthrough in Israeli–Egyptian relations. Publicly, the President's visit was greeted with a kind of stunned disbelief, turning to enthusiasm and hope. In the words of three Israeli journalists, 'Euphoria reigned' (Haber, Schiff & Yaari, 1979). The appearance of Sadat in person – at the airport, in the Knesset, with Israeli leaders, at the mosque in Jerusalem – seemed an undeniable symbol of change and the start of a real opportunity for genuine reconciliation. This impression was in no way lessened by the tough statement that Sadat made to the Knesset. In Israeli government circles there was also a sense that this move of Sadat's marked a genuine turning point. Moshe Dayan recalls that Prime Minister Begin, having pondered Sadat's 'true intentions', concluded that the visit would mark 'a first step on the march to peace and ... an act of historic import-ance' (Dayan 1981 p.76). Even Moshe Dayan himself, who feared that the Egyptians would anticipate a reciprocal 'unprecedented gesture' from Israel, felt that Sadat's action indicated the genuine interest in peace that he claimed to have detected since the ending of the 1973 War (Ibid.).

1   The visit as 'grand gesture'

While reactions to Sadat's move varied widely, depending upon whether it was perceived positively, as a move towards a settlement of long-standing conflicts in the Middle East, or negatively, as a 'sell out' by the leading Arab power in the region, all reactions had certain characteristics in common. Whether one approved of it or not, Sadat's move was generally perceived as dramatic, as unprecedented and as undeniably marking a profound change in Egyptian attitudes and policies towards the main target of the gesture, Israel. Whether one viewed the visit as a concession or as a surrender, there could be no mistaking the fact that it was a major concession – or a major surrender. Sadat, whatever he was perceived as having done, had not done anything by halves.

From his own viewpoint, there can be little doubt that Sadat intended the offer and the visit to be a major gesture of conciliation towards his adver-saries in Israel. Moreover, it was generally perceived as such by those within the target of his gesture, although there were some, such as Dayan, who were sceptical about the substance behind the move. Thus, in the case of Sadat's visit to Jerusalem, we have an example of what one academic observer has termed the 'grand gesture' (Kriesberg 1984 p.483). Moreover, we also have a case of a clear conciliatory move where the intention of the initiator (Sadat) was matched by the perception of the target (Israeli decision-makers and public). For those interested in the beginnings of peace processes and success-ful gestures of conciliation Sadat's visit to Jerusalem seems to provide the par-adigm case of an undeniable gesture of conciliation that started (or, perhaps, re-started) a de-escalatory spiral between Israel and Egypt which, in turn, concluded in the Israeli–Egyptian Peace Treaty signed in 1979.

2   The characteristics of 'conciliation'

At first sight, this argument seems trivial in the extreme. The Sadat initia-tive was so obviously a conciliatory gesture (accepted as such by actor, target and observers – both hostile and friendly – at the time and since) that saying so yet again is both banal and stultifying. Yet, one might ask, why was it so undeniably a *conciliatory* gesture? What characteristics might be found in the Sadat initiative of November 1977 that made that action (and, presumably, other actions sharing those same characteristics) so clearly conciliatory to both targets and observers?

Given that Sadat's visit to Israel seems so universally accepted as an undeniable 'conciliatory gesture', as well as being the start of a major de-escalation process between two adversaries locked in a protracted conflict, it clearly embodies in itself more general lessons for the initiation and, perhaps, maintenance of long-term 'peace processes'. If we are interested in the nature of conciliatory gestures or the beginnings of successful concili-ation processes, then one way of analysing such phenomena is to analyse such an episode and use it to clarify the essential nature of conciliatory actions and concessions.

Alternatively, one can adopt a broader strategy and examine both suc-cessful and unsuccesful initiatives in a comparative fashion. Much can be learned from other actions which may have been intended as conciliatory but which were apparently less obviously so (because they were either not perceived as such by target or observers, or were rejected by the former). In such cases, our question becomes slightly different, although posed within the same framework: what essential characteristics were absent from these initiatives, so that they were *not* recognised as a 'genuine' conciliatory gesture by the target, or were treated with a level of disbelieving scepticism absent from the evaluation of Sadat's move in 1977?

Put slightly differently, can one suggest a model in which intended con-ciliatory gestures fall somewhere along a spectrum of credibility, running from gestures which were undeniably intended as conciliatory and recog-nised as such (Sadat's visit), through those which were (at best) ambiguous, to those which are clearly so incredible to their targets that they are wholly discounted and ignored? Key questions raised by such a model might be, firstly, what determines where a particular de-escalatory initiative falls on this 'continuum of credibility' and, secondly, are there any qualities or characteristics of de-escalatory initiatives that invariably determine the answer to the first question?

This last query implies the possibility of some form of measurement, but the idea can be expressed simply through the concept of ordinality. The Sadat visit was obviously highly *likely* to be perceived and treated as a gen-uinely conciliatory gesture. Which types of action are somewhat less likely to be so treated, which much less likely, and which so unlikely as to be almost not worth the effort, always provided the actor's intention is, in fact, to make a genuine gesture of conciliation towards an adversary?

3   Sadat's previous conciliatory gestures

These questions are neither trivial in a general sense, nor entirely uncon-nected with Sadat's successful initiative in November 1977. While Sadat's action in visiting Israel, and that move's resultant breakthrough, are well known, less well known is the series of previous conciliatory gestures made by Sadat in the preceding seven years from the time he succeeded President Nasser. None of these were nearly as successful in achieving credibility as his triumph in Israel in 1977, so that it is worth asking how they differed from the latter in some (as yet unidentified) key respects. What did previous gestures lack compared with the November 1977 initiative and what might a comparison of Sadat's previous (and relatively unsuccessful) efforts tell us about the nature of conciliatory gestures in general as a preliminary to a theoretical examination of the process of conciliation and conflict resolution?

With these questions in mind, the main purpose of this present study is to analyse the nature and likely effects of *gestures of conciliation* – that is, the first moves in major efforts to bring about the peaceful resolution of protracted conflicts in which adversaries have become enmeshed, and for which no generally acceptable solution appears possible. The literature on diplomacy has many terms to describe such initiatives – 'peace feelers', 'trial balloons', 'olive branches' – and it will be necessary later to discuss the distinctions (if any) between the various forms of conciliatory gestures described in this literature. In tackling this subject, the study will use President Sadat's efforts between 1971 and 1977 as an intellectual 'launching pad' to develop a conceptual framework within which to analyse the general topic of initiating peace processes and what factors might affect the relative success of various kinds of initiatory move. The study will start, therefore, with the reality of Egyptian–Israeli peacemaking efforts in the 1970s and then move to more general considerations of launching and maintaining peace processes.

The first two chapters describe a number of other 'peace initiatives' undertaken by Sadat before his famous breakthrough via the trip to Jerusalem. None of these were as successful as the latter but all were, it appears, quite genuinely intended as some kind of conciliatory signal to Israeli decision-makers. The list includes Sadat's acceptance of the Jarring proposals and his own proposal for a limited withdrawal from the Suez Canal in 1971; his actions prior to and immediately following the ending of the 1973 War; his re-opening of the Suez Canal in 1975; and, finally, an account of the events leading up to the Jerusalem visit and its acceleration of the peace process. In each of these cases, I will briefly examine the nature of the initiative itself; the intentions of Sadat as 'Initiator' of such a gesture; the context within which the initiative took place; the interpretations and evaluations of the initiative by the 'Target'; and the target's reactions, if any, to the initiative.

4   Action or reaction?

One point needs to be clarified before embarking upon this brief review. Concentrating upon Sadat's initiatives will inevitably give the impression that the Israeli role during this period was largely reactive and that they undertook no initiatives themselves. This is not the case. Indeed, when dealing with any long-drawn-out and inter-connected peace process, it is somewhat arbitrary to say what is action and what reaction, or to judge who is reacting to whom or what. It is the case that the various Israeli governments undertook a number of initiatives and sent a significant number of signals themselves during the period 1971–7.[2] For example, during the early months of 1971, the first period examined in Chapter 1, the Israeli Government, having (on 28 December 1970) ended its boycott of the Jarring Mission without a prior Egyptian withdrawal of the disputed missile defences, launched its own 14-point peace plan. Later that year, on 19 April, having rejected Sadat's 4 February proposals, the Israelis submitted to the US Government a plan for an interim settlement and the re-opening of the Canal. A month later, Mordechai Gazit reports that Mrs Meir, the Israeli Prime Minister asked Secretary of State Rogers to arrange for her to meet Sadat in person (Gazit 1983, p.14). None of these initiatives produced any major results, but that they were undertaken indicates that the Israeli Government was not content merely to respond.

However, it does seem to be the case that, on balance, Sadat led the way in initiating moves and putting forward plans and suggestions during the period under analysis. This should not be surprising either empirically or theoretically. Iklé has pointed out that, in any situation involving parties bargaining over acceptable change, the adversaries will often be classifiable as a pro-change and a pro-status-quo party, the latter being more or less content with the existing situation – or, at least, being able to live with it – while the former seeks alteration in some redistributive fashion (Iklé 1989). In long-drawn-out conflicts, of course, the roles of pro-change and pro-status-quo parties can alter, depending upon how the conflict develops. In such a relationship, it will usually be the pro-change party that 'makes the running', putting forward suggestions, making demands, agitating for (usually conditional) negotiations and appealing to others to help bring a little movement into the situation.

It certainly seems to have been the case that this type of situation existed in the Middle East following the 1967 War. Israel was in a position to wait for the Arab governments to make an acceptable offer that would change the post-war situation of advantage which Israeli arms had gained. While the situation following the June War was certainly not ideal for Israel, it was acceptable, far better than the pre-1967 situation, and could be lived with. Israel had no need to accept any change that offered a less satisfactory situation and could wait for others to make offers which could be rejected if unsatisfactory.

Moreover, the changes in Israeli domestic politics from 1971 (Mrs Meir's Labour Alliance Government) to November 1977 (Mr Begin's Likud Government) made it more likely that Israel's posture would be reactive rather than initiatory as far as key foreign policy issues were concerned. Both this factor and the status-quo stance of Israel's external relations provide some explanation as to why the period in question shows a greater weight of activity in search of change from the Egyptian side than from the Israeli.[3]

With this *caveat* in mind, I will now turn to a brief examination of two sets of relatively unsuccessful conciliatory initiatives undertaken by Anwar al Sadat during the early years of his presidency – years when Sadat was still, to some degree, living in the shadow of his predecessor, from which he only managed to free himself following the October 1973 War and its aftermath.

1
Frustration and War: 1970–1973

It has become conventional to assume that what later became known as 'the peace process' in the Middle East only developed seriously after the 1973 War. Then, President Sadat's sudden strike across the Suez Canal and the ceasefire in a position of stalemate gave both Israel and Egypt an interest in a better post-war arrangement and the USA an opportunity to intervene productively to help arrange a more stable relationship between the two adversaries. Abba Eban, in his autobiography, even refers to the period from Sadat's accession to power to 1973 as 'the twilight years' (Eban 1977, p.471).

However, even during this pre-war period it can be seen that Sadat made a number of efforts to signal a willingness to negotiate with the Israelis, and he himself implies that he only gave up efforts to de-escalate and negotiate once his early conciliatory gestures had come to nothing and the 'year of decision' had passed in anticlimax. It is also true that much of the latter part of the period was spent, quite deliberately, in preparing for the attack which eventually took place in October 1973. However, this is not necessarily inconsistent with the simultaneous use of conciliatory gestures. Sadat appears to have been attempting to keep options open.

It should also be recalled that the war of October 1973 was, for Egypt and Sadat, essentially a limited, 'political' war, as well as being a 'psychological' one in its impact. While not necessarily being wholly accurate when he told the People's Council on 16 December 1973 that 'We have fought for peace', nonetheless it is true that Sadat made strenuous efforts to use the stalemated outcome of the war and to involve the US rapidly in a peace process, the goal of which was – at least partly – to restore Egyptian territory conquered in 1967. Thus, both before and after this 'political' war, Sadat signalled a willingness to conciliate and make concessions in the hope of initiating a successful process leading towards an agreement.

1   'The twilight years': 1970–1973

Sadat's first set of initiatives came in what, for the Israelis, must have been a somewhat confusing, multiple package of actions. These began at the start of 1971, three months after the death of Nasser, and took place during the last phase of Ambassador Jarring's effort to salvage his own, UN-initiated mediation mission. In this latter instance, the Jarring process could be said to have re-started with an Israeli action, made rather reluctantly and, according to Gideon Rafael (1981, pp.252–3), in the hope, at least on the part of the Israeli Prime Minister, that it would be rejected. Having refused to allow the Jarring mission to resume until Egyptian violations of the August 1970 ceasefire had been investigated and rectified, Mrs Meir's government relented and issued a formal invitation to the Ambassador to resume his mission. He arrived in Jerusalem on 8 January 1971. Thus the context for Sadat's earliest initiatives involved an on-going mediation process and an Israeli concession, both played out against the background of a temporary lull in the so-called 'Canal War'.

1.1   Renewing the Jarring initiative

Sadat's first public initiative at this point was to agree to renew the cease-fire for another month, which he did on 4 February, two days before the ending of the 90-day deadline. His offer came three days *before* Jarring, in a surprise move of his own, presented identical memoranda to the Israeli and Egyptian UN delegates outlining his own proposals for a solution to the outstanding issues between them. (The proposal was a blend of Egyptian and Israeli ideas culled from position papers presented to the mediator by the two governments during January.) The Jarring initiative was unexpected and irritating to the Israeli government, particularly in respect of his request for 'parallel and simultaneous commitments' from the two governments in order to obtain a peace settlement. In addition, the memorandum called for a full Israeli withdrawal from all Egyptian territory in exchange for a peace agreement and an end to all belligerency between the two countries.

One of the interesting aspects of the Jarring memorandum was Sadat's public response to it. On 14 February, the Egyptian government confirmed its acceptance of the undertakings in the memorandum, declaring that 'Egypt will be ready to enter into a peace agreement with Israel, containing all the aforementioned obligations as provided for in Security Council Resolution 242'.[1] Although perceptions in Israeli decision-making circles seem to have been that this response was made partly as a result of US advice and pressure (Rafael 1981, p.255), it was recognised at the time that this was a major concession on the part of the Egyptians. Rafael describes it as 'far reaching development' and states clearly that the Israelis were 'considerably impressed'. For the first time 'the government of an Arab State had publicly announced its readiness to sign a peace agreement with Israel in an official document' (ibid. p.256). The action was, on this occasion, clearly recognised by Israeli decision-makers as a conciliatory gesture and a not-inconsiderable one.

Unfortunately, recognising an action as conciliatory is a necessary but not a sufficient condition for a target to contribute to a benign spiral of interaction. On this occasion, the Israeli reply to Jarring's memorandum was both delayed and, when it emerged from a protracted and divided cabinet discussion, uncompromising. To an initially flexible Israeli statement on secure, recognised and agreed boundaries between the two countries, hardliners in the cabinet added the intransigent rider: 'Israel will not withdraw to the pre-5 June 1967 lines.' As Rafael himself states, key Israeli leaders had decided that the risks of a peace settlement outweighed its benefits (ibid. p.257). The continuing chasm between Israeli and Egyptian bargaining positions seemed unbridgeable to Jarring. He returned to his post as Swedish Ambassador to the Soviet Union on 25 March, his mediatory initiative at an end.

1.2   Sadat's Suez initiative and Israel's reception

Well before the termination of this final episode in the UN mediation effort, however, Sadat had launched his own, separate initiative towards the Israelis. The basic proposal, made on 4 February in the same speech to the Egyptian National Assembly in which he announced the extension of the cease fire, was for a partial withdrawal of Israeli troops into Sinai and the re-opening of the Suez Canal. Again, it is not wholly clear where the germ of the idea for this conciliatory move originated. For some time, Moshe Dyan had been discussing such a partial withdrawal of the IDF from Suez to a new ceasefire line nearer the Mitla and Gidi passes. This would take the troops away from the canal line, which put Israel into direct confrontation with countries wishing to use the Suez route, quite apart from Israel's Arab adversaries. Eban recalls that this idea was discussed in Washington in January 1971 (Eban 1977, p.472), while others state that it was afforded a cool reception there (Aronson 1978, p.141).

What is certain is that in early January 1971 a close friend of President Sadat had approached the US representative in Cairo to discover whether Israel would be interested in an Egyptian proposal, based upon Dayan's scheme, for a partial withdrawal from the Suez Canal and its subsequent re-opening.[2] The enquiry had been passed back to Washington and thence to Israeli Ambassador Rabin.

The initial Israeli reaction to this indirect and informal initiative from Sadat was to stall. The Israeli government was by no means sure that their US patrons wanted the Canal open, thus facilitating Soviet cargoes en route to Vietnam. Prime Minister Meir interpreted Sadat's offer as the initiation of some form of 'salami tactics' – obtaining sequential, small concessions, little by little, until a great deal has been gained (Ikle 1989) – with Israel gradually being forced to withdraw to the 1967 international boundary without gaining a peace treaty in return (Rafael 1981, p.258). However, on 4 February President Sadat made his offer public in the speech to the

National Assembly in which he accepted a continuation of the ceasefire and characterised his own proposal as an initiative designed to help Jarring's indirect negotiations.

Moreover, Sadat followed up his public announcement in a variety of ways. Firstly, he sent a message to the State Department for onward transmission to Jerusalem emphasising the seriousness of his offer and his intentions (ibid. p.259). Then, after Mrs Meir had given a guarded welcome to the initiative in the Knesset on 9 February, Sadat gave an interview in *Newsweek*, during which he made public further details of his proposals and his longer-term vision of a sustained de-escalation and negotiation process. The public Israeli reaction was to urge Sadat to look more closely at Mrs Meir's Knesset statement, which had indicated a willingness to assist in the re-opening of the Canal and in reducing tensions in the area.

At the public level, Sadat reiterated his proposal again on 1st April (by which time the Jarring initiative had finally come to an end), emphasising that the proposed partial withdrawal was not to be seen as a separate settlement but an 'operative move' linked to a final settlement based upon Resolution 242. The Israelis would withdraw, Egyptian armed forces would cross the Canal, the ceasefire would be extended to enable Jarring to resume the search for a general settlement, and Egypt would begin to clear the Canal. By this time, the public Israeli position had hardened against Sadat's initiative and his linking the move to a final settlement probably reinforced this trend. Mrs Meir formally rebuffed the proposal on 4 April, and tough statements were also made prior to that by Deputy Prime Minister Allon and by Israel Galili.

Two weeks later, on 19 April, the Israeli Government put forward to the USA its own proposals for an interim peace arrangement with Egypt. These included an Israeli withdrawal to an unspecified distance from the Canal *after* it had been cleared and opened for international shipping, in return for an Egyptian guarantee of non-belligerence and an understanding that any interim agreement would be quite separate from the search for a final settlement and a peace treaty. The Israelis were also adamant that no Egyptian military forces would be allowed on the eastern bank of the Canal.

The triangular bargaining among Egypt, Israel and the USA continued until the end of 1971 (when it was overtaken by US–Soviet efforts to develop a formula for settlement), although the initiative for a partial withdrawal was really dead by July 1971, when US Assistant Secretary of State, Joseph Sisco, visited Israel. It broke down over the issues of the distance of Israeli withdrawal, the linkage of a partial settlement to a final peace treaty and the presence of Egyptian forces (or 'armed police') on the eastern side of the Canal (Raphael 1981, pp.264–72; Rabin 1979, pp.195–201). Looking back at the end of 1971, his 'year of decision', Sadat reflected rather bitterly: 'we are back where we started eight months ago ... have lost almost a year ... and the whole story has ended very sadly' (Israeli 1978, p.130).

However, while this particular de-escalatory spiral did not lead to any form of final negotiation, the initiative taken by Sadat can be said to have had some effects in moving Egyptian–Israeli relations into a new phase. Paradoxically, this is implied by Abba Eban who, reflecting on the Israeli Cabinet discussions and decision taken in March 1971 to accept the principle of a partial withdrawal in return for something less than a full peace,[3] argues that, from that point, 'a new era in Middle Eastern diplomacy began. The concept of a partial, interim settlement replaced the previous "all or nothing" approach to peace' (Eban 1977, pp.274–5).

1.3   Reactions and results

It is worth considering briefly why this particular conciliatory effort broke down, a breakdown leading, by the summer of 1972, to a situation where, in Eban's words, all 'political activity concerning the Middle East Conflict was now suspended ' (ibid. p.480), the immediately preceding initiatives having come from the USSR and the USA and from the African Presidents' peacemaking mission to the Middle East. As I noted above, Israeli reaction to Sadat's moves tended, initially at least, to be positive. Egyptian moves were perceived and defined as conciliatory gestures, even if of a rather limited nature, both by the Israelis and by US decision-makers – more so, inevitably, by the latter (Kissinger 1979, p.1279).

Several reasons may be suggested. The first is that the initiatives sent somewhat confusing signals to Israeli decision-makers because they occurred at the same time as a major initiative from the UN mediator himself and thus were difficult to disentangle from that process. Israeli decision-makers had to deal with new inputs coming from a variety of sources and to make sense out of a pattern of signals even more ambiguous than normal. The crucial problem seems to have been the confusing relationship between a partial, interim settlement suggested by Sadat, and a final peace settlement being pursued by Jarring. This confusion seems to have been crucial given the virtually simultaneous start of both initiatives. Just as Sadat seemed willing to talk about a partial settlement, Jarring raised questions of complete Israeli withdrawal and a final peace settlement, thus drawing Israeli attention away from the idea of a limited withdrawal and back to the problems of a comprehensive settlement. Mordechai Gazit, in his account of Israeli policy during this period, points out that Mrs Meir's Knesset response to Sadat's initiative was made on 9 February, only one day after the delivery of the Jarring memorandum and describes the latter as a move 'torpedoing Sadat's proposal by its attempt to return the discussion to the arid pursuit of a general, comprehensive settlement which had eluded the parties since 1967' (Gazit 1983, p.84).

Moreover, Sadat later reverted to linking the idea of a partial settlement to a Jarring-inspired final settlement, just at the time when Mrs Meir seemed on the verge of being willing to accept the idea of a partial settlement not linked to a final, satisfactory (to Israel) peace treaty.[4] This process of swinging between a separate partial settlement and a linked partial settlement undoubtedly made less probable the achievement of either. Henry Kissinger, at that time National Security adviser to President Nixon, says flatly 'Disengagement had no chance of success as long as it had to be negotiated together with an overall settlement' (Kissinger 1979, p.1281).

A second reason seems to have been that many Israeli decision-makers viewed Sadat's offers as less than credible because of their perception that he was responding to US – and particularly State Department – influence. In short, the proffered concessions were not to be relied upon because, to some degree, they were the result of collusion between Egypt and a rather naive sector of the US Government. This impression was probably reinforced by the 'Bergus Memorandum' affair[5] and by Sadat's apparent ability to over-impress – in Israeli eyes – Secretary of State Rogers and Joseph Sisco with his flexibility, reason and desire for a settlement (Rafael 1981; Rabin 1979).

Thirdly, there was the clear perception on the part of many Israeli leaders that Sadat was offering concessions not merely under pressure but also as a way of improving his own position both militarily and diplomatically. Militarily, in the sense that he was trying to get a force over the Canal and get the Israelis to withdraw so far that they would not be able to 'shoot their way back to the Canal' if things went wrong. Diplomatically, in that he was using a 'thin end of the wedge' strategy in that, having obtained a limited withdrawal from Israel as part of an interim settlement, he could use that precedent as a way of pushing it back to the June 1967 boundaries bit by bit, without ever offering a comprehensive peace settlement. Increasingly, in Israeli eyes, Sadat was merely offering 'an empty word ('salaam') for Israeli real estate' (Aronson 1978, p.143).

Another view, outlined by Gazit, was that Sadat's offer and its subsequent elaboration merely represented a tactical ploy to begin a process that would lead to final Israeli withdrawal from all the territories conquered in 1967. Gazit quotes as damning Sadat's MENA interview of 1 April 1971, during which the latter emphasised that the partial withdrawal would be neither a partial nor a separate settlement, 'but merely an operative move that is linked to the [final] solution, on the basis of the Security Council Resolution which provides ... for Israeli withdrawal from all Arab lands occupied after June 5, 1967' (Gazit 1983, p.85).

Fourthly, there was the fact that Israeli decision-makers themselves were fundamentally divided about the risks and potential costs involved in agreeing to a partial withdrawal. Both Dayan and Rabin at various stages of the process offered greater concessions (in terms of distance of withdrawal and acceptance of Egyptian military presence on the Canal's east bank) to US diplomats. However, these concessions were offered off the record and informally, and never became official Israeli offers, as disagreements within the Israeli Cabinet ended with the Prime Minister's more uncompomising line being adopted, with little debate on the issue (Eban 1977; Rabin 1979; and Rafael 1981). While some Israeli leaders wanted to take a risk and respond, others held their more conciliatory colleagues back.

Finally, there was the simple fact that, after his initial conciliatory gesture, Sadat was never able or willing to offer enough to the harder-line Israelis to persuade them to concede what he wanted. The inertial power of the Israeli's then-dominant position demanded greater temptations to move, and – in 1971 – Sadat was not in a position to supply those temptations and to undermine the status quo. Hence, his gestures were perceived and evaluated as concessions by their target, but were not sufficient to sustain a continuously benign process. Many Israeli decision-makers were unable to rid themselves of the perception that a partial, interim agreement was either being offered as a *substitute* for a satisfactory, lasting peace settlement or was merely the first stage of a 'slice by slice' approach that would end by depriving them of the fruits of their 1967 victory.

Moreover, there appear to have been serious doubts in Israel about whether Sadat would have been in a position to 'deliver' any 'serious' concessions that could have led to any negotiated settlement. Sadat was newly in power. He had to contend with serious internal rivals and it was not until mid-May 1971 that he felt secure enough to purge the Ali Sabri group. 'We can never know', argues Gazit, 'whether Sadat had the power in 1971 … to make the concessions that were needed if there were to be serious negotiations' (Gazit 1983, p.84). The issue was never put to the test.[6]

2 Aftermath: October to December 1973

Sadat's initial efforts to begin a conciliation process in 1971 had taken place against a background of a renewed peacemaking effort by the UN, a recently concluded (and disputed) ceasefire and, most importantly, Israeli diplomatic inertia, brought about by the existence of a moderately acceptable status quo. Moreover, Sadat's own political position was unsure in that his survival as President was seen as problematical both by Israeli and US leaders. Relations with the latter were also tenuous and uncertain, a situation based upon US perceptions of a close client–patron relationship with the USSR and worsened by the conclusion of the Soviet–Egyptian Treaty of Friendship and Cooperation signed by Sadat in May 1971.

2.1 The post-war context

By the second half of October 1973, the whole situation had changed drastically and irreversibly. The October War had been fought to the uneasy (and possibly temporary) ceasefire finally achieved on 24 October. Whatever the military situation on that date, there could be no doubt that the structure of political relations in the Middle East had been fundamentally altered by the successful Egyptian assault across the Canal; by the realisation on the part of both Israel's and Egypt's patrons that a Middle East conflict could lead to a nuclear confrontation, so that it was dangerous to neglect any conflicts in the region; and by the Israeli re-perception of their increased vulnerability and the dangers of a status-quo stance and reactive strategy in external affairs.[7] Thus, while any de-escalatory spiral (or individual conciliatory initiatives) had to take place against a background of heightened military tension and suspicion and to deal initially with issues of military disengagement, the broader political contours were relatively favourable to such processes. Movement in the peace process was, paradoxically, more likely than in 1971, as both Egypt and Israel now found themselves in a situation that both wished to change, so that neither could be regarded as a status-quo party.

Against such a background, two major features stood out as likely to affect the nature of any conciliatory gestures made by the Egyptian side. The first was that, by the end of the actual fighting, Sadat was hardly the actor most likely to initiate moves to begin or maintain any de-escalatory spiral. In one paradoxical sense, Sadat had made his initiatory move by starting the October War and launching his assault across the Canal. In retrospect, it is clear that, whatever Sadat's intentions (and there is considerable evidence that he saw himself as upsetting an unsatisfactory status quo not to achieve a complete 'victory' but to move towards a negotiated settlement by redressing the strategic imbalance), the result of the October War was to break an *impasse* and re-start a process of diplomatic bargaining that had been basically deadlocked since he came to power in 1970. One major effect was to engage the USA far more directly and deeply in the central Middle East conflict, so that the US Government became an important source of initiatives and diplomatic activity, proposing disengagement plans, engaging in shuttle diplomacy, offering mediatory services and rewards, and generally pushing forward the peace process in the region. By the start of 1974, the USA (in spite of the effects of the Watergate affair) began to dominate bargaining and diplomacy in the aftermath of the war, and played the major role in shaping relationships between Israel and Egypt.

The second and more immediate feature arose from the military situation at the time of the ceasefire. On the Canal front, both Israeli and Egyptian forces were inextricably mixed together in confusing and potentially dangerous positions (as opposed to the neat separation that had existed at the ending of the Six Day War). The Egyptian Third Army was perilously cut off on the eastern bank of the Canal. Inevitably, this meant that the first stages of any de-escalatory process had to involve some disentanglement of forces, so that initiatives and proposals would involve issues of gradual disengagement to less explosive positions. Moreover, given the position of the Third Army, it was also inevitable that any concessions made by Sadat in the immediate aftermath of the fighting would be the result of the vulnerability of the Third Army and would appear to be (and probably would be) coerced.

Both of these features made it likely that Sadat's behaviour during this period would be *reactive* rather than *initiatory*, and that his room for major conciliatory gestures of the kind carried out previously and subsequently in 1977 would be limited. However, in spite of the features militating against any conciliatory initiatives by Sadat, particularly 'grand gestures', the period immediately after the ending of fighting on the Suez front does provide another example of the kinds of conciliatory initiative that Sadat could take, even in making the best of adverse circumstances.

2.2   Accepting face to face talks

Four instances of conciliatory gestures from Sadat during the period from late October to early December 1973 can be mentioned. The first of these involved Sadat's reluctant willingess to begin direct negotiations with the Israelis in the aftermath of the fighting, a situation which had not occurred since the negotiations on Rhodes to end the 1948/9 Arab–Israeli war, and even then not strictly on a 'face to face' basis. At one level, it could be argued that Sadat accepted the need to make this symbolic but, in Israeli eyes, important concession when he accepted Security Council Resolution 338 calling for the ceasefire that, by then, he desperately needed.

However, the agreement involving this concession did not actually come until some days later, when the ceasefire had finally been implemented and negotiations were going on through the USA and Dr Kissinger to bring medical and food supplies to the beleaguered Third Army. Not surprisingly, the Israeli leaders were using their stranglehold on the latter to extract concessions from Egypt regarding the disentanglement of both armies in the Suez front, while the USA was trying to arrange for the relief of the Third Army as part of Kissinger's strategy of maintaining the military stalemate at the end of the fighting. In the face of increasing US pressure to allow non-military re-supply of the Third Army, the Israeli government was stalling and hoping that time and hunger would result in the Third Army's complete disintegration. At this point Sadat offered to make arrangements to begin direct, face to face talks between the Israeli and Egyptian military commanders in the area regarding arrangements for disengagement.[8] The famous talks at Kilometre 101 resulted from this offer, a concession extracted because of the desperate condition of the Third Army, but one chosen by Sadat rather than the alternative of a military attempt to relieve that force. Whatever the Israeli reaction to this move, Kissinger appreciated its significance, emphasising that the start of the Kilometre 101 talks could and should be seen as a significant landmark in the move towards peace. 'Through our mediation, Israel was about to enter the first direct talks between Israeli and Arab representatives since the independence of Israel. It retained control over the access route to the Third Army … All this in

return for permitting one convoy of non-military supplies to pass'
(Kissinger 1982, p.610).

2.3   The issue of prisoners of war

The second conciliatory move made by Sadat in those early days following
the October War came about during the initial talks at Kilometre 101 and
concerned the issue of prisoners of war, always a sensitive subject to any
Israeli Government. In previous Arab–Israeli conflicts, the exchange of
prisoners of war, sometimes even information about who were prisoners
of war, had been used as a bargaining lever to obtain concessions from
Israel. Initially, this appeared likely to be the case in October 1973. On
28 October, Sadat decided to send his Deputy Foreign Minister, Ismail
Fahmy, to Washington as a preliminary to Dr Kissinger's proposed visit to
Egypt. There Fahmy produced a draft 'framework for negotiations' to be
reviewed by Kissinger. The framework included the following steps: (1)
Israel would withdraw to the 22 October ceasefire lines; (2) all prisoners of
war would be released; (3) Israel would then withdraw to a line east of the
Sinai passes while Egyptian troops remained in place; (4) UN forces would
be deployed between Egyptian and Israeli forces; (5) Egypt would lift the
blockade at Bab el Mandeb; (6) Egypt would begin to clear the Suez Canal;
(7) within an agreed time, Israel would withdraw to the international fron-
tier and belligerency would end (Fahmy 1983, p.36). The crucial initial
point in this framework was obviously that release of prisoners was conditional on an Israeli withdrawal to the positions occupied on 22 October.
Fahmy recalls that, in Washington, he was astonished to learn that the
super-Powers had agreed between themselves that there should be an
immediate exchange of prisoners and that the Soviet leaders had given the
USA a guarantee that the Egyptians would agree to exchange all prisoners
of war 'as soon as possible after the ceasefire became effective' (ibid. p.41).
He then told Kissinger that Sadat had not given such an assurance to the
Soviets.

   On this issue, however, Sadat was willing to make a conciliatory gesture.
The day after Fahmy's initial conversation with Kissinger, and without
informing Fahmy of his intention, Sadat instructed his delegation at the
Kilometre 101 talks to tell the Israeli military team that the Egyptians were
ready to exchange prisoners of war. The Egyptian government also
informed the Soviet ambassador in Cairo, while the Israelis informed
Kissinger, so that there could be no retraction of the offer. Fahmy recalls
that he was dismayed by the move, as, in his eyes, it gave away a major bargaining card[9] as well as seeming to show the USA 'that the Russians indeed
made decisions on Egypt's behalf. The Soviet Union had earlier guaranteed
that Egypt would accept an early exchange, and now Sadat appeared to be
complying with the Soviet decision' (ibid. p.45). He also seems sceptical of
the value of such concessions to the Israelis, taking the view that they

merely encouraged the Israelis to ask for more concessions before agreeing on other issues.

Whatever Fahmy's view of the initiative, it seems clear that Sadat's decision over the return of prisoners of war was another example of a conciliatory gesture, made to have an impact on the Israeli negotiating position. It was also intended to affect US perceptions of Egypt and of its leader, as one willing to pursue a new course towards a negotiated settlement, having taken military action to break a deadlock. That the gesture was made at the negotiations at Kilometre 101 was also significant. I argue later in this work that the *arena* for conciliatory gestures is an important element in the success or failure of an initiative and in this instance it contributed to an accelerating exchange of offers to which I will return below.

2.4   Return to the positions of 22 October

The third important concession agreed to by Sadat during this initial period of sparring about the disengagement process involved the whole thorny question of the ceasefire, and whether the Israeli military had deliberately broken or ignored it for two days in order to complete the encirclement of the Third Army on the east bank. Whatever the ultimate truth of the matter of ceasefire violations following the passage of Resolution 338 and the coming into force of the ceasefire on 22 October, two facts seem clear. The first is that the ceasefire's failure to take hold until 24 October did work to the advantage of the Israelis, enabling them to complete the encirclement of the Third Army, the aim of their original thrust across the Canal. The second is that, again whatever the truth of the matter, their Arab adversaries were convinced that this encirclement resulted from deliberate violation of the ceasefire by the Israelis, so that the initial move in any de-escalation and disengagement had to be a move by Israeli forces back to the positions they had occupied on 22 October. I noted above how the first point in the Egyptian 'framework' of 28 October involved such a return and implied how unlikely this was, given the Israeli determination to use the Third Army's vulnerability as a lever.

Insistence that Israeli forces must first withdraw to 22 October positions (whatever these were) and not maintain their stranglehold on the Third Army was still the formal Egyptian position when Dr Kissinger undertook his first visit to the Middle East on 5 November. Kissinger had already talked in Washington with both Mrs Meir and Foreign Minister Fahmy, who had both presented proposals for interim disengagement arrangements. The Israeli proposals put by Mrs Meir were also approved by the Israeli Cabinet on 3 November (Quandt 1977, p.217). The Israelis would agree to (1) respect the ceasefire, (2) the non-military re-supply of the Third Army (with UN and Israeli inspection of convoys), and (3) the passage of food, water and medical supplies to Suez itself. (In return, they required the exchange of prisoners and a lifting of the blockade.) What they would not agree to was a return to the 22 October positions, although they stated that this could be discussed as part of a general negotiation regarding disengagement.

Kissinger feared that this last issue would be a stumbling block but, much to his surpise, Sadat conceded on this issue, agreeing with Kissinger's argument that it could be bypassed if a substantial disengagement of forces agreement could be rapidly worked out.[10] Mrs Meir's response on learning that Sadat was willing to drop the issue of the 22 October positions was that this was a 'fantastic achievement', although she was less enamoured with Sadat's unwillingness to acknowledge publicly Egyptian lifting of the naval blockade, nor his wish to have sole UN control of the supply road to the Third Army. However, as the main stumbling block of the return to 22 October lines had been removed by Sadat's concession, both these issues were resolved after several rounds of discussion. On 9 November agreement on a ceasefire plan and exchange of prisoners of war was announced and two days later a Six Point Agreement (the original basis for which is claimed by both Israel and Egypt) was signed at Kilometre 101 by Israeli and Egyptian military representatives.

2.5   General disengagement

Finally, Sadat's inclination to use the changed circumstances immediately following the October War as an opportunity for pushing forward a process leading towards a negotiated settlement led to a further set of conciliatory gestures at the talks which continued at Kilometre 101 after the signing of the Six Point Agreement on 11 November 1973. To understand how these progressed towards success and then were finally aborted, it is necessary to emphasise both the central role of the United States and Dr Kissinger in the de-escalation process after the ending of the 1973 war; and the latter's determination that successful disengagement and an eventual settlement would revolve around US efforts and initiatives and no one else's. Having successfully negotiated an initial agreement with Israel and Egypt, Kissinger was determined to keep future exchanges between the Israeli government and its adversaries solely within his control, so that any future disengagement agreement or interim settlements should be achieved through US auspices, thus enhancing American influence in the region.

To this end, Kissinger set up two charades to be played out as a preparation for his own main effort at peacemaking in the Middle East. The first and best known of these was the Geneva Conference, which was designed to establish the principle that formal negotiations *could* take place between Arab and Israeli adversaries, and to satisfy the Soviet Union's desire to continue to play a role in Arab–Israeli relations without giving the USSR any real influence on the settlement process. The second was the continuation of the talks on military disengagement at Kilometre 101, talks which directly involved Egyptian and Israeli representatives on a face to face basis.

It was the unexpected success of these latter contacts which again demonstrated Sadat's ability to make quite significant conciliatory gestures towards his Israeli adversaries, and which caused an alarmed Kissinger to undermine them before Israelis and Egyptians could achieve bilaterally the success that he sought to bring about by US-dominated, trilateral bargaining. On this occasion, it was also the case that Sadat's concessions met with considerable flexibility from the Israeli negotiators, so that a brief spiral of mutual concession-making occurred before a collapse and the bringing of the talks to a halt.

The initial Israeli proposal in the Kilometre 101 talks involved General Yariv suggesting that both sides should pull back from territory that they had gained during the war (the area occupied by the Third Army on the east bank and the Deversoir salient occupied by the Israelis on the west bank), so that a UN force could be introduced into these areas.[11] The Egyptian response was to resort to a proposal first advocated in 1971, namely that Israeli forces should withdraw to the line running from El Arish to Ras Muhammad at the tip of Sinai while Egyptian forces should remain in place. However, the Egyptians rapidly retreated from this inflated demand and General Gamasy suggested that the Israelis should withdraw to the vicinity of the Mitla and Gidi passes, with designated zones for Egyptian and Israeli main forces and lightly armed forces, with a UN buffer zone between them. The Israeli response was to offer to withdraw from the west bank provided that Egyptian forces on the east bank were thinned out.

The exchange of ideas and concessions continued until 29 November. Three days before this, General Yariv suggested that Israel might even withdraw to a position east of the passes if Egypt would reduce its armoured forces east of the Canal to a token level. General Gamasy and the Egyptian delegation showed interest in such a proposal, but insisted that any force reductions would have to be mutual, rather than solely on the part of the Egyptians. On 29 November, the Egyptians discovered that General Yariv had reverted to his original proposal of mutual withdrawal from territory captured. This reversal led to the breakdown of the talks (Quandt 1977, pp.218–19).

It appears that Kissinger, at this stage, became alarmed at the rapid success of the Kilometre 101 bilateral discussions and advised the Israeli government to slow down the talks and reserve their position on disengagement until the planned Geneva Conference.[12] Quandt argues that the reasons for this were a mixture of fear of precedent-setting for later negotiations (with Syria, for example) and delay in the Geneva Conference, as well as a desire to show that a US (but not a Soviet) role was essential for a settlement, together with a need to demonstrate US-sponsored success as a means of lifting the oil sanctions (ibid. p.220). It was also obvious that the Israeli Government felt things were going too fast.[13] Thus, an interesting example of the dynamics of mutually exchanged concessions came to an end. The peace process shifted firmly into US control for the next two years. Kissinger engaged in the shuttle diplomacy and triangular bargaining that brought two Israeli–Egyptian and one Israeli–Syrian disengagement agreements.

2.6   Reactions and results

While these post-war episodes do not provide such striking examples of conciliatory initiatives on the part of the Egyptian President as others, it is nonetheless interesting that they do provide an example of a less dramatic, more familiar process of concession-making and conciliation in the aftermath of an armed struggle which has left both sides shaken and one at a considerable tactical disadvantage. As noted above, de-escalation on this occasion involved a return to a 'normal' situation that had existed before the outbreak of fighting, rather than major conciliatory gestures to break a long-standing diplomatic impasse or to prevent an existing peace process from stagnating. The episode also demonstrates Sadat's capacity for selecting appropriate conciliatory moves to suit existing circumstances, and to use changed conditions to assist in moving towards a process of negotiated settlement, even in the immediate aftermath of a destructive war. His gesture of agreeing to exchange prisoners of war was one which affected a salient Israeli value and was thus calculated to change (or, at least, had the potential effect of changing) Israeli perceptions of Sadat and Egypt in a positive fashion. His willingness to withdraw the insistence upon an Israeli return to 22 October positions showed a grasp of the potential such an issue had for blocking immediate progress and for moving further at a later date if the point was conceded. Finally, the progress made in the aborted second stage negotiations at Kilometre 101 clearly indicated Egyptian flexibility and capability in negotiations with the Israelis, once Sadat had grasped the nettle of agreeing to sit down formally with Israelis in direct negotiation.

Sadat's initiatives during this crucial period may have been minor as the situation circumscribed all actors save the USA, and they may have been coerced gestures forced on Sadat. Nevertheless the initiatives, although minor, were important in helping to begin the process of de-escalating the post-war situation and moving Egyptian–Israeli relationships towards the possibility of substantive negotiations which had been Sadat's goal in 1971 and thereafter.

2
Suez and Jerusalem: 1974–1977

The third set of Sadat's conciliatory moves took place against a markedly changed background from those of 1971 and 1973. The most obvious changes resulted from the long-term effects of the October 1973 war, both political and psychological. The latter had, at one and the same time, made the Israelis less confident of their ability to sustain their dominant position arising from their triumphs in 1967 while making the Egyptians more confident of both their military and bargaining capacities. While not perceiving themselves as equal parties, both Israelis and Egyptians seemed to see themselves as less unequal following the events of October 1973, producing a concomitant willingness to search for solutions on the one hand and a new confidence in dealing with the old enemy on the other.

The other major change in the political context was the greatly increased US involvement in Israeli–Egyptian relations, part of the new US focus on the Middle East occasioned by Sadat's expulsion of the Soviet presence from Egypt, his turn towards the West, the October War and subsequent direct US involvement in the aftermath of that struggle. With renewed US commitment to developing first a disengagement, then a peace process, and renewed urgency and confidence on the part of the regional actors, the context for a process of de-escalation and negotiation seemed far more positive than at any time since May 1967.

However, background changes are not enough to ensure the growth and continuation of what Morton Deutsch has called 'benign spirals' of interaction (Deutsch 1973). After 1973, the peace process frequently faced major set-backs, confronted stalemates and appeared, on occasions, to be wholly abandoned. In such circumstances, parties in conflict often need to undertake initiatives and use conciliatory gestures to maintain or re-start the process. Against such a background, Sadat's moves seem just as worthy of analysis as those made before and immediately following the October War.

1   Suez and the second disengagement: 1974–5

With this in mind, the next set of Sadat's conciliatory gestures to be reviewed is that relating to the final re-opening of the Suez Canal in 1975, an action which was greeted by Yitzhak Rabin (by then Israeli Prime Minister in succession to Mrs Meir) as an 'important and constructive development in concordance with the disengagement of forces agreement between Israel and Egypt' and which, it could reasonably be argued, helped to break the then-existing deadlock over a second disengagement of forces agreement in Sinai.

1.1   Context and purpose

As with the initiatives decribed in Chapter 1, the background for this action was different again from its predecessors, so that the setting against which it had to be evaluated by the target decision-makers has to be understood and taken into account when analysing the move and explaining its impact. Unlike the moves Sadat made in December 1973/January 1974, this Suez initiative did not take place in the immediate aftermath of a war, although the events of October 1973 continued to dominate relations between Israel and Egypt. However, as with the conciliatory process at the end of that war, the possibility of a status-quo stance from Israel no longer realistically existed as it had in 1970–1.

Events since the ending of the fighting in the ceasefire agreement signed at Kilometre 101 had revolved around the US Secretary of State's efforts to disentangle the military forces of the three combatants on the two land borders in such a way as to ensure that there would be no renewal of combat but that no military advantage should accrue to one side through that process of disengagement. To that end, Dr Kissinger had employed a stategy of 'step by step' negotiation and the tactics of 'shuttle diplomacy' between Cairo, Jerusalem and Damascus.

One result of this was that, at least temporarily, the issue of whether to try to achieve a partial or a complete settlement of the issues between Israel, the Palestinians and the Arab states had been decided in favour of a series of partial settlements – ceasefire agreements, partial withdrawals, temporary accommodations. The search for some 'final' peace settlement had been postponed. Hence, any result of a further 'benign spiral' arising from conciliatory gestures from one party or another was likely to be limited to partial settlements of particular issues, rather than grand breakthroughs towards a 'just and lasting' settlement.

Furthermore, on this occasion there was no question that Sadat needed to launch a process of bargaining and negotiation which had been stalled for a considerable time period, as was the case in early 1971. Rather, the situation was one of stalemate and *impasse* in an existing conciliation process involving himself, Israeli leaders and Dr Kissinger as go-between. The US

Secretary of State had spent considerable time and effort at the start of 1975 attempting to produce another step in his step-by-step process of disengaging and eventually making peace between the adversaries in the Middle East, but on this occasion talks had deadlocked on the issues of the extent of Israeli withdrawal to the Sinai passes and away from the oilfields; an Egyptian declaration of future non-belligerency; and control over electronic surveillance facilities. After a final, fruitless effort to obtain concessions from Egypt and Israel, Kissinger had returned to Washington on 24 March 1975, announcing that his negotiation effort was suspended. On the same date, President Ford announced a major re-assessment of US policy towards the Middle East (Quandt 1977, p.267).

With this background, the problem was one of re-starting rather than starting. Hence, the purpose of unilateral conciliatory gestures from either adversary was bound to be very different from those made from the background of *stasis* in 1971 or ceasefire and the immediate aftermath of armed conflict in 1973. Given a desire to continue the process of moving towards another agreement on disengagement and beyond, what might be done by either of the main actors to break the deadlock and resume negotiations?

1.2   Re-opening the Canal

Within this context (what might be described as a 'stalled benign spiral'!) the obvious need was for some conciliatory gesture or set of gestures from one or other adversary. This would re-assure the other party that the initiator remained interested in continuing the peace process and offer something specific in terms of a commitment and a gesture of trust so that the other side would be willing to proceed. As noted above, Sadat had made efforts to use the re-opening of the Suez Canal as an initiative in 1971. Moreover, he had publicly committed himself to clearing and re-opening the canal almost as soon as the guns had fallen silent in 1973.[1] Was it clearly his intention to use the canal re-opening in June 1975 as a conciliatory gesture in order to re-start the stalled negotiations for a further disengagement?

At first sight, this looks unlikely. For one thing, it seems clear from a number of statements made during 1974 and the early months of 1975 that Sadat had been using the re-opening of the Canal and the possibility of allowing through Israeli cargoes or ships as a bargaining counter in the disengagement negotiations being carried out via Dr Kissinger. Implicitly, the Egyptian position was that if the Israelis showed sufficent flexibility about withdrawing into Sinai, away from the Mitla and Gidi passes and the oil fields around Abu Rodeis, then (and only then) would the Canal be opened and Israeli ships and cargoes be permitted to pass through. In effect, and up until 29 March 1975, the formal Egyptian position had been that the Canal would remain closed until Israeli forces had withdrawn *at least* out of artillery range of the Canal and, preferably, away from the two strategic passes. With the failure of the Kissinger shuttle, this result seemed unlikely.

In the final days of March, however, the Egyptian position seemed to change markedly. Sadat explained this proposed alteration of Egyptian policy on 29 March in a speech to the National Council in which he claimed that Egypt now had sufficient military capability in the Canal area to deter any Israeli effort to recapture the east bank territories; and that re-opening the Canal would be to the benefit of the Egyptian people and 'the world at large' (Israeli Vol.3 1979, p.821). However, the bargaining element remained clearly part of this new Egyptian posture, with the passage of Israeli ships and cargoes now the bargaining chip. On the day following, 30 March, the Egyptian Minister for Information stated that Israeli ships would be barred from the re-opened Canal. One day later, Egypt officially let it be known that Israeli cargoes would only be allowed through follow-ing an agreement about further Israeli withdrawals into Sinai. The new Egyptian position could be summarised as offering a carrot that would be available to Israel only after the actual opening of the Canal.

For another reason, Sadat's public utterances over the opening of the Canal seem to make clear that he was using the gesture (at least partly) as a symbolic event aimed at two targets, quite apart from the Israeli govern-ment. On the one hand, he was using the occasion for domestic political purposes within Egypt, hence his use of the date (the anniversary of the Six Day War) and his rhetoric later, at the time of the opening ceremony. Much of the latter concentrated upon the fact that the Egyptian 'glorious crossing of October 6th' 1973 had led to a reversal of some of the defeat suffered in 1967 under Nasser, to a return home of all the refugees from the Canal zone and to a new spirit of confidence in an Egypt that was, unlike Israel, not afraid of peace (Israeli Vol.3 1979, pp.905–8). On the other hand, his target seems clearly to have been the international audience of poten-tial Canal users, particularly the European countries and the USA, to whom he constantly reiterated the twin themes of a re-opening being an act carried out to benefit trading nations using the Canal, but also one to demonstrate Egyptian capability, status and control over its own resources. If, indeed, one of the targets of his gesture was the Israeli government, it seemed to come far down the list.

However, the public reasons for re-opening the Canal, which seemed obvious at the time, may not have been the only or indeed the principle ones for undertaking this action. Even in public, Sadat constantly reiterated a theme which gave a clue to another implicit reason for unilaterally opening the Canal, one which was undoubtedly clear to at least some members of that gesture's principle target. This theme was that the opening of the Canal was designed to move forward the peace process and signal that the breakdown of the Kissinger shuttle should not usher in a long period of stalemate and lack of momentum. Throughout the period from April to June, Sadat regularly introduced this idea into his statements, talking on one occasion of a Canal opening 'in order to lend credence to my peace intentions',[2] on another of the initiative as illustrating 'my intention to tell the world I was not afraid of peace'[3] and on still another of wanting 'thereby to tell the entire world that I was not afraid of peace and that I was acting towards achieving it'.[4] Clearly, whatever other benefits Sadat saw as accruing from the move, opening the Canal was, at least partly, intended as a means of keeping the peace process moving.

It seems evident that Sadat was quite clear in his own mind about the kind of signal he wished to convey to the Israeli decision-makers by opening the Canal. Expressed simply, it was a gesture which involved deliberately increasing Egypt's vulnerability and the costs the country would incur if the peace process went sour and Israel decided to restore military security by a third campaign to re-establish a position on the east bank of the Canal. In effect, and in spite of the defence line that the Egyptians had deployed between the Canal and the IDF in Sinai, Sadat was increasing Egypt's economic (and his own political) vulnerability by returning to economic and social normality in the Canal zone, while Israeli artillery was still within range of the Canal and the Canal towns. The Canal zone had become Sadat's hostage to fortune and, in a paradoxical fashion, a signal that Sadat trusted the Israelis to the extent that they would at least hold to the peace process as far as it had reached.[5]

That Sadat took it as obvious that everyone understood the implications of his initiative seems clear from his prior and subsequent behaviour. As early as May 1971, during the aborted de-escalatory moves of that year, Sadat had indicated his understanding of the nature of the commitment Egypt was making by then trying to re-open the Canal. Talking about an Israeli withdrawal and opening the Canal, he asked US representative Bergus 'if the canal opens, do you think I'll ever start another war?' (Hersh 1983, p.408). Nor was this view solely a personal one of Sadat's. Reflecting on the significance of the re-opening of the Canal and reconstruction of the cities to the west, Foreign Minister Fahmy notes that these measures 'represented added guarantees for the Israelis. If Egypt invested a great deal of money in reopening the Canal and rebuilding the cities, it would hesitate before resuming military operations and incurring new damage. Its international prestige would be adversely affected by a renewed closure' (Fahmy 1983, p.80).

1.3   Reception and reactions

However, it is not necessarily the case that the Israeli decision-makers perceived Sadat's gesture as one of increasing Egyptian vulnerability or an effort to demonstrate trust in Israeli restraint, particularly given the other, more obvious rationales for Sadat's initiative, and also the fact that Israel was under enormous pressure from the US government during this period. Rabin, for example, fails to mention the move at all in his memoirs, although he does note that Sadat's interest in 'renewing attempts to reach agreement with Israel through American mediation', expressed to President Ford at their meeting in Salzburg, was one reason for his own decision to continue contacts with Washington (Rabin 1979, p.26).

Moreover, the initial Israeli reaction to Sadat's announcement of his intention to re-open the Canal was quite negative, in spite of the fact that it was accompanied by Sadat's offer to return freely the bodies of 39 Israeli soldiers discovered by Egyptian reconstruction workers in the Canal zone. (In his own memoirs, Sadat makes a great deal of this as another symbolic conciliatory gesture to the Israelis [Sadat 1978, p.296].) The Israeli response was to argue that the mere re-opening of the Canal would contribute nothing of benefit to Israel nor to the promotion of better relations between Egypt and Israel. The official explanation of the initiative was that it was made for reasons of economic benefit to Egypt, for whom the Canal ensured a source of sorely needed revenue, and to Europe and the USSR.

Economic considerations continued to play a central role in public Israeli reactions to Sadat's initiative. Formally, taking the initiative was attributed to Sadat's dire economic needs, which had led him to bargain for Israeli withdrawal from the Abu Rudeis oil wells (and their prospective revenue) and to re-open the Canal. It was this which, in Israeli eyes, caused him to abandon his stand on not opening the Canal until the IDF had withdrawn to a safe distance from the waterway: 'hard pressed by his economic needs, he yielded in view of the prospect of the promising prospects of high income from the passage fees' (Israeli Vol.3 1979 Intro. p.1). In other words, the gesture was perceived as nothing more than a way of gaining favourable publicity and increasing revenue.

On the other hand, it seems likely that, at least privately, Israeli decision-makers had an alternative evaluation of Sadat's gesture more akin to his original intention. I have already noted Rabin's more positive comments once the Canal had actually been opened, to which he added the hope that Egypt would, in fact, allow the unhindered passage of Israeli cargo. More importantly, three days before the date for reopening the Canal, the Israeli Cabinet held a special meeting, following which it was announced that Israel would unilaterally 'thin out' its troops and equipment on the east bank as a gesture towards easing tension in the region. This pullback was described as a response to Egypt's opening of the Canal. It involved withdrawing IDF artillery to a line 20 miles and missiles to a line 25 miles from the Canal Tanks and troops in the 'limited force' zone would be reduced to 50 per cent of the permitted level. Prime Minister Rabin at a press conference held to announce this Israeli gesture described it as being designed to show 'the world and Egypt that Israel really wants and intends to progress towards peace either by an overall or interim agreement'.[6]

The Israeli response appeared to come as a surprise to President Sadat, who learned of it during his 1–2 June talks in Salzburg with President Ford, describing it there as 'a very encouraging step' (Israeli Vol.3 1979, p.898). The partial withdrawal was completed the day before the opening of the Canal, 4 June. Six days later, on 10 June, Prime Minister Rabin flew to Washington to meet with President Ford and Dr Kissinger for further talks on disengagement. The peace process was in motion again.

2   To Jerusalem; January–December 1977

In this section, I will examine the setting for, and series of events leading up to, Sadat's grand gesture of conciliation – his trip to Israel in November 1977. Of all Sadat's moves reviewed in this portion of the study, this is the initiative which is (and was at the time) regarded as his most successful conciliatory gesture towards the Israeli Government, a move which undeniably signalled to Israel and the world that Sadat was serious when he spoke of his willingness to make sacrifices to achieve peace in the Middle East. It was described as 'daring', 'unprecedented', 'epoch making', 'historic', and 'a major turning point' in Middle Eastern relations so that, even at the time, it was generally recognised as a quite extraordinary move that forced even the most sceptical to re-assess the nature of Sadat's policies and intentions and the prospects for change in a relationship of fundamental conflict that had lasted since 1948.

   However, even though this is one of the most analysed events in recent Middle East diplomacy, some aspects of Sadat's gesture remain ambiguous and seem to defy clear analysis. The circumstances surrounding the move are such as to raise questions about Sadat's intentions when deciding to go to Jerusalem. Evidence of prior contacts between Egypt and Israel in the period leading up to Sadat's journey raise questions about how much of a 'shock' Sadat's surprise announcement was to Israeli decision-makers, and about the interpretations Israeli leaders made of Sadat's reasons for making the move. Finally, amid the euphoria generated by Sadat's visit (and the equally vehement condemnation it aroused in Arab circles), there remain questions about how one might unambiguously isolate the clear impact Sadat's initiative had upon the perceptions, expectations and behaviour of his major adversary; about what other factors influenced such changes; and about whether the move alone triggered a benign, conciliatory spiral of Israeli–Egyptian interaction that led finally to a less hostile relationship between the two countries.

2.1   Context and political environment

Conventionally, the starting point for Sadat's Jerusalem initiative is taken to be his 9 November announcement at the opening of a new session of the Peoples' Assembly in Cairo that he was ready to go to Israel, 'to their house, to the Knesset itself and to talk to them', in order to avoid further violence and bloodshed. The announcement was made almost, it seemed, as an afterthought, at the end of a long speech and in the actual presence of Yasir Arafat, so that the applause that greeted the announcement might have been intended for what was perceived as a rhetorical flourish rather than a serious policy initiative.[7] However, two days later Prime Minister Begin welcomed the idea of a visit in a direct appeal to the Egyptian people. On the 15th November a formal invitation was sent from Israel and on 20th November Sadat was in Israel addressing the Knesset.

One of the striking aspects of this whole, rapid process was that it represented the sudden abandonment – by Sadat and the Israeli leaders – of a process initiated earlier in 1977. This aimed at re-establishing a framework to discuss a general settlement for the Middle East at Geneva, with the aid of both the USSR and the USA. Whereas previous Sadat initiatives had been taken in situations of stalemate and the absence (or breakdown) of diplomatic contacts about a solution or in the aftermath of a military conflict or confrontation, his 1977 initiative occurred while another peacemaking initiative was working its way gradually towards an appropriate formula for a general conference on Middle East peace. Hence, it could hardly be argued that Sadat was using a visit to Jerusalem to break an impasse, to re-establish contacts or to re-start a stalled movement towards substantive discussions. Instead, it was a diversion from, and an alternative to, an existing peace process that aimed at a general peace conference to be held in Geneva in December 1977.

The initiation of the 1977 effort to reconvene a Geneva Conference to discuss a comprehensive settlement in the Middle East originated with the incoming Carter Administration in the United States, and with President Carter's personal determination to search for a final peace settlement. During the summer and autumn of 1977, the US Government invested a great deal of effort in trying to find a formula under which the Geneva Middle East Conference could be reconvened, with December as its target date. The task proved to be long and complex, ostensibly procedural issues (which actually involved important matters of substance) blocking any rapid agreement about a generally acceptable Geneva framework. Key questions included whether the Arab delegations should attend the conference and negotiate separately or as a unified delegation; whether 'the Palestinians' should be represented at Geneva, and by what means; what would be the influence of the provisions of UN Resolution 242 on the agenda of the conference and its deliberations; and what would be the role of the co-chairmen of the conference once convened.

Having conferred with both Israeli and Arab governments on possible frameworks for the conference, the US and Soviet governments issued a joint statement on 1 October, which amended to some degree the provisions of Resolution 242. It was perceived as being partial towards the Arab position on the conference and had the effect of putting considerable pressure on the Israeli Government. The latter promptly rejected the Joint

Memorandum in no uncertain terms. (In contrast, the Arab governments and the PLO generally welcomed the Memorandum.) Subsequent negotiations between President Carter and Foreign Minister Dayan produced a working paper on the procedural issues in dispute in which the Israeli government made a number of key concessions. However, it subsequently became clear that the US Government was prepared to amend this document still further in order to change the Geneva framework. (One alteration discussed by US officials was to allow Palestinians from outside Gaza and the West Bank to attend.) During October, Israeli officials constantly emphasised that they would *not* go to Geneva if PLO representatives attended the Conference, no matter what the latter's disguise.

It seems clear that, by the end of October 1977, the successful convening, let alone concluding, of a general conference on Middle East peace in Geneva was becoming problematical. While the emerging formula for the Conference appeared to be increasingly acceptable to the Arab governments (and even the PLO) in that it put the Israelis in a position where pressure could be brought to bear on them for concessions, the reverse was obviously true for the Israelis. They would be confronted by an Arab delegation made more radical by its coalition structure and a US delegation representing an administration less willing to support Israeli positions than any since 1956. Many observers have subsequently argued that an inevitable outcome of this situation would have been either an eventual Israeli refusal to attend the conference unless the formula was changed radically, or an Israeli walk out from the conference to avoid being forced into unacceptable concessions, or the collapse of the conference in deadlock, followed by general recriminations and an increase of tension in the region. One proponent of this view is quite certain that 'by the end of October, it was evident that even if the Geneva conference could be convened in accordance with the American timetable, a comprehensive peace treaty and a solution to the Middle East conflict would never be the result' (Handel 1981, p.298).

Was this perception of impending deadlock or failure one of the reasons for Sadat taking the decision to break away from the Geneva process and launch his own quite separate initiative by offering the dramatic gesture of his Jerusalem visit? It seems likely that Sadat did not share the general Arab satisfaction with the approach of the Geneva Conference. He may have sensed the likelihood of a resounding failure to achieve progress towards a peace settlement that would not have been offset by the diplomatic 'triumph' of any unilateral Israeli walk out.

If Sadat did entertain such doubts, certainly this was not a view shared by his Foreign Minister, Ismail Fahmy, who resigned in protest against Sadat's proposed visit to Jerusalem. Fahmy subsequently argued that he took this action because Sadat had wrecked a promising process for achieving genuine peace in the region. In his account of the events leading up to

Sadat's Jerusalem initiative, Fahmy argues strongly that a just and final peace was 'on the horizon' (Fahmy 1983, p.215) and that, by autumn 1977, 'the situation in the Middle East was not hopelessly stalemated, but moving forward towards a comprehensive peace' (ibid. p.251). Fahmy's account of events leading up to Sadat's trip includes a long description of how he tried to dissuade Sadat from even considering such a move on the grounds that it would wreck the forthcoming Geneva Conference, which offered the best hope of a settlement satisfactory to the Arabs. It was, he claims, the final destruction of Geneva by Sadat's visit that led to his own resignation (ibid.). Sadat, however, did not share Fahmy's confidence in the Geneva process.

A variety of reasons have been suggested for Sadat's disenchantment with the Geneva process and his wish to break away through some new, dramatic initiative. Firstly, it seems likely that Sadat increasingly realised, as the pre-negotiations for the Geneva conference took place, that such a setting would clearly mean the subordination of Egypt's interests to those of the more radical Arab governments and of the PLO. The Arab conditions for attending the conference, particularly that involving negotiations between Israel and a unified Arab delegation, as well as the low probability of achieving a comprehensive agreement, would mean that any specific agreements that could be worked out on Israeli–Egyptian issues would either be lost in a general failure or (if preserved bilaterally in spite of any failure to reach a comprehensive agreement) would subject Egypt to charges of abandonment of the Arab cause in order to pursue its own interests.

The second possible reason for Sadat's disenchantment with Geneva and the US/Soviet-led peace process involved two aspects. The first was Sadat's increasing doubt about the ability of the US government to put real pressure on the Israelis to make some genuine and substantial concessions at Geneva that would produce a comprehensive settlement acceptable to the Arabs. If Carter could not extract Israeli concessions, then this diminished the attractiveness of such a framework and suggested the need for alternatives. The second aspect involved Sadat's desire to exclude the Soviet Union from any general influence in the Middle East and particularly from having influence over the peace process. Having redirected Egyptian policy towards a rapprochement with the USA, Sadat wanted to keep Soviet influence out of the region, particularly as he was convinced that the Soviet leaders had an interest in the continuation of conflict there, rather than its settlement.

Finally, Geneva may have become increasingly less attractive to Sadat as another alternative – direct bilateral contacts between Israel and Egypt – became a realistic option from May 1977 onwards. Realisation that this might be more than a possibility came through a second process, described in the next section, that took place during the summer and autumn of 1977 in parallel to the Geneva process, but kept secret by both Egyptians and Israelis from their allies and patrons. This is another, neglected aspect of Sadat's November 1977 action and an important aspect of the setting within which the successful initiative was launched. The fact was that the groundwork for Sadat's conciliatory grand gesture had been laid through a series of prior contacts and consultations which took place before 9 November 1977. In the words of one observer, by that date an 'embryonic understanding' existed between Israel and Egypt (Handel 1981, p.319) which could have been wrecked by Geneva.

2.2 Preliminaries: channels and prior contacts

One major aspect of Sadat's Jerusalem initiative clearly sets it apart from other conciliatory gestures and initiatives launched by the Egyptian President from 1971 onwards; the fact that various prior signals may have played a part in preparing Egypt for launching, and Israel for accepting the initiative. The main point that emerges from this account of prior contacts and channels is that, although Sadat's trip to Jerusalem did constitute a most dramatic action in achieving a diplomatic breakthrough, nonetheless some exchange of signals and some contacts had preceded the November move. This might therefore be viewed as the culmination of a preliminary, low-key process.

As usual, there could be considerable debate about the starting point for the process which led up to Sadat announcing his willingness to go to Israel in November 1977. A year previously, Sadat had announced to a US Congressional delegation in Cairo that the Arabs were prepared to make peace with Israel by negotiating a settlement 'on a sound and just basis' without preconditions, and a few days later had called upon President-Elect Carter to help promote a Middle East peace when he took office. Sadat's comments, which were in response to an indirect enquiry about Egypt's view of 'the nature of peace' from Prime Minister Rabin, were ill received in Israel. Rabin commented that they were a diplomatic ploy merely designed to influence US policy and that he hoped that the US would not be fooled by 'beautiful words of peace from Arab states' (Sobel 1980, p.128). Similar views were expressed by Foreign Minister Allon and Defence Minister Peres.

However, given the upheaval in Israeli politics caused by the result of the May 1977 elections, it seems more reasonable to date the start of the process that led to Jerusalem from the coming-to-power of the Begin Government. This was regarded as a major set-back to peace throughout the Arab world, given Begin's hardline reputation, but in the event – possibly under the prodding of his Foreign Minister, Moshe Dayan – Begin proved to be more flexible than anticipated and genuinely interested in the possibilities of a peace settlement. It is probable that his statement to the Knesset on presenting his new government on 20 June 1977 was no more than the usual, ritualistic declaration of willingness to negotiate peace directly with the Arabs used by all new Israeli Prime Ministers.[8] However, subsequent events (although kept well hidden) indicate that Begin was serious in his intentions and prepared to start a peace process if there was any chance for one. A reasonable argument could be made for the position that the process leading towards the Sadat visit was, indirectly, begun by Menachim Begin.

There is some evidence to support the view that the first of Begin's 'behind the scenes' moves was the reported passing of information regarding a threat to Sadat's regime during July 1977. During that month (allegedly on 23 July, Egypt's 'Revolution Day') Mossad is believed to have passed on to Sadat via the USA information about a Libyan-inspired scheme to overthrow his regime and about a terrorist training camp for such a purpose near the Libyan–Egyptian border.[9] As part of this message, Begin is also said to have requested a meeting with Sadat, or some lower-level contacts between the two governments. (Israeli 1985, p.226).

Whatever the final truth of such claims, it is undoubtedly the case that, in late August 1977, Begin took the opportunity of a visit to President Ceausescu of Rumania (who had offered to mediate as early as 1972) to indicate to the Rumanian leader his own desire for peace and a willingness to make meaningful concessions in Sinai to the Egyptians. Later, in an important move, Ceausescu was to convey to Sadat his conviction that Begin was sincere in his wish for peace and that he was a leader who could deliver what he promised; and to convince Sadat that this was an accurate assessment of the new Israeli leader. Begin followed up this contact with Ceausescu with another message, reiterating his willingness to meet Sadat, informally, in Jerusalem, Cairo or on neutral ground (Handel 1981, p.304), although this last action was standard Israeli procedure when in contact with leaders who would meet any Arab statesmen.[10]

While these cautious, preliminary contacts may have had little immediate effect, it seems more than likely that they established some expectation in the minds of both Israeli and Egyptian leaders that the other was ready to talk bilaterally, and would respond to a specific proposal for a meeting. The next move towards a meeting took place in September 1977, when Foreign Minister Dayan had a secret meeting with King Hassan of Morocco and suggested that the King might be able to arrange an informal meeting between Egyptian and Israeli representatives. The King took up this suggestion and a meeting between Dayan and Deputy Prime Minister Hassan al Touhamy duly took place at Fez on 16–17 September 1977. Once again, there is considerable ambiguity about what was discussed and agreed at these exploratory discussions (or what both believed had been agreed) as well as their role in paving the way for Sadat's initiative. There were reports that Dayan paid another visit later that month to arrange a meeting between Sadat and Begin. Whatever the details of the discussions, however, it is possible that the apparent willingness of the Israelis to contemplate concessions (whether transmitted through Ceasescu or by Dayan) might have encouraged Sadat in the belief that any initiative on his part would receive sympathetic consideration by the Likud Government, although Sadat later denied that the Moroccan talks had any influence on his decision about the Jerusalem visit or did anything to prepare for it.[11] Whatever the effect, or absence of effect, of these August and September contacts, for Sadat the choice was becoming one of carrying on with the 'behind the scenes' contacts or undertaking some major initiative in the full public glare.

2.3 Sadat's objectives and expectations

With this background of previous contacts and signals, Sadat would undoubtedly have been reasonably sure of a positive response to any new initiative he might care to undertake, and he also claims to have received a communication from Carter encouraging him to undertake some major move apart from the Geneva process. What, then, were his motives and expectations for undertaking his visit, and how and when did he decide to make this particular gesture?

In his memoirs, Sadat recalls that it was Carter's personal note to him of September 1977 that first directed his thoughts towards the possibility of an Egyptian initiative (Sadat 1978, p.302). However, it was during and following Sadat's visit to Rumania, mentioned above, that an idea began to take a firm shape in his mind, particularly when he learned of Ceausescu's view that Begin was willing to negotiate realistically and could make a settlement 'stick'. He appears to have considered two possible schemes. The first was the idea of inviting the leaders of the big Five to a meeting in Jerusalem at the Knesset with leaders of the Arab states involved (Syria, Jordan, Egypt, Lebanon, plus the Palestinians) 'to make it absolutely clear to Premier Begin that we were determined to prepare seriously for Geneva and ... were now drafting a working paper that included the main guidelines to make a success of the Geneva Conference' (ibid. p.307).

The second was the idea of going personally to Jerusalem, to pray at the al-Aqsa mosque and, as the second version of a dramatic initiative crystallised in his mind, to 'go right to the Knesset ... in order to submit to them the complete facts of the situation, and to confront them with the choice they would have to make if they really wanted to live in peace in this part of the world' (ibid. p.308).

It is interesting that Sadat subsequently claimed that his main objectives in going to Jerusalem had been to break through the psychological barriers (the 'walls') built up between Arab and Israeli by the previous conflicts and wars, to demonstrate to his own people (and the Israelis) his genuine commitment to peace by the symbolic gesture of going to Jerusalem and there praying at al-Aqsa, but also to make clear to the Israelis that any final peace must deal with the claims of the Palestinians and that these were inextricably linked with any hopes the Israelis might have of being accepted securely in the region. If these were, indeed, the conscious objectives underlying his conciliatory gesture, it can be said that he clearly succeeded in achieving his first two aims, even if subsequent events proved that the Israeli leaders could achieve a partial settlement with Egypt which left the fate of the Palestinians still in abeyance.

The exact process by which Sadat finally decided to include the offer to go to Jerusalem in his 9 November speech to the People's Assembly seems to have been rather more tortuous than the clear-cut manner described by Sadat, however. Ismail Fahmy, who was no supporter of Sadat's visit to Israel, recalls that he first learned of Sadat's initial thoughts while the two were on their official visit to Rumania when, following a review of Begin's prior conversations and proposals to Ceasescu (which, Fahmy claims, clearly revealed that Begin was *not* sincere in his desire for a settlement), Sadat casually floated the idea of a visit to Jerusalem 'to deliver a speech and ... come back' (Fahmy 1983, pp.254–6).

Fahmy also recalls that it was he who suggested the idea of a (symbolic) meeting of the 5 Permananent Security Council Members plus the adversaries in East Jerusalem and that Sadat approved of this idea. This account conflicts with Sadat's own recollection of the sequence of events leading up to the 9 November announcement, and with the account given by Sadat to Moshe Dayan after the visit had taken place.[12] It is also plain that Sadat was conscious of the potential opposition, both international and within the ranks of his own advisers, to the proposal. Fahmy recounts how he advised Sadat to float the idea as a 'trial balloon' during the visit to Saudi Arabia, but that Sadat rejected this suggestion (Fahmy 1983, pp.260–1). It was also the case that, returning to Cairo, Sadat mentioned the proposal to a meeting of the Egyptian National Security Council on 5 November, but the only comment from the surprised Council members was a strongly negative one from General Gamasy (ibid. p.266).

One final feature of Sadat's behaviour leading up to his initiative throws some light on his own objectives in making the move and this is the fact that he kept the entire process, including previous Egyptian–Israeli contacts, secret from the United States. (The same, of course, can be said for Begin and the Israeli Government.) To some degree, and especially in the later stages, this can be explained by Sadat's fear that Carter would be annoyed at having his own work in trying to bring about a Geneva Conference undermined and overtaken by a joint Egyptian–Israeli *demarche*, and might try to prevent Sadat's move. However, this fear seems to have played a minor part in Sadat's calculations. Indeed, he seems to have played a curious double game, even with his own advisers, right up to the last minute giving the impression that he was firmly committed to the Geneva process while privately planning his gesture. This reinforces the impression that the direct target of Sadat's move was clearly Israel and the Israeli Government, with a possible secondary target of the Egyptian people themselves who, properly prepared would duly applaud their President's action and thus render his domestic support stronger. In this latter case, Sadat appears to have anticipated likely Egyptian reactions very well. From all accounts, the public enthusiasm for the Sadat initiative in Egypt was only exceeded by that in Israel. At the level of public opinion in the two countries, Sadat's gesture appears to have been wildly successful, whatever reaction might have been in Egyptian elite circles or elsewhere in the Arab world.

2.4   Impacts: Israeli evaluations and reactions

What cannot be in any doubt about Sadat's visit to Israel is the public reaction among Israelis to this first official visit by an Arab leader to the country, and to his address to the Knesset on the issue of Middle East peace. Sadat himself later described the impact of his visit as the beginning of an 'era of wonders'[13] and, at least at the public level, Sadat's tendency towards exaggeration seems justified.

More important for Sadat's conciliatory gesture was the question of Israeli elite and government reaction, for any Israeli response depended very much upon how his initiative was perceived and evaluated among Israeli decision-makers, particularly their interpretation of the reasons for Sadat having made the gesture and the key factors that had led to the visit.

One immediate reaction by some Israeli leaders seems to have been that Sadat made the trip in order to diminish Israeli military preparedness and as a prelude to a renewed assault. General Mordecai Gur, for example, issued a public warning before Sadat arrived in Jerusalem that this, indeed, might be the main purpose of the visit and the Israeli intelligence had had warning of significant Egyptian troop movements in early November. However, this warning seemed to have little impact on the general Israeli euphoria over Sadat's visit.

More generally, official Israeli reaction to Sadat's offer seems to have been overwhelmed by the very fact that Sadat had offered publicly to come, and the domestic political pay-offs to any Israeli government hosting such a visit. The alacrity with which Premier Begin responded to Sadat's initial offer indicates that the Israelis undoubtedly saw the diplomatic advantages of responding positively to the initiative. It would provide them with an alternative to the unsought and perilous Geneva process (with its implications of pressure for concessions from the Carter administration). It would move potential discussions away from Washington (and Geneva) and towards the bilateral discussions between Israel and Egypt, a format which successive Israeli governments had always sought. Finally, it seems plain that Israeli officials were as clear about the implications of the visit as Foreign Minister Fahmy had been when he warned Sadat in Rumania. Having made the visit, Sadat could hardly argue that he had not (at least tacitly) recognised Israel or that a state of belligerence between Egypt and Israel continued to exist. As Ismail Fahmy made clear, there was no going back from Jerusalem.

Aside from this highly positive evaluation of the potential for Israel of Sadat's initiative, there was also the question of Israeli evaluations of *why* Sadat had chosen this particular course of action, rather than – say – continuing with the Geneva process or reverting to a posture of confrontation. There is little contemporary evidence of Israeli reactions to Sadat's visit at the official level, but subsequent analyses have suggested a number of possible elements in Israeli evaluations. One obvious reason for Sadat's initiative, at least in contemporary Israeli eyes, was likely to be Sadat's need for foreign policy success to offset the very considerable domestic troubles he faced from the beginning of 1977, when severe riots erupted in Cairo and Alexandria. Partly, the riots took place over rising food prices, but these were linked to the country's desperate financial position and the need to cut food subsidies. The important factor for Sadat, however, was the degree of hostility directed towards himself and his regime, which obviously had not been offset by his personal charisma or popularity. In Israeli eyes, the domestic crisis faced by Sadat undoubtedly contributed to his search for popularity through external success, and his need for a new, dramatic and popular initiative. As one Israeli observer later wrote: 'Severely shaken by his failure at home, and by the criticism and ridicule he had to endure as a result, Sadat desperately looked for a way out ... He knew full well that without such a lifeline, he would be doomed to sink deeper into the murky waters of his domestic quagmire' (Israeli 1985, p.218).

Another obvious explanation for Sadat's gamble was the sheer damage to Egypt's economy caused by a continued confrontation with Israel. In Israeli eyes, Egypt was bearing the main burden of the Arab confrontation with them, and this was not an inaccurate perception. Since 1967, the military sector of the Egyptian economy had grown to huge proportions, swallowing resources that could have been devoted to economic development, and reducing growth in per capita income to less that 2 per cent per annum. Even in 1967 military expenditure was 25 per cent of GNP. By 1977 the Egyptian national debt was $13 bn and annual economic support from the USA and Saudi Arabia was $5.4 bn. The January 1977 riots were sparked by Egyptian efforts to save $0.5 bn per annum in food subsidies. Too much skilled and educated manpower was siphoned into the armed forces. All this, of course, had occurred while Egypt was receiving no income from the Suez Canal nor any benefit from the oil wells in Sinai. It is hardly surprising that one Israeli interpretation of Sadat's move emphasised potential economic benefits from a genuine peace and argued that 'Sadat and the Egyptian people realised that the time had come to turn inward and tend their sick economy before it was too late. Another war with Israel would only perpetuate Egyptian economic backwardness. The Egyptian President decided to put Egypt first without, if possible, deserting Arab interests' (Handel 1981, p.323).

A third Israeli perception associated with Sadat's visit was that of Egyptian military weakness. The balance of advantage in military terms seemed to have swung clearly in favour of Israel, particularly after the Israelis had extracted massive military assistance from Kissinger as a price of the Second Sinai Disengagement Agreement in 1975. In 1977, Pentagon estimates were that Israel's military strength had increased 160 per cent over 1973, while Egypt's (no longer supported by the Soviet Union) had shrunk to 90 per cent. One obvious conclusion for Israeli decision-makers was that Sadat no longer had a realistic military option either alone or in conjunction with other Arab states. The diplomatic road was the only one open to him both to restore Egypt's territory and economy and to preserve the myth of victory in 1973. One observer comments, 'Aware that he had no viable military option open to him at least in the short run, Sadat preferred to perpetuate his image as the victorious leader of the October 1973 war.' (Ibid. p.320).

Nor, in Israeli eyes, could Sadat have had a Soviet option. In March 1976 Sadat had set the final seal on the break with the USSR by abrogating the Soviet–Egyptian Treaty of Friendship signed only five years previously. To Israelis, this indicated an increasing Egyptian reliance upon the United States, and this was increasingly interpreted as a recognition that only the USA could (1) furnish Egypt with the economic aid needed to avoid economic disaster, and (2) produce an Israeli withdrawal from Egyptian territory. In this interpretation of Sadat's situation, one obvious strategy was to proclaim loudly (and, perhaps, even pursue) a desire for peace with Israel, thus removing domestic objections within the USA towards increased political, economic and eventually military support for Egypt from the US Government. Seen within this framework, Sadat's initiative in November 1977 became – at least partly – a lever to extract concessions and the help from Washington which Egypt desperately needed. At the extreme interpretation, Sadat's visit could be seen as a major move in a strategy to divide Israel and the USA.

Finally, the closure of the Soviet option led to another Israeli view of Sadat's motives for his dramatic action in going personally to Israel. Not merely did Sadat need good relations with the USA (and hence better relations with Israel) for economic and territorial reasons, but he also needed them because the USA provided protection for the Sadat regime against Soviet attempts to have it undermined, overthrown or contained. I have already mentioned the reported help given to Sadat by Mossad in the summer of 1977 and Sadat's desire to remove Soviet influence from the Geneva peace process. All of this was undoubtedly clear to Israeli decision-makers, as was Sadat's concern about the possibility of Egypt's encirclement by pro-Soviet regimes. By 1977 Libya was already becoming a store-house of Soviet arms and had been involved in efforts to subvert Sadat. A coup by the Sudanese Communist Party in 1971 had narrowly been averted partly through Egyptian support for Sudanese President Nimiery. A pro-Soviet regime was in the process of asserting its control over Ethiopia. In Israeli perceptions, the dangers to Sadat must have seemed real and likely to have impelled him more rapidly towards the United States in search of political support and protection. As US political support was dependent on better Egyptian–Israeli relations, this factor might also have played a substantial part in Israeli interpretations of the reasons for Sadat's move.

However, it is probably the case that these evaluations and interpretations of Sadat's motives for making his journey to Jerusalem came after the initiative was over. It seems likely that, like the Israeli public, Israeli decision-makers were also, initially at least, overwhelmed by the gesture that Sadat made in mid November 1977 and felt, as did their voters and Sadat himself, that the initiative was a major and irrevocable turning point in Middle East relations, ushering in a completely new phase in Israeli-Arab relations. Unlike any of his previous initiatives and conciliatory gestures, Sadat's personal visit to Jerusalem seems a clear and unequivocal example of a conciliatory gesture that worked. It initiated a new de-escalatory spiral that, for all its fits and hesitations, ended with a set of complex negotiations and an agreement that, whatever its shortcomings, established a new relationship between adversaries who previously had been separated by hostile behaviour, mistrust and misperception – the 'psychological walls' to which Sadat himself referred and which his Jerusalem visit was designed, in part, to break down.

The historical aftermath of Sadat's visit, discussed in the Epilogue, indicates that even gestures as grand as Sadat's visit are no guarantee of the success of the conciliation process started, or re-started, as a result of the move. What does seem unarguable is the effect Sadat's move had in changing the psychological relationship between Israel and, at least, Egypt, if not the whole of the Arab world. It gave a fresh impetus to the search for a long-term settlement by re-starting a process of conciliation. In that, at least, Sadat's move was a major success.

3   Conclusions

Initially, the most striking thing that emerges from this brief review of the set of conciliatory initiatives and gestures made by President Sadat in the period between his acquiring the Egyptian presidency and his trip to Jerusalem is their apparent diversity in form, content and objectives.

Faced with such wide differences, however, we need to recall that the original purpose in seeking to analyse Sadat's efforts was to discover whether there might be any common characteristics which might *in general* promote or undermine the success of conciliatory initiatives. The diversity revealed in Sadat's initiatives seems to preclude any easy answer to this question, in spite of the useful preliminary, but tentative insights the analysis might reveal. The next chapter, therefore, turns from empirical examples of conciliatory gestures to sundry conceptual and theoretical approaches that might throw additional light upon the issue of 'successful' conciliatory gestures as a key part of conflict resolution processes.

3
Conciliation: Concepts, Frameworks and Models

'Most men in handling public affairs pay more attention to what they themselves say than what is said to them'

François de Callieres *On the Manner of Negotiating with Princes* 1716

Three central themes emerge from the outline of Anwar Sadat's peacemaking initiatives between 1971 and 1977. Firstly, there is the idea that peacemaking often started, or resumed, as the result of a unilateral, sometimes 'stalemate-breaking' initiative on the part of one or other of the adversaries, such moves being part of a broad category of actions or statements which I term 'conciliatory gestures'. Such gestures or actions should be regarded as both the starting point of a peace process and as basic 'building blocks' of the initial stages of inter-party conciliation. Hence, an understanding of the underlying dynamics of peacemaking will have to be based on a clear understanding of the nature and use of conciliatory gestures.

Secondly, it was clearly the case that successful conciliatory *gestures*, such as Sadat's 1977 visit to Israel, only provided an occasion for an inter-party conciliation *process* to begin, or sometimes an impetus for one to be revived. A successful conciliatory gesture will merely begin an exchange of reassuring moves or concessions that will make up a sequence of benign moves by the adversaries, more familiarly known as a 'de-escalatory process'. Furthermore, there seems to be nothing inherent in such initial gestures that guarantees the successful continuation of a conciliation process, even if it only reaches as far as initial contacts through third parties, or preliminary, face-to-face negotiations. The trials and errors of Egyptian–Israeli relations, even after Sadat's dramatic visit, clearly revealed that many other factors influence progress or lack of it towards a resolution of the conflict, beyond that first successful move.

Thirdly, the Sadat initiatives emphasise the supreme difficulty in launching successful conciliation processes which is faced by leaders who are involved in long-drawn-out, intractable and often violent conflicts over fundamental issues – as exemplified by the Arab–Israeli dispute. Sadat's problems, and those facing other leaders whether directly or indirectly involved in seeking a solution to that complex conflict, are all too typical of the obstacles to conciliation between parties locked in what have been characterised as 'protracted social conflicts' – the Cypruses, the Bosnias, the Sri Lankas, the Lebanons that drag on and seem to defy efforts at resolution. Such conflicts have been characterised by Edward Azar as being over identity-related issues, and involve underlying needs for communal recognition, basic security and distributive justice, among other factors. Protracted social conflicts 'are not easily suppressed and continue to be pursued in the long term by all means available, including the possible acquisition and use of destructive weapons' (Azar 1990, p.2). Thus, they present, for a wide variety of reasons, particularly intractable challenges for leaders seeking to begin effective processes of conciliation.

1   Sadat and conciliation: a search for patterns

However, as I noted at the conclusion of Chapter 2, the outstanding feature of the conciliatory moves made by President Sadat in the period between his acquiring the Egyptian presidency in 1970 and his trip to Jerusalem in 1977 is surely their diversity. Firstly, the circumstances in which each occurred appear to have been quite different from one case to another, while different views about the relative 'success' of each initiative were expressed by both observers and by those involved. Can any general lessons be drawn from such a diverse set of cases, with their widely differing outcomes, about factors making for or militating against the use of conciliatory gestures in initiating or maintaining a peace process?

I would argue that this very diversity makes it possible to to take account of the wide range of variables involved in explaining the success of Sadat and others' efforts to launch successful peace processes. For example, consider the issue of the setting for, and timing of, the four conciliatory initiatives undertaken by the Egyptian President. Each occurred at very different stages of the Egyptian–Israeli conflict and were thus intended to have rather different results because of this. In one case, the initiative was undertaken to help overcome an impasse in an on-going mediation effort. In another, the initiative took place in order to begin a de-escalation process at the ending of a short but savage war. In yet another, the conciliatory gesture was made to pre-empt an untrusted peace process being prepared by a patron. All were different in respect of their setting.

This observation regarding the setting for Sadat's conciliatory gestures emphasises that such moves always take place against a complex background, part of which often involves prior coercion and violence. Hence, an initiative's context will undoubtedly affect its likely impact, for good or ill. At the very least, the interaction between the parties in the period preceding any conciliatory initiative is likely to have a significant effect on whether the gesture is actually initiated, and also whether it is evaluated correctly, and reacted to in a positive manner making likely the continuation of a peace process – or reacted to in any manner at all.

If the background for each of Sadat's gestures (for example, its proximity to open warfare or alternative third-party peacemaking initiatives) was different, so were such factors as the nature and form of each initiative, the intentions of Sadat as the 'initiator', and the evaluations of the Israeli elite, as the 'target'. In some cases, the Israelis reacted quickly, in others more slowly, in still others not at all. The channels used for each initiative varied, the degree of publicity was not the same, and the involvement of third parties was dissimilar, even though the US Government tended to be the intermediary most closely involved in the four cases.

Again, however, I would argue that from this range of differences it should be possible to extract a number of working hypotheses about the features (perhaps 'essential qualities') of Sadat's conciliatory gestures that helped to determine whether these particular efforts 'worked', at least in the basic sense of forwarding a peace process. It is also important to recall that the purpose in analysing Sadat's efforts is to discover whether there might be common characteristics which *in general* undermine or help to ensure the success of conciliatory initiatives. The diversity revealed in Sadat's initiatives precludes any easy or comprehensive answers to this question, but a survey of these efforts can reveal useful preliminary insights.

For example, while contextual variables draw attention to the 'when' and 'in what circumstances' issues in launching a hopefully effective conciliatory gesture, the variety of actions undertaken by Sadat clearly indicates that another important set of variables concerns the *nature* of the conciliatory initiative itself, and raises issues about the essential characteristics of a successful conciliatory gesture. Similarly, Sadat's experience immediately raises taxonomic questions, and demands an analysis of the various types of conciliatory gesture available, and of their strengths and weaknesses. Allied to both of these 'what' questions is one which arises from an interest in the continuation of a conciliatory initiative and which queries the nature of successful sequences of conciliatory moves, and the manner in which these either start or maintain the momentum towards a stable peace, or fail to lead towards any long-term solution for the conflict in question. It is a matter of historical record, for example, that the process begun by Sadat's dramatic journey to Israel soon ran into problems and that major efforts to 're-start' the process had to be made by the key adversaries and by third parties.

Further insights offered by the varied initiatives launched by Sadat involve the importance of understanding the nature and variety of obstacles to launching any conciliatory initiative successfully and maintaining a conciliatory 'process'. In the reactions of Israeli and American 'targets' of Sadat's moves and of Sadat's supporters and rivals within Egypt and the Arab world, it is possible to see a variety of factors likely to be present in many adversary relationships, ready to affect the likely success of any move towards a negotiated solution. Misperception and disbelief were constant obstacles to successful conciliation. High levels of mistrust needed to be overcome. Mis-attribution of motives and commitments were present in all of Sadat's efforts and seem likely to be constant obstacles to such initiatives in other protracted conflicts. The problem of establishing and maintaining credibility was a constant problem for Sadat – and will be for other would-be conciliators.

Sadat's efforts thus reveal elements likely to be present in other conciliatory processes and to affect the success or failure of any peace process. I have attempted a tentative comparison of these in Table 3.1 overleaf.

Sadat's varied experience can thus provide a heuristic starting point for thinking about four fundamentals that form part of any analysis of the general process of conciliation in protracted and deep-rooted conflicts, exemplified by that involving Israel and Egypt after 1948:

1 Fundamental concepts, definitions and a terminology for discussing conciliation processes.
2 Basic models of the process, most particularly those which concentrate upon conciliation as one form of communication.
3 The effectiveness of various strategies of conciliation, and the nature of 'success' when conciliation strategies are employed by parties in a protracted conflict.
4 Factors that are likely to affect the 'success' of different types of conciliatory gesture made during protracted conflicts which, as with the four undertaken by Anwar Sadat, will embody a variety of characteristics, be made in very different contexts, employ diverse channels of communication, and face numerous obstacles to their launching, recognition and reaction.

The remainder of this chapter undertakes a preliminary discussion of these four fundamental themes, which are analysed in detail in the remainder of the book. Hopefully, this will at least initiate a discussion of the different interpretations of 'successful conciliation' and, at best, will also suggest a set of characteristics, or a 'profile', associated with success.

2 The components of conciliation: concepts and terminology

The sheer variety of President Sadat's experience, the different actions and reactions involved in his conciliation efforts, all argue the need for a clear terminology that can be used to describe the nature of conciliation. This

Table 3.1 President Sadat's Four Conciliation Initiatives

Conciliation Characteristics	Suez Withdrawal February 1971	Post-October 1973
Background & Context	During ceasefire in War of Attrition along Canal. UN initiative resumed 3 days later. Severe domestic constraints. S. accepts possibility of signing accord.	Immediate aftermath of costly war; precarious ceasefire. US playing key Third Party role. Few domestic constraints given war situation.
Intentions of Initiator	Accelerate seemingly stalled UN initiative.	Accelerate disengagement process leading towards a general settlement.
Nature of Conciliatory Gesture	Conditional promise foll. Israeli withdrawal. Highly revocable & linked to complete withdrawal.	Set of discrete moves, mainly irrevocable, plus proposals for future actions.
Channel Used	Initially private & indirect via USA. Then in a public statement.	Direct talks btwn military leaders re. POW exchange, disengagement & withdrawals.
Target's Evaluation	Mixed but some positive. S. seen responding to US pressure. Israel to lose territory with no gain.	Significant if symbolic concessions by S. but following Israeli counter attack.
Target's Reaction	Public rejection followed by counter offer.	Flexible response by Israeli negotiators eventually negated by US and Israeli caution.
Medium/Long-Term Effects	Partial settlements wd. be seriously considered in future, rather than overall solutions.	Reinforced view of S as someone willing to take some risks to move towards a settlement.

Table 3.1   *continued*

Conciliation Characteristics	Re-opening Suez Canal March–June 1975	Jerusalem Visit November 1977
Background & Context	Disengagement from Oct. '73 position half completed, but stalled. US initiative at a standstill. S. had dealt with all opposition.	Taken during US brokered initiative focused on Geneva Conference, seen by S. as unlikely to succeed. S. in flexible position re domestic opposition.
Intentions of Initiator	Break an impasse in on-going disengagement and settlement process.	Circumvent meeting likely to fail or not deal with Egypt/Israel issues. Initiate bilateral peace process.
Nature of Conciliatory Gesture	Conditional offer to re-open Canal, + sanctions on Israelis if no further withdrawal agreements.	Public, irrevocable and un-conditional move.
Channel Used	Public announcements by S. and Egyptian officials	Public announcements, speeches and actions
Target's Evaluation	Forced on S. for economic reasons, plus need for favourable publicity.	Major domestic & economic pressure plus lack of alternatives forcing S. towards conciliation.
Target's Reaction	Subsequent unilateral withdrawal of Israeli troops and armaments in Sinai.	Establishment of processes and institutions to explore terms for a settlement bilaterally.
Medium/Long Term Effects	Reassurance to Israel re non-resumption of war by Egyptians.	Kept USSR out of Israeli/Egyptian relations and was turning point in Middle East politics and in peace process.

should enable everyday concepts such as 'de-escalation', 'peacemaking', or 'accommodation' to achieve some degree of clarity, and act as a preliminary to constructing a more general framework for understanding conciliatory gestures and their place in the overall process of resolving conflicts, especially protracted social conflicts. What follows is a preliminary attempt to construct a practical terminology for such a framework, which starts by taking into account different levels at which conciliatory processes might be analysed.

2.1   The systems level: process and sequence

Any useful terminology of 'conciliation' will have to acknowledge the fact that whatever peacemaking activities are taking place need to be analysed on at least two levels – on that of the parties engaged in the conciliatory activity, and on that of the overall conflict system involving all the conflicting parties, their interactions and relationships. At this second, systems level it is useful to talk about a conflict system being characterised by overall peacemaking or a peace process, which involves a long-drawn-out sequence of actions and responses sometimes involving years and often initiated by a major 'U-turn' away from a system characterised by almost pure coercive interaction – or, at least, by some lessening of the level of coercion between the parties in conflict. Such changes in the nature and levels of interaction are accompanied by parallel structural and psychological shifts in the units making up the system (the parties involved in the conflict), involving a lessening of tension, fear and suspicion within the adversaries and hence the system as a whole; together with a minimal increase in mutual trust and a shared confidence that certain patterns of damaging events will not occur in the future.

Discussion of the Sadat initiatives indicates that a peace process will not necessarily occur smoothly or even continuously. There may be a number of halts due to some impasse, a reversion to outright coercive interaction, or a gap in which nothing occurs for considerable periods of time and stalemate continues. Hence, it appears sensible to speak of peace processes as involving distinguishable 'sequences', and possibly being marked by noticeable gaps in conciliatory activities, or reversions to coercion and violence.

This argues for the use of the term *accommodative sequences* to describe shorter-term system activity during a peace process. In a more tactical sense, then, peace processes consist of sequences of accommodative interaction in which the parties interact in a manner which contains at least a mix of conciliatory and coercive activities, usually with a balance in favour of the former; or in a manner that is almost entirely conciliatory or co-operative. More familiar terms such as 'de-escalation processes', 'accommodative bargaining', or 'benign spirals' capture many aspects of such accommodative sequences, the central feature of which most often involves the simultaneous use of conciliatory and coercive actions, some pattern of exchange involving the offering or conferring of positive benefits often accompanied, paradoxically, by the threatening or imposing of negative costs.

Long-term *peace processes* can vary in the mix of mainly accommodative or mainly coercive sequences that occur as that process develops over time, and the parties involved employ a variety of conciliatory tactics ranging from sequences of unilateral concessions to the offering of unspecified future benefits, usually in return for immediate sacrifices by their adversary. Accommodative sequences can be varied as the overall peace process unfolds, and in extreme cases can break down entirely, so that the system reverts to a pattern dominated by mutual coercion or even war, as it did for Egypt and Israel in October 1973.

Finally, accommodative sequences within a conflict system will clearly consist of patterns of specific moves, acts or statements by the adversaries. These can be termed *accommodative interactions* that commence, maintain or resume an accommodative sequence and contribute to the development of the overall peace process.[2] In everyday language, such interactions are often referred to as 'peace feelers', 'soundings', 'trial balloons' or 'smoke signals', or characterised as 'concessions' or moves to 'build confidence' or 'reduce tension', each being intended to signal a willingness to proceed with an accommodative sequence and to move forward a peace process, with adversaries envisaging a mutually satisfactory solution to the conflict.

Three distinct concepts emerge, then, at the level of the conflict system itself to help in analysing conciliation and its contribution to conflict resolution processes. Each is relevant to distinct time horizons. Firstly 'peace processes' characterise conflict systems in the strategic long term. At the tactical as opposed to the strategic level, conflict systems may be characterised by 'accommodative (as opposed to coercive) sequences', consisting of patterns of exchange between adversaries that – on balance – contain more benign than malign activities. Finally, at the immediate, behavioural level, a conflict system can be characterised by individual 'accommodative interactions' that begin, maintain or re-start accommodative sequences. The three concepts can thus be viewed as strategic, tactical and behavioural components of conciliation viewed at the level of the conflict system.

2.2   The party level: strategies, tactics and behaviour

However, it is important not to lose sight of the earlier argument that conciliation can also be analysed at the level of the parties themselves, quite apart from the level of the conflict system. Analysed at the 'actor' level, conciliation can also be viewed as having behavioural, tactical and strategic components. As discussions of Anwar Sadat's search for peace indicated, parties to a conflict clearly pursue long-term, *conciliatory strategies*, which can be contrasted with *coercive strategies*, although frequently a party's overall policy can consist of a puzzling mixture of both. Equally clearly, analysis of Sadat's policies shows that parties and their leaders can, in the shorter term, utilise *conciliatory tactics* which, if responded to by the adversary, can produce accommodative sequences of interaction at the systemic level. Lastly, conciliatory tactics will clearly be made up of a number of individual *conciliatory gestures*, used to begin, maintain or re-start a peace process, or initiate or accelerate an accommodative episode. For the sake of brevity, I will use the term *conciliatory initiatives* to cover all three types of actor-level behaviour.

Suggestions about useful terminology can be summarised in a simple table which emphasises that the concepts suggested by the analysis apply to interconnected aspects of 'conciliation' viewed not only from a systemic level but also from the viewpoint of the parties, where they are more usually viewed as initiatives, gestures, tactics or strategies, rather than processes or interactive sequences.

Table 3.2   **Basic Terminology for Conciliation Processes**

	Sub-System Behaviour (what parties do:)	*System Properties (conflict system characterised by:)*
Immediate (Behavioural)	CONCILIATORY GESTURES	ACCOMMODATIVE INTERACTIONS
Short Term (Tactical)	CONCILIATORY TACTICS	ACCOMMODATIVE SEQUENCES
Long Term (Strategic)	CONCILIATORY STRATEGIES	PEACE PROCESSES

The overall scheme outlined in Table 3.2 reinforces the argument at the start of this Chapter that 'conciliatory gestures' can best be seen as the basic building blocks of both a peace process taking place within a system previously characterised by all-out coercion and conflict, and of the accommodative sequences or interactions that make up the overall peace process. To a large degree, the success of any effort by parties in conflict to turn away from coercion and escalation and begin moves towards conflict resolution will depend upon the effective, timely and appropriate use of a series of varied conciliatory gestures and their contribution to starting and maintaining accommodative sequences that lead on to negotiations and towards resolution.

3   Conciliation: a communications framework

One clear implication of much of the above argument is that the employment of successful gestures of conciliation is a matter of accurate communication, although achieving this is often most difficult. Conceptualising conciliatory gestures as signals, and accommodative interactions as an exchange of signals, does, however, suggest both a principle for analysis – namely that conciliation can be viewed as a complex form of communication – and a way of understanding the variable success of conciliatory initiatives, both Sadat's and other's.

Unfortunately, on closer examination, the use and understanding of conciliatory gestures as a form of communicating during a conflict do not appear to be all that straightforward. The process of inter-party signalling via an available range of conciliatory gestures turns out to be fraught with practical uncertainties and theoretical problems. Practically, historical cases involving conciliatory strategies such as Anwar Sadat's seem to have been conducted in an essentially a-theoretical fashion, almost in an 'on-the-job', trial-and-error fashion, at best inspired by some untested hunches about the efficacy of particular moves. Theoretically, there are a large number of levels at which analysis might fruitfully be undertaken, few of which have been minimally, let alone thoroughly, explored.

For example, given the arguments that the successful employment of conciliatory gestures is a matter involving clear and accurate communication, achieving this is obviously of some difficulty, especially in protracted conflicts where the parties involved have previously communicated with each other through a mixture of threats, warnings, and cost-imposing, coercive acts. Taking this into account raises questions about the likely effect of prior political circumstances in which conciliatory gestures might be made – that is, the effects of what has happened in the preceding period before the leaders of one party have decided to do a U-turn and launch a conciliatory initiative. Equally, such a prior pattern of interaction is almost bound to produce psychological conditions among members of both parties that render any immediate recognition of positive, conciliatory gestures very difficult – and very easy the assumption that such gestures, when noticed, are mere traps or public relations exercises.

At another level of analysis, the successful use of conciliatory gestures clearly involves intra-party decision-making processes, for such processes determine (i) whether any de-escalatory initiative will ever be taken in the first place; (ii) if so, what its nature will be; and finally (iii) what will be deemed an appropriate reaction to that move from the target. Similarly, the whole question of reaction to the initial signal, and of continuing reaction to a sequence of signals, involves decision-makers in calculations of alternatives, risks and benefits and, frequently, in internal disagreements and serious political in-fighting over the continuation, suspension or termination of some conciliatory process that might appear to some to be getting 'out of hand'.

A third consideration is that conciliatory gestures involve questions of selecting (if choice is available) the ostensibly most appropriate channels through which to communicate appropriate signals, so that they have the most effect, with the minimum of risk. At this level, questions about suitable message carriers and the role of third parties arise, particularly in regard to the latter's possible impact upon the signals being conveyed between parties seeking an end to mutual coercion and damage. Once again, this level of analysis steers any general approach to understanding conciliatory gestures in the direction of communications theories. It also touches upon aspects of the psychology of conflict that have to do with the recognition and understanding of signals in conditions of high tension and resultant stress upon decision-makers, as well as on their information gathering and interpreting systems.

In spite of this complexity, it would seem foolish to abandon completely the insights likely to arise from a communications approach to understanding the conditions for a successful conciliatory gesture or process. Using a communications framework should play a part in understanding the complexities attending efforts such as Sadat's to move a conflict towards a resolution and should enable us to trace out the influence of different factors on the success or failure of historical attempts to conciliate an adversary. I will return to the opportunities afforded by a communications approach and the issue of success and failure later in this Chapter, but turn now to the issue of how to conceptualise factors that might influence the likely effectiveness of conciliatory initiatives.

4   Influences on successful conciliation: a conceptual model

Leaving aside, for the moment, any question of the precise definition of 'success' in conciliation, the next major issue is how to conceptualise conditions which could be conducive to producing a desired result. Is it possible to advance any tentative suggestions about the necessary and sufficient conditions for success? What circumstances are conducive for the effective launching of a conciliation process? What are the factors that need to be present to make it more likely that any conciliation initiative will achieve what its initiators set out to achieve?

This Chapter started with an attempt to learn from President Sadat's experience and suggested some answers to these questions at least as far as Sadat's four efforts were concerned (see Table 3.1). Moving from the diversity of real-world initiatives, such as Sadat's, to the formality of any kind of model normally necessitates considerable simplification and the conflation of many influences into few determinant factors. Hence, both existing theory as well as common sense and the guidance provided by Sadat's initiatives indicate the likelihood that several discernible clusters of factors play an important role in influencing the outcome of any effort at conciliation between long-time adversaries.

As already indicated, one key influence on outcomes is to be found in the actual circumstances of the conflict at the time the conciliatory initiative is launched – the background or *context of the conflict*. It is one thing to launch an initiative at a time of long-standing coercive stalemate, and quite another to do so in the immediate aftermath of a war. The prospects of success seem initially to be brighter if the initiative takes place at a point where the balance of coercive advantage is stable and somewhat symmetrical rather than when one party appears likely to be about to wrest a major military advantage from its adversary. Whatever the precise details of the variables and the relationships involved, it seems safe to say that any preliminary conceptual model will need to include a relationship between the context of the conflict and the probability of success for any conciliatory initiative.

Similarly, it seems more than reasonable to argue that the form of the gesture or series of gestures themselves – the *nature of the initiative* – must have some bearing on its likely impact, although there have been many occasions when even the vaguest, most ill-considered olive branch has been seized upon by a willing adversary as an opportunity to move towards a settlement[1] – an observation that highlights the need to take into account the interactive effects of variables such as the balance of advantage and the nature of some conciliatory gestures. In most other situations, however, it does seem that the qualities of the initial conciliatory move or series of moves – for example its credibility or transparency – will have some positive effect upon its success in eliciting a similar response and thus moving the adversaries towards a less harmful pattern of mutual interaction.

Similar arguments can be made about other clusters of influences likely to affect the impact of a conciliatory gesture. In the accounts of Sadat's conciliatory initiatives, much attention was paid to the reactions of the Israelis who were the prime target of the intiatives, and notice taken of circumstances within Israel, at both elite and constituency level, when Sadat undertook his actions or made his statements. It may be hypothesised that conditions within Israel or any other target of a conciliatory initiative – the *target characteristics* – will have a major impact on the likely effectiveness of the move. A set of leaders firmly in control are likely to perceive, evaluate and react to a conciliatory move from an external adversary in a very different way from an unstable leadership, beseiged by domestic opponents who scent an end to their time out of office.

A similar point can be made about *initiator characteristics*, a set of variables that will have an impact firstly upon one adversary's ability to contemplate a conciliatory initiative, and on the nature of that initiative, but also on the likely reaction of the target, through the latter's evaluation of the credibility of the move and the trustworthiness of those making it. Undoubtedly, the impact of a conciliatory move will be affected by the target's judgement about whether it was made through force of circumstance or because a significantly large group of leaders on 'the other side' had experienced a genuine and permanent change of ambitions *vis-à-vis* the issues in conflict.

Lastly, President Sadat's experiences in trying to start conciliatory processes also suggest that the manner in which the initiative is launched and continued, or the gesture made, is likely to have a significant influence on its effectiveness. For example, the contrast between the open and almost flamboyant nature of the personal visit to Jerusalem and the low-key, behind-the-scenes exchanges that characterised interactions following the 1973 War indicates how conciliatory processes can vary greatly in how they are made, what communications methods are employed, whether these are multiple or singular, sequential or simultaneous, and whether any third parties are involved as go-betweens. It seems safe to argue, therefore, that another element in any preliminary model must be the means or *channels* used to convey the data, to send the signal, or to convey the olive branch to the other side.

The structure of a preliminary conceptual model based upon President Sadat's – often frustrating – experiences in attempting to launch a process of conciliation seems initially straightforward, although efforts to move it towards the complications of real-world conciliation will undoubtedly make it far more complex at each stage of its development. However, as a basic model for thinking about the general nature of conciliatory processes, I would argue that the key aspects of those processes are reflected in Figure 3.1 and will serve as a starting point and useful framework for analysis.

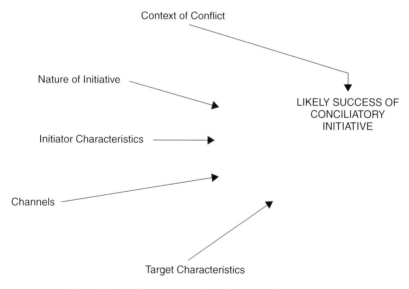

Figure 3.1   **Influences on Conciliation Effectiveness I**

Like all models, the one represented in Figure 3.1. has many limitations, the most significant being its apparent neglect of a key level of explanation. I have argued elsewhere (Mitchell 1995, pp.46–9) that a full understanding of the beginnings of conciliation or de-escalation demands an analysis not merely of structural and behavioural conditions in a conflict system, but also of the interpretation, understanding and evaluation of those conditions by decision-makers involved. What William Zartman, in the context of a conflict's 'ripeness' for resolution, attempts to describe as a move from a 'winning mentality to a conciliating mentality' – a major shift in attitude – depends very largely on how leaders interpret the imperatives of background conditions in the conflict system as well as the opportunities afforded by the behaviour of an adversary (Zartman 1985, p.232).

The model above clearly leaves out a number of intervening variables, mainly at the intra-party decision-making level of analysis, that will explain the likely effectiveness of any conciliatory initiative. Marieke Kleiboer, in discussing what she quite properly calls 'the subjective dimensions of ripeness', talks about the willingness of parties' decision-makers to begin the search for a peaceful solution (Kleiboer 1994, p.115). Similarly, Dean Pruitt's discussion of parties' 'readiness' for a negotiated resolution talks initially about the manner in which structural variables (a hurting stalemate, an impending catastrophe or an enticing opportunity) can produce a *motivation* for conciliation. However it also emphasises that the emergence of a valid (and minimally trustworthy) spokesperson for an adversary and of some new ideas or alternatives for an acceptable solution, can produce a sense of *optimism* among leaders about reaching a supportable settlement (Pruitt 1997, pp.239–40).

Whether one labels key shifts at the decision-making level as changes in willingness, optimism, or motivation – or something quite different – the fact remains that positive alterations in these variables are either necessary conditions for success, in the sense of starting or continuing the kind of positive interactions between adversaries that make up an accommodative sequence or a peace process; or are themselves a somewhat short-term measure of that success. Much discussion in subsequent chapters will be taken up with the issue of whether and under what conditions conciliatory initiatives change such decision-level variables.

It clearly remains the case, though, that firstly this is very much a 'stripped down', parsimonious model; and secondly that it approaches the conciliation process largely from the point of view of the parties to the conflict, either the one undertaking the initiative or the other acting as target. In other words, this is very much an actor-level rather than a system-level model, in the sense that it models the impact of some structural but mainly behavioural factors on adversaries' likely decisions and behaviour. Hence, whether one regards a conflict system as simply being dyadic or – more realistically – as a complex structure of parties, roles and relationships, some of which may be or involve the core parties to the conflict, this model will not throw a complete light upon the process of conciliation at the system level.

What the model does do, however, is to return the discussion to the issue of what exactly is meant by a 'successful' conciliatory process, initiative or gesture – in more formal terms, the nature of the dependent variable of the model. Unfortunately, as I have already implied, what appears to be a straightforward question turns out to be less simple on closer examination.

5   The issue of 'success' in conciliation

A major problem highlighted by using Sadat's conciliatory initiatives as an heuristic device for suggesting fruitful avenues of enquiry into the general nature of conciliatory gestures is that nobody yet seems to have come to any definitive conclusion either about how successful they were or, indeed, about the general nature of 'success' or 'lack of success' resulting from conciliatory initiatives. Does a 'successful' conciliatory gesture mean one which begins a process of de-escalation clearly leading to formal negotiations, irrespective of whether the latter produce an agreement or not? Does 'success' involve producing a major change in the attitudes and expectations of an adversary's elite and/or public opinion? Does it simply involve eliciting a positive, short-term and possibly short-lived response from an adversary?

The everyday criterion of the 'success' or 'effectiveness' of conciliation requires that the process brings about significant changes in the relationship between the adversaries in a protracted conflict, in their attitudes towards one another and, most obviously, in their behaviour. However, another look at the Sadat initiatives suggests that even this everyday conception of effectiveness contains a conglomeration of criteria that may be grouped into two distinct clusters. Firstly, there is the issue of who and what gets changed by the conciliation initiative, and to what degree. This gives rise to queries about the locus, nature and extent of any change brought about by that initiative. Secondly, there is the issue of the longevity of the change, and whether the 'success' of a conciliatory initiative should be judged solely by its long-term impact on the conflict and the parties, or by other, more immediate effects even if these decay rapidly in some situations and circumstances.

5.1   Impacts: locus, nature and extent

By locus, I mean the political location of the change brought about by the conciliatory gesture under analysis, in the sense of 'Who is affected?' Obviously, the most important of the possibilities for an 'initiator' is the direct *target* of the initiative, but Sadat's efforts suggest that others could be added to the list, some of which might be equally important to the party taking the initiative. For example, Sadat's initiatives could be seen as intended to affect:

1 Israeli decision-makers and elites – the direct, primary target.
2 Israeli public opinion – the target's domestic constituents.
3 US decision-makers, elites and public – the target's patrons.
4 Egyptian elites and public – the initiator's constituents.
5 Saudi Arabia, Jordan, the USSR – the initiator's patrons.
6 The UN, France, Sweden, Arab League members – other observers.

All or any of the above targets may be affected by a conciliatory move or series of moves, and the success of such activities can thus be indicated by the number and location of individuals and groups affected by the initiator's actions – that is, how extensive is any change that might take place.

Commonsensically, however, the crucial issue will usually be whether key leaders or elites in the primary target – the adversary – are affected, although, as Sadat's early efforts indicate, other patrons or supporters are sometimes important subsidiary targets. Moreover, although conciliatory gestures are usually aimed most directly at the leaders of an adversary, and only secondarily at an adversary's elites and constituencies, some initiators recognise that within all three levels there are often likely to be divisions, involving powerful factions that are strongly in favour of continuing the struggle (pro-continuation) and others considering alternatives to continued violence and coercion (pro-conciliation). The likely effects of such divisions are considered in detail in Chapter 11, but at this point it is enough to note that one version of effectiveness in undertaking a conciliatory initiative could involve strengthening an adversary's pro-conciliation factions and weakening the influence of those that are pro-continuation.

Other key aspects of a conciliatory gesture's effects involve less the locus of those who change but more the nature and degree of the change, and whether it is possible to discern reliable indicators to show that change has, indeed, taken place. In some cases, the change will be positive (for example, a reduction of hostility or an increase in trust within the target's decision-makers), and in others negative (for example, a decrease in optimism regarding a possible non-violent settlement among the target's elite). For certain conciliatory initiatives, the effect will be intensive, as major changes take place as a result of a move. For others the change will be limited, with individuals in the target making only marginal adjustments to their views or to their actions.

Anwar Sadat's efforts suggest that, at a minimum, 'success' for a conciliatory gesture must involve a positive evaluation of that gesture by those towards whom it is primarily aimed, so that positive evaluation by the target's decision-makers, as well as by the adversary's elites and –

occasionally and provided the gesture is a public one – constituents, becomes a key index of a conciliatory initiative having a successful impact. This does argue for a concentration on the leadership level and – to a lesser degree – on elites when considering at least short-term success.

Beyond that minimum, other impacts may be brought into a broader definition of success by taking other effects into account; for example, whether attitudes change within a target's elites, or whether the target responds with a conciliatory gesture or with a rebuff. Broadly speaking, the following might be useful, general indicators of the 'successful impact' of a conciliatory initiative:

1 Positive evaluation is made in private by target leaders.
2 Positive evaluation is made by elite factions.
3 Positive evaluation is acknowledged in public by target leaders and elite factions.
4 Positive evaluation is made by target's general public.
5 Noticeable change in leaders and elite's attitudes and expectations takes place.
6 Noticeable change occurs in mass attitudes and expectations.
7 Positive reaction by target takes place.
8 Major subsequent change in pattern of target–initiator interaction amounts to an accommodative sequence.
9 Achievement of substantive negotiations.
10 Achievement of acceptable agreement.

Major problems with this list of criteria for 'success' are that it ranges from a perceptual reaction of a small group of leaders to a major relationship change between the adversaries. More particularly, it includes changes that take place immediately following the initiative and others temporally distant from, and far less easy to attribute to, the move. Quite apart from the number of other influences affecting whether or not – for example – parties reach the point of substantive negotiations, ought conciliatory initiatives to be evaluated for their shorter- or longer-term effects?

5.2   Short v long-term impacts

On any scale, the four initiatives undertaken by President Sadat between 1970 and 1977 clearly show very different degrees of long term 'effectiveness', with only the visit to Jerusalem serving to affect Israeli decision-makers, elites and publics in a significantly positive way and resulting in a continuing accommodative sequence that led to direct negotiations but which failed, ultimately, to produce a final settlement. By contrast, the opening of the Suez Canal only seems to have marginally and temporarily altered Israeli elite attitudes and helped to start a new accommodative sequence, while the Kilometre 101 talks produced an aborted accommodative sequence and little change of elite attitudes.

These examples demonstrate the point made above that the same conciliatory initiative can be assessed very differently depending upon whether its effects are evaluated according to long-, medium- or short-term criteria. Logically, there are four possible types of success depending upon whether observers look for shorter- or longer-term impacts:

1 *Immediate effects*, in having the initiative noticed and reviewed by the target's leaders and elites.
2 *Short-term effects*, in beginning to change the leaders', elites' and constituents' attitudes towards the initiating adversary and about views of possible solutions.
3 *Medium-term effects*, in eliciting a response from a target and thus starting or re-starting an accommodative sequence.
4 *Long-term effects*, in achieving some form of direct discussions or negotiations about a solution, perhaps leading to an acceptable final settlement.

Given the difficulty of tracing through the impact of any single change in the long term, and the likelihood that many factors will contribute to the successful conclusion of a peace process, it seems both inherently unfair and theoretically perilous to evaluate the 'success' or 'effectiveness' of a conciliatory initiative according to whether it succeeded or failed in producing a solution or even substantive negotiations. More realistically, when talking about the 'likely success of a conciliatory initiative', reasonably relevant criteria of success would seem best sought in immediate or short-term changes brought about by conciliatory gestures or, at the most, by medium-term alterations in the manner in which parties interact with one another – in other words, whether conciliatory moves initiate an accommodative sequence between adversaries. However, this raises the issue of what immediate and short-term indicators might be used to evaluate shorter-term 'success' in conciliation.

6 'Likely success' in the shorter term

Normally, of course, 'being successful', even in the immediate or short term, involves asking whether a particular initiative has produced the effect desired by the initiator, and to what degree. On the other hand, alternative criteria can exist for making judgements of effectiveness, depending on the framework being used to analyse the relationship. Viewing conciliation as a form of communication thus leads to questions about what criteria are relevant to determining the relative effectiveness or ineffectiveness of communications patterns, and what factors might influence such levels of success.

6.1   Success as 'clarity'

In a communications approach, one fundamental is that conciliation is most appropriately viewed as a signalling process which involves parties in conflict in efforts to infuence each other through the exchange of messages designed to convey information which would structure and then affect a 'target's' future choices and behaviour. It is true that various versions of such a communications 'process' are available, but all share the conception of a number of components making up the complete act of communication.[2] Any communications framework, such as the one illustrated opposite as Figure 3.2, will help to elucidate processes by which conciliatory gestures and initiatives are contemplated, launched, interpreted, argued about and (sometimes) responded to by parties in conflict, and will help any study of elements which affect the relative success and failure of any conciliatory move.

The framework emphasises the number of hurdles any conciliatory gesture must overcome, by referring to various 'screens' which can distort, misinterpret, cut out part of the information sent, and – in some cases – wholly reject a signal from an adversary. Given these organisational, perceptual and psychological obstacles to a clear reading and evaluation of any conciliatory signal, can one regard a gesture that is noted and accurately evaluated by an adversary as 'effective', or must that label be reserved for one that elicits a positive response?

In confronting this question, it needs to be recalled that the process of communicating between parties about conciliation is not precisely analogous to signalling between individuals. There are major differences in signalling between individuals and signalling between individuals who collectively comprise the decision-making 'systems' of complex, institutionalised parties. The latter process confronts all of the problems attendant upon interpersonal communication, such as difficulties of misperception and misinterpretation, but also faces a whole range of additional problems. For one thing, in attempts to begin conciliation between individuals in conflict, it is often difficult to keep track of a target's salient goals and the preference orderings of those goals. (Both can change dramatically and frequently.) The problem is compounded when the process has to try to affect a target within which different individuals or factions possess different goals and preference orderings, so that no single goal hierarchy for 'the party' realistically exists.

Moreover, the problem of *perceptual congruence* is complicated by the fact that the message decision-makers intend to send to an adversary – a symbolic, conciliatory gesture, a minor concession or a move to build trust – may not be the one actually sent. This difference between intended and despatched messages may simply arise because of the need (in complex parties such as those headed by national governments) to separate the *policy choice process* from the *policy implementation process*, a division of labour

53

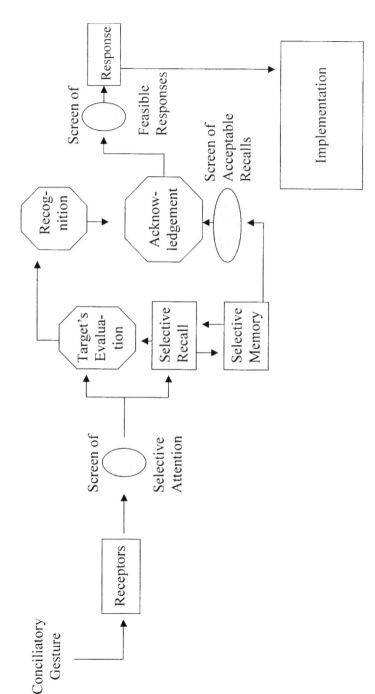

Figure 3.2 **Basic Communications Framework (adapted from K.W. Deutsch, *The Nerves of Government*)**

usually taken purely for 'efficiency' in policy making. In some cases, the implementation of a decision to make a conciliatory gesture may be delayed, transmitted together with other contrary signals, or even inadvertently distorted because of the workings of bureaucratic implementation procedures. This adds another layer of uncertainty and potential misinterpretation to the whole process of signalling. All these stages have to be 'right' if the initiative is to have any impact, an argument which suggests one very simple approach to the issue of what constitutes a 'successful' conciliatory gesture – namely that at its most basic, 'success' involves obtaining a high level of agreement between the message intended by the initiator, the message conveyed by the initiator, and the message received by the target:

Message intended = Message actually sent = Message received

This formulation emphasises once again that, if one is considering the issue of immediate success or effectiveness, then the accurate recognition of a message *and* the fact that it is conciliatory in intent constitutes one basic measure of success for any conciliatory move. At the very beginning of an accommodative sequence, gestures that are not even noticed, or that are misinterpreted as non-conciliatory, clearly achieve something akin to a zero level of effectiveness.

This basic benchmark of 'non-success' also suggests that a target's immediate recognition and evaluation of the gesture is a key intervening factor which determines subsequent impact, and hence short-term effectiveness, which in turn offers some preliminary clues as to characteristics of the initiative likely to increase its influence. Three basic qualities of an initiative seem likely to be important in its evaluation by the target:

1   Whether the conciliatory gesture stands out from other signals emanating from the initiator in such a way as to bring it swiftly to the attention of decision-makers in the target. In other words, a high level of *discernability* seems a necessary precondition for the initiative being evaluated in such a way that it will bring about a positive reaction.
2   Whether the conciliatory gesture achieves an acceptable level of perceived *credibility* within the Target, mainly as regards decision-makers and elites.
3   Whether the conciliatory gesture is seen as increasing decision-makers' ability (and hence willingess) to respond by helping to overcome barriers within the target. Conciliatory moves vary according to their perceived *respondability* and the degree to which they offer riskless opportunities to react.

Thus increasing *discernability*, or 'recognisability', *credibility* and *respondability* seem to be key requirements for parties thinking about initiating concil-

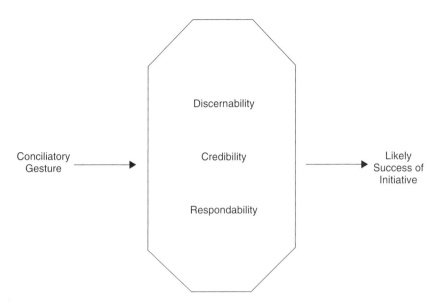

Figure 3.3   **Target Evaluation as an Intervening Influence**

iatory moves and concerned with increasing the chances of a successful first step.

Having the signal detected, recognised and accurately evaluated as being at least minimally conciliatory seems a far cry from achieving a negotiated solution to the conflict, but it can act as one basic criterion for determining immediate success. Moreover, it does imply that other benchmarks may be found to indicate the degree of short- and medium-term effectiveness, and to provide sequential indicators of success in a communications/conciliation process by indicating how far along this sequence an initiative might reach.

6.2   A sequential approach to short-term success

The idea of treating any conciliatory gesture as a sequential form of communication raises both practical and conceptual questions about each part of the sequence. For example, who chose the particular 'signal', who implemented it, and were these the same person or institution? What 'noise' accompanied the signal and how did this affect the ambiguity of the signal or the consistency of a series of signals? At the receiving end of the process, how effective were the target's sensors in picking up the signal and its interpretive systems in accurately evaluating it?[3]

Conceptually, it should be relatively easy, at least in principle, to tell how far the signal moved beyond a formulation stage to one at which it was actually sent, to one where it was detected relatively noise free, interpreted accurately, and then responded to by the target, thus extending the first conciliatory move into a process. Unarguably, the most 'unsuccessful' signal is the one that is never sent, a not-unusual phenomenon, given the dangers and uncertainties surrounding the launching of any conciliatory initiative, well illustrated by the risks Sadat had to take in undertaking some of his efforts. With this in mind, the very first, basic benchmark of success might not be a target's recognition of the gesture but simply that of conceiving the possibility that a conciliatory move might be worthwhile. This is not something that readily occurs to leaders engaged in a violent, protracted conflict, so that the fact that such an option is even given some attention is not to be denigrated. Contemplation of a possible move might not, however, lead to its being undertaken, given the risks and constraints that normally exist when parties are focused on the justice of their struggle and the effective use of coercion to obtain their rightful goals. Hence a second degree of success could well be the overcoming of political, organisational and psychological obstacles and the implementing of some conciliatory move by some of the leaders of an embattled party. This suggests a second, rather minimal benchmark of success, that of the signal that actually gets sent, to which others can be added, including – as I have previously suggested – the actual detection or recognition of a signal by the Target and its accurate evaluation as regards the sender's intentions. Passing these 'benchmarks' would indicate increasing degrees of short-term effectiveness, and the whole sequence could involve stages of:

1 *Contemplation*, in that some key leaders or decision-makers in one of the adversaries begin to consider the possibility of launching a cautious conciliatory move as a serious alternative to continuing the struggle through existing coercive means.
2 *Initiation*, in that a conciliatory move is planned and launched, a degree of success that raises fundamental queries about what determines the willingness of one party to a conflict to risk initiating a peace process by undertaking (at least) one conciliatory gesture, and what affects the nature of that gesture and its smooth implementation.
3 *Recognition*, discernment or detection, in that at least some leaders in the target actually recognise the initiative as being conciliatory. This leads to a series of questions, such as what affects the likelihood that the target of a conciliatory gesture will, in fact, recognise that an initiator's perceived action is intended to be conciliatory rather than having some other purpose (for example, a public relations gesture).
4 *Acknowledgement*, in that leaders in the target indicate in some way, either publicly or within decision-making circles that they recognise the nature of the signal. The stage involves questions about what determines whether those perceiving the initiative as a serious conciliatory gesture

will be able to acknowledge this publicly (at the very least to the point of admitting it to fellow decision makers or to opinion makers).

5 *Reaction*, in that the target responds to the signal by returning some communication of its own, raising questions about what determines whether a target will respond with a positive move rather than a rejection or a rebuff.

6 *Interaction*, in that both parties continue a sequence of non-coercive signalling in an accommodative sequence, setting off a longer term peace process and a mutual search for a solution. This raises issues of what factors determine whether this initial conciliation process will continue in a reciprocal exchange of concessions leading to a benign 'spiral' of interaction, possible negotiations, and the eventual resolution of the conflict.

Using a sequential approach based on the principle of 'degrees' of success, a conciliatory gesture that is actually sent as a signal to the adversary and is recognised and responded to positively can be viewed as more 'successful' than one which is misinterpreted as a piece of public relations and completely ignored, although the latter might be counted as more successful than an initiative that is simply not picked up because of the surrounding noise of self-justification, threat and vilification.

In short, a communications framework suggests the possible utility of an ordinal scale of short- to medium-term success for conciliatory gestures, if not for more complex conciliatory processes, running from least to most successful:

1 Conciliatory gesture is contemplated as a viable option;
2 Gesture is initiated (conceived and made);
3 Gesture is received and clearly recognised by target;
4 Gesture is internally acknowledged as credible by target;
5 Gesture is reciprocated by target;
6 Accommodative sequence ensues, with exchange of positive moves and signals.

While not forming a 'scale of effectiveness' that would be recognised by any serious social science methodologist, the sequence of 'benchmarks' outlined above does provide some rough and ready means of determining relative levels of short term success for conciliatory gestures. Moreover, it is based upon a communications approach that usefully opens up a number of different ways into the question of what might help and what hinder an understanding of why some conciliatory initiatives do initiate accommodative sequences, however brief, while others merely alter evaluations and perceptions or fail to break through a target's stony indifference. The last question for this chapter is – How will all or any of this be used?

7   Format for the study

While the discussion of determinants, definitions and indicators of success-ful conciliation has covered a wide variety of possible approaches and frameworks, the major focus for the rest of this study will remain the question of what factors make it more likely that conciliatory initiatives will achieve any measure of success – however the latter is defined. In carrying the discussion further, therefore, I will use two of the basic approaches outlined in this chapter:

1 a *communications* framework, which treats the issue of conciliation as a process of communication, and success in conciliation as dependent upon success in signalling and in overcoming obstacles to launching, receiving and interpreting a conciliatory signal, as well as the target's acknowledging and responding; and
2 a *causal* model, which attempts to connect five major variable clusters with the likely success of conciliation, viewed in the short term as a positive evaluation of the initiative by the target and in the medium term as the start and maintenance of an accommodative sequence.

From this point on, the study will adopt a short-term and somewhat elitist approach to the nature of success and the question of the effectiveness of conciliatory moves. It will be short term in the sense that it will focus on issues of change (most often marginal shifts) in the perceptions, attitudes and expectations of adversaries; and on short-term behavioural responses to conciliatory gestures that start, continue or help to re-start accommodative sequences. It will be elitist in that it will concentrate attention on changes in decision-makers and elites within adversaries who become initiators or targets for conciliatory moves. The arguments for this approach are that, at this stage of a peacemaking process, it is normally elites and decision-makers who play a crucial role – although Anwar Sadat's visit to Jerusalem should be a reminder of indirect influences on the process that can arise from mass publics. 'Success', hereafter, will be regarded as having a 'positive' impact on decision-makers and elite views and in initiating or continuing co-operative behaviour in an accommodative sequence.

It may be argued that such a study will be concentrating only on the initial stages of a peacemaking process, so that it can hardly explain why one activity contributes to the ultimate resolution of a conflict, while others do not. Even a casual acquaintance with the problems of conflict resolution in the real world of protracted and violent conflict will indicate how complicated and lengthy is that overall process. On the other hand, almost any systematic attempt, however preliminary, to understand any part of such a complex process will be none the worse for starting modestly and concentrating upon basic issues before moving on to more complex problems.

Subsequent chapters will examine the characteristics of conciliatory gestures, their effects and side effects, and the constraints on initiating and responding to such initiatives. Most importantly, they will seek to illuminate the factors affecting their successful use as signalling devices and as efforts to influence the behaviour of an adversary in such a way as to initiate and sustain a successful peace process.

The next chapter will discuss the context of conciliatory initiatives and the way in which this shapes their launching and reception. Subsequent chapters will consider the form and content of particular types of conciliatory gestures. Most particularly, these chapters will deal with how conciliatory gestures might contribute to the diminution of mistrust between erstwhile adversaries. They will also examine factors that might contribute to its non-reception or faulty interpretation by a target, an examination that will inevitably cover psychological factors that contribute to the recognition or rejection of gestures intended to be conciliatory.

Later chapters will deal with the divisions and constraints within initiating and target parties that might account for a lack of clarity in signal *content*, as well as the level of *noise* accompanying the signal. The latter discussion will inevitably involve some consideration of the effects of various kinds of channel on the interpretation and reaction of the target, a discussion which will also involve consideration of the role of third parties in communicating, endorsing and amplifying conciliatory signals. Finally, I will attempt to bring these interlinked ideas together into a framework that will help in the general understanding of conciliatory initiatives, and their role in accommodative sequences and peace processes as well as in the overall process of conflict resolution.

The next part of the study turns from the empirical example of conciliatory gestures used by Anwar Sadat to concepts, propositions and approaches that might throw additional light upon the issue of 'successful' conciliatory initiatives viewed as an integral preliminary to 'successful' peacemaking.

4
Contexts For Conciliation

'It is circumstances and proper timing that give an action its character and make it good or bad.'

Agiselaus from Plutarch's *Lives*, Book 23

In Chapter 3 I argued that accounting for the success or lack of success of any conciliation initiative involved focusing on five sets of factors likely to influence the manner in which the conciliatory gesture was contemplated, initiated, recognised, acknowledged and reacted to. The five were: the context of the conflict itself, the nature of the initiative, the condition of both the initiator and the target and the channels through which the initiative was conveyed from the former to the latter. In this chapter I will discuss the first of these clusters of variables in an attempt to delineate key influences on likely success from within the *context* of the conciliatory move, and then propose a heuristic model of contextual dimensions to guide further investigation. Chapter 4 thus concentrates upon one aspect of the original causal model.

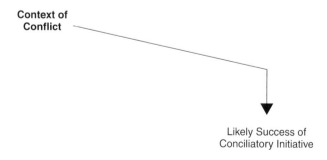

Figure 4.1 **Influences on Conciliation Effectiveness II**

1   The setting for conciliation: background factors

The review of Anwar Sadat's conciliatory initiatives between 1971 and 1977 in Chapter 3 emphasises that such moves take place, almost by definition, within an adversary relationship and against a background of prior interaction, involving coercion and violence. Hence, at the very least, this short-term context will frequently affect the move's likely effects, for good or ill, the interaction between the parties in the period immediately *preceding* any de-escalatory initiative being more than likely to have a significant effect on whether a conciliatory gesture is actually initiated, and also whether it is evaluated accurately and reacted to in such a manner as to make likely the continuation of a peace process.

Apart from Sadat's experience, conventional wisdom also holds that the context for a conciliatory move always has a significant effect on its likely degree of success. To take two contrasting examples, making effective conciliatory gestures at the height of a war is a very different process (and presents very different problems) from making similar gestures at the end of a long period of isolation and relatively tranquil stalemate. Initiating or responding to conciliatory moves in late October 1973 was, for both Israelis and Egyptians, a wholly different matter from making them in 1977, after three years of military peace and the comparative success of the mutual disengagement process arranged step by step through the efforts of US Secretary of State Kissinger. Different factors also play a role during a pre-negotiation period preceding face-to-face negotiations, when the parties confront a deadlock, the prospect of agreement recedes, and some move is necessary to get around this impasse. Again, it obviously makes a considerable difference whether decision-makers are trying to defuse a rapid and dangerously developing crisis or to restore normal relations after an inconclusive military confrontation, followed by a long period of tacit isolation and petty harrasment (the situation between the USA and the CPR when President Nixon and Premier Chou-en-Lai began to send out cautious peace feelers in 1969–70). At the very least, the urgency in the former setting is likely to result in major and multiple gestures – but also in missed and misinterpreted signals. The latter case is likely to be susceptible to more discreet 'soundings', over a longer time period, without the same sense of urgency or impending disaster.

Quite apart from the Sadat initiatives, then, any list of occasions on which parties in conflict have conveyed 'olive branches' or floated 'trial balloons' would suggest the potentially wide variety of circumstances in which adversaries might launch de-escalatory initiatives through a variety of conciliatory gestures, with each likely to have its own particular features and its problems to be overcome. These would range from conciliatory moves made during a major crisis, such as the Cuban missile crisis of October 1962, through those made during temporary lulls in long-drawn-out wars

(Iran or Iraq following the first stage of the first Gulf War in 1981); to those contemplated after the cessation of actual hostilities but where relations remain tense and dangerously volatile (Anglo–Argentine relations after the 1982 war in the South Atlantic).

Any review of the backgrounds against which conciliatory initiatives have been undertaken will reveal a very 'mixed bag' of situations that seem minimally comparable. Very different answers would be offered in each case to questions such as: Are the adversaries attempting to defuse a crisis situation before violence has been employed or are they looking for a way out of an on-going, 'hot' war or a cold confrontation? Has there been a cessation of coercion via some truce or cease-fire? Are there formal, bilateral channels through which conciliatory gestures might be made? To what extent is the psychological condition of the parties still affected by having recently been the targets of mutual (and probably destructive) coercion? What is the relative balance of advantage between the adversaries?

Trying to answer such questions demonstrates some of the problems of constructing a *typology of contexts* that might be useful for comparative analysis of the backgrounds for successful and unsuccessful conciliatory moves. For example, one simple approach would be to take as a key dimension organised and purposeful violence and classify contexts for conciliation according to whether they broadly involve situations pre, during or post-violence between the adversaries, given that the threshold of purposeful violence is generally a key practical and a symbolic 'marker' in patterns of interaction between conflicting parties. (What might be called the 'first blood' principle.) A slightly more sophisticated taxonomy might posit five basic contexts for conciliation in protracted and deep-rooted conflicts (Table 4.1).

Table 4.1   **Levels of Violence in Contexts for Conciliation**

Pre-Violence	During Escalating Violence	During Continuing High Level of Violence	While Violence Abating	When Violence Terminated
US–Iran 1979–80	Cuban Missile Crisis 1962	Korean War 1953	Lull in Iran–Iraq War 1981	Post South Atlantic War 1982

Perhaps more fruitfully, analysis could take up the old adage that 'change begets change' and posit that conciliation is most likely to occur successfully when the context for the conflict has become more fluid than previously, thus offering leaders of the parties an occasion for a major reconsideration of policy, a greater degree of flexibility than they enjoyed in previous time periods, and the opportunity (at least) for adopting new patterns of behaviour. Returning to the four cases involving Anwar Sadat, two underlying themes seem clearly revealed. All four seem capable of being classified either as initiatives undertaken following (or in anticipation of) some major form of change, or as apparently undertaken following some ostensible form of long-drawn-out *stasis* or deadlock, which presumably led to a high level of decision-making frustration.

In fact, the former, *dynamic* type of context seems to predominate in our examples. In the four Sadat initiatives, the contexts can be summarised as:

1   Made in anticipation of a resolution of a major UN initiative (the Jarring Mission, second stage).
2   Made when moving from a situation of armed combat to a ceasefire and post-combat negotiations (following the 1973 campaigns).
3   Made during the continuing failure of the second round of the US brokered disengagement process.
4   Made in anticipation of an imminent third party process that increasingly seemed likely to fail, and involved the reintroduction of a formerly ousted patron (the USSR) as a major influence (at the proposed Geneva Conference).

I would argue that this approach via differential change is, theoretically, the most interesting, as it leads on to further suggestions about causal connections between contexts for conciliation and the likely success of conciliatory initiatives.

2   Change as a key feature in contexts for conciliation

The principle that major prior, imminent or anticipated change is likely to be a common feature of contexts in which conciliatory initiatives will probably be successfully initiated and maintained is a straightforward one. In essence, it arises from an argument about the nature of decision-making during protracted and deep-rooted conflicts, which starts from the empirical observation that decision-makers facing an adversary and attempting to obtain their goals (that is, to 'win' the conflict) by chosen policies to which much time and effort have been devoted rarely pause to reconsider fundamentally either goals or policies. In other words, as I have argued elsewhere (Mitchell 1991, p.36–8), decision-making during a protracted struggle usually concerns the day to day conduct of operations designed to make the adversary quit, and to counter their efforts at making 'us' quit.

Typically decision-makers in conflict utilise an *incremental continuation* mode of decision-making, which is based on Herbert Simon's process of 'satisficing', and is typified by the incremental adjustment of existing policies. However, the decision to initiate some conciliatory move or to plan an accommodative sequence clearly is not a minor decision as it involves a major reversal of strategy – or, at least, of thinking about alternative means

of attaining goals. On such occasions, the whole focus and scope of decision-making changes to a more fundamental reconsideration of basic goals
and means, which I have characterised as a *comprehensive reconsideration*
mode (Mitchell ibid. p.37), but this is not an exercise likely to be undertaken easily or often. Hence, there needs to be some 'occasion for reconsideration' by decision-makers, which provides a context for a major
re-evaluation of the conflict and 'the weighing of options, ends, means,
costs, benefits and probabilities' (ibid.). It follows that the most likely circumstances bringing about such an 'occasion' will involve some major
change or discontinuity. This will swing at least the decision-makers in one
party to the conflict into a comprehensive reconsideration mode which
will possibly (but not inevitably) lead to some conciliatory gesture,
however small, and may then lead to an accommodative response by other
parties in the conflict system.

The argument that some change is likely to lead to reconsideration and
conciliation seems inherently plausible, but it immediately raises the question of what kind of change and change in what. If prior dynamism is a
necessary, even if not a sufficient, condition for conciliatory gestures to be
made by the parties and accommodative sequences of interaction to begin
to characterise the conflict system, what is the nature, direction and intensity of that change, and how does it differ from other types of change that
might lead on to an intensification of coercion and violence, rather than
efforts to move towards a mutually acceptable solution?

Empirically, a whole variety of changes suggest themselves as providing
contexts for conciliation. A major crisis or other form of escalation that has
just been averted, exemplified by the 1962 Cuba Missile Crisis, often seems
to lead to a subsequent lessening of tension and the sending out of some
form of 'peace feeler'. A lull or change of intensity in the level of fighting
or other form of coercion provides another such context. The period following a mutual or unilateral set-back or disaster is another time of change
in many conflicts that has provided the occasion for efforts to conciliate.
Paradoxically, the breakdown of one peace process and a resumption of
mutual coercion often seems to lead to renewed efforts to start another
accommodative sequence. The defection or ejection of an ally of one of the
adversaries is another common change that often leads one side or the
other to send out signals indicating the possibility of a major change
of strategy; so is the involvement of one of the adversaries in another,
separate conflict.

Many analysts, most notably James Rosenau (1990), have argued that
change produces both unpredictability and uncertainty for decision-
makers, including those involved in conflict systems, and hence may lead
to changed actions and goals. However, while it seems a reasonable starting
point to argue that *all* forms of exogenous change will afford the leaders of
parties in conflict an opportunity, at least, to initiate conciliatory processes,

it seems equally reasonable to assume that different types and degrees of change will afford greater or lesser opportunities for altering the course of a protracted conflict and moving it towards a solution. Different effects, for example, are likely to follow change that takes the form of a marked discontinuity with past patterns of interaction from that which involves crossing some significant threshold for the parties in conflict.

Types of change can differ in scope, speed, continuity, reversibility and effects,[1] so that – for example – it is likely that rapid change will have a different impact than change which is gradual, while the same can be said about change which is smoothly incremental compared with that which is abrupt and discontinuous. As a working hypothesis, it would seem reasonable to argue that different effects are likely to flow from a major change that is abrupt and discontinuous (such as the defection of an ally) as opposed to one where the change is gradual but continuous (such as the gradual erosion of financial resources available to prosecute the conflict or the downgrading of a goal once deemed essential).

With this in mind, I propose four key characteristics of change in conflict systems that seem likely to provide a context in which conciliatory initiatives might be launched most successfully:

1 Abrupt as opposed to gradual change.
2 Extensive as opposed to limited change.
3 Irreversible as opposed to reversible change.
4 Discrete as opposed to continuous change.

With regard to the impact of such different forms of change, Rosenau has cautioned that it is always necessary to recall that it often takes decision-makers some time to recognise that major change has occurred and thus for it to have any effect on goals, attitudes or subsequent behaviour, conciliatory or otherwise. For example, it often takes time for decision-makers to recognise that some irreversible change has, indeed, taken place, although Rosenau also notes that 'Sometimes ... the breakpoint is so widely perceived that the changes wrought by it are explicitly defined as new continuities, rather than possible departures from past practices' (1990, p.84). Hence, it is not surprising that recognition of change and reaction to it are frequently *lagged* rather than *immediate*. It is an important principle in analysing the effects of different types of change to recall that 'thresholds are reached and crossed when people become aware that things are fundamentally different' (ibid.). Moreover, it is also the case that cognitive factors play a part in decision-makers' *anticipation* of change, which – as Sadat's initiatives demonstrate – can also be a powerful influence on the launching of conciliatory gestures.[2]

Paradoxically, the concept of *lagged* reactions to change suggests that even initiatives that seem to occur during a period of stability and little change may be the results of major prior change, the irreversibility of which has only tardily been recognised as such by the affected decision-makers, who take time to recognise that they confront an entirely new and different situation. Conciliatory moves arising from Zartman's well know 'hurting stalemate', for example, may be the result of a belated recognition by decision-makers that a previous period characterised by fluctuating balance of advantage or by a gradual 'overtaking pattern' has come to an end, and been replaced by a situation involving stasis, stalemate and accumulating costs. There seems a strong possibility that, in many cases, there will be a refusal by leaders to recognise that the adversaries now face circumstances involving long-term, stable symmetry, and an assumption that this temporary situation of 'no change' will rapidly revert to a familiar 'overtaking pattern' or moves towards long-term dominance by one side or the other.[2]

Of the four key characteristics of change, I would argue that, while all four are likely to provide a helpful context for conciliation and to affect the likelihood of conciliatory gestures being forthcoming, the primary influence will arise from the *scope* or intensity of change. This does not necessarily mean that scope should be interpreted as a system affected by a large number of relatively minor changes over a short period of time. Clearly, many sudden minor discontinuities often provide tactical occasions for conciliation efforts but, while the sheer number (and variety) of such minor changes is often very large (particularly if attention is concentrated upon short-term, incremental changes in tactics or behaviour), this does not always indicate significant change likely to encourage conciliatory initiatives by parties facing a completely new and different set of circumstances. Such minor changes in a conflict system might best be regarded as *system fluctuations*, and while these may represent some degree of change and do afford an opportunity for conciliatory moves, it seems far more likely that some forms of change bringing about conflict *system transformation* will provide a context more conducive to conciliation and a search for solutions. Hence, what is needed analytically is some organising principle to distinguish change that will strongly affect a conflict system and bring about a context for conciliation.

In this regard, it would be helpful to distinguish among three levels of change which represent, in themselves, different *intensities* affecting the state of a conflict system, of the parties involved, and the likelihood of a successful conciliatory initiative being launched and an accommodative sequence developing. These are:

1 Structural changes in the conflict system itself.
2 Strategical changes in the relationship and patterns of interactions between the adversaries and between the adversaries and their environments.

3 Tactical changes, in the behaviour, actions or statements of the adversaries, or their style of conducting the conflict. Graphically, the levels are modelled in Figure 4.2.

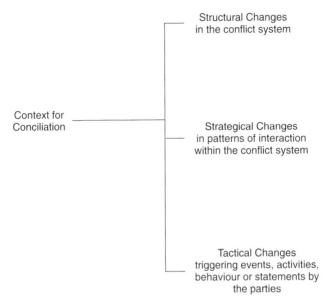

Figure 4.2 **Contextual Dimensions**

Obviously, the nature of change (as well as its direction, rate and frequency) at each of these levels is likely to vary greatly, with tactical changes occurring more often and more readily than change at either the strategic or, particularly, the structural level. However, the overall scope of change in a conflict system (and the existence of a context for conciliation) can range from changes in the structure of the conflict system itself, which are of major significance when they occur, to changes in action and behaviour from week to week (or even day to day) which are regarded as minor unless they 'add up', over time, to changes at the strategic level.

Interconnections between changes at the three levels are inevitable over both the long and short term. For example, the involvement of new parties as additional elements in the structure of a conflict system will rapidly alter both the pattern of interactions between the other elements, and the tactical behaviour of at least some of the latter. In the longer term, incremental, tactical changes in the activities of one party may succeeed in dividing another, so that additional elements are created. All of these various types of interlinked change will, in turn, have an effect on increasing or decreasing the likelihood of conciliatory processes beginning or continuing.

Anticipating a later argument, it seems likely that structural changes will produce a context for conciliation that makes it more likely that conciliatory initiatives will succeed than would be the case with a context only involving strategical changes. Short-term tactical changes may present briefly open 'windows of opportunity' for starting successful conciliation processes – as long as it is recalled that windows close as easily as they open.

3   Structural changes in conflict systems

Structural change in a conflict system can take a variety of forms. For example, the collapse of the Soviet Union in the early 1990s and the termination of its major role as a patron or interested intervener transformed a number of conflict systems in widely different regions of the world, from the Middle East to South Africa and Northern Ireland, paving the way for major subsequent changes in those systems. Similarly, the linking of the conflict system involving Iran and Iraq to another, involving Iraq, Kuwait, Saudi Arabia and a coalition of mainly western governments led by the USA, exemplified major, structural change and resulted in the rapid termination of the former conflict.

Providing examples of major structural change illustrates the main argument of this section of the study, but for more systematic analysis some general principles of conflict system transformation that could be linked to the development of a context for conciliation in such systems are needed. Initial ideas arise from the work of organisational theorists, who argue that changes in system *complexity* can produce turbulence, uncertainty and a potential for major change between and within the actors making up the system. These theorists (Rosenau 1990, pp.61–2; La Porte 1975, p.6) have argued that important changes in the level of complexity sufficiently significant to constitute 'system transformation' and to effect major changes in both system dynamics and actor behaviour usually involve changes in:

1 The number of actors in the system, with a greater number increasing the resultant intensity and complexity of interactions.
2 The variety of actors in the system, with a greater variety leading to more elaborate interactions.
3 The degree of interdependence among the actors in the system, with greater interdependence leading to greater intricacy in the interactions between actors.

It is certainly the case that these three types of change in system *complexity* are likely to produce a greater willingness on the part of some of the actors to initiate conciliation processes, but I would argue that there are other types of major changes in a conflict system equally likely to have a similar effect, so that structural changes other than the three types outlined above can also produce a context for conciliation. At the very least, changes in the following structural characteristics of conflict systems are likely to produce unpredictability and uncertainty in the minds of decision-makers that could lead towards conciliation:

1 **Complexity** – defined as the number of separately distinguishable parties centrally involved in the system. In conflict systems, these usually consist of two major adversaries, (sometimes themselves involving coalitions of separate actors) together with allies or patrons, and other actors playing a variety of 'third party' roles, such as advocates, conveners or intermediaries.
2 **Isolation** – defined as the degree to which the system is connected with other conflict systems. It is not unusual, for example, to find at least one of the adversaries in one conflict system participating in other significant but unconnected conflicts, which all become 'interlocked' (Kriesberg 1980, p.102).
3 **Interdependence** – defined as the degree to which the adversaries are interdependent or could survive in isolation from one another. Clearly, what holds adversaries together in some conflict systems is their adversary relationship which, should the conflict be ended, will dissolve and the parties become thoroughly isolated (for example, Israel and Egypt). In other systems, it is not realistically feasible for the parties to attain complete isolation; some new relationship other than one of conflict will have to form part of the solution (for example, Israel and Palestinians).
4 **Salience** – defined as the importance of the issues in conflict to the adversaries.
5 **Range** – defined as the number of issues in contention between the main adversaries.
6 **Convergence** – defined as the degree to which the adversaries agree on the nature of the issues in dispute (in other words, what the conflict is about).
7 **Intensity** – defined as the degree of coercion and violence involved in interactions between the main adversaries.
8 **Volatility** – defined as the level of significant fluctuations in system interaction.
9 **Symmetry** – defined as the balance of resources available for the prosecution of the conflict (material, personnel, financial). A highly asymmetric conflict system involves adversaries that are very unequal in the (coercive) means – whether inherent or 'borrowed' (for example, from a patron or ally) – by which the conflict can be pursued.

The system characteristics listed above[3] fall naturally into 3 sub-groups. The first of these concerns the number of units involved in the system, their interconnections with other conflict systems, and their existing inter-dependence or 'other-than-conflict' relationships with each other.

The second sub-group concerns the conflictual relationships between the actors, the salience of these relationships to them and the degree of coherence in their views of what the conflict is 'about'. Many scholars writing about various forms of conflict resolution have argued that one of the key variables affecting the likely success of mediation or facilitation, for example, is 'the nature of the conflict', and the range and equivalence of the conflict system are dimensions that capture different aspects of this catch all conception of the 'nature' of the conflict.

The third sub-group concerns the nature and level of interactions that characterise conflict systems and involves a dimension of intensity of such interactions, together with one that concentrates upon the volatility of that level, together with a dimension that characterises actors' ability to interact equally with the other core actors in the system.

My contention here is that all of the above structural characterisitics of conflict systems can, from time to time, change, even if they are not inherently dynamic, and that it is certain kinds of change in these structural characteristics that confront rival decision-makers with a new and unpredictable set of circumstances in which a 'change of course' in the direction of conciliation is most likely to take place. The key question is what might be the nature and direction of change in each structural characteristic that would be most likely to produce conciliatory gestures and set in motion some accommodative sequence. I discuss this question in the following section before moving on to strategical and tactical changes and their effects in producing favourable conciliation contexts.

4   Structural changes conducive to conciliation

There has been little analysis directly focused on the connections between the changing structure of conflict systems and the propensity for these to be characterised by conciliatory activities. Some recent literature on conflict resolution and on international mediation has devoted a little attention to connections between structural aspects of the conflict – number of parties, nature of the conflict, level of the conflict – and the likelihood of resolution initiatives being successfully launched and concluded (Bercovitch, 1996; Wall and Lynn, 1993; Bercovitch and Langley, 1993). The same lack appears to be true of research into connections between contextual factors and the escalation of disputes to higher levels of violence. Siverson and Miller in a recent article lament this lack and argue that 'sooner or later it will be necessary for a sustained enquiry into the effects of context on interaction' (Siverson and Miller 1993, p.80).

4.1 Changes in the 'level' of conflict

Part of the limited amount of work on this context/interaction connection involves a debate about 'key' factors in determining efforts to settle or resolve protracted conflicts. For example, many have argued that a necessary condition for beginning successful resolution or undertaking successful mediation is the parties' prior convergence on an agreed definition of the issues (what the conflict is 'about') rather than the maintenance of widely divergent views about the nature of the issues in contention. Another familiar, if ambiguous, argument involves the relationship between the 'level' of conflict and the likelihood of successful resolution, with conventional wisdom holding (with Wall and Lynn 1993, p.176) that, as the 'level' of conflict increases, the likelihood of successful mediation decreases.

The problem with this latter argument that high levels of conflict decrease the chances of a non-violent resolution is the tendency of two factors to be conflated in the conception of 'level'. For many writers, 'level' implies the degree of violence – or some other aspect of coercive, inter party behaviour – present in the system. There appears to be a great deal of evidence to support the not-implausible argument that the more *intense* the conflict, in the sense outlined above, the less likely to develop are a context for conciliation or a successful mediation process.[4]

On the other hand, other writers interpret the concept of 'level' to mean the importance of the issues to the parties – what is defined above as the conflict's *salience* – arguing that this factor is also inversely related to successful third-party mediation and, by extension, to creating a context for conciliation.[5] At the level of international conflict, for example, some research points to the hardly surprising conclusion that when vital issues are involved (threats to territorial integrity or political independence) there is a tendency for greater escalation of violence, hardly a background against which conciliation can be effective (Gochman and Leng 1983). Bruce Bueno de Mesquita has argued that the salience of the issues involved in a conflict will overcome even a major imbalance of military capability, so that decision-makers will choose to wage war – and, presumably choose to continue to wage war rather than conciliate – even when their subjective (or real) prospects of victory are very small if they care enough about the issues in question (Bueno de Mesquita 1980 and 1985). The Finns fighting alone against the Soviet Union in the 1939–40 'Winter War' might be an apposite historical example of this phenomenon.

Others challenge this contention, however, arguing that the greater the salience of the issues to the parties the greater the likelihood of efforts to settle the conflict non-violently, through such processes as mediation and conciliation. Among a variety of writers Ott (1972) and La Tour *et al.* 1976 advocate the view that the greater the salience of the conflict, the greater the pressure for and likelihood of a successfully mediated outcome. Similarly, Bercovitch *et al.*'s (1991) analysis of data on international mediation supports a generalisation that conflicts fought over 'core' interests, such as territory or security, are more, rather than less, amenable to mediation than those fought over issues such as ideology or independence – so these issues are presumably more likely to contribute positively to a context for conciliation.

Whatever the validity of such general hypotheses about connections between the various static aspects of conflict system structure and the success of mediation processes, it is probably necessary to re-emphasise that the focus of this current analysis is on the dynamic aspects of that structure. The main contention of this chapter is that it is particular changes in systemic characteristics that increase the likelihood of successful conciliation, while other changes in, for example, degree and direction, could have the opposite effect.

In spite of the arguments of Ott and LaTour, I would argue that the changing salience of the conflict (or importance of the issues to parties) is directly related to the intransigence with which they continue to pursue their goals via their chosen means, once they have embarked on a course of mutual coercion; and thus to their unwillingness to consider the possibility of abandoning or even modifying strenuously coercive efforts to achieve essential goals, vital interests or core values.[6] Envisage even a rough continuum of issues ranging from the most to the least salient:

1　Conflicts involving the destruction of an adversary.
2　Conflicts involving the conversion of an adversary.
3　Conflicts involving the incorporation of an adversary.
4　Conflicts involving separation from an adversary.
5　Conflicts involving the immiseration of an adversary.
6　Conflicts involving minor reductions of an adversary's resources.

It seems obvious that the most unlikely context for conciliation – or for anything else, other than a Carthaginian peace – is an existential conflict in which the issues continue to be perceived to be the continuation in being of one (or both) of the parties. However, the suggestion here is that it is a particular transition from one magnitude to another which is of interest in explaining the likelihood of conciliatory initiatives being taken – for example, when a government accepts a set of 'rebels' as a legitimate negotiating partner, or secessionists publicly acknowledge the ultimate unity of a country. This means that it is the direction and degree of alteration in conflict salience that is crucial in providing a context for conciliation, as opposed to one for greater commitment or intransigence.

The most plausible hypothesis arising from this approach is that a diminution of issue salience – particularly a large one – is a change likely to produce a context encouraging some consideration of conciliation, while a change in the opposite direction will have quite the opposite effect.

This is easy to propose conceptually, but how is this likely to occur in the real world? The basic dynamic behind such change usually arises from altering evaluations of goals, rather than from alteration or abandonment of the goals themselves. For example, there is clearly a linkage between the costs and likelihood of achieving particular goals and the evaluation of the goals themselves. Leaders can have a major influence on 'goal inflation' and 'deflation'. Other goals can replace those underlying a conflict or, at least, overtake the latter in the preference hierarchies of leaders, elites and followers. New leaders can come to power with different goals and aspirations. Leaders can die and generations change. People learn, so that interests once deemed 'vital' no longer seem so. Technologies can render long held goals and interests irrelevant. All of these factors can produce a shift either in the direction of making goals seem more important, in which case no context for conciliation is likely to emerge, or to make them seem – often quite suddenly – relatively less important, so that conciliation is more likely to become a considered alternative.

4.2   Structure, dynamism and conciliation

A similar analysis can be offered in the case of changes in the complexity of the conflict system. Major shifts in this can occur in the direction of greater complexity (more parties being drawn in on one side or the other, major divisions within adversaries appearing over the best ways of prosecuting the conflict and so on) or of greater simplicity (patrons withdrawing support and interest, allies collapsing), so that a multi-party conflict becomes a relatively simple dyad. Again, it appears plausible to argue that a change in the direction of greater complexity *may* afford decision-makers the occasion to reconsider the possibilities of conciliation, but – given the introduction of new parties with their own goals and agendas (sometimes with little connection to the original conflict) – it seems more likely that greater complexity will lead towards greater commitment to existing strategies, or to an inability to agree on anything save the 'lowest common denominator' of continuing coercive activity aimed at 'unconditional surrender'. In contrast, the defection of allies with their own agendas and often with valuable resources for continuing the struggle seems likely to lead to uncertainty and more serious consideration of options, including conciliation. Such a change is likely to increase the parties' flexibility, as not having to take into account the interests of allies or patrons is also likely to expand the number of alternatives available to decision-makers.

Similar arguments can be applied to changes in the seven other structural variables discussed above. In all cases, whether structural change in the conflict system does produce a context for conciliation or not seems likely to depend upon both the direction and extent of the change. The defection of several allies – the Front Line States abandonment of the Zimbabwean Patriotic Front in 1980, for example – is more likely to produce a serious reconsideration by a party's leaders than the defection of just one.

Suggestions about the likely impact of various types of structural change in conflict systems, and the probability that they will contribute to a context for conciliation, are summarised in Table 4.2 opposite, reproducing the type of analysis attempted with conflict system salience and complexity above. I have also included in the Table some suggested ways in which various types of structural change might come about.

What this table does not directly include are the implications of Rosenau's argument about leaders' and constituents' perceptions as a key part of any complete analysis. It leaves out the fact that it may not be the existence of structural change that brings about a context for conciliation, but decision-makers' perceptions and evaluations of that structural change, which can either take the form of leaders' prescient anticipation – in which case conciliation may occur *before* the system actually experiences major change, as in Zartman's 'imminent catastrophe' model – or (unfortunately more likely) an inability or unwillingness to recognise major structural change, so that conciliatory moves are lagged and take place well *after* such change has occurred. The connection between structural change and leaders' recognition and acknowledgement of its importance is further discussed in a later chapter.

4.3   Structural contexts for conciliation

What the main features of Table 4.2 do suggest is a number of ideas about a likely context for conciliation, although some key ambiguities remain about the effects of changes in structural symmetry within conflict systems. For example, one key proposition is that a structural change in the system that reduces its complexity will produce a context in which conciliatory moves become much more likely than either a stable level of complexity or a change towards greater complexity. Similarly, an alteration in the salience of the conflict, as issues become less important and goals diminish in absolute or relative importance, is more likely to increase the chances of one or other adversary initiating an accommodative sequence of moves than a situation in which either the salience of goals remains stable or increases for the parties. Thirdly, the table suggests that a promising context for conciliation will be brought about if one conflict system changes so that it becomes a less isolated dispute through one or more of the adversaries becoming involved in other salient conflicts which demand attention, effort and resources.

Unfortunately, Table 4.2 also suggests that many types of structural change could produce effects that lead either towards a more propitious or a less propitious context, depending on circumstances. Changes in the direction of greater symmetry between the adversaries,[7] for example, might

Table 4.2 Changes in Conflict System Structure

System's Structural Characteristics	Direction of Change in Structure	Possible Sources of Change	Likely Effects of Change#	Likely Contribution to Creating a Context for Conciliation**
1. Complexity Number of core actors in system	H → L	Withdrawal of patrons* Third Party abandons mission	Narrower range of issues in contention. Decrease in expectations of success via coercion	POSITIVE
	L → H	Cleavages appear within adversaries	Parties abandon own core responsibility for finding solution	NEGATIVE
2. Isolation Degree of inter-connection with other conflict systems.	L → H	Adversaries resolve other conflict	Parties now able to concentrate efforts on one conflict system	NEGATIVE
	H → L	Adversaries become involved in other conflicts	Parties now have to weigh relative importance of conflict systems Efforts to extract themselves from intractable conflict system	POSITIVE
3. Interdependence Degree of parties' non-conflict inter connection with one another.	H → L	Technological innovations Discovery of alternative markets/suppliers/employers	Solution can be sought without regard to future relationship	NEGATIVE
	L → H	Alternative partners no longer available Exhaustion of own resources	Future relationship becomes a factor in leaders view of a 'successful' solution	POSITIVE

Table 4.2 *continued*

System's Structural Characteristics	Direction of Change in Structure	Possible Sources of Change	Likely Effects of Change#	Likely Contribution to Creating a Context for Conciliation**
4. Salience				
Importance of issues involved in conflict	H → L	Other, more central issues arise	Alternative outcomes to outright victory can be considered	POSITIVE
	L → H	Sacrifices render goals more salient & valuable	Other possible outcomes are ruled out as 'success' begins to equal survival & only viable outcome	NEGATIVE
5. Range				
Number of issues involved in conflict	L → H	New issues involved through other parties joining in. Expansion of arenas for confrontation.	Greater complexity in number of goals to be achieved makes most available outcomes sub-optimal	NEGATIVE
	H → L	Issues abandoned as unrealistic	Alternative solutions possible, if remaining issues appear compromisable	POSITIVE
6. Convergence				
Degree of parties' agreement on nature of issues in dispute	H → L	Change of leadership in one party	Divergence of views makes it hard to envisage any solution not involving imposition of one view	NEGATIVE
	L → H	Collapse of one side's 'culture of justification'	New, shared definition enables major reconsideration of options by the parties' leaders	POSITIVE

Table 4.2 continued

System's Structural Characteristics	Direction of Change in Structure	Possible Sources of Change	Likely Effects of Change#	Likely Contribution to Creating a Context for Conciliation**
7. Intensity				
Level of coercion involved in the inter-action	H → L	Exhaustion of resources Intra-party protest/disunity	Lessening of mutual/unilateral coercion leads to 'breathing space and opportunity for a reconsideration of options	POSITIVE
	L → H	Intra-party anger against adversary Acquisition of new resources	Rise in coercive level likely to lead to efforts to resist and counter coerce	NEGATIVE
8. Volatility				
Fluctuations in level of interactions in system	H → L	Existence of stalemate Reduction of resources for both sides	Gradual certainty re inability to succeed via continuing coercive strategy	POSITIVE
	L → H	New resources introduced Equalisation of capability	New uncertainties and risks; revival in beliefs about possibilities of 'victory'	NEGATIVE

78

Table 4.2 *continued*

System's Structural Characteristics	Direction of Change in Structure	Possible Sources of Change	Likely Effects of Change[#]	Likely Contribution to Creating a Context for Conciliation**
9. Symmetry				
Balance of capability in prosecuting the conflict	H → L	Strategic success Involvement of patrons New resources for one side	Tendency for party losing capability to search for alternatives; gainer to reinforce current policy	POSITIVE
	L → H	Catch up by dominated party	Equalisation brings occasion for reconsideration; either might choose new strategy – or not.	POSITIVE

Notes:

* For all of these, opposite changes are likely to produce reverse effects.

\# Change does not have to affect *both* parties for it to provide 'occasions for reconsideration'

** This says nothing about the eventual success of any conciliatory gesture launched as a result of a propitious context for conciliation developing.

well lead to greater coercive efforts on the part of both parties through a 'catch up' phenomenon, with one side striving to avoid the balance of advantage swinging against it, while the other increases its efforts to overtake the first. This argument echoes that of James Morrow with respect to escalation, when he states that leaders 'choose to escalate a dispute into war when they hold a temporary military superiority over their opponent that is beginning to slip away as their opponent begins a new armament program' (Morrow 1989, p.507). It also echoes Organski's classic theory of 'rear-end collision' (Organski 1968).

On the other hand, the party being overtaken might well decide that the time had come to offer some 'olive branch' before the situation became one of its being at a significant disadvantage, so that a structural change in the direction of symmetry would produce a context in which conciliation might at least begin. Whether it continues into an accommodative sequence would, however, depend upon the overtaking party *not* declining the proffered olive branch and waiting until it could 'negotiate (that is, dictate) from strength'.

Table 4.2 also raises questions about the interactive and reinforcing effects of changes in the structure of a conflict system. Presumably, it is reasonable to argue that a more propitious context for conciliation would come about if a number of appropriate structural changes took place at roughly the same time as when, for example, patrons abandon one or both of the adversaries, adversaries become involved in other, unrelated conflicts and the issues in conflict become less salient or (at least) appear to be resolvable. (In the terms used in this study, the conflict system becomes less complex, isolated and of lesser – but not insignificant – salience.) Clearly, this would provide a context in which, at the least, the initial moves of an accommodative sequence could easily take place and might lead towards a negotiated or facilitated resolution. On the other hand, the effects of other roughly simultaneous changes might be more mixed and less easy to anticipate, as when patrons defect but increased sacrifices make issues *more* salient, while new issues become involved in the conflict system, thus widening the range. With these complications in mind, an appropriately cautious approach seems to be one which argues that: (1) in isolation, a number of structural changes in the system are more likely to produce a propitious context for conciliation than others, and these are illustrated in Figure 4.3 overleaf; and (2) in combination, all or some of these changes will reinforce one another to produce a highly propitious context for conciliation.

So far, the argument makes clear that there are a number of aspects to the development of a more or less propitious 'context for conciliation', at least at the level of the structure of the conflict systems. Thus, recognising a promising context for a conciliatory initiative to be both launched and sustained involves examining nine 'dimensions' that contribute to the

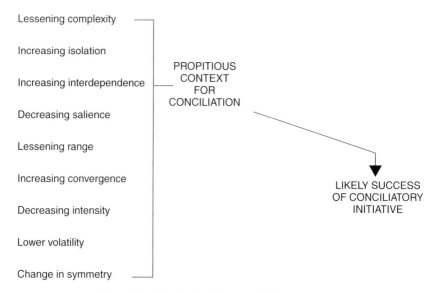

Figure 4.3   **Conducive Structural Circumstances**

existence of a positive context for conciliation in protracted and deep-rooted conflicts. These are summarised in Figure 4.4 below.

However, while it is reasonable to argue that structural changes in the conflict system are most likely to create a radically new context within which decision-makers are likely to contemplate alternative, conciliatory initiatives, it should be recalled that there are two other levels of change which may well

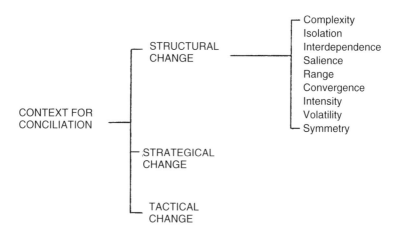

Figure 4.4   **Structural Aspects of Conflict Context**

help to produce the same effect, the strategical and the tactical. Much of this study's subsequent analysis focuses on these two levels, so the remainder of this chapter will briefly introduce arguments about common strategical and tactical changes likely to contribute to conciliatory moves and processes.

5   Strategical change and conciliatory contexts

If the changes most likely to bring about a context for a reassessment of goals and means by the leaders of parties in conflict are those involving the actual structure of the conflict system itself, a similar if perhaps less intense effect is also likely to arise from significant changes, actual or anticipated, in the patterns of interaction between the adversaries. My argument here is that, in creating a climate of 'uncertainty and unpredictability', alterations in patterned behaviour at the strategic level will also provide decision-makers with occasions for a reconsideration of their chosen means and methods, and that this reconsideration may, depending upon the nature of the strategical change, lead to them undertaking conciliatory initiatives or starting accommodative sequences. For example, the ending of a period of intense combat – as in October 1973 – marked for both Anwar Sadat and the Israeli leaders a major strategical-level change and an opportunity to choose alternatives to continued mutual violence and coercion.

5.1   Linkages between structural and strategical change

As with many concepts, the line between structural and strategical change is not always unambiguous. For example, a major change in strategic inter-action in a conflict system will arise with the entry, re-entry or withdrawal of a third party, which has been discussed earlier as an example of struc-tural change in the system. However, such structural changes will also bring about a major alteration in the strategical pattern of interaction, usually changing its form from bilateral to trilateral (or vice versa if the third party withdraws, as did Dr Jarring and his UN initiative in 1970).

On most other occasions, however, the distinction is a clear and useful one, the key differences being the relative speed with which strategical change can occur and its potential for being reversed. One rule of thumb for making the distinction is to utilise the familar basic model of the three dimensions of a conflict illustrated in Figure 4.5 and to regard structural change as an alteration in the conflict situation while strategical change is a major alteration in the behavioural dimension.

Expressed in systems terms, structural change involves a transformation of the conflict system, while strategical change refers to 'changes in the processes that go on within the parameters of a given structural configura-tion' (Genco in Holsti *et al.* 1980, p.71). The latter, therefore, involves some form of major discontinuity from the pattern of interaction that had gone before, but not the kind of 'step level function' involved in a transforma-tive change of the actual system itself.

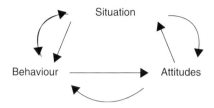

Figure 4.5   **Basic Conflict Structure**

5.2   Types of strategical change

What typical types of 'within system' change appear frequently in protracted and deep-rooted conflicts, what frameworks might be developed to
categorise and understand them and what might be the characteristics of
those most likely to develop a positive context for conciliation? Again, the
analysis of Sadat's efforts in the 1970s provides interesting empirical examples for consideration. Clearly, one common type of strategical change in
protracted conflict is the move from mutual coercion through violence to
some lull or tacit ceasefire, following intense efforts at mutual coercion.
The literature on international crises also suggests that the reverse of this
change from coercive violence to its absence is also an example of major
strategical change. Hence, an approaching crisis, involving an escalation of
threatening moves and statements, is another example of major strategical
change that calls for new thinking from decision-makers. The example of
the Cuban crisis in 1962 also suggests that an averted crisis is likely to be
the kind of strategical change that leads towards a context for conciliation,
although both the literature on international crises and on industrial
conflicts suggest that a crisis which has 'come to fruition' and led to quali-
tatively different efforts to coerce an adversary produces a context for continued coercion rather than for conciliation.

Moreover, both Sadat's experience and the literature on hurting stalemates suggest that another form of strategical change is both the experience and the anticipation of some major, but highly undesired event which
changes current patterns of interaction. The exhaustion of resources by one
or both sides is the kind of precipice discussed in Zartman's work on
hurting stalemates (Zartman 1984, pp.), as is the sudden cutting off of
needed weapons supplies through an embargo or the imposition of sanctions by a previous supplier.[8] Historically, changes in the pattern of interaction represented by the proposed re-convening of the 1977 Geneva
Conference, and the re-entry of the Soviet Union directly into the
Egyptian–Israeli conflict, constitute another example of an anticipated dis-

continuity that created the occasion for a conciliatory initiative. Similarly, the failure of an outside peace process may, paradoxically, provide another kind of discontinuity that leads decision-makers to consider another form of conciliation process, perhaps in a different arena.

The variety of historical circumstances that can exemplify strategical change is inevitably very large – crises (approaching or averted), lulls in activity, failures of campaigns or peace processes, diminished activity through exhaustion of resources, loss of partners, addition of patrons, imposition of sanctions. Analytically, what seems to underlie many of these empirical changes might be summarised by arguing that they are all examples of three major types of strategical change:

1 changes in *intensity* of interaction;
2 changes in *content* or *balance* of interaction (that is, in the mix of coercive or other forms of behaviour);
3 changes in *direction* or *pattern* of interaction (i.e. in the number of actors principally involved in the exchanges).

The first – a major alteration in intensity – is the most common of these basic changes in patterns of adversary interaction and includes such alterations as diminished intensification represented by lulls, impasses, deliberately engineered pauses, and stalemates; or increased levels of interaction such as approaching crises, major intensifications through escalation of effort and extension of arenas for interaction, or increased exchanges of information about aspiration and justification in a propaganda campaign.

Equally familiar is the second type of strategical change – major alterations in the balance or mix of the pattern of interaction – as when changes occur in the level of coercion contained in the overall exchange between adversaries, or the level of justification offered for actions and statements by one side or the other. A common approach to this type of change is to compare the 'mix' of co-operative or conflictful acts or statements, and to note any marked or sudden change in the mix, or to note similar changes in the 'range' or diversity of the acts and statements used by adversaries in different time periods.

With regard to changes in *both* the intensity and the mix of interactions, it should be recalled that one significant form of change that might well lead to parties undertaking conciliatory initiatives is a change from volatility to stability. In other words, while most of the examples discussed in this section involve change from one pattern of interaction to another, it is quite possible that a period in which change does not take place might, in contrast to a previously volatile period, offer an occasion for reconsideration and new initiatives. Paradoxically a time of 'no-change' might represent such a major alteration from a period of 'much change' that the stability, in itself, could bring about some reflection about optimum goals and means by decision-makers.

The third major type of change – in direction and pattern – is somewhat less obvious but can be highly important in creating a context for conciliation. There are a variety of ways in which changes in direction and pattern can occur. For example, as I mentioned above, a major change in the pattern of interaction can be brought about by the introduction of an active 'third' party into the system, either as a direct ally of one of the core actors or as some form of intermediary seeking a solution to the conflict. Depending upon the number of previously external actors that cross the boundary from the environment to become part of the conflict system, the pattern of interaction can change quite rapidly from a bilateral to a trilateral or a multilateral one, thus creating major strategical change. Such a change, of course, is an illustration of the manner in which alterations in conflict system structure are thoroughly interconnected with strategical changes within the system, the increase in the number and variety of parties affecting the way in which the elements in the system interact.

A similar change in the pattern of strategic interaction involving an increase or decrease in system complexity can arise as a result of 'sub-system' changes within the adversaries themselves through processes of disintegration or integration. For example, internal divisions within a revolutionary movement can result in the emergence of two organisations where one existed previously, thus adding to the number of core actors and a major change in patterns of interaction within the conflict system. Internal divisions become cleavages, cleavages become splits and from the splits emerge new organisations or movements to add to the number of actors in the system and complicate both interactions and decisions. For example, the emergence in 1993 of the ill-named Liberia Peace Committee and of the Lofa Defence Force added two new major actors to the already complex, multi-party system making up the 'Liberian civil war', and made the starting (or, more accurately, re-starting) of any comprehensive peace process, embracing 'all the parties', a much more difficult undertaking. Alternatively, the integration of previously separate (and often rival) organisations can produce a simplified pattern of exchanges that significantly alters interaction patterns, as when ZANU and ZAPU, the two Zimbabwean liberation movements, combined as the Patriotic Front in their struggle against the Rhodesian Government.

Another way in which altered relationships or patterns of interaction can provide occasions for adversaries' reconsiderations of goals and strategies and give rise to conciliatory moves involves a re-ordering of relations among elements which are already part of the system. For example, the increasing cooperation between the Irish and British Governments during the early 1990s over the conflict in Northern Ireland, culminating in the 1993 Downing Street Declaration, significantly altered the context within which the British authorities, the Nationalists and the Unionists were carrying out the complex, violent struggle in the province, and accelerated the exchange of conciliatory moves, culminating in the 1994 ceasefire (Mallie and McKittrick 1996, pp.256–75). Changes in the alignment of parties already in the system can, on occasions, have a greater effect even than the introduction of new parties to the system.

5.3   The impact of strategical change

My main argument at this point is that any of these types of strategical change outlined above can be important in helping to create a context for conciliation. Hence, the final question concerning this second level of change is what effects might the various forms of strategical change have upon decision-makers' willingness to initiate conciliatory moves or sequences. At this stage of research, only a few rough rules of thumb can be suggested and these have to be heavily qualified by the circumstances of each historical case. Taking our framework of strategical changes falling into three basic categories, initial hypotheses might take the following forms.

Diminutions in the intensity of interactions provide a positive context for conciliatory gestures, so that the most likely circumstances for conciliatory gestures to be made or initiatives launched involve lulls, averted crises, disengagements, and impasses. Increased levels of interaction, on the other hand, are likely to lock the parties' leaders into a pattern of decision-making dominated by *incremental continuation*, as they concentrate upon continuing, or responding to the high level of activity. Hence, periods of escalation, an intensive propaganda campaign, or a major diplomatic 'offensive' within any organisation involved in conflict are likely to occupy the time and attention of leaders, and prevent what will appear to be a time consuming and fundamentally irrelevant reconsideration of options or a possible reversal of course.

Unilateral diminutions – whether intended or not – in the relative coercive content of interactions are more likely to lead to the launching of conciliatory gestures than are increases in the balance of coercion. In such circumstances, initial conciliatory moves could come from the party whose 'mix' of coercive and other forms of activity has changed or from its adversary in response to such changes. However, the connection suggested here is by no means an unambiguous one. For example, a decline in ability to coerce may, in some cases, lead to a greater determination not to appear weak by making conciliatory moves. In other cases, a period immediately preceding the offering of some olive branch may be characterised by an increase in coercive activity, as the party planning the conciliatory move seeks to signal that the move is not being made from a position of weakness. Hence, although the principle that a major change in the balance of interactions between the adversaries offers a context for conciliation remains, the likelihood that particular changes will lead to conciliatory gestures being made is by no means clear.

As noted above, alterations in the pattern of interaction within a conflict system can take a wide variety of forms, so that delineating the impact of such changes beyond the principle that any such changes can offer an occasion for decision-makers to launch conciliatory 'trial balloons' is difficult. It seems sensible to start with the broad argument that an increasingly complex pattern of interaction might well work against new initiatives, as decision-makers do engage in a major reassessment of their goals, options and best methods but probably decide to keep to current policies until the implications of the new pattern become clearer. With a new pattern emerging from the disintegration of an adversary, the temptation might be to hope that this process will have a weakening effect, thus affording opportunities to extract concessions through escalation. With a new pattern emerging from the involvement of a major intermediary, the temptation might well be to retain one's options, to wait and see and to leave the intitiatives to the newcomer. In the case of a new patron entering the conflict system, this seems likely to increase the determination not to yield on the part the party newly assisted, while its adversary is likely to seek for its own patron to counter-balance that of its rival. On the other hand, it may be that any of these changes in patterns could also provide occasions for conciliation, as when the decision-makers of one party hope that the involvement of a cautious or conservative patron of its adversary might have a dampening effect on the aspirations of that client.

Simplifying the pattern of interaction seems more likely to be the kind of change that leads in the direction of conciliation, however. The integration of a previously divided rival might, in the eyes of the other party's decision-makers, increase the possibility that the new unity might enable a deal to be struck and kept. The entry of an intermediary might encourage parties to launch their own conciliatory initiatives, perhaps in support of the third party process or – if the intermediary's activities are less than welcome (as in the case of the joint US/Soviet initiative in 1977) – to forestall the intermediary's unwanted activity.

Once again, the logical extension of these hypotheses is the argument that, when several of the characteristics of change are present in any situation, these will reinforce one another to produce a highly propitious context for conciliation. Hence, while single changes in, for example, the intensity of conflict system interactions might well lead to the launching of conciliatory gestures, a more likely starting hypothesis is that the most propitious context for conciliation is likely to involve a pattern of strategical changes – not necessarily associated from or arising as a result of structural changes – that involves:

1   a diminution of interaction levels;
2   a lessening of coercive activity so that the balance or mix of interaction has changed; and
3   a simplification in the pattern of interaction.

An increase in intensity, a change in balance towards coercion and an increase in complexity are likely to have the opposite effect, so that – while this type of change might produce an occasion for reconsideration – the end result is likely to be a move away from conciliation and towards intensification of current policies through the creation of a 'context for coercion'.

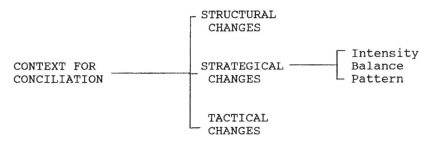

Figure 4.6 **Strategical Aspects of Conflict Context**

Finally, while changes in systems structure and in patterns of interaction provide occasions for reconsideration and help develop a context for conciliation, it is also the case that events at a tactical level can also contribute to the development of a context for conciliation. On occasions, some isolated and unconnected actions or events can have a major impact on creating a context for conciliation and lead to equally dramatic initiatives – although whether these tactical-level happenings serve as 'triggers' for conciliatory moves on their own, or only as elements within some mix of structural, strategical and tactical factors is by no means clear. The last section of this Chapter examines the nature of tactical level changes that can trigger conciliatory moves and sequences, thus completing the discussion of what contributes to a context for conciliation.

6   Tactical changes: triggers, thresholds and symbols

Paradoxically, often the most immediately noticeable aspects of the existence of a context for conciliation are those discrete events that initially appear not to be directly connected with the waging of the conflict, but which nevertheless provide an occasion for the subsequent launching of a conciliatory initiative or accommodative sequence. Apparently isolated events or 'one off' changes sometimes serve as opportunities for conciliatory gestures by one or other party to a conflict. These occasions may seem to be very different in nature from the systemic or structural changes in the conflict system already discussed, but such 'triggers' or 'thresholds' may have a far greater impact than their basic nature suggests.[9]

The effects of single 'significant' events on triggering a change of behaviour policy has been frequently recognised in even protracted and deep-rooted conflicts. For example, the British strategist, Liddell Hart, once argued that 'Decisive results may come sooner from sudden shocks than long drawn out pressure. Shock throws the opponent off balance. Pressure allows him time to adjust to it' (Liddell Hart 1947, p.31). Brian Tomlin provides an alternative rationale by suggesting that many peace processes start with 'an event or change in conditions that causes a restructuring of the values that attach to alternative outcomes by one or more parties' (Tomlin 1989, p.22). Other writers have argued more specifically that a common trigger for decision-makers to consider (at least) embarking on an alternative policy of conciliation often takes the form of a major disaster, such as occurred for the British at Yorktown or for the French at Dien Bien Phu in 1954.[10]

Empirically, significant 'triggers' that have helped to create a context for conciliation have taken on such a wide variety of forms that it is tempting to argue that trigger events or 'significant discontinuities' can only be seen as specific to a particular conflict or, at least, to the cultures of the parties involved in particular conflicts. It may be, however, that events or discontinuities that help to produce a propitious context for conciliation do share certain basic features and that it is not unlikely that, in their fundamental characteristics, they resemble deliberately made – and successful – conciliatory gestures (an argument taken up later in this study).

In the absence of any systematic analysis of historical 'significant discontinuities', I would suggest that most of such triggers fall roughly into three categories: sudden major shocks, the crossing of significant thresholds, and the lowering of leaders' – and, sometimes, followers' – levels of commitment.

6.1   A major shock model

This approach to significant triggers contends that decision-makers will usually consider a significant change of course in the direction of conciliation after their party has experienced a major, negative change of circumstances or after they have observed a similar negative shock affecting their adversary. (Hence the conciliatory gesture may come from either party, the one experiencing the shock or the one observing it.) The 'shock' can involve the loss of a key leader, the rapid diminution of a key resource, a major strategic disaster, or the collapse of intra-party support for continuing the struggle.

All or any of the above are likely to produce a rapid diminution in the leaders' perception of available options and lead to a decision to reconsider current strategies and – possibly – to initiate a process of conciliation. Again, it should be recalled that some leaders may also be able to anticipate an imminent shock and to recognise the rapid diminishing of some commodity essential for continuing to wage the struggle. In some cases, this commodity may even be time, as when parties in conflict find themselves facing the 'deadline' phenomenon, with the approach of the end of one's term of office, the end of the campaigning season or the expiration of an agreement or a treaty.

6.2 A threshold model

If the 'deadline' phenomenon does not involve a practical or material termination, it may be an example of the second type of trigger event which tends to be symbolic in nature. This approach suggests that leaders are likely to consider initiating a major reconsideration of policy as the result of approaching or passing some symbolic point or threshold, which sets off some alarms – often cultural or national – in the minds of decision-makers, causing them to ask: 'Is it worth continuing, or should we try alternative methods?'

Lewis Coser has written about some types of key thresholds that can serve as significant 'termination' points in violent conflicts (Coser 1961), some of which can be negative (the loss of a capital city, the penetration of key defence lines, the capture of some symbolically important resource), while others are positive (the gaining of a long-sought strategic goal, such as the Golan Heights, or a culturally significant prize, such as east Jerusalem). Others might have to do with time, as when a significant anniversary is approached (ten years of struggle, or an annual holiday such as Christmas or Ramadan), or when a time limit emphasised as significant by leaders comes – and goes (Sadat's own 'Year of Decision', for example).

The point usually made in connection with this type of trigger is that the approach or crossing of some threshold, even if it is only symbolic, can become the occasion for leaders to reconsider policy or, by anticipating a reconsideration by their adversary, lead to a context for possible conciliatory changes.

6.3 A new leadership with lowered commitment model

Both approaches discussed above have in common exogenous events that are likely to produce the result of an existing leadership reconsidering options, goals and policies. The third type of trigger, in contrast, does not involve an existing set of leaders 'changing their minds' through the impact of external shocks or symbols. Rather, it suggests that the advent of new leaders may touch off a re-evaluation of present policies and give rise to an initial move in a peace process.[11]

A number of arguments are used to support this hypothesis, most notably the one that holds that new leaders will not be committed to the policies of their predecessors (indeed, they may want to distance themselves from such policies), so that they will find it easier to 'change course' if this is desired. Again, it is often argued that new leaders cannot be held responsible for the policies (and often the policy failures) of their predecessors, so that change is easier because it is less costly in political terms.

Lastly, the very advent of new leaders usually produces an expectation of change and these expectations in themselves may create a context in which change becomes easier, often through the operations of some form of self-fulfilling prophecy. Paradoxically, this last phenomenon may lead to the advent of a new leadership in one party producing a policy reconsideration in another, as the latter's decision-makers consider the best means of utilising this change.

In contrast, changes in leadership (or even in the balance of influence within elite circles) may not lead to changes in basic policy, or even to considerations of such changes. Often, new leaders' legitimacy depends upon them assuming the mantle of those they have replaced, especially if the old leaders are established and well regarded. Sadat, for example, had to proceed with great caution before making any kind of a break with the policies of his predecessor, especially regarding Israel. Moreover, it is not necessarily the case that a change in leadership and a subsequent review of options, goals and policies will result in the adoption of a more conciliatory pattern of behaviour. Quite the reverse may be true, so that new leaders may escalate the conflict and pursue success through victory. However, these caveats and ambiguities do not render our heuristic model any less useful as long as they are kept in mind.

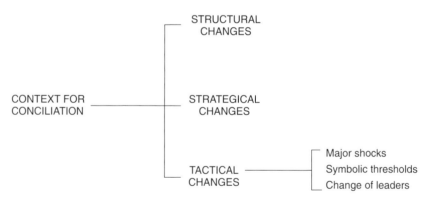

Figure 4.7   **Tactical Aspects of Conflict Context**

7   Conclusion

Whatever the nature of significant triggers in particular conflicts, it remains clear that, at a tactical level, certain events and changes can and do have a major impact in producing a context for conciliation, while a cluster of such events may act in a mutually reinforcing way to push decision-makers in the direction of policy change and the search for a non-imposed, negotiated solution. These tactical triggers and thresholds may operate in isolation or they may be closely connected with major strategical and structural changes in the conflict which in themselves will produce levels of uncertainty and unpredictability likely to lead towards a propitious context for conciliation.

In this chapter, then, I have suggested a number of initial guidelines that, hopefully, help to clarify the extent to which a particular set of structural, strategical and tactical circumstances – a context – is likely to lead to the launching of a conciliatory initiative and also (by extension) to its successful recognition and some kind of response, so that an accommodative sequence begins. However, an appropriate context at a structural, strategical and tactical level merely makes the launching of a conciliatory gesture and a later positive reception more likely. It does not make the initiative a certainty. Nor does the existence of an appropriate context do much to guarantee that the gesture itself will be successful, in the sense of beginning a fruitful peace process. As I discussed in Chapter 3, other factors outlined in our basic model come into play and influence the impact of any initial move towards conciliation, chief among them being the nature of that move (or series of moves) itself. The following chapters discuss possible qualities of conciliatory gestures that lead to their successful launching and positive reception as well as the maintenance of a sequence of interactions leading in the direction of a peaceful solution.

5
Varieties of Olive Branch

'There is Nothing makes a man Suspect much, more than to know
little. And therefore Men should remedy Suspicion by procuring to
know more ... Certainely, the best Meane, to cleare the Way in
this same Woode of Suspicion is franckly to communicate them to
the Partie that he Suspects. For thereby he shall be sure to know
more of the Truth of them than he did before.'

Francis Bacon *On Suspicion* Essays XXXI

While such factors as the actual state of the conflict or the existing relationship between the adversaries form part of the context working for (or
against) conciliation and are powerful influences on the effective use of
conciliatory gestures and their development into accommodative
sequences, a second set of influences clearly arises from the nature of the
initiative itself. The contrast between Anwar Sadat's conditional offer to
reopen the Suez Canal and his later personal visit to Israel is obvious, as is
the different impact these initiatives had upon the prospects for a resolution of the Egyptian–Israeli conflict. It is almost tempting to start consideration of this particular influence on successful conciliation by proposing a
general rule of thumb that the more 'dramatic' the gesture, the more likely
it is to have the initiator's desired effect, although the number of conciliatory gestures, even some of those containing elements of high drama, that
have failed to move forward a peace process, or even begin cautious accommodative moves, warns against easy generalisation. While dramatic gestures may achieve a high degree of recognisability, the key issue is whether
they invariably achieve similarly high levels of credibility and respondability with members – and particularly leaders – of an adversary; and whether
'drama', however defined, is a necessary characteristic of successful conciliatory gestures.

The basic question about conciliatory initiatives clearly remains crucial.
All other things being equal, what characteristics of gestures intended to be
conciliatory increase the probability of success for that move – defined in

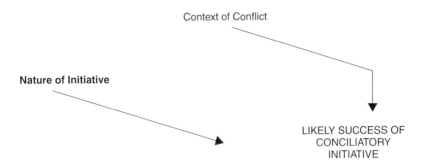

Figure 5.1 **Influences on Conciliation Effectiveness III**

the short term as achieving recognition and acknowledgement as a genuine conciliatory move, or in the medium term as eliciting positive reaction by the target, or in the long term as advancing an accommodative sequence or a peace process?

Combining possible answers to that question with the observations of Chapter 4 on positive or negative contexts for conciliation leads naturally to a second, rather more practical query. If it is possible to determine which qualities make it more likely that a conciliatory gesture will be successful, how might these best be enhanced so that such gestures might succeed even in contexts not particularly conducive to the start of a conciliatory process? These themes form the focus of the next chapters, which deal with key characteristics of successful conciliatory gestures, focusing on the second element of the model of factors affecting the outcome of a concilia-tory initiative, that is, the *nature* of that initiative – see Figure 5.1.

In this Chapter, I first outline a variety of traditional approaches from different literatures to try to discern possible common features of sucessful conciliatory gestures. Next, I review some taxonomies of traditionally con-ceived conciliatory moves, and then some ideas regarding the employment of a series of such moves as part of typical accommodative sequences. Finally, I discuss the manner in which such conciliatory initiatives have commonly been combined (often counter-productively) into an overall strategy aimed at achieving a lasting solution to protracted conflicts.

1   Signalling conciliation: some empirical examples

During the early stages of President Nixon's efforts to restore normal rela-tions with Peking, a wide variety of conciliatory signals and messages were employed by the White House to indicate a willingness on the part of the US Government to begin a dialogue with the Chinese Government and to move towards an ending of the long period of muted hostility interspersed with direct confrontations that had existed since 1949. Like President

Sadat, President Nixon was searching for some conciliatory move that might effectively initiate a process leading towards a less adversarial relationship with China.

One such signal was sent during a visit of President Ceausescu of Rumania to Washington when, during a toast at an official dinner, President Nixon mentioned 'the People's Republic of China'. This was the first time that the official title of the regime in Peking had been mentioned by an American President, a point that was not lost on the Rumanian President (then serving as a contact point betwen the USA and CPR) – nor, apparently, on Soviet Ambassador Dobrynin.[1] As a conciliatory gesture it was symbolic rather than substantive but, being both discreet and effective, was one of the more subtle indications of a willingess to talk that were then pouring out of the US administration in the direction of Peking. (Hersh 1984, p.365)

The tactic of using an official title claimed by an adversary but never used before is only one example of a wide variety of essentially symbolic signals indicating a willingness to talk, to conciliate and to compromise, developed within the international community as various parties therein signal to each other using symbolic messages and gestures to convey both information and intention. Some signals and indicators are so well understood as to have become almost ritualised, such as the expulsion of diplomats or the formal breaking of diplomatic relations to indicate displeasure not sufficiently high to warrant costly sanctions; or state visits to indicate generalised goodwill between two countries. However, the variety and subtlety of much diplomatic signalling frequently goes beyond such 'broad brush' gestures. Robert Jervis has mentioned the distinction made by some scholars between a language and signalling systems (Jervis 1970, p.21), the basis of differentiation being the flexibility and subtlety of the former compared with the latter.[2]

As I noted in Chapter 3, conceiving of conciliation as a process of communication draws attention to a number of important aspects of that process when it is being used to move an on-going conflict into a different pattern of interaction. One such aspect is the nature and content of the communication. Clearly, the actual nature of any conciliatory communication can take a variety of forms, but at the level of international diplomacy much communication takes place through a 'code' – that is, a repertoire of familiar and generally understood signals (almost a shared 'sign language') that are part of a diplomatic 'culture' and which can be used in a variety of situations. In the case of conciliatory initiatives, the code can consist of a variety of shared signals, which range from those thoroughly understood by all, through those well understood by certain decision-makers (Presidents Nixon and Ceausescu), to those less well understood in a general sense and to a residual category of those which are unique or case-specific signals, having a meaning only in the context of the relationship between particular adversaries and even the particular time at which the signal is sent.

If such a code of signals does exist for conciliatory initiatives in intense and protracted conflicts, what sorts of signals are typical and is it possible to suggest a simple classification scheme of types of conciliatory gesture used frequently during the initial stages of any accommodative sequence? Alternatively, is conciliation typified by case-specific signals so that no common pattern can emerge?

Part of the problem of answering these two questions is that, at first sight, the range and variety of historical signals launched – even if not responded to – seem almost bewildering. Governments signalling concessions and conciliation have used signals, symbols and actions varying from the most subtle and nuanced to the most blatant and unsophisticated. On the one hand a regime has announced a major run down of troops in a given region; on the other, a government has left out a familar phrase from a press statement. In one instance a political leader has launched a noisy and public campaign for peace; in another, a head of government has studiously refrained from answering the latest attack on his administration and its policies. At one time a minister closely associated with a hawkish posture towards an adversary has been summarily dismissed; at another an official known for his 'reasonable' approach to a conflict has been quietly promoted to head a special task group charged with planning for the aftermath of an on-going dispute.

With such an endless variety, the search for common characteristics of successful conciliatory gestures seems overly optimistic. While the United States' attempts to signal a desire for accommodation to the Government of the CPR during President Nixon's administration, and President Sadat's efforts between 1970 and 1977, provide useful sources of historical data on successful conciliatory moves, can they alone indicate anything about the general characteristics of successful conciliatory gestures?

Fortunately, historical cases of conciliation are not the only existing source of ideas. There has already been a considerable, if disparate, amount of analytical work undertaken into various types of conciliatory gesture and accommodative sequence, so that, for example, the literatures on de-escalation and on negotiation provide initial clues about the basic nature of conciliatory gestures during protracted conflicts. Paradoxically, one area in which some systematic attention has been paid to the whole issue of conciliation, accommodation and peacemaking processes has been the literature on coercive bargaining, limited war and crisis management, although more recent literature on peacemaking, negotiation, conflict management and arms control has also produced ideas that might be useful in a systematic study of the use of conciliatory gestures. Perhaps the most immediately relevant ideas can be gathered from literature on negotiation processes and from work on the reduction of tensions in situations of confrontation as a preliminary to disengagement and the start of a series of arms control measures. Such ideas do need to be treated with caution, however, given the very different situations existing in the pre-negotiation and negotiation stages of any peace process.

2 Conciliatory gestures: traditional taxonomies

Whatever the most fruitful source, a useful start highlights four basic ideas from the general literature on disengagement that have immediate relevance as types of 'move' held likely to play a major part in any peace process, especially one in which tacit bargaining during an accommodative sequence takes place:

1 concessions;
2 symbolic gestures;
3 tension reducing measures (TRMs);
4 confidence building measures (CBMs).

Unfortunately, part of the problem with using these ideas is that – partly because they have been used in distinct fields of study – their meanings tend to overlap and, in some cases, it is not clear where one concept ends and another begins. For this reason, I will briefly discuss the nature of each of these ideas and then attempt to provide a set of clear definitions showing how each differs from and relates to the others.

2.1 Concessions and concession-making

The most thorough work on the nature of concessions and the process of concession making can be found in the literature on negotiation. From this source comes the key characteristics of a 'concession' – that it represents some retreat from an established bargaining position, known and clearly visible to a negotiator from a rival party. A large literature has grown up upon the nature, rate and range of concession-making in face-to-face bargaining and its influence on the outcome of negotiation. (Brown and Rubin 1975; Pruitt 1981; Druckman 1996 for examples). This considers issues such as whether it is 'better' to begin negotiation with a major concession or hold out until the adversary makes a major retreat from his public bargaining position. Some writers have argued that an essential feature of a concession is that it is a forced retreat and that the party making it would be unwilling to take such a backward step if it had not been made to do so (Kriesberg 1981). This distinction between a coerced and a voluntary retreat is an important one, although sometimes the line distinguishing the two is blurred.

Concessions can also be made during pre-negotiation accommodative sequences, however, although the context for making such a gesture is usually very different from that surrounding making a concession during an on-going negotiating process.[3] The making of an obvious concession can be the beginning (or an important accelerator) of a peace process. The problem with such actions as 'concessions' is that, if the central defining characteristic is a clear retreat from a previously clear position, the 'giving up' of something already possessed, then many conciliatory processes begin from situations in which both parties possess initially vague public bargaining positions (or, at least, bargaining positions in which there are many ambiguous areas), so that selecting an action as a 'concession' to be proffered and its recognition as such by a target may depend on the clarity of the initiator's previous stand on a particular issue. As I noted elsewhere (Mitchell 1990), when a party's position, limits or lines ('resistance points', 'maximum concession levels') are clear, retreat is also clear, but the reverse is also true. If positions and limits are ambiguous, identifying a retreat is much more difficult.

An alternative way of expressing this idea is that the use of 'concessions' implies the existence of a clear and agreed 'reference point' or initial demand to serve as a bench mark against which to evaluate the degree of 'movement' represented by the proffered concession (Druckman 1990). In the absence of such a clear standard, most retreats offered as concessions are open to substantial misinterpretation, especially by the target of the gesture. In other situations, the adversaries may possess quite different reference points, so that a proffered retreat may seem nothing of the sort to the target. In many cases, a successful party will proffer a retreat from the current situation, while an unsuccessful one will require a return to some previous status quo before being able to perceive further retreats as 'real' concessions. For example, offers of the return of parts of a captured territory are rarely seen as concessions by the party originally losing that territory. Secessionist movements rarely perceive offers of limited autonomy as concessions, given that their reference point is the illegitimate original inclusion of their people within the then-existing state. The inevitable conclusion seems to be that conciliatory gestures that take the ostensible form of 'concessions' have a greater chance of success if adversaries can agree on a common reference point from which to 'retreat'.

Bearing such caveats in mind, a suggested definition for the concept of a 'concession' would, therefore, be:

> Any retreat from a previously clearly laid out public bargaining position. This may involve dropping a demand or prior condition, lessening the magnitude of some recompense demanded or decreasing some level of activity wanted from the adversary either before or during subsequent negotiations.

The successful use of concessions is, therefore, likely to be associated with the extent of the retreat; the clarity of the previous bargaining position; and the acceptance of common reference points by the adversaries. A concession is more likely to be recognised and evaluated as 'genuine' by the Target the more is given up or abandoned and the more clearly the previous position is understood by the target's decision-makers. Qualities of clarity, distinctiveness and degree of change thus seem important in the likely success of any concession. The larger and more obvious the retreat, the more likely the move is to be recognised and then responded to.

2.2   Symbolic gestures

A large number of moves made to begin a process of conciliation and move towards a negotiated compromise do not necessarily involve any retreat, clear or otherwise, from a previously well-laid-out bargaining position. President Nixon's use of the formal title of the Chinese Peoples' Republic; the dropping of a leader associated with a particular line of policy as when, in May 1939, Stalin forced his pro-Western Commissar for Foreign Affairs, Maxim Litvinov, to 'resign' as a signal to Adolf Hitler; President Gorbachev's November 1985 announcement that he would open Soviet space weapons laboratories to US inspection; all these represent forms of conciliation that do not involve abandonment of a previously enunciated bargaining position at major cost to, or sacrifice by, the initiating party.

Such actions come under the broader heading of symbolic gestures, and on many occasions moves of this type have been used by parties to send up a trial balloon: to send out a peace feeler; to indicate their own willingness to initiate or push forward some de-escalatory process; or to get round an impasse in a peace process. Some gestures are mainly designed to indicate a willingness to proceed, some to reassure, and others to signal continued interest in a conciliatory course of action.

Similar functions can, of course, be performed by concessions, but it seems useful to make a distinction between the two forms of move, and to regard symbolic gestures as a second category of actions within the general category of 'conciliatory gestures', both being intended to initiate or forward a peace process, and each being used when appropriate to carry out this task (Mitchell 1990). It is usually the case, however, that symbolic gestures display two basic characteristics. Firstly, they are new – and somewhat unexpected – and so are innovative in a sense not available to concessions, which by definition arise from issues that have a history of 'being on the agenda' of the adversaries, however vague their nature or place on that agenda may have been. Secondly, symbolic gestures 'stand for' or represent something beyond themselves, and it is usually this underlying meaning that is influential rather than the intrinsic nature of the action itself. Compare, for example, the implications of even the reluctant handshake between the Prime Minister of Israel and the Chairman of the PLO on the White House lawn in 1993 with the US Secretary of State ostentatiously refusing to take the hand of the Prime Minister of the CPR in 1954.

A working definition of symbolic gestures would, therefore, take the following form:

> Any symbolic or token (as opposed to practical) move, intended to signal a willingness to begin, continue or accelerate a process of conciliation. The signal usually occurs in an arena in which no definite bargaining position yet exists for the party making the gesture, is frequently innovative and creative and represents something more than the intrinsic act itself.

Symbolic gestures can involve a wider range of possible acts than concessions, involving behaviour ranging from the release or return of prisoners to refraining from the customary condemnation of an adversary. Nixon's 1970 speech mentioning 'the People's Republic of China' was, for example, preceded by an easing of travel restrictions on US citizens visiting China, by an increase in the amount of dollar purchases permitted while travelling there, and by positive references to the CPR in the President's special report on foreign policy to the Congress. The crucial factor is whether the message conveyed by the action is, in some sense, 'larger' than such an action would normally imply, but the key quality needed to overcome barriers of suspicion and mistrust would appear to be the surprise nature of the move. The more unexpected, distinctive or innovative the action, the more likely it is to be recognised, given high credibility and enable a positive response to be made.

2.3 Tension reducing measures

Studies of ways to reduce the dangers posed by the confrontation between NATO and the Warsaw Treaty Organisation in Central Europe in the 1980s gave rise to a new range of concepts to do with mutual disengagement and a reduction of the chances of an outbreak of open fighting, perhaps leading to a nuclear exchange. Two ideas seem particularly helpful in any consideration of de-escalatory moves, the first being that of tension-reducing and the second confidence-building measures.

Taken literally, TRMs refer to any action or statement by a party to some form of dangerous confrontation, whether brief or long lasting, with the intended effect of lessening the sense of fear, alarm or apprehension felt by all participants and observers of the confrontation. Hence, while concessions are specifically retreats from bargaining positions intended to signal a willingness to negotiate during a mutual search for a solution, TRMs aim at signalling some form of general reassurance to an adversary regarding the risks and dangers of the situation and (presumably) the non-lethal or non-violent intentions of the initiator. Moreover, TRMs achieve this through their being practical, workaday moves where the intended signal is closely articulated to the nature of the action, unlike symbolic gestures which are characterised by their ability to signal through their representative nature.

In many cases, TRMs are usually employed prior to concessions in that they are assumed to be necesary to remove generally debilitating feelings and attitudes from a target and to enable that party's leaders to recognise other forms of conciliatory gestures, which may later include some clear concessions. TRMs may include such moves as restoring communication with an adversary, abandoning particular activities which the target may view as potentially threatening or damaging, or agreeing to accommodating moves suggested by third parties.

TRMs may therefore be defined as:

> Concrete moves or statements made to avoid or reduce the dangers arising from situations of crisis or confrontation (usually involving coercive force) which have a high probability of escalating towards new levels of violence.

It is almost a tautology to argue that TRMs are more likely to succeed in advancing a peace process the greater the level of reassurance they convey to a target, and such a statement says nothing about inherent qualities in TRMs that ensure that such a sense is conveyed. An initial suggestion might be that TRMs which unilaterally and unconditionally self-impose limitations on those undertaking them are likely to be most reassuring to adversaries – especially if such limitations are clear, observable and extensive (the quality of transparency mentioned in many works on TRMs). Hence, the degree of precision in self-limitation or commitment to particular non-harmful actions, so that observing any violation is simple and unambiguous, will be a quality which enhances the likely success of any conciliatory gesture that takes the form of a TRM.

2.4   Confidence building measures

The second conception to emerge from academic contemplation of Cold War confrontation in central Europe was the idea of the confidence building measure (CBM). As various writers have pointed out, this idea can be interpreted in either a broad fashion to mean almost any move intended to improve relations between adversaries by building up their confidence in and diminishing mistrust of one another; or in a narrower, strictly military sense, useful for analysing conciliation processes and differentiating CBMs from more general activities aimed at reducing tension.

In this second, narrower sense, CBMs refer to actions which help to develop the level of confidence in a target that certain things are less likely to happen – in other words, reducing the target's estimation of the probability of unpleasant actions from 'quite likely' to 'most unlikely' or (in extreme cases) 'virtually impossible'.[4]

CBMs thus operate at two levels, by unilaterally reducing the Initiator's physical capability of undertaking certain harmful actions, and by unilaterally demonstrating to the Target the Initiator's lack of intention or motivation for undertaking the feared act. Some writers refer to the added benefit of increasing a target's broader 'trust' of an adversary, but while this might be another advantage, it is not strictly necessary that this form of conciliatory initiative should have this additional effect. CBMs are intended to build a target's confidence about what it need no longer fear.

Broadening slightly the strictly military aspects of traditionally conceived CBMs, this form of conciliatory gesture can be defined as:

> Unilateral actions taken with the deliberate intention of either (irretrievably) removing, abandoning or destroying some means of inflicting damage on a target; or demonstrating an absence of intention of utilising such means, thus increasing the present confidence of the target about the low likelihood of such damage and future confidence about the actions and intentions of the party initiating the CBM.

As with TRMs, it seems plausible to argue that CBMs are most likely to fulfil their intended function in building confidence and initiating (or continuing) an accommodative sequence when the removal of resources underlying the threatening capability is most thorough and when their degree of self-limitation is highest. With such moves, threats and dangers are reduced for the target and perceived risks are minimised. Hence, the larger the threat removed and the more irrevocably it is removed, the more credible to the target will be the CBM. It also seems likely that a sense of confidence and a lowering of mistrust by the target is likely to follow the implementation of the kind of confidence-building measure that cannot be rapidly reversed or easily withdrawn. Confidence is not likely to be increased by an initiative that can be revoked rapidly and at little cost to the party undertaking the original move.

2.5   The array of conciliatory moves

As I argued earlier, it seems clear that concessions, symbolic gestures, TRMs and CBMs can all be fruitfully viewed as different forms of conciliatory gesture, each having its own unique features. However, all such moves do share the characteristic that they are, at least, intended to signal to an adversary a willingness to stop a pattern of confrontation or coercive bargaining, and to initiate (or resume) a conciliation process. Some stop at conveying that message, others are intended to signal additional information about motivation or capability. The spectrum of conciliatory moves thus includes a number of different types of signal from an initiator to a target, ranging from simply indicating a willingness to begin (or continue) conciliation, to an attempt to build up a target's confidence that certain things cannot or will not occur. The range of moves is summarised in Figure 5.2 overleaf.

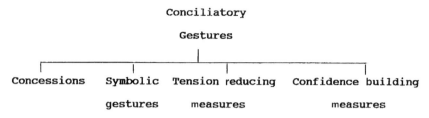

Figure 5.2 **Main Types of Conciliatory Gesture**

Historical examples of conciliatory gestures do not always fall neatly into one or other of these four basic categories, however. President Sadat's visit to Jerusalem appears to have been mainly a symbolic gesture, although it could also be viewed as a major concession if one takes the Arabs' refusal to acknowledge the existence of a State of Israel as the key reference point. Sadat's return of prisoners may have been symbolic but was also a tension-reducing measure. His reopening of the Suez Canal was a major concession, given the conditions that the Egyptians had previously imposed on that option. In the light of such examples, the categorisation scheme offered by this conventional typology of conciliatory gestures seems at best a very loose one and at worse nothing more than a simple set of labels derived from different fields of study.

Moreover, while it may be reasonable to view these four types of 'move' as the basic forms of conciliatory gesture, the imprecision of the categories involved makes it difficult to discern common properties that might affect the likelihood of their successful use. A preliminary scan suggests some clues but no definitive answers. Qualities of degree of change and distinctiveness seem likely to enhance the probability that a concession will be successful in eliciting positive reactions from an adversary, while novelty, engendering a sense of surprise in a target, seems an important quality in any symbolic gesture made with serious intent. Others may be revealed on closer examination. I return to this theme at the end of the chapter.

3   Conciliatory tactics and accommodative sequences

While the account of President Sadat's peacemaking activities between 1971 and 1977 emphasised his individual gestures or moves, much of the current literature on the opening stages of peacemaking stresses the practical necessity of initiating a series of linked gestures in a tactical pattern so that a clearly conciliatory direction is discerned by an adversary. A varied range of conciliatory gestures, it is argued, may be used sequentially or simultaneously by any party seeking to diminish tension, build confidence and trust, or successfully move towards a solution to the conflict.

In line with this thinking, I suggested in Chapter 3 that, while individual gestures could be viewed as the basic 'building blocks' of a conciliatory process, it was also necessary to think beyond the immediate to the tactical and the strategic levels of conciliation, and to pay close attention to the sequence of gestures used in conciliatory initiatives which – through their continuity – would contribute to a continuing accommodative sequence, a successful peacemaking process and the ultimate resolution of a conflict. Conventionally, most conciliatory strategies have been viewed as necessarily being a mixture of several types of initiative, usually in different proportions or sequences. Hence, it is important to be conceptually clear about current thinking regarding the various tactics forming part of any conciliatory strategy.

3.1 Patterns of conciliatory tactics

Much of the recent effort devoted to describing the various tactics underpinning conciliatory initiatives or accommodative sequences tends to have been undertaken by experimental psychologists who have used laboratory simulations, often variations of the classic Prisoners' Dilemma, to study the nature and relative success of alternative tactics in bargaining relationships. Many of their findings involve indications of stable relationships between such variables as the rates at which concessions are made during simulated bargaining and the achievement of better outcomes – for example, Druckman and his colleagues' findings about the success of positively accelerated concession rates in negotiations where parties are under time pressure (1972 and 1976).

While these and other findings arise from simulations and laboratory experiments, many of the tactics they have delineated possess an inherent plausibility when applied to historical cases of both coercive and accommodative bargaining as well as to conciliatory initiatives and strategies – at least in the sense that decision-makers seem to follow such tactics implicitly, even if not consciously. A list of basic conciliatory tactics derived from this literature would include:

1 Unilateral restraint (UR), either by deliberately refraining from making a coercive move, as when President Eisehower unilaterally took a decision to refrain from ASAT development in the 1950s, or by ceasing some ongoing coercion unconditionally; or by refraining or ceasing conditionally, perhaps for a specified time period (URC);

2 A set or series of unilateral conciliatory moves, as when President Gorbachev announced to the UN in 1988 that the USSR would reduce its armed forces by 500 000 troops and 5000 tanks (CO-OP);

3 An initial conciliatory move, followed by concession for target's concession, but coercion for target's coercion (Tit-for-Tat or TFT);[5]

4 An initial conciliatory move, followed by larger concessions in response to target's reactive concession (Geometric Acceleration or +n%);
5 'I will make a concession if you will make one – first' (I-will-if-you-will or IFU);
6 'I will do x, but to *enable* me to do this, you will first have to do y.'

This last could be called 'enable me to be nice to you' tactic, but Alan Newcombe has coined the expression the *Ankhesnamun Initiative*, after an Egyptian queen of that name who offered to conclude a treaty with the Hittite Emperor by marrying one of his sons, *if* one were to be made available (Newcombe and Stolfi 1979) Hence the form: I will, if you first make it possible – or ANK.

In some historical situations, a single type of conciliatory 'tactic' may be elevated into an overall strategy, as when one party decides that its position dictates a policy of complete collaboration with its adversary in reaching some settlement. In others, basic tactics seem to have been used in a variety of combinations to produce a complex strategy intended to forward a peace process. 'GRIT' strategies, as I argue below, consist of a combination of unilateral concessions and TFT, structured in a series of sequential stages, each dependent upon its predecessor for continuation. 'Carrot and Stick' strategies are mainly based upon TFT, although they frequently commence either with some unilateral conciliatory gesture by the initiating party, or with some version of an IFU offer.

3.2   Conciliatory tactics: an initial analysis

One can differentiate among commonly used conciliatory tactics on the basis of a number of criteria. These would start with the question of which party initiates a particular move or gesture, whose choice it is to continue the sequence, and how specific a response is demanded from the party reacting to the initiative. (The last would involve questions of what choice of response is given to the reacting party, and whether there is any flexibility in the selection of a response.) Other differentiating features could include the tolerance for delay in responding and the question of how easily defection by both initiator and target might be detected – that is, how clearly it could be seen that a target has not responded 'satisfactorily' to the demands of the initiator, or the degree to which the initiator has reneged on an initial offer, whether conditional or not.

3.2.1   Co-operative tactics

In the cases of both UR and CO-OP, the first move obviously has to come from a party willing to initiate, and the continuation of the de-escalatory process will depend upon: (i) the number of gestures or moves that party is willing to make before requiring some response from the target; and (ii) whether an acceptable, sufficient reaction is, indeed, forthcoming. The nature of that 'acceptable' reaction is usually established by the initiator and tends to be case specific. Historical examples suggest that unilateral sequences tend to be short, often consisting of a single act or statement serving as a 'trial balloon'; and terminated abruptly if a clear, acceptable reaction is not forthcoming relatively quickly, although parties in a conflict do differ in their tolerance for non-reciprocity.[6]

The matter of initiation is not so clear as regards the +n% tactics, and while the commitment in principle to increase benefits to any reacting adversary is reasonably clear in theory, it will inevitably be less clear in practice as the value placed upon each of a sequence of concessions or conciliatory moves is likely to differ greatly in the eyes of those making them and those on the receiving end.

3.2.2   Conditional tactics

In the case of TFT and URC, any sequence usually begins with a unilateral gesture on the part of one party with an implied offer of further concessions if this is reciprocated by the target. (Sometimes the tactic is preceded by an unambiguous IFU move.) Continuation of the process then depends upon the alacrity and clarity with which the target responds to the initial move. Delays frequently result in the initiative being overtaken by other events and lost in the on-going prosecution of the conflict. To some degree, the ease with which the Target can respond to the initial move, and keep the TFT or URC process going, will depend upon the specificity of the demand for a reaction made by the initiator. This is also a feature of IFU tactics discussed below.

One of the problems with the IFU tactic is that it is frequently used as a part of a generally coercive strategy in order to demonstrate that the initiating party is flexible and willing to seek a peaceful solution – and that the target is not. Hence, many IFUs are merely attempts to put targets in a bad light and demand preconditions and prior moves from an adversary which the initiator knows beforehand the adversary is unlikely to make. The problem for the parties in conflict is distinguishing genuine IFUs from coercive probes, publicity ploys or straightforward traps – a problem compounded by perceptual difficulties that might lead initiators into asking for concessions which they perceive as 'reasonable' but which, in the target's frame of reference, either appear highly unreasonable or completely out of the question.

Even genuine IFU initiatives have the decided disadvantage of placing the onus for initiating action on the target. Their basic message is; 'You act first and then, when you have shown you are ready to conciliate, we will act.' This shifting of the onus on to the target often undermines efforts to begin or continue conciliatory processes.

On other dimensions, IFU has certain advantages, in that it can be specific about what will happen, once the initial barrier of the first move has been overcome, it being clear to target and onlookers what reaction is required and what the initiator's response will be once it has occurred. In a sense, an IFU tactic has some minimal safeguards for the target in that it is usually clear when the other party is reneging. Moreover, some IFUs can combine the advantages of a promise of a specific response with flexibility in prior demands for target reaction. Instead of taking the form 'I will do x if you do y', some IFUs can preserve an adversary's own discretion in the matter by taking the form 'If you make *some* conciliatory gesture to demonstrate an interest in de-escalation, I will do x.' In this latter case, the target retains responsibility for determining what constitutes a feasible conciliatory gesture (with inevitable attendant problems of determining what the adversary is likely to regard as 'enough' for x to take place). This characteristic can materially assist internal decision-making processes involving doves and hawks by minimising the external appearance of giving in completely to pressure.

3.2.3   Permissive tactics

Finally, while ANK tactics closely resemble IFU, they differ in that they attempt to put greater pressure on the target by implying that a conciliatory gesture from the 'initiator' is simply not possible without some prior, enabling act by the target, after which the gesture will be forthcoming. Again, as with IFU, the responsibility for the initiative is placed on the target, and it is an increased responsibility in the light of the proclaimed helplessness of the initiating party. Similarly, ANK can be quite specific in that the initiator is promising a particular move which is enabled through a specified prior move by the target. Both know what is supposed to happen in the sequence, once target takes up the initiative. Furthermore, reneging is quite clear.

Some historical examples indicate that the ANK tactic is used frequently in protracted conflicts, both as a genuine attempt to begin de-escalation and move towards negotiation, but also, unfortunately, as a public relations exercise or as a trap for an adversary as part of a broader, coercive strategy. One way of distinguishing the genuineness of the tactic might be to differentiate between those prior enabling actions which are (i) *logically necessary* before the promised move can take place; and those which are (ii) *politically desirable*, in that they make the move easier to carry out. There seems to be an important difference between moves which are awkward to make because of internal opposition, the loss of future bargaining reputation or the prior existence of a clear, public commitment to an intransigent position, and those which are literally impossible without some prior action by an adversary.

Clearly, President Sadat's visit to Israel fell into both the logically necessary and politically desirable categories of ANK tactics. In the first sense, it was clearly impossible for Sadat to fly to Israel without guarantees of a safe passage for an Egyptian plane. It was also necessary, from a political point of view, for a prior invitation to be issued by the Israeli Government. Sadat's offer, in fact, took the form of saying; 'I will come to Jerusalem to visit Israel (and, by implication, recognise the country) but to do that you must first make my visit possible by inviting me.' As such, it seems a clear case of the use of the ANK tactic.

Discussion about the various conciliatory moves and accommodative sequences leads to a point where these have to be fitted into conceptions of overall strategies of conciliation and long term peace processes. How have current analysts fitted specific moves, tactics and accommodative sequences into models of an overall conciliatory strategy – if at all? What conceptual difficulties arise when such behaviours can also form part of continuing coercive efforts to win protracted conflict?

4 Conciliatory strategies and peacemaking: traditional approaches

The line between strategical and tactical behaviour in peacemaking processes is a vague one. Existing literature on both escalation and de-escalation confuses terminology so thoroughly that it is virtually impossible to envisage any coherent taxonomy. In much of the literature, however, a common approach assumes that the underlying process can be charac-terised as long distance, tacit bargaining, in which communication and sig-nalling plays a key role, whether one party is engaged in: (i) trying to coerce an adversary into surrender or; (ii) both coercing and persuading an adversary to negotiate; or (iii) conciliating an adversary with a view to working out a compromise solution.

The use of such terms clearly indicates the extent to which thinking and writing about 'peacemaking' has been influenced by the assumptions of the realist, 'peace-though-strength' school of thought, in which the fastest and most secure road to peace lies through coercion and the triumph of one party to the conflict over the other. So pervasive is this way of thinking about the achievement of peace that much analysis of alternative strategies treats such alternatives to peace-through-successful-threat (or violence) as a minor, if interesting, aspect of the wholly dominant mode – the peace imposed by the strong. It is the kind of thinking that clearly underlay President Sadat's military efforts in 1973, when the Egyptian leader per-ceived that the best means of making a satisfactory peace with Israel was ini-tially to redress the coercive imbalance left over from the 1967 June War.

4.1 Mixed strategies; coercion and conciliation

Traditionally, the study of long-term, tacit bargaining strategies has been dominated by a concern with the communication and use of coercive threats or acts, employed with the aim of cowing an adversary and bringing about peace through victory and surrender. Paradoxically, some writers (Snyder, 1972; Schelling, 1966) have made a clear distinction between coercive bargaining and accommodative bargaining strategies, the latter associated with the offering of concessions and conciliatory gestures in a manner consonant with long-term conciliatory strategies.

However, there are more things in heaven and earth than ever suggested by the taxonomies of social scientists. It is more usually the case that parties in conflict 'signal' to each other by a mixture of coercive and conciliatory actions or statements, used simultaneously or in overlapping sequences, in an attempt to achieve some satisfactory settlement of their dispute. Colloquially, this strategy is frequently referred to as a strategy of 'carrots and sticks', which seems a perfectly accurate and acceptable description of the nature of that particular pattern of offers, actions and counter-offers. Other writers (Thies, 1980) have also made a distinction between the use of carrots and sticks and the strategy of coercive warfare on the grounds that, while the former contains a mixture of cost imposing actions and genuine concessions (carrots and sticks), the latter merely offers a target the choice between further coercion or some diminution or cessation of the existing level of coercion, damage and pain as the inducement for moving towards an 'acceptable' negotiated settlement (smaller sticks).[7]

In plainer words, it is possible to conceive of a situation in which one party to a conflict pursues a strategy of deliberately coercing and damaging an adversary, partly to undermine the latter's will to continue the dispute, but also in order to have the option of beginning an accommodative sequence by abandoning specific forms of previously imposed coercion as a 'concession' to the target.[8] 'Conciliation' then becomes merely a matter of relief from imposed coercion: 'We will stop hurting you when you cease doing x and agree to negotiate reasonably – but if you don't stop, we will hurt you even more.' Coercive Warfare strategies often contain a conditional promise to decrease the pain – or, at least, to keep it at its present level – plus an implied threat to increase it!

Whether this particular strategy, or the unconditional if temporary abandonment of violent coercion, such as a bombing pause, is viewed by the adversary as a 'conciliatory gesture' seems open to doubt.[9] Targets seem to take the attitude that such negative benefits merely place the relationship back on an equivalent footing rather than offering 'genuine' concessions. Mai Van Bo, the North Vietnamese ranking diplomat in Paris during the period of coercive warfare conducted against his country by President Johnson's Government, expressed this view succinctly when, in September 1965, he passed a message to the US Government via French intermediaries to the effect that

> The essence of the American propositions is the stopping of bombing under conditions. The American bombing of the DRV is illegal. The US

should put an end to the bombing and cannot impose conditions ... The American message has been communicated after an escalation of the attacks against Hanoi and under the threat of continuation of the attacks against Hanoi. It is clear that this constitutes an ultimatum ... It is only after the unconditional stopping by the US of the bombing and all other acts of war against the DRV that it would be possible to engage in conversations.

Clearly, these are not the views of someone who regards the ending of imposed pain as a meaningful concession or as an acceptable peacemaking strategy.

Within this whole 'peace through coercion' school, Thies' distinction between carrots and sticks and coercive warfare (the latter being a strategy where the only 'carrot' consists of *not* using the 'sticks') is a useful one, especially as it clearly reveals some of the existing and widely shared assumptions about how one 'makes peace' or 'resolves a conflict' (Thies 1980). With this intellectual background, one should not be surprised at conflicting parties' practical tendencies to use mixed strategies of coercion and conciliation in order to 'find a solution'.

4.2   GRIT and other alternatives

Apart from carrots and sticks and coercive warfare, however, other conciliatory strategies exist which involve an overlap between coercive and accommodative bargaining. One of the better known is that originally advanced by Charles Osgood as Graduated and Reciprocal Initiatives in Tension Reduction (GRIT). This is a strategy which Osgood advocated as a way of extracting parties from deadlocked confrontation when neither dare make the initial conciliatory move for fear of being exploited by the adversary. As a strategy, GRIT – discussed in detail in Chapter 7 – clearly falls into the category where coercive and accommodative bargaining overlap, as it utilises tactics of both unilateral concession and tit-for-tat responses, the latter including coercive activities if such appear necessary because of exploitative responses by the adversary.[10] It is also the case that GRIT is a far more structured approach to the business of conciliation and de-escalation than other strategies, with greater emphasis on the accommodative aspects of the interaction than on the coercive. Hence, in any taxonomy of strategies, GRIT would fall towards the more accommodative end of the continuum.

This argument leads to the suggestion that one taxonomy of peacemaking strategies could consist of a continuum of mixed activities including both coercive and accommodative actions. We need to consider what would be the limiting points of such a continuum, particularly the strategies that would be most and least accommodating. Clearly, one end of any continuum of bargaining strategies would be that which offered complete co-operation to the other party, 100 per cent compliance with its wishes and an equivalent level of collaboration with its activities. Glenn Snyder discusses this as a strategy of 'capitulation', and such a strategy would be exemplified by any wholly pacifist response to the goals of another party. In our Israeli–Egyptian case, such a strategy would have involved the Israelis, for example, in an acceptance of UN Resolution 242 and complete withdrawal from territories captured in 1967 before peace negotiations began.

While some governments may, on occasions, have approached the use of such a pure accommodative strategy, the only historical cases appear to be those occurring after defeat in a major war. The opprobrious terms reserved for such behaviour, such as 'capitulation', 'appeasement' or 'collaboration' indicate the popular reaction to such limiting cases, but it has to be recognised that most parties involved in peacemaking processes can employ strategies that contain heavy elements of collaborative tactics, short of outright appeasement. Moreover, in other contexts tactics that are essentially similar to capitulation are much more frequent and treated with much less contempt. As Pruitt and Rubin have pointed out, at the level of interpersonal and small-group conflict, parties frequently employ tactics of yielding (lowering aspirations and submitting to the wishes of the other party) or withdrawing, particularly when the withdrawing or yielding party is concerned about the general well-being, if not the particular aspirations, of the other (Pruitt and Rubin 1985).

Purely for symmetry's sake, it is easy to see that the limiting case at the other end of any coercion–accommodation continuum would be a strategy of complete coercion with no conciliatory initiatives to encourage negotiation. The strategy would merely involve dogged use of cost-imposition until the adversary gave up completely. Historically, this seems difficult to envisage until one recalls the Allies' strategy of 'unconditional surrender' during the Second World War, clearly enunciated and actually put into practice as far as Hitler's Reich – if not Italy or Japan – was concerned. Similar strategies often typify revolutionary wars or wars of national liberation, struggles in which the existence or survival of one party appears to be at issue. They are not uncommon – at least on the part of political incumbents – in secessionist struggles, such as the American Civil War. Hence, strategies of 100 per cent coercion aiming at an adversary's capitulation are perhaps less uncommon than strategies of 100 per cent collaboration, although it is difficult to see how such strategies can ever realistically be counted as 'peacemaking', save in the sense of making a desert and calling it peace.

5   Traditional taxonomies and key attributes

The fact that some attention has been paid to the nature and form of conciliatory gestures, tactics and strategies is encouraging, but it has to be admitted that not much systematic, analytical work is currently available to the student of conciliatory behaviour, short of labelling and distinguishing some conciliatory activities, and dissecting others that use coercion and damage as preliminaries to an imposed 'solution'.

Even if attention is focused on individual conciliatory gestures themselves, the existence of conventional classifications involving 'confidence building' or 'tension reducing' actions throws only a little light on why particular actions reduce tension and others do not, or why particular statements build confidence, while others signally fail to have that effect. In the existing literature on conciliation there are only occasional hints of explanatory theory that seek to link characteristics and impacts in any systematic way, or even to go beneath the surface of individual examples of conciliatory actions to look for common qualities or shared attributes.

A start could be made by suggesting how it might be possible to use existing thinking to answer the central question of this present study: what determines the success of conciliatory actions or initiatives? At this stage, one possibility would be to take existing ideas about types of conciliatory gesture and produce a simple classification scheme to bring some order into the apparently haphazard variety of behaviours that constitute historical gestures of conciliation.

Without wishing to over-simplify a complex variety of conciliatory gestures and actions, one approach would be to suggest that most conciliatory gestures in the real world of protracted conflict could be classified under one of three headings: as gestures of *Abandonment*, *Acknowledgement* or *Initiation*.

5.1   Abandonment

The defining criterion of gestures of abandonment is simply that they all involve the withdrawal of something from somewhere. This can be the withdrawal of an accusation, a claim regarding some object or material good not already possessed, or from a particular bargaining position put forward as non-negotiable or as the furthest limit of concession. Equally, the gesture could involve the withdrawal of some presence (such as troops, military/technical advisers, observers) or of support for a client. Again, gestures of abandonment can involve the withdrawal (by dismissal) of a key official or office holder, a representative identified with a prior policy of coercion, or some objection to a course of action delayed by that objection.

The key conception underlying gestures of abandonment is that the gesture is some action that a party does to something of its own. The initiator abandons his own position, argument, or objection as a move towards conciliation and dialogue.

5.2   Acknowledgement

Conciliatory gestures in the category of acknowledgement involve a party employing some form of behaviour, physical or verbal, that indicates acceptance of something about the adversary. This acceptance may merely involve taking notice of the official existence of an adversary (President Sadat acknowledging the state of Israel; the Israeli Government acknowledging the legitimate existence of the PLO as a representative political movement), which may be achieved merely by communicating directly with them. (Recall the effects of the United States UN Representative Andrew Young talking to PLO representatives.)

On the other hand, acknowledgement may take the more official form of some kind of 'recognition'. In other circumstances, a gesture may consist of the acceptance of some claim or demand by the adversary (going far beyond merely 'taking notice' of existence), or recognition of some right possessed by the adversary or some wrong done to them in the past, as when President Kennedy's American University speech implicitly acknowledged that the Cold War could be seen as the fault of both the USA and the USSR, not merely the latter.

It might be argued that there is no clear difference between abandoning one's own claim to something and acknowledging an adversary's claim to the same something. However, it does not seem unreasonable to hold that the way gestures are made or expressed will have a major impact on the way in which they are recognised, evaluated and reacted to, and it is this difference that justifies the distinction used here. If, in abandonment, a party gives up something of its own, in acknowledgement the party accepts something of the other party's.

5.3   Initiation

As opposed to gestures of abandonment and acknowledgement, which both tend to be 'backward looking' in the sense that they pertain to behaviour from the past, gestures which can be classed as initiation look to the future and make suggestions about future activity either by the initiator, by the target or jointly. Conciliatory moves that involve offers of future benefit, moves that will ease tension and build confidence, plans or proposals for future consideration and discussion, suggestions for mutual meeting places, arenas of possible agreement about future activity or future means of arriving at some solution to the conflict.

Although the distinction is not quite so clear-cut as in the last two cases, it still seems plain that initiatory gestures involve the party making them in proposing something definite for the adversary and/or the conciliator to do separately or jointly in order to move towards a solution. In that sense, this third type of common conciliatory move can easily be recognised and distinguished from the other two major types.

5.4   Gestures, typologies and the issue of 'success'

It can justifiably be argued that in the messy, real world of international and intra-national conflict, the way in which a conciliatory gesture is made, transmitted and perceived is not likely to involve a clear-cut case of its being seen as one or other of the three types outlined above. A gesture may be intended to show abandonment, be implemented to indicate acknowledgement, become distorted en route to involve elements of initiation, and finally be received and evaluated as some combination of all these. All are quite possible, given the likely distortions in communication and interference from background noise that was emphasised in the communications framework discussed in Chapter 3.

Moreover, given the need to discern linkages between the nature of the initiative undertaken by one of the parties in conflict and the likelihood of its success in starting an accommodative sequence or carrying forward a peace process, beginning with any typology of strategies or of gestures seems unlikely to reveal essential or even influential qualities linked to success. Classification can say only a little about causation. Are gestures of abandonment more likely to be successfully initiated and recognised than gestures of acknowledgement or initiation? What impacts are gestures of acknowledgement likely to have on a target's elites or constituents? Are gestures that initiate activities afforded greater credibility by an adversary's leaders than those which simply acknowledge what those leaders have regarded as self-evident truths from the very start of the conflict?

Although the distinction between these three types of conciliatory gesture, or between the familiar empirical forms, might be useful as an initial attempt to differentiate among a wide variety of conciliatory moves, something more complex is required in order to investigate links between different types of conciliatory gesture and their likely effectiveness. Some clues have already been provided by the analysis of the historical types of conciliatory gesture discussed above in Section 2. There it seemed clear that the magnitude of the retreat from a previous position involved in any concession made success much more likely, while a lack of conditionality also enhanced a gesture's chances of being perceived as credible by a target. Similarly, the degree of transparency in TRMs and the voluntary nature of all forms of conciliatory gestures were likely to be qualities that increased an initiative's credibility in the eyes of an adversary's leadership. Lastly, the discussion of the manner in which gestures could differ in the degree of flexibility they allowed targets in choosing their own response to an olive branch also suggested another quality likely to increase not only the credibility of a conciliatory initiative but also its respondability. These qualities, it was implied, were likely to make for greater success in launching a peace process.

This line of thought is followed up in Chapter 6, which discusses these and other characteristics of conciliatory gestures likely to be essential qualities that increase effectiveness.

6
The Nature of the Initiative: Characteristics and Impact

'He who thinks that, among great men, new benefits cause old resentments to be forgotten makes a great mistake.'

Machiavelli, *The Prince*

Previous discussion of the various types of conciliatory initiative undertaken in Chapter 5 began to suggest a number of attributes possessed by successful moves in situations of protracted conflict. This raised at least the possibility that an observer could look for certain qualities associated with greater or lesser effectiveness, while a practitioner could examine any planned or proposed gestures, or those used by an adversary, to see whether they conform to certain guidelines. For example, discussion of 'concessions' suggested that the larger the retreat, the more likely it is that the initiative will obtain the desired response, while 'symbolic gestures' clearly have to articulate with the values and assumptions of a target. The more transparent a TRM and the clearer the voluntariness and unconditionality of a CBM, the more credible and respondable they will be to a target.

Further key aspects of the nature of the initiative may be discernible from analysis of other conciliatory moves, so this chapter opens with a brief examination of another example of a gesture of conciliation, taken in the aftermath of violence but well before any settlement of the conflict in question.

1 A recipe for failure?

On 6 July 1985, three years after the end of a short but vicious war over possession of the group of small, sparsely populated islands in the South Atlantic known in London as 'the Falklands' and in Buenos Aires as 'Las Malvinas', the British Government made what at least some of its members thought was a major gesture of conciliation towards the recently elected government of President Alfonsin in Argentina. It lifted the embargo on trade with Argentina which had been imposed at the beginning of the actual war in 1982 and not subsequently removed. The move was announced simultaneously in Rio de Janiero by the British Foreign Secretary, Sir Geoffrey Howe, and in the House of Commons in London by his deputy, Timothy Renton.

The British move was clearly intended to be a conciliatory gesture, and in government circles in London the hope was privately expressed that the initiative would lead on to the start of discussions and negotiations over the outstanding issues in the South Atlantic – in other words, to a peace process. The British move was initially described as a 'concession', although it was open to interpretation whether the removal of an embargo imposed unilaterally during a stage of overt inter-party violence would be viewed as such by the target of such an action. In the terms used in Chapter 5, the British initiative is probably best viewed as a symbolic gesture, intended to signal a willingness to begin a process of conciliation, although the move obviously involved practical side effects, especially for companies prevented for three years from trading with their partners in the other country.

Whatever the type of initative, there is no doubt that the British hoped that this gesture would begin a process of restoring normal relations between Britain and Argentina, the official British statement emphasising that this was a 'fresh step to promote improvement' in Anglo–Argentine relations (even though a late, Prime Ministerial addition to the draft statement insisted that the British Government was not willing to discuss sovereignty over the Islands, in Argentine eyes the central issue in the dispute). Equally, there can be no doubt that the Argentine Government failed to perceive this gesture as anything but posturing and certainly not the major 'concession' that was intended in London. The British move failed to be seen in Buenos Aires as 'conciliatory', did little to relieve the continuing tension between the two governments, and did almost nothing to build confidence. It failed to begin an accommodative sequence of actions and reactions. A peace process did not get under way.[1]

There are many ways in which the British conciliatory gesture of July 1986 can be contrasted with President Sadat's visit to Israel in 1977. The British initiative was low key; it merely restored a status quo which had existed (to the advantage of both parties) before 1982; it contained a firm re-statement of a British position on the central issue in dispute that was wholly unacceptable to any Argentine Government, although in this it was very similar to Sadat's speech to the Knesset; and it was interpreted by the target as largely a propaganda ploy to impress an international audience increasingly impatient with what was seen as British intransigence over the Islands. Finally, the outstanding feature of the gesture, compared with Sadat's, was its complete failure to initiate any peacemaking process between the two governments, in spite of the fact that (certainly compared with Israel and Egypt) they had enjoyed friendly relations right up to the outbreak of the war.

Comparison of the British July 1986 initiative and Sadat's initiative in October 1977 returns our argument to the more general question of why some conciliatory gestures 'succeed' (at least in the sense of starting an accommodative process) while others fail, even in this minimal sense. Past history is littered with conciliatory gestures that were ignored or (apparently) not even noticed; with concessions that were rejected or damned as attempts to steal some advantage over their target; and with tension-reducing or confidence-building moves that only succeeded in making the target more suspicious and, as a result of the target's reaction, the initiator more convinced of the target's intractability. As I have noted previously, based purely upon anecdotal evidence, there is much to commend the proposition that far more conciliatory gestures fail to begin accommodation (even from relatively low levels of tension and hostility) than succeed. The question is: why should this be so and what might be done to increase the probability of success for well-intended conciliatory initiatives?

Unfortunately, as also noted in Chapter 5, conventional understanding of conciliatory gestures, accommodative sequences and peace processes tends to be merely descriptive or taxonomical. Simply labelling an action or series of actions as 'a concession' or as 'tension reduction measures' is little help in understanding why some initiatives 'succeed' while others do not. At the very least, it ought to be possible to indicate the circumstances in which a practical concession rather than a symbolic gesture is needed to start a de-escalation spiral, remove a negotiating log-jam or reduce the danger of re-escalation, although even this slightly increased level of sophistication would be of little help in adding information to the basic causal model, which is illustrated in Figure 6.1 below.

However, the argument that there are certain forms of conciliatory moves that have a greater chance of success than others, almost irrespective of the context in which they are made remains a reasonable one, but

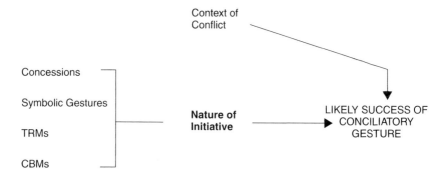

Figure 6.1   **Influences on Conciliation Effectiveness IV**

focuses attention less upon the type of initiative undertaken and more upon fundamental attributes of the gesture itself. 'Essential qualities', rather than the type of conciliatory gesture made – or using a communications approach, the *content* of the signals sent – will be one significant influence on the success of any conciliatory initiative, so the key issue becomes an analytical rather than a taxonomic one. The British Falklands initiative undoubtedly diminished its likelihood of success by containing an intransigent statement about the central issue of sovereignty and by the fact that it was announced by the Foreign Minister (and not Prime Minister Thatcher) in a location easily construed as an arena chosen for its proximity to a very large and attentive Latin American 'gallery'. In contrast, the Sadat initiative succeeded, at least partly, because it involved an implicit, major concession – recognition of Israel by physically going there – carried out by the Egyptian Head of State in a location that could not have been more central to the target of the gesture. The issue is whether it is possible to generalise from a few examples of success and failure in order to outline general characteristics of conciliatory initiatives that make them more rather than less likely to succeed. Hence, it is necessary to confront three basic questions:

1 Analytically, how is it possible to conceptualise those attributes of conciliatory gestures that contribute to their effectiveness?
2 Theoretically, which seem likely to be the most salient characteristics that affect the likely success of conciliatory initiatives?
3 Practically, how might it be possible to reinforce the impact of such salient characteristics, thus increasing the probability that the conciliatory initiative will be successful?

It might be noted that answering the first two questions outlined above focuses on what the literature on attributional processes calls 'processing of information', that is on what factors affect the interpretation of messages in terms of another's intentions in sending the message. The third question concerns practical issues of 'the management of impressions', or how the initiator of a message might go about ensuring that the signal has the desired impact on the target's perceptions or evaluations (Druckman 1990, p.556). Clearly, the nature and attributes of the 'message' sent will affect its likely impact, so for an initiator the practical question becomes one of how to 'manage' the conciliatory move so that it has the right 'mix' of attributes to achieve the optimum desired effect. This and the following chapters deal with both the analytical and the practical aspects of these processes, beginning with the issue of what attributes of conciliatory gestures might have maximum impact on a target's ability to process information about an adversary's gesture in a clear and positive manner.

2   Characteristics of effective gestures: preliminary conceptions

Chapter 5 tentatively suggested a number of qualities likely to enhance the effectiveness of conciliatory initiatives, whatever taxonimical label was placed on the actual initiative itself. These can be summarised as qualities of:

1 *Magnitude* of the change represented by the initiative;
2 *Articulation* of the initiative with the values, culture and history of the target;
3 *Transparency* of the initiative so that performance can easily be monitored by the target;
4 *Unconditionality* of the initiative, in that performance does not depend on commitments or actions by the target;
5 *Voluntariness* of the initiative, in that it is not seen as a reluctant move, wrung from the initiator by prior coercion.

In searching for other characteristics of successful conciliatory moves, it would be helpful to return initially to the communications approach outlined in Chapter 3. Any successful efforts to start a conciliation process inevitably involve parties in conflict communicating with one another, in one way or another, with one level of impact or another. Yet, clearly, messages intended to be sent via any type of conciliatory gesture often turn out to be quite different from those actually picked out and perceived by the target.

Hence, it is necessary first to enquire what are the qualities of signals that increase the likelihood that the target's interpretation will accurately match the initiator's intention. Some conciliatory gestures seem, by their nature, to be more likely than others to be recognised accurately for what they are by a target.[2] At one extreme, what Snyder (1972) refers to as total 'capitulation' is highly likely to be recognised accurately by the target of any communication about the initiator's willingness to abandon the struggle completely. At another, minor changes in wording of statements concerning a contentious issue, even in the most propitious of contexts, seem less likely to be so easily recognised. So, what assists or ensures the effective communication of intent so that intentions and interpretations match, and a conciliatory move is 'successful'?

To simplify this problem a little, recall that I argued earlier, and at length, that a conciliatory initiative can be 'successful' at six levels, quite apart from whether it leads – eventually – to a final resolution of the conflict. The first two involve an initiator contemplating making a tentative gesture and then actually initiating one; the next three a Target's accurate recognition of the initiative, its internal evaluation of the move, and its reaction through a conciliatory move of its own. The final stage of success is continuing interaction in an accommodative sequence, or a process of de-escalation characterised by decreasing coercion and hostility. I deal with issues of contemplation and initiation in a later chapter, so at this stage merely confine analysis to issues of recognition, evaluation and reaction, asking, what are the inherent characteristics of 'conciliatory' actions or gestures that are more likely:

1 to be picked out and attended to by the target (*discernability*);
2 to lead the target to attribute a genuine, stable and long-lasting change of interests, goals or (at least) means to the initiating party (*credibility*);
3 to begin altering the attitudes, cognitions or expectations of the target regarding the conflict and its adversary (*credibility*); and
4 to make it easier for the target to make a conciliatory response (*respondability*)?

Clearly, the first hurdle to be overcome for intital effectiveness in making a conciliatory gesture is simply having it noticed by the target, on the not unreasonable grounds that an unnoticed signal is unlikely to have much impact on the target's beliefs, goals or behaviour. In communications terms, the signal has to break through the screen of selective inattention erected by all parties in conflict. This raises issues of a gesture's 'recognis-ability' and implies that a basic task for an initiating party is to increase the distinctiveness of the signal. To anticipate a later argument, this require-ment indicates that at least one feature of the initiative should be its prominence, especially within the perceptual framework of the target, a quality that links clearly to that of articulation in the list of important characteristics or features.

The second hurdle to be overcome involves success in altering attitudes and cognitions of the target to some degree – at least as far as cognitions of the target's adversary and the conflict itself are concerned. Many have argued that for peacemaking to succeed, it is necessary for the parties to increase both 'trust' and 'confidence' in each other, so that one essential effect of a conciliatory initiative and the resultant accommodative exchange is that both alter (at least minimally) the target's attitudes (both evaluative and cognitive) towards its adversary. Others hold that such atti-tude change is too much to expect and, anyway, is not necessary to move towards a resolution.[3] However, Kelman (1985, pp.224–34) has argued per-suasively that conciliatory gestures or accommodative sequences should have the capacity to alter at least the target's expectations about the future of the conflict. This might be achieved: (1) by breaking the psychological barrier erected by a sense of hopelessness that the conflict will inevitably continue as it has in the past; and (2) by convincing those involved that alternatives do exist as the adversary is not quite as previously conceived.[4]

What all such arguments appear to have in common is their sense that – in order to break through perceptual and political barriers – any conciliatory gesture must be characterised by a considerable element of surprise or novelty, at least as far as the target's decision-makers are concerned. Michael Handel (1981, pp.71–80) has argued that, to achieve maximum impact, initiatives have to involve a major change (magnitude), but equally importantly be new and be unpredicted, achieving maximum impact through their 'unexpectedness'. I suggest that one can conceptualise these ideas by arguing that, to achieve any level of success, a conciliatory move needs to be characterised by a high degree of novelty or to be clearly precedent-breaking.

In this connection, it is interesting to recall that, on coming to power in April 1977, Israeli Prime Minister Begin himself issued an open invitation to all or any Arab leaders to meet him for peace talks in Jerusalem – or anywhere else. However, such an invitation had almost routinely been issued by all incoming Israeli Prime Ministers, so the move had become almost something of an accepted ritual and probably no one would have been more surprised than Mr Begin if the offer had been taken up!

While characteristics of novelty and magnitude seem likely to have an effect on the discernability of a conciliatory gesture, other qualities, while also enhancing recognisability, are also likely to increase or decrease its credibility – that is, to convince an inevitably sceptical set of rival leaders that those responsible for the initiative are genuine in their wish to seek an alternative way of achieving goals and relating to their adversary. Thus, a third approach to the question of what seems likely to affect possible 'success' underlines the need for an initiator to ensure that any chosen gesture leads the target to attribute a genuine alteration in the initiator's own objectives (for example, a compromise rather than victory) or, at least, in its view of appropriate means of achieving unchanged goals (for example, via negotiation rather than coercion). The initiative must make it more probable that the target will perceive the initiator as newly (but firmly) committed to a different strategy, and no longer to old means or goals. Of course, given the intractability of many conflicts, the nature of 'commitment' and the difficulty of altering entrenched images, this is perhaps the most difficult hurdle to overcome. However, an initiative that can project the characteristic of commitment, is likely to increase its chances of achieving some degree of success.

While the inherent quality of commitment in a conciliatory initiative is likely to increase that move's credibility by affecting a target's evaluation of the initiator's intent, a simpler connection can be made between a move's credibility and the capacity of the initiator to carry it through. As with threats, a basic question about conciliatory initiatives, especially those involving offers about future actions or conditional promises, is whether the initiator has the resources – materials, information, skills, finance – needed to implement what is on offer. A second, of course, is whether the leaders making the gesture can overcome intra-party constraints when the time comes to implement the offer.

True, it is often the case that initial conciliatory moves do not demand much in terms of resources, time or effort. In 1973 all the Egyptian Government presumably required to return Israeli prisoners of war were lorries and some minor logistical support, while in November 1977 President Sadat merely required the means to travel a short distance to Ben Gurion Airport. Other kinds of gesture, however, can require rather more, so that perceptions of an initiator's capacity can play a major role in determining an offer's credibility.

Closely linked to this issue of capacity is a target's evaluation of the way in which making the move affects the fortunes, resources and position of the party carrying it out – and especially the fortunes of those leaders responsible for the making or endorsing of the move. Moves that impose a high cost on either the party or the leadership making them are likely to be both noticed more easily and viewed more positively than those made at little cost, or even some benefit, to the originator.[5] The likely costs to Sadat of making his trip to Jerusalem were obvious to everyone following the announcement of his intention. On the other hand, the costs to the British of lifting the trade embargo with Argentina, unpopular with both their own business interests and their partners in the European Community, were minimal, and some Argentine commentators even argued – with some justification – that lifting the embargo benefited the British just as much, or even more, than the Argentinians (Mitchell 1991, p.414). Hence, the quality on *costliness* seems one that can have a major impact on whether and to what extent a conciliatory initiative succeeds, although in a paradoxical fashion in that the potential costs of moves yet to be made are likely to diminish the credibility of the proffered initiative, while the costs of a move once made are likely to increase the general credibility of the initiator and the specific credibility of future initiatives.

Further associated with the quality of costliness is the matter of risk. Targets seem often to ask what degree of risk, and risk of what, attaches to the offering of some olive branch. The risk to core interests posed by the British lifting of the embargo appeared minimal to Argentine leaders and as the announcement was accompanied by a firm reassertion of the most intransigent British position on the key issue – sovereignty over the Islands – the move seemed to lack most of the characteristics making for any degree of success. The risks to President Sadat were many, central and obvious. At the risk of mixing metaphors, to offer a successful olive branch one has to go far out on a limb. Hence, the degree of risk posed by an initiative to a party's core objectives and interests, and to the position and future of a set of leaders, is likely to affect the success of a conciliatory gesture. Degree of riskiness in a move thus seems likely to affect probability of success.

From a somewhat different perspective, a further quality likely to increase probability of success is one that concerns a gesture's effect on the target's ease of response, rather than ease of discernment or of positive evaluation. Even though the conciliatory gesture may have been recognised, evaluated positively, and brought about a shift of expectations among at least some of the target's decision-makers, it may ultimately fail due to the latter's unwillingness or inability to react positively. Hence, a conciliatory gesture that makes the target's decision-makers want to respond positively but also assists or enables them so to react, perhaps by lowering the risks and costs of so doing to key leaders or factions within the target, appears more likely to elicit the desired response than one that lacks such characteristics. To some degree, as I have argued above, an initiative's characteristic of unconditionality is likely to have a positive impact on the decision-makers in a target by allowing them both the choice of responding or not, and the defensive argument – against intra-party critics – that they are responding voluntarily because such a response seems an optimal reaction, rather than because they are surrendering to an adversary's pressure.

There seems to be much merit in the argument that maximising a target's flexibility of response – rather than demanding a specific reaction either before or as a response to a 'conciliatory' initiative – provides decision-makers with both a psychological and a political rationale for reacting with a conciliatory move of their own. Psychologically they can tell themselves that they are not having to react to coercion, but have a choice about whether they respond and in what manner. Politically, they can argue to critics who wish to reject any move by the adversary out of hand that they are participating freely in an exchange which is not one-sided, yet retain the option of withrawing from the process of their own volition.

Similarly, it can be argued that a conciliatory move that cannot be reversed or withdrawn is also likely to have an impact on the ability of a target's leaders to react positively if they so choose. The characteristic of irrevocability will not only contribute to the credibility of an initiator's action but will also increase the respondability of the adversary's leaders by providing them with the justification that the other side has already committed that action or expended the resources in a manner which cannot be reversed. Sadat could not go back to the previous position of denying the existence of the State of Israel after visiting the place and talking with its leaders. It would have been very difficult, although not completely impossible, for the British to reimpose the trade embargo on Argentina once they had announced they were lifting it. Other conciliatory moves are more reversible, but again there seems to be good sense behind the argument that the less the ability of an initiator's leaders to reverse their gesture – that is, the more irrevocable it is – the greater the likely effect on the target's ability to respond.

3   Success: some tentative conclusions

It is always perilous to claim to have discerned general patterns from one or two cases but, on the other hand, one needs the real world in order to start drawing out some generalisations. Hence, tentatively suggesting ideas about what qualities in conciliatory gestures might well be associated with effectiveness seems a reasonable procedure – provided the emphasis is on the 'tentativeness'. As the old saying is, 'One has to begin somewhere'.

So far, my argument has been that, if one looks at some empirical examples of conciliatory initiatives and processes, a number of features emerge that suggest that initiatives characterised by a discernible range of qualities have more chance of having a positive effect on a target and of eliciting a positive response from a target's decision-makers than others lacking those qualities. Up to now, I merely list likely qualities as being worthy of further investigation and would be reluctant even to place them in any order of importance, or argue that they form either necessary or sufficient conditions for successful conciliation.

On the other hand, some of the characteristics discussed above do have a surface plausibility that derives credence from either their presence or absence in historical examples. I would argue that it would be best to abandon a simple taxonomical approach to analysing why certain conciliatory initiative succeed, even if only to some degree, while others fail. Instead, it is more fruitful to examine conciliatory moves from the standpoint of inherent characteristics and to propose a list of key 'attributes' that have a major impact on the gesture's probability of success. The preliminary list begins with the magnitude of the change in, or retreat from a previousy outlined negotiating position, set of conditions or general stance regarding the conflict in which the parties are engaged. It includes such attributes as a gesture's transparency, unconditionality and irrevocability. Adapting our basic model, I would suggest that Figure 6.2 shows the characteristics of conciliatory gestures which are usually and identifiably present to some degree, and which together make up 'the nature' of particular conciliatory gestures and influence the probability that a particular conciliatory initiative will be effective.

The adapted model raises a whole host of further questions, mainly concerned with explanations of why these particular characteristics play a part in determining whether or not conciliatory moves will succeed. I have already implied a tentative rationale for some of them, for example, by suggesting that the unconditionality and irrevocability of a gesture will give a target's decision-makers the needed flexibility to be able to choose their own response, a process that can (all other things being equal) ease some of the intra-party constraints on reacting.

Another approach to answering the 'why' question is to use one of the communications models outlined in Chapter 3 and to suggest that the

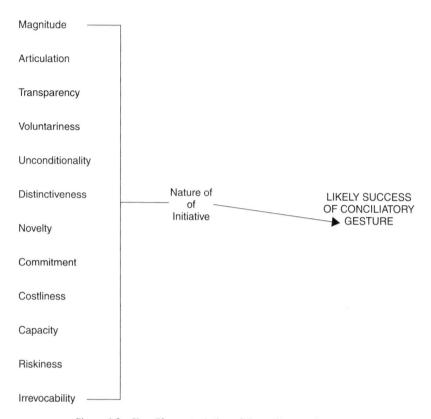

Figure 6.2   **Key Characteristics of Conciliatory Gestures**

presence of certain inherent qualities in a conciliatory initiative is likely to affect a target's cognition of the move, and to make success greater by having a positive effect on the target's recognition, perceived credibility and perceived respondability. The pattern of likely influences in Figure 6.3 is, again, only a tentative model but one which follows from the earlier discussion in this chapter.

An acceptable answer to the 'why' questions must, surely, be a theoretical one and, moreover, one that traces through the effects of particular characteristics of a conciliatory initiative on the target's decision-makers, in both a psychological and political sense. The theoretical issue of why, for example, a gesture's level of commitment has the effect of increasing its credibility in the eyes of an adversary's leaders links with the practical issue of how an initiator might best demonstrate this attribute in launching an actual conciliatory move. I discuss both these and other issues in Chapter 7.

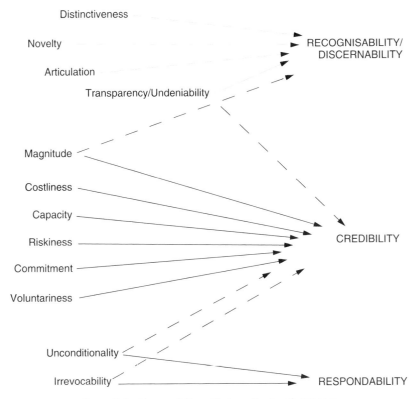

Figure 6.3   **Focus of Conciliatory Gesture's Impact**

7
Increasing Recognisability

'Promising and not fulfilling causes needless emnity.'

Arab proverb

At universities in the United States, students have the habit of 'highlight-ing' important phrases or sentences ('bits of information') in their text-books by blocking them in with a yellow pen to make them stand out against less important material.[1] A somewhat similar task confronts the leaders of a party to a conflict that have passed through some process of contemplation and decided to undertake a conciliatory initiative as a move towards peacemaking, although – to be metaphorically accurate – the ini-tiator's task more resembles that of the actual author of the textbook, using differing type faces and sizes to draw attention to key points and passages in the argument. The initiator's task is one of the 'management of impres-sions' in such a way as to simplify the target's 'processing of information' and thus ensure that the initiative is recognised and an 'appropriate' evalu-ation made.

The principle is easy to enunciate, but how is it possible for initiators to make such a gesture 'stand out' from the remainder of the flow of signals, messages and information parties in conflict inevitably transmit to one another and to third parties, most of which will be received and need to be evaluated by the adversary they are trying to affect? How can decision-makers 'flag' or 'underline' the initiative to make it stand out among the 'noise' of normal, conflictual communication flows? Is it possible to imitate US students and highlight the important part of their overall messages, par-ticularly in view of the fact that their 'textbook' is the somewhat uncoordi-nated product of multiple (and sometimes contending) authors? In short, how can individuals such as President Sadat or collectivities like the British Government make their statements and actions firstly more distinctive, and thus more likely to be recognised, and secondly more credible, and thus more likely to be believed?

1 Obstacles to making effective conciliatory gestures

The first problem for decision-makers signalling to their opposite numbers in a target is to ensure that their conciliatory gesture is even noticed among all the noticeable information available for the target to receive and devote attention to. Basically, this task is crucial to the third of what I described above as a six-stage process for decision-makers trying to communicate conciliatory intentions to a target and initiate an accommodative sequence. Many writers tend to treat it as a simple two-stage – or, as Robert Jervis (1970, p.24) terms it, a 'two-level' – problem. That is, the recognition stage involves having the signal noticed and attended to by the target, but also, as Jervis points out, the target determining 'what message the sender is trying to convey' (ibid.), a much more complex procedure than the label 'recognition' suggests. However, even a six-stage model may be over simple. The final stage of reaction involves a complex set of inter-related decision-making processes that range from an evaluation of the costs and risks involved in a set of possible responses – including not responding at all – to the feasibility of different actions.

I discuss these latter dilemmas in subsequent chapters, but they actually arise only when an initiating party has managed to pass through the recognition and evaluation stages successfully – that is, has had the gesture initially noticed and interpreted as something sufficiently unusual as to have it placed on the agenda for serious consideration by the target's decision-makers. This impact is by no means easy to achieve. There are likely to be practical obstacles to the signal being picked up and attended to, particularly at the height of any conflict when the amount of information available, both positive and negative, is likely to be more than abundant. Equally important are the psychological obstacles or 'cognitive barriers', firstly to attending even to 'out-of-character' signals and secondly, for lower-level decision-makers working in the information-gathering and processing agencies of a party in conflict, to placing such signals on the agenda of a party's leaders.

At all levels, there will be a psychological tendency to fail to notice (or ignore) incoming signals that do not fit in with the accepted view of the adversary, its interests, goals and tactics or, if noticed, to suppress such discrepant signals as irrelevant, as they fail to conform to what is already 'known' about that adversary. Jervis argues strongly that, at the state level, leaders' expectations create predispositions leading them to notice certain things about others' behaviour and to neglect other things. Hence they quickly, and often unconsciously, draw inferences from what is noticed and find it difficult to consider alternatives. (Jervis 1970)

Moreover, this resistance to non-conforming information can be very strong in the best of circumstances, but relationships involving a high level of conflict, hostility and mistrust are hardly those. Jervis also comments that 'when a statesman has developed a certain image of another country he will maintain that view in the face of large amounts of discrepant information' (Jervis 1976, pp.145–6), but this is equally likely to be true of bureaucrats and analysts who man a party's receptors and are responsible for monitoring and interpreting the acts and statements of an adversary.

For these and other reasons, any party seeking to change the way in which its adversary perceives its goals, objectives, methods and priorities, as well as its degree of commitment to them, will face interpretative barriers that resist change almost as a function of the intensity of the conflict. Anwar Sadat himself once referred to these as 'the other walls', self-erected between enemies. Many writers, among them Kenneth Boulding (1956) and Leon Festinger (1957), have observed how, even under normal circumstances, decision-makers, as well as rank-and-file followers, possess cognitive structures which tend to reject non-conforming or 'discrepant' information and which are thus highly resistant to change. Whether these cognitive structures are described as 'images', 'belief systems', 'cognitive maps' or simply 'attitudes', and whether the process of accounting for the general desire to retain them undisturbed and to avoid psychological stress is described as the avoidance of 'cognitive dissonance', the search for 'cognitive consistency', or the desire for 'psychological balance', the outcome of strong psychological resistance to change and the rejection of non-conforming data is almost universally recorded.

Moreover, as others such as Ralph White (1970) and Ole Holsti (1962) have pointed out, decision-makers in conflict (that is, in situations of often-considerable stress) have an increased tendency to exhibit symptoms of extreme closed mindedness (Rokeach 1960) and to be particularly prone to clinging to established beliefs and images, even in the face of considerable amounts of information that could lead to the disconfirmation of these beliefs. Images of the nature of 'the enemy' and of the latter's own belief system, goals, objectives and preferred means, become firmly embedded in the minds of leaders, elites and rank-and-file constituents from other parties to the conflict. The images are all usually highly negative (unsurprising in view of the nature of the conflict relationship) and especially resistant to change, particularly because conflicts 'lock in' adversaries to a pattern of mutually coercive behaviour following initial escalation, thus confirming the negative images of 'an enemy' originally created by the simple existence of mutually exclusive goals and the frustrations engendered by encountering opposition.

Jervis (1976, pp.187–8) again summarises these arguments neatly, saying that

> the original organisation of the stimuli strongly structures later perceptions. Some cognitive processes can only be reversed with great

difficulty. Once a belief has taken hold, new information will not have the impact it would have had at an earlier stage. Earlier, when the person is trying to make sense out of the evidence, he will experiment with different interpretations of incoming information. Later, when he thinks he understands the stimulus, he will automatically perceive new information as having a certain meaning'.

For example, Holsti (1962) has reported in detail the ability of US Secretary of State, John Foster Dulles, to fit major changes in Soviet policy, behaviour and attitudes during the Krushchev era into his (Dulles') own belief system about the unchanging nature of the Soviet Union and its leaders, their implacable hostility to the West and their inability to change ultimate objectives, interim goals or basic strategies and tactics. Evidence from other cases seems to confirm that Dulles' resistance to discrepant information in such situations is by no means unusual.

All of this is obviously relevant to parties in conflict considering some conciliatory process and moving towards a negotiated settlement. Normally, the initial conciliatory move will be launched at a target who will have developed a highly negative image of the other party, who will be anticipating information which merely confirms the negative image and fits in with what the target already 'knows' about the adversary, and who will thus be particularly prone to reject even a non-conforming conciliatory signal because it fails to fit in with the structure of the negative belief system that has been built up as a result of the conflict. Common sense, plus a great deal of evidence from psychological research, indicates that it is extremely difficult for conflicting parties that have systematically been using coercion and threats against one another to change tactics by initiating a positive signal, perhaps involving a promise, and to have the latter noticed and then believed (Heilman, 1974). It is more than likely that positive signals will be lost in a sea of continuing negative acts and in the memories of past injuries.

For these and other reasons, even markedly 'discrepant' information will be easily ignored; rationalised as a trap, probe or publicity seeking move; explained as a move forced on the reluctant adversary and to be abandoned as soon as feasible; dismissed as a meaningless gesture brought about by internal unrest; or re-interpreted as an indication of the adversary's loss of will or concern over diminishing resources.[2] These likely reactions all contribute to the original problem of achieving initial recognition or later credibility for a conciliatory initiative.

2   Strategies for increasing distinctiveness

Given the likely resistance of decision-makers in conflict to altering their beliefs about an adversary as the result of non-conforming information, especially signals arriving directly from that adversary, what might parties wishing to begin conciliation with an effective gesture do to increase its effectiveness and to break through the psychological resistance of a strongly structured, negative belief system? How can they 'manage impressions', so as to ensure an initial degree of success for their move?

A commonsense answer to this problem of unrecognised or ignored conciliatory initiatives is obviously to make the signal stand out in some way, so that a target's receptors have little choice but to pick up that signal and then pass it upwards as worthy of attention. A more detailed answer was outlined in the previous chapter, when it was suggested that initiatives characterised by a high degree of distinctiveness, novelty, undeniability, articulation and magnitude (or degree of change) were most likely to be recognised by a target. On this basis, one immediately obvious strategy is to make any initiative so unusual that it cannot easily be ignored, through achieving a high level of:

1   *Novelty* and *magnitude*, for example by ensuring that it involves such a major and especially unpredicted change from previous patterns of behaviour that its very lack of conformity and the degree of surpise involved in its initiation make it 'stick out' in an unmistakable manner;
2   *Distinctiveness*, for example by having it performed by someone whose own status or prominence makes it a signal that has to be noticed, or in an unexpected manner or a prominent arena that ensures it cannot be ignored by the target's decision-makers, at a time which will ensure its prominence, and against background activities that highlight its difference;[3]
3   *Undeniability*, for example by having the statement or action take place 'in the open', so that evidence of the gesture having been made or the commitment undertaken is clear and on record;
4   *Articulation*, by ensuring that the initiative takes into account and utilises key historical, cultural and ethical aspects of the cognitive framework (or filter) of the target which the latter will use in identifying and later evaluating the move.

In all cases, I would argue that the success of an initiative arises from an important basic principle, which is to make the gesture as discrepant or dissonant as possible with what has gone before, and as unexpected as possible. This argues firstly for gestures that are (at least) precedent breaking and, hence, dissonance creating in the extreme – as unusual, eye-catching and dramatic as intra-party constraints permit. According to this principle, an optimum, if idealised, move is the one likely to create the greatest dissonance among the target's decision-makers while remaining relatively unobtrusive to rivals and to rank-and-file followers within the initiator.

For example, one such move might involve some action that deliberately reveals the existence of internal doubts and divisions within the initiating party. This may have a major impact on a target's image of its adversary (although the normal attitude towards undertaking such a move is that it will only be evaluated as indicating 'weakness' to an adversary and so should be avoided at all costs). As Jervis has pointed out:

> Actors see each other as more internally united than they in fact are, and generally over-estimate the degree to which others are following a coherent policy. The degree to which the other side's policies are the product of internal bargaining, internal misunderstandings or subordinates not following instructions is under-estimated. (1968, pp.475–6)

Information that reveals such internal divisions and processes may have the usually negatively evaluated effect of demonstrating a lack of unity. Equally, it may have a positive impact by undermining the common image, described by Ralph White (1970), of an implacably opposed adversary with whom one cannot reason or negotiate.

Unfortunately, while the strategical rules for making a *novel* or *distinctive* gesture are clear in principle, in practice their very nature means that there are significant obstacles to their implementation. Obviously, the clearest and least ignorable signal is one which involves the maximum non-consistency with previous behaviour patterns (visiting Israel as opposed to calling for new Egyptian/Israeli discussions without specific details of when, where or what); and the maximum degree of surprise in the manner of its performance. Equally, this type of signal is the most difficult for a party to a protracted conflict to make, both for reasons of internal vulnerability and of indicating weakness to an adversary. Hence, parties wishing to make a non-ignorable conciliatory gesture need to search for an action that is novel and distinctive while not being (i) *risky*, either to their own intra-party status or their future bargaining position with the target, or (ii) *costly*, in terms of retreating too far or giving away too much (although, as argued in Chapter 6, these latter qualities also enhance a conciliatory initiative's credibility).

Similarly, it is easy to propose the principle that the distinctiveness of an initiative can be increased if the gesture – whatever it might be – is made by some prominent person or institution, but this is often difficult to implement for a variety of reasons, including the limitations leaders have imposed on themselves by prior declarations and the consequent dangers involving risk and costs to persons and institutions. However, there are ways in which these and other types of limitation can be overcome. For example, it could be arranged for the gesture to be made privately, but through a non-involved leader or a spokesman previously used as a trusted channel to or by the target, a strategy often accompanied by prior indications that this particular source will be used to convey an important message. Alternatively, subtle prior signals from prominent leaders – heads of state or a government – could be used to ensure attention to later moves and messages, although too frequent use of this tactic can degrade it while too effective use can diminish the other desirable quality of undeniability. On other occasions, the principle source of the signal can be highly distinctive, but the initiative launched from a less than distinctive arena – regular press briefings, statements to legislatures, speeches to domestic audiences or to international bodies.

For example, the speech with which President Kennedy inaugurated the 1963 accommodative exchange leading to the Test-Ban Treaty and the 'Hot-line' agreement (and, it has been argued, the US/Soviet detente of the 1960s) was made to an academic audience at the American University in Washington DC. Even the high profile Sadat initiative of 1977 began in a low-key but un-ignorable action – President Sadat's speech to the People's Assembly in Cairo on 9 November of that year. Both examples indicate that, on occasions, distinctiveness can be increased because of the arena for the signal or the channel chosen for delivery, quite apart from the the the signal's source, its content or its lack of consistency with past behaviour.[4]

Given the argument that all five qualities of undeniability, articulation, magnitude, novelty and distinctiveness of any conciliatory gesture are all important, it is the latter two that are most directly related to its dissonance creating capacity through the extent to which they break precedent. But what are the various ways in which this principle might be used in practice? Four broad strategies mainly intended to increase an initiative's distinctiveness and novelty, and hence the likely success of conciliatory initiative, can be outlined.

3   The strategy of the grand gesture

Bearing in mind President Sadat's 1977 visit to Israel as an obvious example of a dissonance-creating initiative (or a precedent-breaking move), it seems reasonable to argue that conciliatory initiatives will have the greatest chance of being highly distinctive, and overcoming decision-makers' resistance to recognising and evaluating them, if they are important single signals rather than a series of small, minor conciliatory moves made in a series. What Louis Kriesberg has referred to as the use of the 'Grand Gesture' (1981) clearly combines elements of an initiative that unpredictably makes a significant break with previous behaviour, is undertaken publicly by a major figure among a party's leadership, and is performed in a manner that permits no retraction should the initiative not succeed in eliciting the desired response from the target.

Moreover, while again acknowledging that it is just this kind of conciliatory initiative that is often difficult to make because of intra-party constraints, the argument for the likely effectiveness of this type of gesture is simply that it is less easy to reject out of hand, either psychologically or politically, than smaller, less 'radical' moves. Decision-makers' belief systems, as noted above, are highly resistant to information about incremental changes in an environment that they are psychologically structured to interpret in a consistent fashion. They find it far more difficult to reject or trivialise information about major changes, although decision-makers with particularly 'closed' belief systems seem able to reject almost any amount of disconfirming evidence, whether about central organising concepts, such as an adversary's basic nature or fundamental goals, or about more peripheral items such as that adversary's means and methods. However, in general, conciliatory initiatives might well be framed with Jervis's argument in mind that

> Greater change will result when discrepant information arrives in a large batch than when it is considered bit by bit. In the former case, the contradiction between it and the prevailing view will be obvious. But when discrepant information arrives gradually, the conflict between each bit and what the person believes will be small enough to go unnoticed, be dismissed as unimportant or necessitate, at most, slight modifications. (1976, p.308)

Apart from Sadat's Jerusalem visit, other illustrations of the use of the 'Grand Gesture' include the Khrushchev/Bulganin visit to the West in 1958, which caused a major – if temporary – re-evaluation of the nature of the Soviet leadership; and the Fascist Grand Council's overthrow of Benito Mussolini in 1943 in Italy as a signal to the Allies and a prelude to Italy's withdrawal from the Axis Pact. Such examples do reinforce the argument that, through their dissonance-creating capacity, such actions achieve a high level of novelty and distinctiveness and can break through the 'recognition and acknowledgement barrier', be counted a success at this level, and often initiate an accommodative sequence of conciliatory exchanges.

4   The strategy of the prominent point

Another common but little-analysed strategy for enhancing the distinctiveness of conciliatory gestures is to use, or occasionally deliberately create, some *prominent point*. This can be used either as part of the content of the gesture or as a salient 'platform' from which a gesture could be launched with a greater chance of its being picked up and noticed.

The idea of a prominent point as a 'natural' starting – or stopping – place for a process, or as a threshold at which some associated major change might be made or anticipated, has been examined by a number of scholars concerned with ending conflicts. Lewis Coser, for example, employed the concept to try to indicate when parties are likely to be psychologically ready to consider seeking peace or to anticipate a peace feeler from an adversary. He suggests that there are some common and generally accepted points which indicate victory or defeat, such as the loss of a capital city or a key province, the defection of an ally, or the passing of some point in time to which the parties attribute significance. On the other hand, he also suggests that some prominent points may be specific to a particular culture or party so that, for example, the final inability of the Boer commandos to obtain horses to continue their guerrilla campaign against the British in 1902 was – to them – a symbol of their ultimate defeat much more than the loss of their major cities and towns two years earlier (Coser 1961).

Similarly, Tom Schelling (1960 & 1966) has argued that there are common break points in a bargaining process (a 50/50 split, or losses exceeding some symbolic figure) that serve as thresholds in the minds of decision-makers, and thus can be utilised in a process that involves reversing course or converging on an agreed stopping place. In everyday life, round numbers appear to be psychologically prominent, a finding that seems to have been born out in experimental games involving the 'entrapment' process. Barry Staw (1976), for example, has found a tendency for role players in one of his entrapment simulations to invest round figures of $1, or up to thresholds of $10 or $20, but not between or beyond. Again, Brockner and Rubin (1985) report in one of their variations of the similar 'Dollar Auction' game that there was a tendency for participants to stop investing at 500 points, which represented both the value of the prize, half the player's total allocation of points, and a round number.

What is suggested here, however, is that decision makers can (and, indeed, do) use psychologically prominent points to help make de-escalatory initiatives sufficiently distinctive as to be recognised – and responded to – by the target of that initiative. The use of prominent dates (for example, anniversaries) for the launching of initiatives or the beginning of conciliatory activities is a well-known example of this strategy. Truces begun at Christmas or at Tet have been used to emphasise the importance of such pauses and the fact that they provide further opportunities for reciprocation and subsequent de-escalation. Pauses in military activity once salient geographical prominent points have been reached (the Golan Heights, the Jordan River) have indicated that one party to a conflict – at least – is willing to stop violence and begin negotiation.

A second way in which another type of 'prominent point' might play a role in increasing both recognisability and credibility of a conciliatory gesture is suggested by those aspects of *prospect theory* that emphasise the significant way in which an individual's or a group's choices are much affected by their selection of an 'anchoring' or 'reference' point from which to compare events, offers or alternatives. The choice of a salient 'anchoring point' will very much affect whether, for example, a concession or other form of conciliatory gesture will be perceived as involving a potential gain or an avoidable loss and, according to the theory, also affect whether the party in question will perceive a strong incentive to compromise or conciliate and be more or less willing to take a risk. There is much evidence to the effect that people generally treat potential losses and potential gains very differently, and that losses loom much larger than gains, so that people generally will make serious efforts to avoid outcomes viewed as loss incurring (Kahneman and Tversky 1979). Moreover, it also seems to be the case that people value things that they actually possess far more than 'comparable' things they do not have (Levy 1992, p.175), and this to such a degree that over-evaluation of current possessions has been called the *endowment effect* (Thaler 1980, pp.43–7). All of this lends great importance to the nature of the anchoring point from which comparisons are made, and existing offers or choices 'framed' as involving potential gains or losses, such a point often being one from a wide range of possibilities.

In one illustration of such alternative points, Max Bazerman (1983) has argued that a union negotiator might well compare a current management wage offer with at least five possible anchoring points: (1) last year's wage level; (2) management's initial offer; (3) his estimate of management's maximum concession level (MCL); (4) the union's maximum concession level; or (5) the union's publicly announced bargaining position. Each of these anchoring points will help to determine the union's views of whether the current management initiative is seen – 'framed' – as a gain (over last year's wage level, the initial offer and – possibly – the union's MCL) or as a loss (over the union's estimate of management's MCL or the union's public demands). Framing around any one of these points will affect whether the initiative is seen as a sure, worthwhile gain or an unacceptable loss.

In a simpler version of the same principle, adversaries' reactions to conciliatory moves could be significantly affected by whether their anchoring point is (1) where one started (past position);[5] (2) where one is now (current situation); or (3) where one aims to be (future aspiration).

Prospect theory would posit that in 1970, Israeli attitudes towards any conciliatory moves regarding Sinai, the West Bank and Jerusalem – the 'gains' from the Six Day War – would vary depending on whether these territories were regarded as (1) additions to Israel's pre-1967 territories; (2) fully incorporated as part of Israel proper; or (3) parts of an essential yet incomplete Israeli security zone.

Each anchoring point could be, and probably was, different for each of the conquered territories – Sinai, the West Bank, Golan, Jerusalem – and also 'coded' differently by individual Israelis. Each would produce a different evaluation and a different response to any conciliatory offers from Egypt or anywhere else, depending upon whether the anchoring point framed such offers as gains or losses compared with that point. In the case of Sinai, any arrangements beyond those existing pre-1967 were easy to frame as a gain, the anchoring point being April 1967. In the case of

Jerusalem, any changed arrangement that altered its contemporary status as fully part of Israel would almost inevitably be framed as a loss, and resisted totally.

Robert Jervis has suggested that there is a tendency for gainers to adjust quickly in their acceptance of a new 'status quo', while losers take very much longer to accept the results of their loss, so that their 'status quo' continues over a long period to be one existing in the pre-loss past (Jervis 1992, p.199). I suspect that what Jervis terms 'renormalisation' – the length of time it takes parties to adjust to a new status quo – is affected by many other factors, so that different aspects of gains and losses become the accepted 'norm' at different rates. For Israelis, given Jewish history, East Jerusalem seems – psychologically – to have become part of a status quo from which only losses could occur the day after it was conquered, a process that took much longer for the West Bank and which never fully occurred for Sinai or the Golan. In these, as in many other cases, however, the principle holds good that effective 'prominent points' have to be those which an adversary is overwhelmingly likely to use as 'anchoring points' in evaluating an offer as leading to a gain rather than a loss.

In all this welter of complex, often competing theory, what does seem clear is that, if appropriate prominent points can be built into the content of conciliatory gestures, either as anchors or symbols, this is likely to enhance their distinctiveness, and the probability that they will be noticed by the adversary and at least considered and evaluated (if not finally responded to). An offer of talks is likely to be that much more distinctive if it is accompanied by the release of prominent prisoners, or by an offer to pay workers a Christmas bonus irrespective of the outcome of a strike. A gesture is also likely to be recognised and given credibility if it suggests an anchoring point for an adversary that enables the latter to frame the offer positively as involving some gain. Finally, it is also more likely to be noticed if it takes into account the beliefs, values and cognitions of the target.

5   Articulation and prominent points

Keeping in mind the previous argument about the manner in which the characteristic of articulation increases a conciliatory initiative's chances of recognition, it goes without saying that to be effective, a conciliatory gesture that employs a prominent point must do so in terms of the target's belief system and cognitive map; it must 'articulate' with the values, beliefs and perceptions of the target. A 'point' (whether temporal, spatial, social or political) must be prominent in terms of the target's image rather than the initiator's – a guideline often (apparently) forgotten by some decision-makers intent upon demonstrating their willingness to conciliate but using their own framework of signs and symbols. Crudely a 'Christmas truce' is unlikely to have much impact on an Islamic adversary.

One good example of this *articulation principle* at work is the all too brief, 'military expenditure' de-escalation carried out between the Kennedy–Johnson administration and the USSR in 1963–4. Ruth Sivard (1978) argues that this was initiated at the suggestion of members of the US Arms Control and Disarmament Agency, who argued that informal de-escalation of military expenditure might best be carried through without formal agreements because of the symbolic importance of the annual military budget to both governments. At the time, it was argued that reduction in one military budget would be clearly noticed and possibly responded to in kind by the other, a hypothesis which was proved initially correct and which led to reciprocal budget reductions for a brief but confirming period, until the exigencies of the Vietnamese involvement forced President Johnson to ask in May 1965 for a supplementary budget increase, effectively ending this accommodative sequence.

Sivard's example is one where the instigators of a conciliatory initiative were careful to select what would be a prominent issue area both to them and, more importantly, to their adversary so that the gesture would be recognised and, eventually, responded to in kind. As such, it seems to be a good example that illustrates the utility of another aspect of prospect theory which links individuals' or groups' estimates of the likelihood of future events (in this case, a continuation of a downward spiral of arms expenditure) to the ease with which examples or associations come to mind as models or indicators (the arms budget as an indicator of future military policy).

Whether deliberately or not, the ACDA originators of the US/Soviet accommodative sequence seem to have employed the principles of what became known as the *availability heuristic*, and to have applied these so as to ease the cognitive tasks of their Soviet opposite numbers, and thus have their own budgetary gesture recognised and reciprocated. In brief, the availability heuristic argues that decision-makers (and other individuals) estimate probabilities of future events occurring (that is, how credible concessions, promises or future outcomes might be) according to the 'ease with which instances or associations come to mind' (Taylor; 1982, p.191) or 'the ease with which they can recall or cognitively construct relevant instances' (Levi & Pryor 1987, p.220). In estimating some likelihoods, the heuristic usually depends upon the frequency of retrievable events from the past, so that the process involves what has become known as the retrieval of instances. However, in conflict situations it is far more likely that the situation will involve wholly unique actions and events and the process of estimating likelihoods will involve the construction of examples or scenarios. In this case memorised examples which are salient, vivid or easy to imagine will determine how 'available' certain scenarios might be when compared to others. As Taylor remarks, 'The ease with which examples or associations are brought to mind provides an estimate of likelihood ...

which in turn provides a basis for making other social judgements such as evaluating another, imputing causality or responsibility, describing another's attributes, categorising others or describing oneself'. (Taylor 1979, p.198). Or, I would add, evaluating the likelihood of an adversary's offer being genuine.

I will come back to the availability heuristic and what actions an initiator might take to ensure that its use enhances the credibility of a conciliatory move later. At this stage I simply want to point out that its probable use by a target of a conciliatory gesture suggests that, for an initiator, an important rule of thumb is to present an initiative in such a way as to make it more rather than less likely that the target in question will be easily able either to retrieve prior instances or to construct a scenario that produce a strong likelihood in the minds of the target's decision-makers that the initiator's move is distinctive and intended seriously. The gesture must 'articulate' with scenarios in the target which are available, salient and vivid, although clearly the precise nature of these will vary from target to target. What results in the construction of a positive scenario in one case may have quite the opposite effect in another.

Of course, in a protracted conflict there may be no easy way of producing such an effect. Salient and vivid scenarios involving an adversary in such circumstances are likely to be highly negative and to ensure that, to a target, the adversary's move is not distinctive, novel or serious. However, the example of the ACDA decision-maker's choice of budget reductions to obtain the attention of Soviet decision-makers and then develop a degree of credibility for their conciliatory initiative does indicate that thoughtful gestures can overcome barriers to recognisability and credibility, and bring the desired response provided the move articulates well with the cognitions and memories of those it is intended to affect. It is also likely that conciliatory gestures could be shaped to articulate with positive scenarios drawn from parallel experiences of the target that do not directly involve the adversary, but rather an ally, patron or respected other. The manner in which the Basque guerrilla organisation, ETA, and its linked political party, Herri Batasuna, employed Sinn Fein and the IRA as a reference point in many of their policy debates in the 1990s may be an example of how such easily available parallels are used in devising conciliatory gestures in the conflict over the degree of Basque independence from Spain.

6   Using appropriate frames of reference

This discussion of the need for initiators to select an appropriate 'prominent point' from which to launch a conciliatory gesture is merely one example of a third, more general strategy aimed at increasing recognisability as well as credibility through effective articulation with the history, values and cognitive frameworks of adversaries. The apparent rarity of such 'calibrated' moves does underline that parties instigating conciliatory initiatives seldom seem to consider very carefully what impact their gesture is likely to have on their adversary, given the latter's frame of reference. However, 'prominent point' examples do emphasise the general need for initiators to pay attention to this 'management of impressions' aspect of conciliatory gestures. This implies using a strategy which articulates well by using relevant frames of reference for a target, making it easier for the latter to recognise the move as non-consistent, distinctive and unexpected, so that the effect achieved at least approximates to the one desired.

However, many observers have stressed that initiators themselves often need to overcome their own psychological obstacles to success in sending a meaningful message to their target, quite apart from those facing the target in observing and interpreting the signal. Senders of signals have a tendency to assume that, if the message is clear to them and fits neatly into their own frame of reference, it must be equally clear to the target – so that failure to notice, understand, or respond is a matter of perversity and intransigence rather than misinterpretation. As Jervis argues, this is partly because, having usually put a great deal of time and effort into thinking about their own decision and action, the initiators understand its nature and nuances thoroughly. They thus assume (often incorrectly) that it will be equally plain to a target which, unfortunately, lacks their own background knowledge and assumptions and has *not* put the same amount of time and effort into observing and evaluating the signal.

Moreover, the tendency to assume that targets will share relevant and clarifying background information is particularly prevalent in the case of conciliatory gestures which initiators are quite open about, at least as far as the adversary is concerned. Initiators assume that this very openness is a guarantee that their gestures will be seen clearly and understood thoroughly. As Jervis summarises the argument, 'When actors have intentions that they do not try to conceal from others, they tend to assume that others accurately perceive these intentions. Only rarely do they believe that others are reacting to a much less favourable image of themselves than they think they are projecting' (1968, p.477).

Of course, this tendency to over-estimate the clarity and distinctiveness with which initiating parties signal concessions is a general problem for starting an accommodative process, and will affect the level of success of other strategies and signals. It seems particularly relevant at this first stage of the process, when initiators are trying to get targets merely to recognise that they are being signalled to in a positive manner. The argument reinforces the necessity for parties to consider their intended signals within the frame of reference likely to be held by the target. Conciliatory moves can be made more distinctive by making them conform to background assumptions and reference points in the target's cognitive structure.

This argument that, in seeking a really distinctive signal to initiate a conciliatory process, parties must use their adversary's frame of reference appears straightforward in principle, but what are its implications in practice? As noted earlier in this chapter, some clues about the means by which a conciliatory initiative can most effectively influence the adversary's decision-makers – who will clearly be affected by the way in which any gesture presents the problem of making a choice – arise from prospect theory (Kahneman and Tversky 1979), and from its findings that the same basic message can be interpreted or 'framed' differently by its recipient, and therefore elicit very different reactions. This argues the need for parties hoping to initiate an accommodative sequence to consider the form of any initial conciliatory initiative carefully and in great detail before making it.

In one of its most relevant aspects, prospect theory posits that any party initiating a signal, suggestion or other gesture needs to take into account that the target's decision-makers will either tend to be risk-averse or risk-seeking. If the former, they will be willing to quit or change course when confronted with a conciliatory option which is 'framed' to emphasise its potential for maintaining actual gains from that course of action (they will not want to lose what they have). Conversely, if they are risk-seeking they will be willing to continue a coercive course of action – even if this appears not very likely to lead to success – when the conciliatory alternative is framed so as to emphasise any losses (they will be unwilling to accept long term the losses they have up to then sustained).

The theoretical implications of this aspect of prospect theory for any party contemplating the launching of a conciliatory gesture clearly involve the need for an initiator to try to ensure that the initiative is couched in such a way as to make it as easy as possible for the target to use an anchoring point that frames the option positively, as providing gain, and more difficult to use one that leads to a negative frame, which would emphasise loss. Max Bazerman argues strongly that a negotiator 'should always create anchors that lead the opposition into a positive frame and negotiate in terms of what the other side has to gain' (Bazerman 1983, p.215), and the same is true for any party wishing to begin a conciliatory process that moves towards that negotiation.

The major practical problem for a party seeking to shape a conciliatory initiative so that it maximises the likelihood that its adversary will consider the move within a positive (gains emphasising) frame is that, throughout most early stages of protracted conflicts, both leaders and followers will regard anything short of 'victory' – or the complete achievement of their goals, the anchoring point – as a loss and hence be willing to carry on the struggle in order to avoid suffering those losses permanently. This tendency will persist in spite of there being a low perceived probability of success through coercive means. A key turning point, at least at a psychological level, will be when some decision-makers, at least, come to frame offers and other initiatives from the other side in terms of potential gains from either past anchoring points or the present unsatisfactory status quo. In other words, the anchoring point has shifted at least for these decision-makers.

Such a change should make it more likely that a conciliatory gesture will be recognised and viewed favourably as offering a gain over the present situation, rather than a loss in terms of aspirations about the future. Of course, many other leaders and followers are likely to continue to view any offer leading towards an outcome of less than complete success as a major loss, and to call for continuing the struggle.[6] In the Northern Ireland conflict, for example, the issue for the nationalist parties has constantly involved considering how to evaluate the current status quo on offer – proportional access to political office and considerable influence in decision-making, guaranteed civil rights, and substantial influence from Eire. Should it be compared with the situation at the start of the 'Troubles' – a dominated minority with no civil rights, subject to widespread discrimination and firmly within a province of Britain- or with the goals and aspirations of the historical nationalist struggle – a united Ireland? For much of the thirty-year struggle, the anchoring point was that of a united Ireland. It is only in the 1990s that more and more members of the nationalist community have made the psychological jump to considering the status quo post the 1985 Anglo-Irish agreement, or now post the Good Friday Agreement of 1998, primarily as a gain on the pre-1967 situation.

Switching for a moment to the initiating party, the question is how an initiative might be shaped to make 'positive' framing of the move more likely. Can anything be done by a single gesture or even a series of moves to change the dominant frame within an adversary, particularly if the 'victory or nothing' view predominates, as it usually does in at least the initial stages of a conflict? Practical examples of this difference in framing conciliatory gestures are difficult to envisage at first, but might be illustrated by contrasting preambles to conciliatory proposals such as:

(a) 'In view of the present costly stalemate, which is costing all parties resources they can ill afford, of the lack of likelihood that either party will achieve its goals within the foreseeable future, and of the fact that the government of X has failed to fulfil any of the objectives for which it began the present conflict, we would suggest' (leads to negative framing); and

(b) 'The government of X has, at this present time, succeeded in obtaining general international recognition for its claim to have its grievances with regard to A considered in a fair and judicious manner, and has also called attention to the previously neglected issues of B and C; we therefore suggest' (Leads to positive framing).

Again, the practical paradox of this argument is that it is just such features of the situation – the gains of the other side – that a party's decision-makers are least likely to want to emphasise in front of their own followers. For that audience, in order that they should frame the situation in such a way as to make them averse to the risks of continuing and desirous of quitting now to preserve what they have achieved, their leaders must emphasize the positive gains involved in the present situation, together with the risks of loss entailed in continuing to pursue the current course of action. Once again, decision-makers wishing to de-escalate a conflict confront the familiar multi-audience dilemma.

7   The strategy of multiple gestures

The 'multi-audience' problem arises yet again in the fourth strategy which initiators of conciliatory gestures use to enhance the recognisability of preliminary initiatives – that of making a series of gestures, usually close together in time, so that the moves reinforce one another and increase the likelihood that they will be noticed by the target's receptors. Again, with this strategy, a practical problem is to try to ensure that the signals are plain to the target, but are less than obvious both to intra-party rivals and critics – for reasons of domestic status and political survival – and to rank-and-file followers – for reasons of loss of morale and possible mobilisation of feelings of betrayal.

In many ways, the idea of a sequence of (perhaps small) conciliatory gestures is based upon the assumption that one isolated move is unlikely to be noticed by the target, but that the repetitive signalling of small moves will have a cumulative impact by creating a pattern more noticeable than one gesture. In this sense, the strategy is one of repetition and reinforcement, both characteristics helping to highlight the message that the party's decision-makers are trying to convey to the target.

One clear example of this particular strategy in operation can be found in Osgood's GRIT scheme mentioned in Chapter 5 (Osgood 1962). This starts with a pre-announced series of small, de-escalatory moves carried out across a wide range of issues and arenas. GRIT is somewhat unusual in that the sequence is to be announced in detail beforehand to the target, and consists of actions that are easily verifiable by the target. In this way, a prior announcement – Osgood implies that this should be a public announcement, as was Kennedy's statement that the USA would begin a moratorium on atmospheric testing of nuclear weapons in his American University speech of 1963 – and a subsequently implemented series of moves produce a signal that is difficult to miss or to ignore, even if there is no response from the target.

In one way, Osgood's suggestions regarding the GRIT strategy illustrate an example of what might be called the 'prior eye-catching gesture, reinforced by smaller moves' sequence. In the case of GRIT, the prior eye-catching gesture is the announcement that a series of concessions is about to be made, thus alerting the target to the series. The initiating party then hopes that the cumulative effect of both gesture and series will bring about some alteration in target's attitudes and willingness to undertake some response. In other situations, prior gestures have been less 'eye-catching' but have, nonetheless, been made, often in the form of quiet soundings or contacts indicating that some gesture or series of conciliatory moves is about to be made. The Soviet/US military budget de-escalation initiative mentioned above was, in fact, preceded by President Kennedy sounding out Soviet Foreign Minister Gromyko about possible Soviet reactions to such a move by the USA, which had the effect of alerting Soviet decision-makers to the possibility of some such move on the part of the US Government (Sivard 1978).

An alternative, but perhaps equally effective, sequence reverses the order of GRIT-type initiatives and begins with a set of small, continuing gestures of conciliation, possibly increasing in frequency and scope as a preliminary to some major move which could be difficult for the target to miss on its own, but is doubly so if preceded by such a set. The logic behind this arises from findings in psychology about the manner in which attitudes change, the argument being that both images and attitudes are highly resistant to discrepant information in small amounts, but that repetitious increments of non-consistent information can have the effect of 'softening up' a recipient so that a substantial amount of such information becomes much less likely to be ignored, and more likely to have the desired impact than even a major gesture *not* preceded by minor, preparatory moves. This alternative sequencing might be termed the 'constant dripping followed by the eye-catching gesture' approach. I will discuss it in more detail in Chapter 8, in connection with the problem of altering a target's perceptions and attitudes.

Finally, many observers have suggested that one variant of the strategy of multiple gestures is to make a number of moves, or even a single conciliatory gesture, but to have it or them conveyed to the target through multiple channels, to maximise both the likelihood that the move will be noted and its impact upon the target.[7] This particular strategy has the double advantage of ensuring that the move will at least be noticed by the target, but also that there is built up an implicit and transferable consensus among those acting as channels that this move is – at the least – worthy of notice and some careful consideration by the target's decision-makers.

8   Connecting recognisability and credibility

The four strategies outlined above are mainly aimed at overcoming cognitive barriers within a target so that an initiator's conciliatory gesture or set of gestures is recognised and afforded some attention by receptors and decision-makers within the target. However, our discussion of the strategies themselves and the theories underlying their use has also involved occasional comments on the effect such strategies might have on the credibility of the conciliatory initiatives, implictly making the point that it is often difficult, both practically and intellectually, to separate a strategy's impact on the recognisability and the credibility of an initiative. It is not necessarily the case that a gesture which is distinctive, novel, well articulated to the cognitive frame of its target and impossible subsequently to deny will also be highly credible in the eyes of the decision-makers in that target, but it is clear that some characteristics of a conciliatory initiative that increase its recognisability also increase its credibility.

The issue of credibility, however, is an important and complex one, and many historic cases, apart from the failed 1985 British initiative over the Falklands/Malvinas, show clearly that a conciliatory gesture that is recognisable by its target is not necessarily credible. The practical question of what characteristics increase the credibility of a conciliatory initiative, and the theoretical question of why this should be so, deserve separate and careful consideration. This is undertaken in the next chapter.

8
Enhancing Credibility

'Of great importance for our picture of the social environment is the attribution of events to causal sources. It makes a real difference, for example, whether a person discovers that the stick that struck him fell from a rotting tree, or was hurled by an enemy.'
Fritz Heider *The Psychology of Interpersonal Relations* 1958

Assuming that the decision-makers for a party intending to begin an accommodative sequence have selected a conciliatory initiative which has succeeded in engaging the attention of the decision-makers in their adversary, further success will depend upon the gesture's capacity to elicit from the target's decision-makers a positive (and generally shared) evaluation that the signal 'accurately represents what the sender *will* do in the future' (Jervis 1970, p.24 emphasis added), that it is perceived as being genuinely 'conciliatory', and that it indicates genuinely changed priorities and commitments. I have argued directly in Chapter 6 and indirectly in Chapter 7 that this involves a gesture achieving a high level of 'credibility' and that this is more likely to be attained if it is, at least, significant, costly, contains elements of risk for those undertaking it, is uncoerced, and also difficult to reverse.

In achieving high credibility, one major obstacle that an initiative must overcome is the undoubted scepticism with which decision-makers of one adversary will view any signal purporting to indicate that the other has undergone some genuine, major change in its objectives, views of appropriate means, and expectations about likely outcomes from the conflict in which both are engaged. There are many mechanisms which operate to produce a negatively biased assessment of offers from an adversary, but one that seems particularly relevant is that involving the reactive devaluation of any conciliatory initiative. Lee Ross and his colleagues have investigated this phenomenon in a variety of situations (Ross and Stillinger 1991), and have concluded that there is a general tendency among parties in conflict to 'devalue' offers and compromises once it is known that they have been made by the adversary.[1] This will certainly be the case with an initiator sending some form of signal directly to an adversary. They suggest that this tendency may simply be the result of the target possessing an automatic assumption that any conciliatory initiative by an adversary must be relatively advantageous to 'them' and therefore less advantageous to 'us'. This leads on to a belief that the adversaries have given up nothing of real value 'to them', so that nothing of real value 'to us' should be contemplated as a return gesture. Alternatively, the target may apply negative interpretations to any ambiguous aspects of the initiative, and bring in evaluative criteria different from those of simple advantage or disadvantage ('justice', 'rights' or 'equity') in weighing the move. Finally, and in line with the processes discussed in Chapter 7 associated with prospect theory, unless the initiator makes successful efforts to frame the gesture appropriately, there will be a tendency to evaluate the offer in terms of potential losses rather then potential gains. Whatever the underlying mechanisms, the effects of reactive devaluation mean that any unilateral conciliatory move will, in Ross and Stillinger's words, 'face a formidable obstacle' (ibid. p.395).

Given the wide range of political and psychological obstacles to a conciliatory move's achieving credibility, ranging from common scepticism about adversaries' motives to reactive devaluation of their moves, an initiator's gesture has to be such that its nature optimises the chances that the target will feel it truly indicates a change from the former's previous goal priorities and commitment to winning through coercive means. Only if the target's decision-makers gain this impression can the initiative be said to be 'successful' in any continuing sense.

There are a variety of approaches to increasing the credibility of conciliatory initatives that might prove helpful in throwing some light on the question of how the characteristics of conciliatory gestures help or hinder the impression of their having arisen from a party – or some, at least, of its leaders – developing new priorities and new commitments:

1   Characteristics of the gesture that help a target attribute positive motivations for a gesture, and are likely to elicit an accommodative response rather than disbelief or rejection;
2   Characteristics of the gesture that enable the target to identify a new commitment on the part of its adversary, at least towards a non-coercive strategy and possibly a willingness to consider a settlement involving concessions and compromise;
3   Characteristics of the gesture which make it difficult for the initiator to retract, even if the underlying motivations for making the gesture prove to be tactical, tentative or transitory. For each of these, there are relevant theories and principles that might indicate how practical initiatives could be shaped or selected to increase the likelihood of a positive impact on the target. The rest of this chapter discusses each in turn.

1   Attributing 'positive' motives, causes or reasons

A variety of scholars have, in recent years, considered the processes by which people explain to themselves why others behave as they do – in other words, what causes one type of behaviour rather than another. Heider (1958), Jones & Nisbett (1971), Kelley (1973) and many others have all made contributions to explaining this process of causal attribution and have developed a number of hypotheses about factors likely to affect the way in which observers (or targets) of behaviour are likely to view causation – why parties act as they do – particularly the locus of cause.[2]

As far as conciliatory initiatives as part of a peace process are concerned, the general relevance of attribution theory is clear. Firstly, there is much evidence that a search for causal explanations usually only arises when people face deviant, unexpected or incongruous events (Weiner 1985, p.81). The making of a conciliatory gesture amid a protracted conflict seems a paradigm case of such a situation. Secondly, to a considerable degree, a target's reception and interpretation of a conciliatory gesture from its adversary will depend upon that target's view of why the gesture is being made; that is, what factors have contributed to persuading the adversary's decision-makers to make some ostensibly radical alteration of strategy in a conflict, up to that point undoubtedly characterised by fairly consistent coercion. Assuming that the gesture is not actually intended by the initiator merely to probe for weaknesses on the target's part, and that it represents some genuine desire to start a benign spiral, the question for the target's decision-makers is whether the initiative conveys some 'real' change in the goals, aspirations or internal dispositions of the adversary's elite, or whether it has been brought about simply by changes in the latters' circumstances – which can change back again – so that the gesture is a response to externally generated pressures, leaving basic goals, interests and expectations wholly unchanged.

As far as the locus of causation for another's acts is concerned, *attribution theory* makes a basic distinction between two possibilities: (a) Actions which arise from the internal dispositions of the actor and which thus accurately represent those dispositions – underlying attitudes, 'personality traits' or fundamental beliefs – for example, benevolence, compliance, trustworthiness. (b) Actions which arise through the operations of external factors and which thus do not represent internal dispositions of the other party but which only continue if the new external circumstances themselves remain unchanged.

Attribution theorists are agreed that, in assigning causes for the actions of others, people have 'a fundamental tendency to underestimate the role of context' and to 'the over-estimation of personal or dispositional factors' (Jones 1979, p.107). This tendency has become widely known as the 'fundamental attribution error' implying, in a protracted conflict, a strong tendency for those involved to assume that the causes of their adversary's hostile and coercive behaviour lie deep within the latter's structure, character, beliefs and aspirations. If this is the case, are there any ways in which the leaders of any party seeking to initiate a conciliatory process can credibly signal to an adversary that they have undergone at least some relevant modifications of their basic dispositions and that the cause of a conciliatory initiative can be correctly assigned to some genuine change on their part?

In this connection, Harold Kelley and others have suggested that observers – including, presumably, targets – of behaviour will tend to attribute causation according to two basic principles. The first is the *discounting principle*, which implies that a party's behaviour – for example, in making a conciliatory move – is more likely to be attributed to a (changed) disposition to seek a negotiated compromise when alternative, external causes – exhaustion of resources, defection of patrons – can be ruled out. Thus, 'out of' or 'against' role behaviour will accurately reveal underlying dispositions. Behaviour that breaks rules or departs from convention is more likely to be regarded as representing a party's true disposition than are actions which conform to roles and norms.

Secondly, the *augmentation principle* suggests that a person's actions will be taken to be more truly expressing an underlying disposition if they involve risks of potential loss, or actual costs to the initiator. Hence, anyone who runs risks or harms their own interests by undertaking an activity, such as launching a conciliatory initiative, is more likely to be seen as being genuinely 'disposed' against a continuation of conflict and towards some compromise alternative. The connection of this argument with the previous inclusion of 'costliness' or 'riskiness' as credibility-enhancing characteristics of conciliatory gestures will be obvious.

Reversing the argument arising from these two principles, cases in which conciliatory gestures are made when a target can see alternative, external reasons – exhaustion of resources, domestic discontent – for an initiator making a conciliatory gesture, or with no cost or risk attached to the move, are likely to lead decision-makers in the target to assume that there has been no real change in the initiator's basically hostile 'disposition' *vis-à-vis* themselves or the conflict. On the contrary, actual or promised changes in behaviour represented by a conciliatory initiative can accurately be attributed to the adversary's reluctant, and possibly temporary recognition of necessity forced by change of fortunes or circumstance.

Theoretically, then, the ideal characteristics for a high credibility gesture are those which indicate a major change of disposition – goals, aspirations, attitudes and expectations on the part of the initiator. Hence, in line with basic attribution theory, the more a party can employ conciliatory initiatives which clearly are *not* the result of externally generated problems or difficulties, but which are potentially risky and clearly costly to the leaders, the more likely it will be that the target's decision-makers will find such gestures credible, attributing them to an overall change in their adversary's disposition. In these circumstances, all other things being equal, a target's leaders should be inclined to evaluate the move as genuine and to consider responding positively.

Practically, the issue then becomes how the initiator's leaders can select a conciliatory move which maximises the probability that the target will attribute the underlying causes to a changed disposition to seek a non-violent, compromise solution, rather than to elements in a party's changing environment that have forced its leaders to adopt a new course of action while leaving basic dispositions intact.

Unfortunately, even acknowledging the evidence from interpersonal attributions cited by Kelley and his colleagues (1980 & 1983), it seems most unlikely that attributing a conciliatory gesture to fundamentally altered dispositions on the part of an initiator will occur easily, following a long and costly conflict during which the adversaries have tried all they can to harm one another, both physically and psychologically, and have come to firm negative conclusions about the adversary's fundamental 'dispositions'. Anecdotal evidence from international conflicts seems to show overwhelmingly that decision-makers attribute peace feelers and trial balloons to 'change of circumstances' – contextual necessity – rather than 'change of heart', unless it is so clearly the case that the conciliator is running very substantial risks to person and position.

For example, over a number of years in the late 1980s, the general reaction of leaders, elites and followers in the United States to the series of conciliatory gestures used by the Soviet leader, Mr Gorbachev, was initially to attribute them to external factors such as domestic economic problems, fear of being technologically outbuilt by the USA, or problems with allies in Eastern Europe. A second explanation, which represented another common response to finally undeniable changes in an adversary's behaviour, was that the changes were very much the result of idiosyncratic leadership on the part of Gorbachev, and that they would inevitably be reversed once he left office. Those advancing these views about the reasons for Soviet efforts at a *rapprochement* were, as in many other cases, falling victim to what Lee Ross, among others, has termed 'the fundamental attibutional error', the pervasive bias mentioned above that sees key individual people with their own enduring dispositional attributes as major causal agents, rather than a mixture of personal, social and situational variables (Ross; 1977). The very last explanation offered was that the new leadership in Moscow represented a widespread change in basic dispositions within a new generation of Soviet leaders quite as profound as that represented by the changeover from Stalin's regime to Krushchev's in the mid-1950s – a change that was also originally denied and then attributed to the exigencies of Soviet agricultural failures and the Sino–Soviet split.

The conclusion which arises from this example is that, except in very rare circumstances, it is likely that changes in the direction of greater conciliation – at least in protracted and violent conflicts – will usually be attributed to force of circumstances rather than fundamental changes of a party's basic dispositions towards a conflict and its adversary – unless the leadership of that party changes prior to the initiative. Even then this is no guarantee of internal attribution, as has been argued in the case of Mr Gorbachev. The crucial issue then becomes whether changes in the initiator will be ascribed by the target to: (1) circumstances that have arisen independent of the conflict and particularly independent of the target's own efforts – such as exhaustion of resources, change of internal leadership, withdrawal of support by a patron, bad harvests, act of God; or (2) circumstances which *do* appear directly to be the result of the target's efforts in the conflict – changing balance of advantage, successful acquisition of support, widespread condemnation of the adversary.

It then becomes reasonable to hypothesise that the former case is more likely to lead a target to view a conciliatory gesture as genuine, stable, – if the external changes seem permanent –, and hence credible so that a positive response can be contemplated. If the latter interpretation is made, then the target is more likely to conclude that its own efforts are a cause for this gesture, which cannot then credibly represent a significant or permanent change of circumstances or of basic goals and dispositions. The move will then be interpreted as the first sign of weakness, vulnerability or diminishing resolution on the part of an adversary and a sign for intensification of effort rather than a reciprocal conciliatory gesture.

With these arguments in mind, attribution theory suggests that highly credible conciliatory gestures (those targets are more likely to attribute to factors which enhance rather than reduce the appropriateness of a positive response) involve:

a   some obvious element of risk and cost to the initiator;
b   some element of against-role behaviour by the initiator, as well as some element of norm breaking; and
c   some clear implication that the gesture is being made because of external circumstances not directly connected with the efforts of the target and that these circumstances are not transitory.

There remains some ambiguity about the likely influence of the permanence or impermanence of such changes in external circumstances. On the one hand, it seems reasonable for a target to feel that it will be necessary for such changes to be permanent in order to prevent the adversary reverting to old goals and methods once an unstable or dynamic external environment changes once again. Parties in protracted conflicts usually need a high level of reassurance before themselves risking a significant response to a conciliatory move engendered by contextual change. On the other hand, it may be that a target could be persuaded to respond to an initiative made as the result of transitory circumstances, through its accepting a 'window of opportunity' argument. If a target recognises that the external circumstances calling forth changed behaviour from its adversary are likely to be transitory – and out of its control – then this may equally provide a reason for viewing the initiative as 'credible' and responding to it positively, particularly if the target's decision-makers also take into account ideas connected with the development of a stable commitment to a new course of action discussed in the next section.

2   Indicating genuinely changed commitments

A second major task for a conciliatory initiative being evaluated positively by the target's decision-makers, is to convince the latter that it is a sign of a genuine commitment to a new strategy of accommodation aimed at a negotiated settlement. The question for the initiating party's decision-makers is how their initial move can be structured so that it conveys their party's commitment to a changed line of policy in an unmistakable and credible manner, provided that policy has, indeed, changed.

There is a two-fold problem in analysing this issue. The first of these is conceptual and arises from existing intellectual confusion about the concept of 'commitment' and the manner in which this attribute might best be identified. The second is the practical issue of how best to convey some changed commitment to an inevitably sceptical adversary.

The conceptual problem arises from the fact that there are two linked but different conceptions of what constitutes 'commitment'. As Katzev and Wang (1994, p.14) emphasise, the common and everyday definition of a commitment implies that someone has taken a decision and, often, made a formal, public pronouncement that pledges or binds them to a particular course of action or set of objectives. The second conception involves a more generalised internal attitude that involves a desire for some object, a belief in some position or a condition of feeling bound to some form of action. It might best be regarded as 'a state of being committed' (ibid.) and while it can be reinforced by a public announcement of the commitment, it can exist separately from such a pledge yet remain a major influence on a pattern of behaviour.

The problem for any party in conflict that wishes to initiate a conciliatory process is that it will be necessary through behavioural actions, perhaps including commitments in the first sense, to convince an adversary that this second, underlying form of attitudinal commitment has altered significantly. In the terms used in this present study, making a credible conciliatory gesture – in the sense that the target comes to believe that its adversary is now, barring rejection and other set-backs, likely to be committed to conciliation and negotiation – involves clearly transmitting believable signals about a change of underlying commitment on the part of the initiator.

Paradoxically, the issue of one party's perceived commitment enters into the process of conciliation in at least two ways. First, it is in the degree to which a target is convinced that an initiating party is irreversibly committed to the goals in conflict and to coercive means of achieving them at the expense of target. In most protracted conflicts, given the resources previously expended by its adversary in pursuit of these goals, a target is likely to perceive the actor's commitment to continuing this course of action as very high. Secondly, it is in the degree to which a conciliatory initiative reveals a new, altered commitment on the part of the initiator, if not wholly to abandoning original goals, yet certainly to altering the means of achieving them.

At first sight, the crucial issue appears to be the degree to which a target perceives the other party to be newly committed by the conciliatory initiative and whether the initiator's decision-makers can undermine the target's belief in the continuation of their original commitment and replace it with a new belief about a changed commitment.

Regrettably, things are not as straightforward as this, for the target also is usually committed, sometimes heavily and irretrievably, to a perception of the relationship and an associated pattern of reactive behaviour. To understand this, it might be useful to go back to the distinction between two conceptual approaches to the nature of commitment made above, both of which have implications for conciliation and successful de-escalatory moves. I will deal first with the approach that centres around the idea of the psychology of being (or becoming) committed, and secondly with the ostensibly more relevant approach which involves behaviour that indicates a high degree of commitment to a line of action.

2.1   The psychology of being committed and of decommitting

Much of the work on the nature of commitment is tentative but does suggest a number of interesting insights into barriers that a party's leaders might have to overcome in convincing an adversary that their previous commitment to a line of action has been modified. The basic principle, outlined, for example, by Kiesler (1971), is that behaviour in pursuit of a goal or in support of an attitude has the effect of psychologically committing the person carrying out such behaviour to that goal, belief or attitude. The argument, in fact, turns virtually on its head conventional psychological wisdom that attitudes affect behaviour, for it hypothesises that behaviour (particularly voluntary behaviour, undertaken as the result of an unfettered choice, publicly carried out and performed repetitiously – or in various forms, if it is in support of a particular belief) will affect attitudes by producing an internal 'binding … to behavioural acts' (Kiesler 1971). Kiesler's argument is that an actor's commitment to an attitude, belief or set of goals is established and then increased through the act of behaving to achieve those goals. This involves a justificatory process, internal rather than external, particularly if the behaviour is subsequently challenged. In these circumstances, the alternative to justifying one's activity is to admit that the behaviour was wrong or misguided, so the more frequent tendency is to justify it as a result of an attitude or belief, to which the party initially becomes committed and subsequently even more committed.

If it is, indeed, the case that public behaviour in pursuit of a set of beliefs or attitudes further commits individuals or groups of individual decision-makers to those beliefs or attitudes – and makes it more difficult to abandon them – then there are a number of ways in which commitment (in this psychological sense) might affect the likely success of conciliatory gestures made by a party trying to convince an adversary about its abandonment of an old commitment and the adoption of a new one.

Firstly, this line of argument starts with the not unreasonable assumption that, during the conflict, a target's decision-makers will have carried through a persistent pattern of behaviour to resist what they perceive as their adversary's objectives and to achieve 'victory'. Commitment theory will hold that target's decision-makers will thus themselves have become firmly committed to a negative view of their opponents, but also to a perception of those opponents' own intransigent commitment to specific goals and particular strategies. Any conciliatory gesture that opponent might initiate will have (somehow) to overcome the target's commitment to a negative set of beliefs and attitudes which will strongly influence and, in turn, be influenced by, their own previous behaviour.

On the other hand, commitment theory would also hold that an initiator's very action in undertaking a conciliatory move, particularly a public one, will itself reinforce its own commitment to this new line of policy – on the basis that actions affect attitudes and reinforce the strength with which the latter are held and defended. The *justification hypothesis* implies that decision-makers in an initiating party who begin a new conciliatory policy, even if they do this tentatively or without much optimism and sometimes just as a tactical ploy, will become both politically and, equally important, psychologically committed to the beliefs and attitudes implied by that policy the more publicly they act, the more frequently they act, and the more they act through their own choice rather than because they feel forced to act in such a manner. This last factor adds further weight to the importance of the voluntariness of the gesture made by the initiating party. Provided a target understands the effects of conciliatory gestures freely and publicly made on an initiator's attitudes and likely future behaviour – that is, an increase in the initiator's own sense of commitment to a conciliatory line of policy simply because this was a freely made choice, rather than an expedient – the fact of a gesture being undertaken could carry its own credibility.

The argument in support of this conclusion hinges on the hypothesis that the psychological processes of commitment will operate on a party's decision-makers to make their initiative become one to which they are increasingly committed both internally and publicly. Furthermore, this could be recognised by an aware target. The effect would be increased if, as is likely, the move and its underlying 'philosophy' are domestically attacked.[3] Paradoxically, this could help a target give credibility to the notion that the leaders of its adversary are genuinely no longer committed to a coercive strategy, even if they might still be committed to its basic goals in conflict. On the target's part, there could be a clear realisation that the very undertaking of a conciliatory initiative would commit the initiator's decision-makers more and more to a belief in the efficacy and worth of this conciliatory course of action and to a policy of continuing because of their public, political acts of commitment. The more both initiator and target embark upon a mutually conciliatory pattern of behaviour, the more committed – at least psychologically and, probably, politically speaking – both will become to accompanying beliefs and attitudes, as well as continuing behaviour. The resemblance of this process to one of entrapment, at least in a benign sense, will become evident when I discuss this latter phenomenon in Chapters 10 and 11.

The crucial factor in the likely success in starting a conciliatory process through a process of decommitment and recommitment thus seems to be a combination of a clearly conciliatory initiative from one party in a conflict and the target's realisation that this very initiative will itself increase commitment to a belief in conciliation and compromise on the part of those undertaking it. In this way, the conciliatory behaviour itself might carry its own credibility, given the appropriate theoretical knowledge among the target's decision-makers.

2.2   Committing behaviour

A somewhat less convoluted and paradox-ridden, as well as more familiar, approach to the concept of commitment involves the issue of what actions a peacemaking party might take to convince a target that it was genuinely seeking a reduction of coercion and tension and the start of a process leading towards a negotiated solution. For any party signalling to a target and seeking to increase the credibility of the signal, the question takes the form of asking: What kind of behaviour – apart from simply making a pledge or a promise – will indicate a high degree of commitment to a different and inevitably dis-believable course of action?

This issue returns the argument to questions about the nature and definition of 'commitment' and to the qualities exhibited by 'committing' acts. A simple dictionary definition suggests commitment involves 'making a pledge to do something in the future' which, in the context of an accommodative sequence would involve a continuation of conciliatory gestures and not a reversion to coercion when this suited the party ostensbibly committing itself. This central idea of a promise of *self-imposed* obligation to a future action or strategy involves consistency and continuation, and the principle of deferred benefits – that is, of ignoring specific benefits now for more generalised rewards in the future. It also implies a characteristic of irrevocability, this time in the sense that committing oneself to a course of action denotes that there will be no turning back or aside.[4]

Perhaps the most useful, practical suggestions regarding committing acts come from writers such as Tom Schelling (1966) who have suggested that one way of indicating and underlining a party's commitment to a course of action is to increase the size and automaticity of penalties that will be suffered if the course of action to which it pronounces itself committed is, after all, abandoned. It is seldom the case that a course of action can be made so costly that there is absolutely no chance of its being reversed. (Schelling talks about 'burning bridges behind one' as a way of ensuring that retreat is physically impossible, and Sadat's visit to Jerusalem may be one such example, in that the Egyptian President could never deny that such a visit had occurred, nor could he undo the effects of having been seen to make the visit.) However, it is often possible to make the 'costs of reversal' very high, and deliberately (and publicly) to increase those costs as a way of demonstrating a high level of commitment so that everyone – constituences, adversaries, observers – realises what the costs might be of turning back. Again, this process of deliberately 'escalating commitment' can in itself become an entrapping element, although a consciousness of this effect can be an element that undermines the psychological aspects of this process.

Decision-makers often attempt to increase the costs of reversal by 'committing' their prestige, status or reputation to a course of action, in the sense that abandonment will lead to a diminution of these ascribed qualities. Other tactics involve some form of penalty clause for withdrawal or change of policy which will automatically take effect irrespective of the future wishes of either party involved. Finally, it may be possible to involve some third party as a guarantor, in the sense that the party making the commitment will lose something through actions by that guarantor if the commitment is not kept up. The whole point about such methods is to increase the credibility of an initiative through making a commitment, the future abandonment of which has deliberately been made highly costly by and for the initiator.

3 Making the irrevocable move unconditionally

Inherent in some conciliatory gestures is the clear fact that, once undertaken, they cannot be reversed or rescinded. The case of Sadat's 1977 visit to Israel and his addressing the Knesset is a clear case of an irrevocable initiative in that, having undertaken the visit and dealt directly and personally with the Israeli Government, Sadat could hardly go back to the position of not recognising the existence of Israel or the need to negotiate a settlement with Israeli leaders. In contrast, the British gesture of lifting the trade embargo on Argentina was less irrevocable. The embargo could have been re-imposed had there been no positive response from Buenos Aires, as indeed turned out to be the case, but it would clearly have been politically difficult to do so in the absence of any more hostile Argentine move than the rejection of the British overture. Other types of conciliatory initiative are even more reversible. Truces and ceasefires can end and coercion be resumed with relatively little difficulty. Bombing pauses can be ended simply by resuming operations for which plans and preparations have often already been made. Verbal promises to refrain from harmful actions can be withdrawn with the excuse that circumstances have changed, or the other side has done something that makes the promised inaction no longer appropriate.

As I argued in Chapter 6, both the respondability, but also, to an important degree, the credibility of a conciliatory initiative is directly related to its irrevocability. All other things being equal, the less the possibility of the move being reversed, the more it is likely to be viewed as a genuine indication of changed commitment or changed strategy, even by the suspicious and mistrusting set of leaders of a long standing adversary. Clearly, there are two major differences between conciliatory gestures that take the form of promises of future action: those that take the form of reversible actions taken 'for the time being', until some deadline or in anticipation of some specific (or even unspecified) response; and those which take the form of an action irrevocably undertaken and unilaterally executed. These differences will affect a gesture's level of credibility.

Another characteristic mentioned earlier that can contribute to, or undermine the credibility of, a conciliatory gesture is whether it is contingent on some form of reciprocation by the target (especially if the offer made is dependent upon a prior contingency), or is made in a wholly non-contingent fashion. In Chapter 5 conciliatory tactics were discussed as either being non-contingent or as involving various forms of contingency such as IFU proposals or tit-for-tat sequences. Elsewhere, I have put forward the argument that different levels of credibility are conveyed by the differences between promises and contingent promises; between actions and contingent actions; and between actions contingently followed by further actions and contingent actions followed by further actions (Mitchell 1991). The principle emerging from this is that there is a clear connection between the credibility of a conciliatory intitiative and the degree to which its performance, or its continued performance, depends upon actions by the target. Moreover, targets take this into account when evaluating both the credibility of a gesture and the ease with which they might respond to it.

All this leads to the conclusion that a party initiating a conciliatory move, and wishing to convey credibly to its adversary that it is genuinely committed to a changed strategy, would be best advised to carry out some action that it cannot, of its own volition, cancel or rescind. In addition, the more the action can be undertaken without the compulsion (or even at the suggestion) of the adversary – in other words as a voluntary action – the more it is likely that this will add to its credibility. Thirdly, the fewer conditions attached to the performance of the initiative, the higher the probable credibility. Finally, further credibility is likely to be added the more costly the action is to the party taking the conciliatory initiative. Sacrifice appears to add considerably to the probability that an act will be viewed as a genuine effort to engage in a meaningful conciliation process. The greater the sacrifice involved in a voluntary, irrevocable unconditional action, the more likely it will be evaluated by an adversary's decision-makers as a credible change, rather than a tactical ploy, an effort to win support for the initiator's claims or position, or simply an effort to confuse the adversary's leadership, and put them 'off guard'.

4   Framing and credibility

Part of the discussion in Chapter 7 involved a possibly important relationship between the way in which a conciliatory gesture was 'framed' by both the initiator (in the sense of 'presented') and the target (in the sense of 'interpreted'), and its recognisability. There were further indications that the framing of a conciliatory gesture would also have an impact on its credibility and that insights from prospect theory might throw some light on other factors that increase or decrease the likelihood that an initiative will be viewed as 'genuine'. Whether framing factors will be influential enough to overcome the negative expectations of an adversary in all circumstances, especially at the height of a protracted conflict, is another matter. Apart from the commonsense observation that positive offers from an adversary are usually viewed as insincere at best and dangerous traps at worst, there is much experimental evidence that the obstacles created by being in an adversarial relationship are frequently proof against even the most subtly positive framing processes. Madeline Heilman, for example, argues that it is extremely difficult for credibility to transfer from a party whose normal mode of interaction was through threats, should such a party choose to switch to making promises. Her data indicates clearly that, at least at the interpersonal level, 'a reputation for matching deeds with words did not always guarantee that a new influence attempt would be credible', and that credibility gained through fulfilling threats could actually impair credibility when making a promise (Heilman 1974, p.323). Heilman's general conclusion is that once a coherently negative reputation has been built up, it is difficult to have positive moves believed by the target and she expresses it, at its simplest, as the belief that 'Bad people are rarely good.'[5]

On the other hand, Beggan and Manelli (1994) have sought to examine directly the impact of framing on the credibility of threats and promises, beginning with the hypothesis that one's expectations about the kind of tactics that an initiator would use in a given context would strongly affect the perceived credibility of a particular move, depending on how it was framed. Thus, in a context where threats between adversaries were viewed as normal, an offer presented as a promise would have much less credibility than the same offer presented as a threat; while in a context characterised by friendship or partnership, the credibility of an offer would increase if framed as a promise compared with framing as a threat (ibid. pp.168–9). Their data did, indeed, indicate that framing an offer as a promise was less likely to be credible in a context of protracted conflict, where expectations led decision-makers to view threats as the norm.

Prospect theory does, however, suggest a number of other useful ideas about how the credibility of a conciliatory gesture, particularly one involving the offer of some possible future benefits, might be increased – an example of the general problem of how decision-makers estimate the likelihood of future events. I touched upon one aspect of this in Chapter 7 when discussing the way in which the availability heuristic might influence a target's ability to recognise a conciliatory initiative through its being presented as another case of some salient and available class of events – a 'constructed example, or scenario' in terms of the theory (Kahneman and Tversky 1982). For example, the availability of the vivid and salient example of the unilateral 1994 and 1997 IRA truces in Northern Ireland clearly affected the thinking of ETA's leaders considering a possible offer to the Madrid Government.

A similar line of argument serves to illuminate what might increase the credibility – or the perceived likelihood – of the initiator carrying through on any promise involved in a conciliatory initiative. A great deal of recent work on what affects decision-makers' estimates of the perceived likelihood of promises being carried out has followed two alternative lines of thought. The first of these follows the classical theory that argues that a decision-maker's contruction of scenarios – with which current offers, events or results will be compared – will be based on how easily available stored and retrievable models might be. As Levi and Pryor express the idea, 'the more easily the event can be constructed or imagined, the higher the probability estimate the individual will assign to it. (1987, p.220). This line of research suggests that higher credibility will be assigned to initiatives that can easily be identified with similar – and presumably positive – scenarios, salient and hence easily retrievable by a target's decision-makers.

However, a second line of research has explored the possibility that the availability of causal arguments, or reasons for the event or the offer, will also increase decision-makers' estimates of its likelihood. As Levi and Pryor make the argument, given that a probability estimate is a belief, 'the availability of causal arguments for an event should increase probability estimates for the event' so that 'the more reasons generated in favour of an outcome, the higher the probability estimates for the outcome.' (ibid. p.221–2). Moreover, they also argue that decision-makers' 'self-generated' reasons will have considerable effect on probability estimates (possibly more than reasons put forward by others, including the adversary's decision-makers); and that the availability of causal arguments will have a far greater effect on views of likelihood – and hence credibility – than simple ability to imagine an outcome or be aware of similar examples. The author's experimental data provide some support for all these ideas and provided considerable encouragement for anyone clinging to the old belief that decision-makers often do act on the basis of not-too-irrational calculations. As Levi and Prior conclude, 'when individuals are provided with reasons for a particular outcome, their probability estimate for that outcome increases', but when they 'Simply imagine a particular outcome, their probability estimates are not affected' (ibid. p.230).

Not unexpectedly, the effect is even more marked when the reasons are consistent with prior expectations about the sources, offer or event, but this does raise a problem for situations in which a target is evaluating the likelihood of a conciliatory move – for which many reasons may be available – being genuine, in spite of prior expectations of an adversary's intentions and likely behaviour being wholly negative. However, at the very least, this particular line of research does suggest that one way of diminishing the influence of such negative prior expectations is by accompanying a conciliatory gesture by many causal arguments regarding the reasons for its being made and, hence, for its being genuine. If credibility and perceived probability are, in the words of Levi and Pryor, 'based primarily on the extent to which numerous reasons or causes for the event's occurrence can be imagined' (ibid. p.221), then the obvious strategy for an initiator is to supply, or even simply hint at, such reasons and causal arguments.

5   Enhancing credibility: a summary

In his analysis of the impact of the 1977 Sadat initiative, Herbert Kelman has argued that the making of major conciliatory gestures (the *strategy of unilateral reward,* is likely to have a number of self reinforcing impacts. These effects include; (i) serving as a reinforcement, by strengthening a target's preceding behaviour; (ii) creating an incentive for further conciliatory behaviour; (iii) contributing to the reduction of tensions; (iv) establishing an obligation to reciprocate; and finally (v) changing the image a party has of the party making the gesture (Kelman 1985, p.217). As I argued in the preceding sections of this Chapter, many of the effects that Kelman outlines depend for their occurrence on the conciliatory initiative being both recognisable and, equally importantly, credible to the target of that move. Moreover, any permanent change in a target's image of the initiating party is likely to increase the more dissonance-creating the conciliatory initiative, and the more the initiative takes the form of a reinforcing series of gestures, a theme to which I return later in this work.

5.1   Key characteristics and increased credibility

This chapter has attempted to set out some of the influences on the likely credibility afforded a conciliatory initiative by a target whose leaders will, inevitably, be highly suspicious and prone to disbelieve any positive move coming from another party that has habitually employed threats, coercion and violence in its efforts to achieve its own goals and deny those of the target. By outlining some of the obstacles to an adversary's initiative attaining a high level of credibility, I have emphasised that, even if the characteristics of a conciliatory gesture conform to those previously discussed, this will merely increase the probability of success, in the sense of having the signal recognised and evaluated positively by a target's decision-makers. Nothing guarantees certainty.

However, it seems reasonable to argue that conciliatory initiatives will be more credible if they that have the characteristics of size and salience; of being costly to the initiator and of involving some risk; of being undertaken without coercion; of being unconditional and irrevocable; and of indicating changed commitment to a new line of policy. In addition, as Roger Fisher argued in the 1960s, it is clearly important that conciliatory moves should also demonstrate capacity, specificity and anticipation (Fisher 1969, pp.112–27). Capacity, on the grounds that a promise for which a target can see no clear means of implementation will no more be believed than a threat without commensurate capability. Specificity, on the grounds that making an offer or promise that is ambiguous will present a target with some difficulty in determining whether the initiator has, indeed, fulfilled what was offered; while making one that is specific as regards details will indicate that time, thought and effort have been invested in the offer, all of which indicate that the initiator deemed it serious enough to warrant such investments. Anticipation, on the grounds that transparent, public preparations, or contingency plans, for implementing an offer are likely to convince the target of the seriousness of that offer, and to add to its irrevocability by making it less deniable.

Since Fisher outlined these sensible preliminary ideas, many have argued that the key to credibility, and hence to obtaining a positive reaction, lies in a conciliatory move's ability to enhance its target's belief in the initiator's commitment to a changed strategy.[6] If this is the case, then findings from studies of the psychology of commitment suggest that practical moves characterised by the following qualities have the best chance of increasing the initiative's credibility and of convincing the target of a genuine commitment to some peacemaking process:

1 The public nature and explicitness of the action, which diminish deniability and increase the need for internal self-justification and external justification for the new commitment;
2 The degree of freedom of choice enjoyed by those undertaking the initiative, and the initiator's range of alternatives, as perceived by the target;
3 The degree of irreversibility or irrevocability of the act, as perceived by the target.

From ideas about committing behaviour, the following are important:

1 The costs for discontinuation of a conciliatory line of policy should the initiating party abandon conciliation and return to coercion; and
2 The penalties for abandoning the conciliatory policy which the initiator deliberately builds into the new pattern of behaviour to indicate commitment, with particular stress on the size and inevitability of these penalties.

As set out so far, these ideas, together with those discussed in Chapter 7 dealing with enhancing the likelihood of a gesture's being initiall recognised by a target, hardly provide a detailed blueprint for infallibility when starting an accommodative sequence or a peace process. Nor do they address directly the third prerequisite of 'success', namely factors leading to a high level of respondability on the part of a target's decision-makers, and hence a positive response to the initiator's move. (These factors will form part of the later discussion of links between target characteristics and successful conciliation.) However, they do begin to suggest some general principles for the launching of initiatives likely to be successful at the level of recognition and credibility.

5.2 Conciliatory gestures and changes in attitudes and beliefs

On the other hand, the conception of conciliating an adversary does also carry a common language connotation that one of the results of such behaviour is likely to be a longer-term alteration of a target's attitudes regarding the conciliator. A pessimistic approach posits that conciliatory behaviour will only increase the feeling of contempt towards, or dislike for, the party attempting conciliation (in line with the negative connotations attached to the term 'appeaser'), and thus lead to increased coercive behaviour on the part of the target. I have earlier suggested some circumstances in which the attribution of reasons for conciliation will lead to such a reaction.

However, a more positive hypothesis holds that alterations in the target's attitudes towards a conciliator can be positive, with fear, mistrust and hostility being gradually replaced by more positive perceptions – respect, a working trust and even, in the long run, approval. Such changes may lead to or accompany continuing and reciprocal conciliatory moves, an accommodative sequence of interactions and a successful peace process.

In situations of protracted and intense conflicts, the likely resistance of decision-makers' cognitive structures to fundamental change will be very high. This will especially be the case if the change concerns that part of a belief system involving the nature of an adversary and of that adversary's previous (inevitably coercive) activities. For each decision-maker and each member of a party's rank and file, this will involve a large number of inter-locking dimensions of belief concerning both adversary and conflict. It seems unreasonable to expect that these fundamentals of shared cognition within an embattled party's leadership, its elites or its overall membership, will alter positively in the short term, whatever initiatives are undertaken by their adversaries. (For some, hostilities and suspicions will long remain, even following an extended period of peace and co-operation.) It seems particularly unreasonable to expect any change at all as the result of a single conciliatory gesture or even a series, no matter how dissonant, compelling or dramatic these might be, and even if the continuation of that process is recognised as being dependent on changes in the target's assumptions about its adversary's ambitions, hostility or trustworthiness.

Even accepting the argument of some scholars that the necessary change 'merely' involves – in the first instance – a decrease in the target's mistrust of its adversary, the task for any conciliatory initiative, not just in obtaining a reaction from the other decision-makers that starts an accommodative sequence but in changing the latters' fundamental attitudes towards an adversary, appears formidable indeed. I have argued that the penultimate stage of 'success' for any conciliatory initiative involves obtaining a positive behavioural reaction from the target. However, why should any gesture – or even a linked set of gestures – have any additional, significant impact on attitudes towards, and beliefs about, an adversary when a long series of preceding interactions have inevitably fostered negative feelings and images, including high levels of hostility, suspicion, fear and dislike on the part of all concerned, decision-makers, elites and rank-and-file followers alike?

At the very least, for the continuation of a conciliatory process beyond an initial gesture from one side and some form of positive response from the other, some diminution in levels of fear and suspicion must surely occur. While it is unlikely that adversaries' cognitive structures and attitudes towards one another will change completely in the medium or even the longer term, it does seem necessary for some basic attitudes to alter – at least to a degree – so that a conciliatory process can continue. One key change that many mention involves a diminution of the level of suspicion and mistrust on the part of the adversaries, and much discussion of conciliation implies a hypothesis that the process will not continue without the development of a sense of minimal trust in one another's commitment to a strategy of accommodation and a negotiated, non-violent solution for the conflict.

This raises the inevitable question of how parties in a protracted and violent conflict might be able to diminish the level of mistrust sufficiently to push on with an accommodative sequence, when the rest of the relationship continues to be founded upon an unwillingness to believe anything but the worst about the adversary, or to assume in self defence a worst-case-scenario for each one of the adversary's moves. The following chapter takes up this difficult issue of suspicion and trust and discusses possible means of lowering mistrust between parties in conflict, suggesting a few principles upon which longer-term trust building might be based.

9
Reducing Mistrust

'Shall I join with other nations in alliance?
If allies are weak, am I not best alone?
If allies are strong with powers to protect me,
Might they not protect me out of all I own?
Is a danger to be trusting one another
One will seldom want to do what other wishes
But unless some day somebody trust somebody
There'll be nothing left on earth excepting fishes!'

The King and I. Act I, Scene 3

The possibility of a clear connection between conciliatory gestures and the reduction of mistrust between adversaries mentioned at the conclusion of the previous chapter briefly returns the argument to the issue of 'success' and the impact, or 'effectiveness' of conciliatory gestures. Up to now, the discussion of effectiveness, has concentrated upon short-term issues such as whether the initiative has been recognised as credible and worth responding to by the target, and whether an accommodative sequence of mutually reinforcing benign behaviour occurs. There are, however, longer-term considerations involved, especially in considering the effects of accommodative sequences. Surely another criterion of 'success' is whether a particular conciliatory initiative is one which brings about at least some positive changes in the attitudes, aspirations and expectations of leaders, elites and constituents within the adversaries? Admittedly, it seems unlikely that any major or permanent changes will be effected by a single conciliatory move, even one as dramatic as Sadat's trip to Israel, so that changed attitudes, expectations and beliefs will clearly be largely dependent upon subsequent patterns of behaviour. No single conciliatory gesture is likely to wipe away years of fear, suspicion and hostility developed during a protracted and violent conflict; this will only result from a prolonged and self-reinforcing peace process, often extending beyond even the point of a successful negotiation producing a compromise solution.

At best, a 'successful' conciliatory initiative may begin or contribute to a number of key, longer-term changes within and between the adversaries at behavioural, psychological, and structural levels, such as a diminishing of violent behaviour and hostile rhetoric, a lessening of fear and suspicion, and a decrease in desires for revenge or one-sided 'justice'.

However, while it may be true that many of the psychological and structural effects of successful conciliation will inevitably be long term, it does seem to be the case that one necessary short term psychological effect, on which many others depend, involves significant change in the level of 'mistrust' between the parties in conflict. Most of the other medium- and long-term effects of conciliatory initiatives depend upon the parties achieving some minimally higher level of 'trust' within the decision-making circles of the adversaries, at least as far as key aspects of both initiating and target parties' intentions and future behaviour are concerned. To begin a successful accommodative sequence, the high levels of mistrust inherent in a relationship brought about by protracted and damaging conflict must be reduced, if only to a point where communications about possible non-coercive solutions can be exchanged. To echo Trudy Govier, 'given that we cannot successfully communicate and co-operate without at least a moderate level of trust and given that ... there are compelling grounds for distrust, how can we progress from a situation of warranted distrust to one of well founded trust?' (Govier 1992, p.18). Greater trust is a necessary precondition to any progress towards any solution.

There is much practical and not a little experimental evidence to support this contention. For example, Zand (1972) in his study of problem-solving groups in organisations – who are, of course, not in any form of highly conflicted relationship – argues that the existence of a high level of trust between members of such group generally increases open-ness, reduces defensiveness and increases the effectiveness of a group in solving problems. In contrast, other studies indicate that a high level of intra-group mistrust will result in distortion of 'messages', inaccurate perceptions of motivation, and difficulty in concentrating upon received messages (Gibb 1961); in an inability to recognise and accept good ideas (Parloff and Handlon; 1964); and in a lasting decrease in problem solving effectiveness (Meadows *et al.* 1959).

Zand argues that the reasons for these negative effects of high mistrust arise from:

1 A party's willingness to 'disguise facts, ideas, conclusions and feelings that he feels will increase his exposure to others' (Zand 1972, p.230; emphasis added);
2 A party's efforts to 'resist or deflect the attempts of others to exert influence' (ibid.); and

3 A party's efforts to minimise his dependence on others. He will 'feel he cannot rely on them to abide by agreements and will try to impose controls on their behaviour when coordination is necessary to attain common goals, but will resist and be alarmed at their attempts to control his behaviour' (ibid.).

Zand's basic argument is that mistrust produces an intense sense of vulnerability and consequent efforts to reduce this which, in turn, interfere with creative problem solving. Unfortunately, it is precisely these conditions that conflict analysts encounter in the relationship between parties seeking a solution for a protracted conflict. Hence, a crucial problem for the initiation and maintenance of a conciliatory process becomes how it might realistically be possible to lower the high level of mistrust between adversaries, rather than the more idealistic notion of creating some higher level of trust between them. In any potentially productive accommodative sequence, first one and then the other party needs to develop a minimal level of perceived trustworthiness, at least as far as one another's commitment to de-escalation and negotiation are concerned, even if general mistrust continues high between them. Each party's expectations about the other have to become less negative, at least to some limited and focused degree, and decision-makers' assumptions about inevitably hostile reactions less certain.

The extent to which this can be accomplished will depend, to some degree, on the parties possessing a clear understanding of the ways of achieving and granting trustworthiness and the successful use of conciliatory tactics to achieve 'sufficient trust'. The problem is to achieve this in circumstances of prolonged, intractable and violent conflict.

1   The nature of trust

To a large degree, how one deals with the 'sufficient trust' problem depends firstly upon one's view of the nature of trust and mistrust, and secondly how a party might go about proving itself trustworthy. Scholars who have written about the concept have very different views about the essential nature of trust, most taking the position that it should be regarded as a multi-dimensional or multi-aspect concept but all sharing some ideas about the essential qualities of the concept; and the characteristics of those seen as 'trusting' or deemed 'worthy of trust'. For example, Deutsch (1958 and 1973), Giffin (1967) and Pruitt (1965) all focus on the idea of trust involving confidence in the motives (and hence the related behaviour) of another party in a situation involving risk, while Riker (1974) argues that trust involves a willingness, and mistrust an unwillingness, to be dependent upon another party.

1.1 The functions of trust and mistrust

Whichever way one looks at the matter of trust or mistrust, Niklaus Luhmann (1979) is certainly correct when he argues that the normal function of trust in any social system is the reduction of uncertainty, and an increase in ability to predict the future. As Luhmann points out, if people did not have some level of trust in the predictability of others and in the stability of surrounding natural, social and political systems, they simply would not be able to function:

> trust goes beyond the information it receives and risks defining the future. The complexity of the future world is reduced by the act of trust. In trusting, one engages in action as though there were only certain possibilities in the future. (ibid. p.20)

Paradoxically, as Luhmann also argues, mistrust fulfils the same function of reducing uncertainty and a sense of insecurity. 'Distrust … is not just the opposite of trust; as such, it is also a *functional equivalent* of trust' (ibid. emphasis added). We make sense of the future by predicting that other(s) cannot be trusted to perform in particular ways, perhaps ways to which they openly commit beforehand.

If this is true in situations of intractable conflict, then the argument goes that each party simplifies its decision task and deals with uncertainty about the future from a basis of almost total mistrust of the adversary. Hence, any move away from systematic mistrust represents a move into risk and uncertainty for those undertaking that move. Risk-avoidant leaders (or even 'average' leaders) are, therefore, likely to find it difficult to abandon a position of mistrust, which is at least safe and certain, for the uncertainties of even partial trust.

While Luhmann is correct in his argument that the major function of trust is to reduce uncertainty in a relationship, this does not mean to say that it is the only function. Extending his argument only a little implies that trust also functions to reduce complexity in the situation being confronted. Trust *and* mistrust are simplifying mechanisms that work directly on expectations. More importantly, from the viewpoint of conflict analysis, trust must also function to reduce a person or party's sense of vulnerability and actually to diminish the number of dangers that must be guarded against. In this last sense, mistrust is no longer the precise functional equivalent of trust, as the kind of high mistrust that characterises conflictful relationships will help to pinpoint and highlight the sources and nature of threats and dangers, and allow the mistrustful party to concentrate efforts on reducing those dangers and thus its own sense of vulnerability.

Implied in this discussion of the functions of trust and mistrust are some ideas about the nature of the phenomenon. Two major features are involved. Firstly there is predictability, which helps to reduce uncertainty about the future and about the level of risk in future action. It should also be noted that 'predictability', in this sense, involves an expectation that others will not deliberately mislead one, quite apart from the straightforward aspect of being able to forecast future situations reasonable accurately. For this reason, the predictability/unpredictability dimension of trust tends to incorporate a deceit/veracity dimension, which is often neglected in studies of trust.

A second general feature of trust involves a competence dimension, in the sense that the person, group or organisation is being trusted as having the capacity to carry out the assigned task, or promised action. In other words, the party is trusted to do something on the grounds that those trusting perceive that the trusted has the capability of carrying out the task assigned to it, or promised by it. Other key aspects of trust and mistrust can be sought in the literature on social relationships.

1.2   Trust and trusting in collaborative relationships

Unfortunately for students of protracted social conflict, the general conception of trust has usually been analysed as an aspect of relationships that are co-operative rather than adversarial. It is usually discussed as being something which exists, or doesn't exist to the degree desired, between persons or organisations in some co-operative enterprise. Questions are usually asked about why people engaged in such an enterprise should or do trust one another; what is meant by 'mutual' trust in interdependent relationships; what are the signs of persons possessing others' trust or conferring trust on others; and how one loses or diminishes trust in relationships of co-operation.

Most commonly, the development of a sense of trust within individuals (or shared trust within groups and organisations), and a relationship characterised by trusting behaviour, is discussed as it affects a variety of co-operative dyads, such as:

1   Relatives or friends – the argument is frequently made that we first learn to trust within the family, and this sense of trust can be specific or general, as in (for example) 'I trust my daughter/ son with the new car', or 'I trust my son/daughter not to do anything to dishonour the family name'.
2   Collaborators or loosely defined 'partners' – where the trust can take the form of a belief that the person/organisation in question will do nothing to harm 'our' persons or interests.
3   Those in some contractual relationship – trust being usually expressed in the form 'I trust my partner to fulfil the terms of our agreement in good faith'.
4   Professionals and their clients – in which case the trust takes the form of an expectation that one's doctor, for example, will make an accurate and

informed diagnosis and recommend the most appropriate medical action, while the doctor trusts that his advice will be accepted as professionally competent by the patient; or that the Honorary Treasurer of a society will handle the finances with due diligence and competence, and not run off with the funds; or, more generally, as in 'I trust my broker to make the best investment decisions for me.'

5 Leaders and their followers – which is probably the most obvious example of *generalised* trust, in that leaders try to develop within their followers a shared sense that all the leaders' actions are intended to benefit rather than harm the followers (at least in the long term, so that trust, in this relationship, has the function of conferring freedom of action on one party); but also that the leaders are competent to tell what is in their followers best interests and pursue it effectively.

Clearly, all of the above types of trusting relationship demonstrate mutual expectations of predictability in the other's behaviour and intentions (not to deliberately deceive), as well as competence in their activities. However, a further basic element is revealed in most of these approaches to the conception of trust, and this is the characteristic of benevolence. Trust is felt for and conferred upon those whom we deem well disposed towards us, who will look after our interests and goals not merely competently and in a predictable and undeceitful manner, but also with our best interests at heart and with no desire to do us harm. A generally accepted view of the nature of trust and a trusting relationship seems, therefore, to involve identifiable features of competence, benevolence and predictability, and is invariably characterised by mutuality[1] of the parties involved, and a continual exchange of trusting actions or behaviours. Trust itself then becomes a psychological state in which someone has expectations of another entity (and the latter's attitudes and behaviour) that involve elements of predictability, competence and benevolence.

Trusting behaviour involves actions that indicate that one party holds attitudes of trust, *vis-à-vis* the other, and will act according to expectations of certainty and low risk. Zand characterises such behaviour as that which 'conveys appropriate information, permits mutuality of influence, encourages self-control and avoids abuse of the vulnerability of others' (1972, p.238) and, following Morton Deutsch, defines trusting behaviour as 'actions that (a) increase one's vulnerability (b) to another whose behaviour is not under one's control (c) in a situation in which the penalty (disutility) one suffers if the other abuses that vulnerability is greater than the benefit (utility) one gains if the other does not abuse that vulnerability'.[2]

The themes of benevolence, competence, predictability and unexploited vulnerability are again echoed in Barber's major work on the limits of trust (1983), which also emphasises the key element of expectations with a basic definition of trust as being 'the expectations that actors have of one

another' (ibid. p.9). Barber then goes on to discuss three types of expectation as being particularly relevant to 'trust' in its 'fundamental' sense:

1 the persistence and fulfilment of the natural and the moral social orders;
2 technically competent role performance; and
3 partners in interaction will carry out their fiduciary obligations (that is,
   their duty) in certain situations to place other's interests before their
   own.

Ignoring the first of these expectation types as too general to be of much
use in understanding the reduction of mistrust in a situation frequently
characterised by a complete absence of moral order (although a conflict
between one party that holds such an expectation and one which does not
would pose some interesting conceptual problems), the second clearly
echoes our theme of competence, while the third puts some interesting
detail into the theme of benevolence by operationalising 'benevolence'
into a duty to sacrifice one's own interests rather than those of the trusting
party.

However, Barber's approach does indicate how little deconstruction of
the traditional conception of 'trust' offers to anyone seeking to develop
trust where its opposite exists. What is the 'technically competent role performance' of an adversary? How likely is it that a party in an adversarial
relationship will recognise any prevailing duties towards its adversary, let
alone put such 'duties' above its own goals and interests?

1.3   Mistrust and mistrusting between adversaries

For those seeking to initiate conciliatory processes, the problem with many
conventional views about trust, trusting and trust building is that they start
at a point from which trust can (relatively) easily be built, or at which a
considerable level of trust already exists. The whole point about a conflict
situation is that the relationship between the individuals, groups or organisations involved is an adversarial one, frequently characterised by a complete absence of trust (or an absolute level of mistrust) which precludes any
movement towards conciliation, de-escalation or resolution.

In short, an adversarial relationship is characterised by the complete
opposite of the kind of collaborative, high trust relationship outlined
above. In such a relationship, adversaries handle uncertainty and the problems of prediction by assuming high levels of mistrust, often under the title
of pursuing 'worst-case scenarios'. They deal with the problem of competence or capability by assuming an almost infinite capacity for harmful
action by their opponent. They deal with the issue of benevolence by
assuming constant, steadfast and generalised malice on the part of their
rival.

In most protracted conflicts, then, it is prudent to assume an absence of trust between the adversaries. The central problem for any party seeking to initiate a conciliation process thus becomes one of engaging in mistrust-reducing activities in a situation of high mistrust, where efforts to build some level of trust will (initially at least) require parties to abandon the clarity and certainties of absolute mistrust for a situation in which risk is prevalent and unpredictability to be expected.

In other words, for a conciliatory process even to begin, there have to be answers to questions such as, who has to be trusted, at what sort of a level, to carry out what sorts of activities, and how can this activity safely be brought about?

2   Principles and practices for reducing mistrust

For anyone involved in initiating and maintaining conciliatory processes, the problem of starting such a process is usually portrayed primarily as a matter of increasing trust between the adversaries, at least to the point where representatives will agree to meet with some expectations that any contacts or meetings will not be used by the other to inflict harm on them, and that some benefits might arise from such discussions. I have argued so far, however, that the problem is best conceptualised as one of decreasing mistrust between the adversaries by engaging in credible behaviour that moves the relationship at least a little way from one characterised by mutual expectations of malevolence, predictable deceit and competence in doing harm. The procedure is normally summarised as moving at least some among the adversary's leaders from attitudes of secure mistrust to those of insecure minimum trust – where 'trust' itself is usually treated as some kind of generalised and undifferentiated concept, without asking questions about trust in what, how developed and reinforced.[3]

2.1   Risk and uncertainty in reducing mistrust

Analytically, it might be helpful to think about the dilemmas of decreasing mistrust between adversaries by concentrating on two of the major components of the generalised conception of trust, namely predictability and benevolence.

In Figure 9.1 overleaf, I have simply taken the idea that mistrust and trust both involve a predictability and a benevolence dimension and hypothesised that it is possible to locate a (potentially) trusting party somewhere along these two dimensions. In case A1, a potential truster can, at one particular time, have a view of the adversary as wholly malevolent and absolutely predictable in its malevolence. In case D2, the trustee can be viewed as somewhat unpredictable and unfriendly, but tending towards the

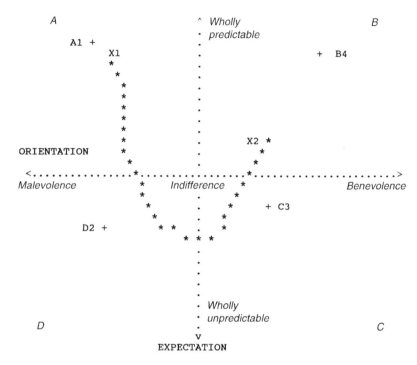

Figure 9.1   **Expectations of Trusting and Mistrusting Parties**

indifferent in its attitudes and behaviour towards the truster. In Case C3 the trustee is viewed as unpredictable but largely benevolent while in Case B4 the party is highly predictable and almost completely benevolent.

From a strategic point of view, the task of any conciliatory process involves moving the expectations of adversaries in a conflictual relationship from somewhere in Quadrant A firmly in the direction of Quadrant B, all the while being aware that arriving there will be a long-term achievement and that the tracks of the adversaries are likely to:

1 display a large number of turns backwards towards the extreme end of the malevolence dimension;
2 begin inevitably by moving sharply towards the unpredictable end of the vertical dimension as each party becomes more uncertain regarding its expectations of its rival; and
3 remain for a long time in the lower half of the unpredictability dimension, even when (or if) each party comes to the conclusion that the other is indifferent or marginally well disposed to the first's survival, security and good fortune.

I suggest that the most usual kind of path for an effective process of mistrust reduction via conciliation in any protracted conflict is likely to follow a track similar to that sketched out in the Figure from X1 to X2.

A similar analysis of necessary changes in the level or, at least, the direction of movement of the third major component of the trust and mistrust concept, namely competence, seems bizarre, but I would argue that, as it is a fairly general phenomenon that adversaries in a conflictful relationship regularly attribute undoubted capacity to do harm to their opponents, a move towards an increased incapacity to do such harm should (all other things being equal) produce a decreased expectation of continued coercion on the part of that adversary and, if capacity to do so is seen as purposefully decreased, an increased willingness to trust at least to a minimum level, based upon a perception of decreased malevolence and decreased capacity for harm. The odd principle that emerges from this argument is that, at least in the initial stages of a conciliatory process, increasing incompetence (or incapacity, to be more accurate) on the coercive dimension, represented by activities that remove coercive options from consideration through abandonment of capacity, will play a major role in diminishing mistrust, a general principle in line with some of the specifics suggested by the 'transparency' and 'self limiting capacity' arguments connected with TRMs and CBMs. Later in the process, as I argued in Chapter 6, demonstrated capability to undertake benevolent actions is likely to increase a move's credibility, partly, at least, through its effect in lessening mistrust.

2.2   Strategic principles for mistrust reduction

Once again, much of the available literature on developing trust (and reducing mistrust) concentrates on the former process and treats it as though the prior relationship between trustee and truster was collaborative or – at least – non-conflictful. Little has been written about reducing mistrust in adversarial relationships, although some clues to possible tactics can be found in some of the work carried out on trust-building.

Most interestingly, Sven Lindskold (1978) has suggested that there are at least four ways in which a sense of trust can be built up. A party attempting to create such a sense through conciliation might well, therefore, concentrate upon developing that aspect deemed most affectable in a given situation. Lindskold discusses four basic tactics with differing aims.

2.2.1   *To affect the sense of objective credibility*

That is, that the trusting party needs to be brought to the point where it has developed a sense that the other's behaviour follows a pattern and can be relied upon to continue that pattern. The usual special sense of the pattern is that the party's actual deeds will correspond with his previous words (no deceit or manipulation), so that the latter can be relied upon.

Clearly this approach ties in with the dimension of trust that focuses on predictability and veracity and with the argument that, to be increasingly viewed as 'trustworthy', a party has to carry out promises and refrain from actions it has foresworn. This 'truthfulness' aspect of trust corresponds in many ways both with Rotter's idea on 'interpersonal' trust[4] and also with the simpler approach advocated by Gordon Tullock (1967), who argues that trust is essentially a matter of being able to predict behaviour accurately – having perfect confidence that A will do x and not y or z.

Unfortunately for our purposes, this approach to mistrust reduction seems less than useful as, during a coercive conflict, the pattern of behaviour displayed (at least up to the point of the conciliatory move intended to engender trust) will have been both coercive and such as to demonstrate a pattern of the basic faithlessness (not to mention malevolence) of the adversary. Hence, while it may be possible to build up trustworthiness of a party (in the sense of predictability of positively benevolent behaviour) in the later stages of a conciliatory process, it is unlikely to be applicable, in this sense, to the opening moves of such an initiative when the issue is how to switch from predictably malevolent behaviour – which is, at least, credible in an adversary – to a much more incredible set of actions. Some form of conciliatory initiative similar to Osgood's GRIT could have the suggested impact, as the underlying concept is based upon a linked set of moves undertaken after a prior announcement of action and an invitation to reciprocate, so that a reputation for tested trustworthiness – based on completed commitments – could begin to be developed. However, it is usually the case that obstacles within an initiator will militate against the offering or carrying through of announced sets of moves, particularly in the absence of some form of reciprocation, no matter what effects these might have in reducing an adversary's sense of mistrust.

2.2.2   To affect presumed benevolence

That is the trusting party has to be brought to the point of being able to presume that the other is basically motivated to help, reward or (at the very least) not cause harm or impose costs on the first. As I argued above (and as Lindskold himself points out) these first two senses of trust can operate independently of each other. It would be perfectly possible for one party to feel that another was interested in maintaining the first's welfare but also to feel that the other's behaviour is likely to be erratic or, at least, unpredictable.

Again, this strategy for trust building seems less than useful for parties seeking to initiate a conciliatory process, or maintain it in its early stages. It is hardly likely that an adversary will have developed much of a perception of the inherent benevolence of the party which may now be seeking an accommodation but which, up to that point, will have displayed an almost limitless capacity for hostility, emnity and desire to harm. Again, minimal attributions of benevolence may emerge after the accommodative sequence is well under way, but even here the degree and robustness of this feeling of trust is not likely to be very great.

2.2.3   To convey an absence of manipulation

In this way, the party seeking trust must act to convince the other that it is not the victim of covert efforts to move it in a direction it would avoid. This is a double source of trustworthiness in the sense that a party (i) does not appear to be in a position to gain from the other party's actions or statement (a disinterestedness dimension); and/or (ii) does not appear to be deliberately seeking to control the outcome of the other party's decisions (a manipulativeness dimension).

Once again, however, this strategy for developing a sense of trustworthiness does not appear very relevant to the stage of initiating conciliation. It is obviously the case that an adversary offering (tentatively) an alternative route to a settlement of the conflict is being manipulative as well as being highly interested in the reactions of the party in whom the sense of trust is being (hopefully) created. There seems to be no way in which trust in the sense of not being manipulated by an interested party can be achieved, unless it can be arranged that the initiative for the de-escalatory process appears to come from an intermediary or other disinterested third party (a possibility that I discuss in a later Chapter).

2.2.4   To emphasise the existence of potential costs

For this strategy a party seeking trustworthiness needs to place itself in a position of increasing its own losses as a result of its failure to fulfil verbal promises or commitments by subsequent deeds. This may seem (intuitively, at least) a misuse of the concept of 'trust', but a number of writers have argued that a party will obviously trust another's intention to fulfil commitments the greater the costs for not carrying out the initial promise. As Lindskold (1978) emphasises, the parties' perceptions of the probabilities of detection and that the costs will be levied are usually major factors in determining the level of trust-through-cost-for-defection.

2.3   Trustworthiness and the costs of defection

Of the four strategic approaches to decreasing mistrust outlined above, the last one seems to be the most relevant for the search for conciliatory initiatives between adversaries in situations of protracted and intense conflict, where there is a generally shared consensus that 'being trustworthy' involves at least some aspects of benevolence, predictability and competence.

Even in circumstances in which parties have developed an unshakable perception of each other's malevolence and deceit, the fact that defection from some conciliatory course of action, or a failure to follow through on a promise of benefit transfer, will result in heavy and inevitable costs to the defector should increase the sense of trust that the acts will be performed.

This may be a very limited sense of trust, and one confined to that single set of interactions rather than involving a broad sense of predictability, veracity, benevolent intent or disinterested non-manipulation that make up 'trust' in a more general sense, but it may be all that conciliatory gestures can achieve in the early stages of a peace process.

Hence, the leaders of any party seeking to increase its own trustworthiness in the eyes of an adversary can, according to this 'trust through defection costs' hypothesis, best do so by unilaterally, publicly and deliberately increasing the potential costs to themselves of reneging on promises made as part of the conciliatory initiative. This approach echoes Schelling's conception of commitment and increasing costs for non-performance although here we are concerned with the psychological impact on the target and on the target's perception of the actor's trustworthiness. It also connects with the paradoxical utility of risk, in the sense that the most important and difficult situations calling for trust are, as Virginia Held points out (1968), those involving uncertainty arising from the fact that the party requesting trust always has a choice of harming or not harming the one conferring trust.

It is also the case that this minimalist conception of trust and of mistrust reduction, with its attendant lessons on strategy for those seeking trust from others, connects neatly with Swinth's interesting treatment of the subject (1967). The core idea in this work is that a party seeking trust from another can do so most effectively by initiating a strategy of deliberately exposing itself to the other by assuming a position of vulnerability. Hence, the target can, if so moved, take advantage of the initiator and impose costs on the latter without either running any risks or suffering any costs himself.

Swinth suggests that there are two variants of this strategy of attaining trust through self-imposed vulnerability. The first consists of the initiator deliberately giving something to the target which cannot be taken back (usually while implying or expressing the hope that the target will make some reciprocal transfer in exchange) – a central feature of GRIT-based strategies and clearly connected with the quality of irrevocability discussed in earlier chapters. The vulnerability in this case is a definite one, in that the initiator will already have made a transfer (which may be either material or symbolic) and experienced the loss. There may be a return, but that decision is entirely in the hands of the target, which will clearly have some impact on the target's options, its sense of being pressured and hence the gesture's respondability. A major part of the vulnerability for the initiator is transferring the responsibility for reciprocation (and continuing the process) wholly to the target. The initiator can also, in this case, begin to tell whether this strategy of trust-building is succeeding, depending upon whether the target responds or not – the response being a signal of the target's own desire to trust.

The second variant of this strategy involves vulnerability not simply through cost but through risk, in that the initiator's loss is potential rather than definite, so that it is the aspect of risk that becomes the test of whether the target has accepted the initiator's indication that he wishes to be trusted and is desirous, on his part, to trust the target. In this strategy, the initiator places himself in a position such that the target *can* take advantage and impose costs if he chooses. However, the initiator's losses are uncertain and depend upon the target's decision to take up or ignore the offer to begin building a less mistrustful relationship. (Thus, in the first case, the target's decision is whether to reciprocate, whereas in this case it is whether to take advantage.) If the target does not take advantage of the initiator's deliberately self-imposed vulnerability, then this becomes the signal that the target is, indeed, interested in trusting so the process may continue fruitfully from then on.

What does all this imply for the discussion of trust building and mistrust reduction? It seems clear that any party in a conflict wishing to begin to appear trustworthy – at least as far as a reliable commitment to a strategy of conciliation is concerned – will probably have only a small chance of developing a sense of benevolent intent, non-manipulation or veracity in the minds of an adversary. It may be that the target can develop a sense of trust-as-predictability after experiencing a number of benefit-conferring interactions in an accommodative sequence, but this appears unlikely in its initial stages. What is left is a strategy of attempting to obtain trust for a conciliatory process by deliberately making oneself vulnerable to the target, and being willing to bear the costs if that target, as is not unlikely, takes advantage of that vulnerability. As Worchel (1979) points out, revealing something about oneself always gives the other party some power over the disclosing one, but there is some evidence that, the greater the power one party has over another, the more likely the first is to engage in trusting behaviour. His view that 'Self disclosure is reciprocal; it indicates a basic trust in the other which, in turn, obligates the other to reciprocate' (1979, p.181) may be overly optimistic in cases of protracted conflict, but it does offer a principle that could be cautiously used in reducing mistrust. The issue must be to strike a balance between vulnerability and effectiveness in lessening mistrust.

The two variants of what is colloquially known as 'sticking one's neck out', discussed above, both involve either imposing a deliberate cost on oneself (a unilateral concession or reward) or deliberately running a risk of losing a benefit if the target takes advantage of vulnerability. For example, one can make a gesture of conciliation by abandoning a claim publicly. Or one can indicate that one might be prepared to abandon such a claim, thus weakening a previously certain commitment, should the adversary want to pick up and publicise this hint.

One general lesson seems to be that the only path likely to be available for diminishing mistrust in the initial stages of a conciliatory process is to be prepared to make sacrifices and run risks which are obvious to the adversary. Of course, these are precisely the kinds of move that render decision-makers most vulnerable to internal criticism and dissension, especially if the move fails and the target declines to reciprocate or takes advantage in a situation where such a choice is offered.

This last point leads to another issue. I have tended to concentrate upon the question of what a party desiring to develop trustworthiness or reduce untrustworthiness in the eyes of an adversary can do to forward this objective. However, it is also the case that a major responsibility for the development of a trusting relationship rests with the target of conciliatory actions. Trust can only be developed if one party is willing to give a trust-seeking adversary an opportunity to prove that it is worthy of trust. If mistrust is so strong that one party will never give the other the least chance of proving that it can be trusted, even in discrete and carefully demarcated arenas, then there will be no way of modifying the blanket belief that the adversary cannot be trusted. Similarly, if the target of moves designed to initiate a mutual decrease in mistrust responds by taking advantage of the initiator's deliberate vulnerability, this will merely confirm the latter's hawks and doubters, at least, in their expectations of predictable malevolence. The crucial event is the target's not taking advantage. As Luhmann notes, the process of diminishing mistrust is largely a learning process, which 'is not completed until we have had the opportunity to betray trust and have not used it' (Luhmann 1979, p.44).

In some circumstances, it may even be the case that a target might itself run an initial risk by indicating it is prepared to trust its adversary, at least to some minimal level, even though the other has done little yet to warrant such trust. Such a strategy would resemble, in principle, the kind of therapeutic trust discussed by Horsburgh (1960) with regard to individuals, where a person deliberately puts trust in someone, even though the latter is not particularly trustworthy and, indeed, has given many examples of untrustworthiness. The aim in this case is to encourage the other party to a positive-self sense of reliability and honesty and thence to further trustworthy acts and attitudes (Govier 1992, p.27). Whether such a strategy might work in protracted and deep-rooted conflicts is open to question. However, there is evidence that, in many situations, the experience of being trusted as a pattern of reciprocal behaviour does lead on to sequences characterised by growing trust and, as Lewis and Weigert express it, 'behavioural displays of trust implying actions help to create a cognitive platform of trust. When we see others acting in ways that imply they trust us, we become more disposed to reciprocate by trusting them more' (1985, p.971).

Such arguments suggest that, in the absence of a target's willingness to risk some small experiment, there is little likelihood of any major reduction of mistrust or substantial growth of stable trust developing in an adversarial relationship. At worst, conciliation efforts will fail and the adversaries will remain locked in a malign spiral of interaction where the only solution to their conflict will be victory for one and defeat for the other – unless there is an alternative approach to the conception of mistrust reduction when neither side wishes to risk even a minor increase in its own vulnerability.

3   Symbolic elements in mistrust reduction

One possible alternative to strategies that involve ostensibly dangerous increases of vulnerability involves the use of appropriate symbolic moves either in isolation or in association with other, substantive actions. Although the effectiveness of symbolic gestures was mentioned in Chapter 5, I have, up to this point, discussed the development of a sense of trust, or the lessening of mistrust, essentially as though these processes can be understood as decision-makers' careful assessment of whether a level of risk or vulnerability is acceptable in terms of the material benefits achieved from a move's impact on another party – what John Aguilar (1984, p.3) describes as the development of 'rational trust'.[5]

However, many writers, including Aguilar himself, have pointed out that there is a second type of 'psychological trust and mistrust', denoting 'relatively stable dispositions to experience emotionally directed perceptions of the absence or presence of danger with respect to a ... range of persons and situations' (ibid.); and much affected by symbolic factors as well as material ones. This distinction seems especially helpful if one is trying to understand the means by which mistrust might be diminished in an adversary relationship, when neither party wishes to run the risks of becoming vulnerable by having a conciliatory move rebuffed or a costly action undertaken but not reciprocated. Wishing to avoid material losses, a party hoping to begin a process of mistrust reduction can fall back on cautious symbolic actions, following the axiom that 'trust may be created through the exchange of symbolic goods of various types' which have 'the capacity to symbolise' both an existing relationship and also the desire to change one (Haas and Deseran 1981, p.3).

Obviously it is the case that, in any situation where goods are exchanged, the exchange can be evaluated on two dimensions, the utilitarian and the symbolic, both of which convey some information to the target about the initiator's intentions. However, the point about successful symbolic gestures is that they are less important for the actual material good involved than for the message that the party making the gesture is willing to invest time, attention, effort and care in establishing or, in the case of adversaries, changing the relationship.[6] Some writers have argued that the symbolic importance of a gesture can be enhanced if the material costs of the good or token to the initiator (a further indicator of investment and intentions) is much higher that the utilitarian value to the target – an imbalance at the material level that can be offset by the importance to the latter of the symbolic value. In this view, the crucial factor is the information conveyed to the target by the gesture – and also back to the initiator by its acceptance or refusal.

As mentioned in Chapter 5, the precise nature of appropriate symbolic gestures in reducing mistrust is often a matter of the relationship involved and the culture of the parties. Symbolic exchanges take place in structured social settings and between individuals or parties who are often 'occupants (or would be occupants) of named social positions with recognised responsibilities and relationships to other such positions' (Haas and Deseran 1981, p.6). While the latter constraint may be less true of enemies or adversaries, particularly in protracted social conflicts, it seems reasonable to argue that cultural factors will very much affect what is perceived as an important symbolic gesture in a given conflict, and make it difficult to generalise about gestures likely, in general, to help to reduce mistrust. Haas and Deseran have suggested five types of symbolic gesture that might form the basis of what they term a general 'vocabulary of symbolic exchange', three of which might be useful in adversary relationships:

1 Food and drink, the exchange of which, or even the sharing of which, can act as a powerful symbol of strengthened or restored relationships.[7]
2 Gifts, which can be used cautiously to initiate a search for a new relationship, particularly if the gifts in question are unexpected, or given on occasions other than those when exchange of gifts is clearly required by the cultural pattern.
3 Attendance and attention; Haas and Deseran express this as 'attendance at formal ceremonies and some kinds of visits' and they make the indisputable point that such a presence – for example at an independence day celebration or at a state funeral – can express considerable commitment or, indeed, a major change of commitment. I would add the idea that attention, interest and concern can also demonstrate a commitment or investment in a way that clearly sends a message about a party's intention, in much the same manner as studied indifference conveys the opposite message. One recalls, for example, the well-publicised example of PLO Chairman Arafat watching on television the funeral of the assassinated Israeli Prime Minister, Yitzak Rabin.

The last section in the suggested vocabulary involves the refusal or rejection of symbolic exchanges and Haas and Deseran review some interesting arguments about when such refusals do or do not undermine an existing relationship of trust or, more importantly from our viewpoint, indicate that the target of a symbolic gesture involving exchange refuses to contemplate the changed relationship being suggested. Clearly such rejection can be unequivocal and, in many cases, humiliating and costly for an initiator.

The British reaction to the Argentine rejection of their removal of the 1982 trade embargo was to assume that the Argentines were simply not interested in the restoring of normal relations between the two countries. At a more personal level, the refusal of US Secretary of State Dulles even to shake hands with PRC Premier Chou En Lai was a universally understood snub by one government to another and an indication that there was no way in which the existing enmity was likely to be modified.

If the representatives of adversaries in an intense conflict can shy away from the implications of even shaking hands with one another, are there any ways in which even symbolic gestures can be used to initiate a low-risk process to lower mutual mistrust? Unfortunately, as I already noted, much of the literature on trust concerns its increase within relationships of partnership or amity. However, Aguilar's work on the 'psychology of trust' offers some suggestions, as his research concerns social situations in Mexican peasant societies that are characterised by intense mutual mistrust and by 'relatively stable dispositions to experience emotionally directed perceptions of the ... presence of danger in respect to a wide range of persons and situations' (Aguilar 1984, p.3). Thus, Aguilar's peasant society resembles a conflict system, consisting of parties in protracted conflict, in that it is peopled by individuals that are non-trusting, and the 'non-trusting person has expectations of harm. He is always at least a little wary. The common affective experience is fright, for the world is perceived as a dangerous place.' (Isaacs *et al.* 1963, p.465).

For Aguilar's peasants, as well as for decision-makers of parties in conflict, the problem is how to establish relationships based upon some level of trust rather than mistrust; how to discover persons in whom one can have the *confianza* to engage in reciprocal exchange; how to initiate a process of mistrust reduction that does not expose one to exploitation by another party likely to betray the initial efforts at building a minimal trust level. The means by which this is achieved in the society studied by Aguilar involves a process of gradually testing whether another member of a society in which there are few resources to share and in which mistrust, secrecy and betrayal are the norm, might be willing to enter into a relationship of mutual trust and thus build up a necessary network of support making a person and his family less vulnerable to hardship and disaster. The chief features of this process are, firstly, establishing a relationship of mutual *confianza*, through a cautious process of testing whether another would be willing to assume this relationship. Tactics include:

- sending the target person or family gifts;
- communicating 'political' agreement or alignment through gossip, sharing negative evaluations of others and so on;
- inviting the target as a guest of honour (*invitado*) to a domestic or religious fiesta;

- extending unsolicited aid to a person or family in need;
- consistently extending cordial greetings in public.

The function of all such moves is to begin to define an altered relationship with the target by communicating actions designed to redefine the existing relationship. Weinstein and Deutschberger (1963, p.465) and Hewitt (1976) both refer to this activity as *altercasting*, an effort 'to pursue goals by attempting to create a role for another that supports those goals', for example by 'treating people as special friends, confidants or intimates in order to secure their cooperation' (Hewitt 1976, pp.136–7). The ultimate aim of the strategy is at once to display oneself as a person interested in, and worthy of, the target's trust and also to test out whether the target is interested in and worth establishing a relationship of *confianza*.

A second important feature is ensuring, through the establishment of an initial relationship of trust and reliance, that the parties in the relationship understand the importance of maintaining one another's self esteem, dignity and reputation, whenever one is making or receiving a future request for assistance. Both Aguilar (1984) and Goffman (1967) refer to this sub-process based upon mutual tact as 'face work', and emphasise that it involves a symbolic exchange whereby one person's 'self esteem and dignity needs are protected in return for the protection of the other's reputation.' (Aguilar 1984, p.21). The exchange is carried on in such a way as to 'decontaminate the refusal of its negative social meaning by serving as an invitation to the petitioner to return in another time of need' (ibid.).

The ideas discussed by Aguilar and other anthropologists both emphasise the importance of symbolic elements in conciliatory gestures and provide some indications of how symbols might be used in the initial stages of a conciliatory process to avoid the risks and costs inherent in a 'rational mistrust' strategy involving vulnerability on the one hand and failure to reciprocate on the other. Some of Haas and Deseran's and of Aguilar's suggestions recall such powerful symbolic actions as Sadat's returning unasked the bodies of the Israeli soldiers, or the sending of the US table tennis team to participate in championship matches in the CPR. The final handshake between Prime Minister Rabin and Chairman Arafat following the signing of the Oslo Accords, and the reluctance with which it was undertaken, emphasise the importance of symbolic actions in altering relationships and beginning to diminish mistrust on the part of erstwhile adversaries. Clearly, one task for would be conciliators and students of conciliation is to examine what types of symbol are most effective in what cultures and what situations. From that analysis it might be possible to extend and particularise the 'vocabulary of symbolic exchange' and provide some tools for those seeking to move adversaries towards a level of mistrust that at least permits some further trust-building activities which may involve temporary vulnerability. What that minimum level might look like is discussed in the next section.

4   Achieving minumum or sufficient trust

Many scholars and practitioners have argued that a successful resolution process must involve the initial establishment of a 'minimum' or 'sufficient' level of trust between the adversaries, enabling the process to continue, once begun. It is also generally agreed that the achievement even of this level of trust must involve an incremental process by which mutual trustworthiness is cautiously built up over time and over a series of moves. As Peter Blau (1964) expresses this idea, trust is built up and mistrust diminished by a series of gradually increasing 'investments' in the relationship, in which the partners can demonstrate their trustworthiness to each other. A similar approach is suggested by Worchel (1979, p.181) who talks about 'a sequence of steps involving reciprocal self-exposure and reinforcement', and by Bennis *et al.* (1964, p.217), who describe a process by which two people expose more and more of their own 'selves' to one another. More recently, Roy Lewicki and Barbara Bunker (1995) have suggested a three stage, trust development model in which parties are led from a stage of trust based on calculation (what others call instrumental or cognitive trust), through a stage of trust based on knowledge and predictability, to a stable, final stage of trust based on identification – parallel, in some respects, to emotional trust. All of these schemes share the problem that they tend to start from a presumed absence of any prior relationship and ignore an axiomatic stage for adversaries in which there already exists a high level of mistrust, so that a crucial question is how to break through this 'mistrust barrier' to a stage of instrumental, rational or calculus-based trust. Once this is done, even if a trust building process involves suspicious adversaries, it will at some point reach a minimum trust level at which joint consideration of solutions to the conflict might begin.

But what is a 'minimum level of trust' that can lead to subsequent, increasing trusting behaviour between erstwhile enemies and thence to a search for a mutually acceptable settlement? Conceptually, the level must lie somewhere between a total absence of trust between the parties, characterised by expectations of constant malevolence, deceit and coercion, and total trust in which one party attributes to all members of another party constant benevolence and competence, steadfast veracity, and a complete absence of manipulation over all issues and interests. Clearly there must be conditions that lie somewhere between total trust and total mistrust, but how might this be conceptualised and how might one begin to develop possible indices of different levels of trust, identify 'sufficient' or minimum trust, and suggest means of achieving such levels?

4.1   Minimum trust across a number of dimensions

One answer might be that when one comes to look more closely at the idea of trust as an expectation on the part of some person or persons, it quickly becomes clear that trust can be viewed as being characterised by a large number of different qualities or dimensions – for example how focused or specific trust might be.

'I trust his technical competence but not his impartiality' is a phrase not infrequently heard about another person, and the fact that it is possible to trust a person's judgement and competence, but not his veracity or honesty, indicates that one can have different expectations (and levels of mistrust) about different aspects of the same person's character or behaviour. On the other hand, one can often find people saying – even if they don't always follow through behaviourally – that they trust another person 'completely', which implies on every possible dimension and in all circumstances.[8]

This sort of approach to conceptualising trust is very close to that used by Malim Akerstrom in his study of treachery and betrayal (Akerstrom 1991). He clearly involves conceptions of predictability and benevolence in his work on trust and the betrayal of trust, but also expresses an idea that trust can be focused on, or specific to, one or more issues – in his case, trust to maintain agreed norms and to keep secrets – rather than being generalised across all and every aspect of a relationship. (This particular formulation of the specificity of trust is reflected in the everyday phrase 'He will do what he says he will, but he can't keep secrets.')

However, Akerstrom's approach also echoes my point that trust can be disaggregated and viewed as a divisible phenomenon. Moreover, trust or mistrust can be applied differentially to different aspects of another's anticipated behaviour *or* to different members of the same group, collectivity or organisation ('X is alright; you can trust him, at least – but don't trust any of the others!').

All of this suggests that one can think of trust in terms of its being distinguishable according to its generality. People can trust other people either in a limited fashion, over specific issues or aspects of their relationship, or – at the other end of the scale, and probably only possible in an idealised world – they can trust others in a complete, absolute and diffuse manner, over all possible aspects of their relationship.

In searching for a conception of minimum or sufficient trust, then, it may be helpful to think about trust as being characterised by a number of such dimensions as generality. This approach can help to differentiate the types of trust that might exist in a relationship – even one characterised as an 'adversary' relationship. For example, there is a useful distinction to be made, surely, between trust which takes the negative form of believing that the other will *not* do certain things and that which takes the form of believing that the other will undertake certain (presumably beneficial) actions.

DIMENSIONS OF TRUST

DEGREE

Absolute   Minimal
< . . . . >
100%   5%

DIRECTION

Positive   Negative
< . . . . >
X will do what   X will not do what
he says he will   he says he will not

FOCUS

Diffuse   Specific
< . . . . >
Generalised: over   Limited: focused
all relationships   on one aspect or
and issues   issue only

LIMITATION

Unconditional   Conditional
< . . . . >
X will not commit any   X will carry out his
harm, even without a   promises to confer
specific commitment   benefits or refrain
                                            from harm

SCOPE

Inclusive   Exclusive
< . . . . >
Trust conferred on   Trust only conferred
all members of   on limited and
trusted entity   identified members
                                            of trusted entity

Figure 9.2   **Dimensions of Trust and Mistrust**

For a start, I would suggest that it might be helpful to think about trust as being characterisable – and differentiated – along the five dimensions illustrated in Figure 9.2 above. Other useful dimensions will emerge from further analysis but even this initial sketch helps to throw some light on the possibility of delineating minimum trust, and the way in which initial conciliatory gestures might move a relationship between adversaries away from absolute mistrust to a point at which further, mutually reinforcing initiatives might be undertaken.

4.2   A sketch of minimum trust

It is probably easier to say what minimum trust is not, rather than what it is. Certainly it is not absolute and diffuse trust in the sense that the parties trust one another completely across an entire range of issues and all aspects of their relationship. Given that the starting point for any conciliation is usually zero trust – even as regards isolated issues, such as the organisation of relief or the exchange of prisoners – minimum trust can only involve some level of trust (at least above a perceived even chance that the adversary will do as promised) involving very specific issues (such as the provision of information about numbers of A's refugees in territory controlled by B).

Similarly, minimum trust is likely to involve, at least initially, a reasonably secure expectation that the adversary will refrain from taking certain harmful actions but only if the leaders have made specific commitments to that effect. Thus minimum trust has to begin by being negative and highly conditional.

Lastly, as I noted above, the objects of minimum trust seem most likely to be limited in numbers and differentiated only slightly from both the majority of an adversary's elite and the bulk of the rank-and-file followers. In minimum trust, the scope of the trust is likely to be very limited, confined to 'doves' on the other side, who have probably become thoroughly mistrusted by their fellow leaders and by their followers, and the occasional but very important 'owl', who is able to retain the trust of followers while gaining some trust and respect from the adversary, at least as far as certain specific issues and levels of predictability are concerned.[9]

It seems likely that, in the initial stages of any conciliatory process, the most that can be expected will be to move away from an absolute level of mistrust towards a slight increase in unpredictablility and a minimal lessening of malevolence, through a conciliatory, mistrust-reducing initiative that produces a level of trust characterised by its:

1   small scope (covers a few key individuals);
2   mainly negative direction (what adversary will *not* do);
3   minimal degree (slightly over 50 per cent confidence);
4   high conditionality (tied to specific promises to refrain); and
5   Considerable specificity (concerns limited issues).

The initial stages of any conciliation process therefore seem, at least as far as gestures to lower mistrust and build up minimum trust are concerned, to confront the standard dilemma of how to do enough to obtain a response from a target while not doing something likely to be risky. Moves that may well be tailored towards achieving minimum trust will also be those with low discernibility and low credibility, so the question is one of doing 'enough' in the exploratory stage to overcome these two initial obstacles. Subsequent stages in an accommodative sequence could involve the tactical moving of adversaries towards larger scope and general diffusion, plus unconditionality and more positive direction.

4.3   The ideas of 'working' and 'transferred' trust

These principles for trust building are in line with ideas of many unofficial third party facilitators, who have organised informal preliminary discussions or workshops involving non official participants from warring parties. They argue that such initial exchanges should not be aimed at creating high levels of trust between adversaries, nor even interpersonal trust between particular individuals who have participated in discussions.[10] Rather, Kelman and others have developed the conception of *working trust* which is 'based on the recognition of common interests despite profound differences that allows participants to engage in the work of analysis and joint problem solving' (Kelman 1991, p.154). The characteristics of working trust, then, are that it is limited and specific, being confined only to certain processes, situations and results, and negative in the sense that certain things will not happen (ranging from personal danger to participants while participating to subsequent leaks, publicity, or use of information for coercive advantage) once the discussions are finished. It is also limited in scope to those members of the adversary party attending the workshops.

In another context entirely, Trudy Govier (1992) has suggested some interesting guidelines for working collaboratively with a 'partner' on a common task. The 'partner' may be different in many ways (and will be if, prior to this task, he, she or they have been an adversary) – in goals and interests, emotional style, attitudes and beliefs, communication patterns or favoured strategies. However, Govier argues that collaboration will be possible under certain minimum conditions, involving:

1 an ability to communicate fully and openly;
2 a willingness to listen and appreciate communication even if initially not being disposed to agree;
3 an unwillingness to distort other's information or deliberately to suppress or conceal one's own;
4 a refusal to use other's information to harm, betray or manipulate;
5 a readiness to credit the other with honesty, competence, sincerity and integrity;
6 reliability in fulfilling commitments.

'Partners', argues Govier, 'communicate openly and effectively, share goals, co-operate, co-ordinate activities, rely on each other's promises and commitments, and make efficient dependable arrangements that do not presuppose constant surveillance and supervision.' (Govier 1992, p.30) At this point, it seems as though Govier's ideas have more to do with friendly and co-operative partners than with adversary partners who are, reluctantly, cooperating to find their way out of a protracted conflict. Nonetheless, her ideas do set some goals for the level of minimum trust that might be aimed for as the result of a successful conciliatory process.

Other forms of minimum trust do not set such high standards for adversaries. For example, Kelman has also made the interesting observation that such problem-solving procedures are able to make their contribution to a conflict resolution process partly because of a process of transferred trust, a process which may not be confined to informal workshops but which probably plays a major role in many third party initiatives aimed at conflict resolution. By this, he means that adversaries, while continuing to mistrust each other thoroughly, are able to attend such discussions because of their trust of the third party.

Kelman notes that third parties play 'a vital role in this regard by serving as a common repository of trust in this situation'. He adds, 'Their common trust in the third party enables the participants to proceed with the assurance that their interests will be protected, that their sensitivities will be respected and that their confidences will not be violated' (Kelman op. cit 1991, p.154). There are problems even with this argument, however, and there is much evidence that there is no automatic transfer of trust even to third parties, many of whom are often viewed with high levels of mistrust by adversaries. There is a fuller discussion of the 'transfer of trust' problem in Chapter 11.

5   Conclusion

It seems clear that, at the very least, minimum trust must ultimately be developed to a level which would permit representatives of parties in conflict to meet one another without the fear of physical harm befalling one or other set of representatives. The constant refusal of faction leaders in the Liberian civil war to meet one another seems to have been based on very straightforward concerns for physical survival if they were to meet at some site where they were physically vulnerable.

In such circumstances, the problem is not the conventional one of how to maintain trust or how to increase it, but rather to create it within an environment of total mistrust. For leaders such as Anwar Sadat and others thinking of employing a strategy incorporating conciliatory gestures, the problem remains how to begin a process of establishing even the minimal levels of trust necessary to 'jump start' a conflict resolution process.

Our predictability–malevolence model suggests that, to some extent, how a leader goes about this task will depend on whether the adversary's leaders inhabit Quadrant A or D of the model in Figure 9.1. In the case of Anwar Sadat, did he face a key Israeli leadership that perceived Egypt and its leader as (1) highly predictably malevolent or (2) somewhat unpredictably malev-

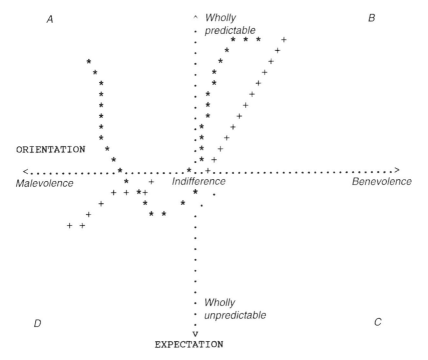

Figure 9.3 **Mistrust Reduction Paths for Anwar Sadat**

olent? The latter might involve a record of either random or sporadically malevolent actions together with occasional benevolent acts. Paradoxically, a completely malevolent record might make initial trust-building actions easier, in that a conciliatory gesture or a series of benevolent acts will stand out in stark contrast to what went before. If the situation for Sadat and the Israelis did, indeed, fall within Quadrant D, then a major act of benevolence will be required to stand out and have much impact, hence the necessity for Sadat's dramatic move in 1977.

However, theories of both cognitive consistency and attribution tell us that non-conforming acts that clash with expectations are likely to be 'rationalised' away, so that it is possible that even in Quadrant A either a major non-conforming action will be required or a series of actions which move the situation initially towards Quadrant D (see Figure 9.3 above).

Precise tactics for diminishing mistrust and achieving sufficient or working trust will undoubtedly be highly situation specific. Although some general principles underlying mistrust reducing actions could be developed, moves based even on these will need to be made with caution. Zand suggests, for example, that even 'behaving with high trust towards others who are not trusting will not necessarily induce trust' (1972, p.237), and quotes experimental evidence that efforts by a leader to be open about intra-party constraints affecting him can be interpreted by mistrusting others as a means of deflecting blame for an unacceptable stand or policy.

Such general principles will be the subject of my concluding chapter, but it would be as well at this point to recall Zand's warning about trust and mistrust even within a relatively homogenous group: 'mutual trust or mistrust among members of a group are likely to be reinforced unless there is marked and prolonged disconfirming behaviour' (ibid. p.238). Some experimental work involving individuals with high or low predispositions towards trust – the latter, surely, quite characteristic of enemies and adversaries – comes to the hardly surprising conclusion that 'low trusters' need the substantial and consistent evidence of a series of co-operative moves before they diminish mistrust to the point of reacting co-operatively (Parks *et al.* 1996).[11] However, Zand is being very realistic when he continues: 'Exactly what disconfirmation is needed and how much requires further investigation' (ibid.).

10
Obstacles to Clear Signalling

'We have suffered and sacrificed too much to turn back now.'
Arthur Scargill, President of the National Union of Mineworkers, at the height of the NUM–National Coal Board conflict in 1985 in which the miners were decisively 'defeated'

Previous chapters have discussed two of the major influences on the likely success of a conciliatory initiative, the context within which the initiative occurs and the characteristics of the initiative itself, the latter affecting the recognisability and the credibility of the move. Two further important sets of factors are likely to have a major influence on the likely initiation of some conciliatory move and its probable impact. The first of these involves a range of political and psychological conditions within the initiating party, particularly within elite and decision-making circles, but also at the levels of opinion leaders and rank-and-file constituents; the second the

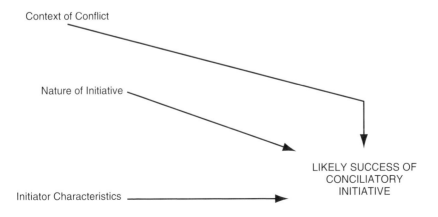

Context of Conflict

Nature of Initiative

Initiator Characteristics

LIKELY SUCCESS OF
CONCILIATORY
INITIATIVE

Figure 10.1   **Influences on Conciliation Effectiveness V**

conditions within other parties, but particularly the adversary, the targets of the conciliatory gesture or set of gestures launched in the hope of starting an accommodative sequence. Both mainly affect the respondability of the move; both resemble one another, but there are sufficient differences to prevent them being exact mirror images, explainable in precisely the same manner, and amenable to precisely similar remedies (see Figure 10.1).

The importance of these two sets of factors on the likely success of any conciliatory initiative is perhaps best explained by returning initially to the communications approach outlined in Chapter 3 and using that to consider possible intra-party obstacles to successful conciliatory activities, either in situations where parties involved need to initiate a de-escalation process from high levels of violence, tension and mistrust, or to re-start fruitful communication after a previously failed peacemaking process and a subsequent period of stalemate and lack of communication. What, then, are some of the major intra-party constraints on conciliation?

1   Dilemmas of initiation

A communications approach emphasises the centrality of clear and unambiguous signals from an initiator to a target if the conciliatory initiative is to be successful in making an impact on the latter and beginning a process of action and reaction which eventually constitutes one of Morton Deutsch's 'benign conflict spirals' (Deutsch 1973). Initially, the approach draws attention to issues discussed in Chapters 5 through 9, such as the content and nature of the signal, the consistency with which a series of conciliatory signals are sent, and the effects of 'noise' on the target's ability to pick up, interpret and recognise the signal for what it is meant to be. However, as the discussion in Chapter 3 emphasised, any process of conciliation begins in consideration and initiation stages, well before any conciliatory gesture is actually made. The decision-makers (or at least some of them) of one party to the conflict have to have come to the conclusion that outright 'victory' (however defined) is no longer a possibility; that the costs of continuing the conflict, whether escalating to new levels of coercion and violence or stalemated in some unsatisfactory impasse, are likely to outweigh the benefits; and that the time has come to explore the possibility of a negotiated settlement with their adversary. It is a matter for speculation when, exactly, Anwar Sadat reached this conclusion, although his early efforts to signal the possibility of a major change in Egyptian strategy indicate that he may even have entered office with this possibility in mind.

The broad circumstances in which leaders of countries, communities and other complex parties in conflict come to such a conclusion were discussed in Chapter 4, which dealt with contextual factors arising from the conflict system itself that were conducive to a search for alternatives and a subsequent decision to quit unbridled coercion in pursuit of a unilaterally imposed solution. However, there are a number of features, both of the decision-making process and of the decision to seek a negotiated solution itself, which can have a major, adverse effect upon leaders' ability to signal consistently and unambiguously to their adversary, and which place major intra-party constraints on any ability to make convincing gestures which clearly signal a willingness to talk to the adversary.

Firstly, the process of deciding to abandon a particular coercive strategy (war, limited war, economic coercion or other form of sanctions), by recognising that it has not achieved its aims and is becoming counter productive, is an agonisingly uncomfortable one for individual and collective decision-makers, who have become politically and psychologically trapped by, and committed to, a particular line of policy. Each heavily committed decision-maker finds it hard to accept the necessity for peace feelers or other conciliatory gestures towards a mistrusted adversary, and will often change this stance only very slowly. In any conflict, a decision to switch from a strategy of coercion to one of possible conciliation involves a profound degree of change. This is not an adjustment of policy, nor a minor alteration of means or direction. I have previously argued that such a change calls for decision-making characterised by comprehensive reconsideration as opposed to incremental continuation.

In a somewhat broader field, talking about changes in foreign policy, Charles Hermann uses the term 'fundamental redirections in ... policy', differentiating three types of such change – in programme, in goals and in overall orientation – from simple adjustments to the level of effort or the scope of activity (Hermann 1990, p.5). He makes the point that, in many cases, the only way in which such a major alteration of policy can occur is through regime change, 'when new governments with different perceptions of the environment and new agendas come to power' (ibid. p.4). However, most of this and subsequent Chapters will concentrate upon situations in which existing leaders decide upon a major switch from coercion to conciliation, or self-correcting change in Hermann's terminology. Whatever the term, many obstacles can abort the process.

One major obstacle arises from the likelihood that different individuals within a set of leaders will reluctantly come to a conclusion that a change of policy is needed at different times during a conflict. (Some never do and would fight on to the end, no matter how bitter this might be.) Hence, fierce divisions are likely to arise within a decision-making elite over the necessity for conciliation, accommodation and – finally – negotiation. Factional differences will arise over the issue of fighting on or settling through negotiation, and bitter in-fighting is likely to take place over this question.

The intra-party debate frequently takes the form of a dichotomy over 'carry on or quit' or sometimes over escalation or de-escalation. At least one faction will argue for additional effort so that the conflict can be ended once the adversary has been placed in an unambiguous position of disadvantage – what Fred Iklé has called 'peace through escalation' (1989) – while the other argues for the opposite course of action and for the need to make at least some minor concessions to an adversary in order to start talking and to stop suffering the continued costs of fighting. Japanese army leaders in 1945, for example, argued for a strategy of awaiting Allied invasion, defeating it thoroughly and then approaching the Allies with a peace offer rather than trying to make peace that summer (Sigal 1988).

The effects of in-fighting tend to be two-fold. For one thing, the nature of the issues will inhibit those seeking accommodation and a negotiated settlement from using full freedom of action to pursue their new goal. This option will often involve a complete U-turn from the previous policy for which they are often (at least partly) responsible, and for which they have argued in the past. Furthermore, while no political leaders relish being charged with inconsistency, even less do they relish being called traitors by those of their erstwhile colleagues who wish to continue the struggle. Frequently, 'premature' efforts to make peace have cost political leaders their reputation, their following, their office and sometimes even their lives. As Marguerite Yourcenar's Hadrian writes, 'to be right too soon is to be in the wrong' (Yourcenar 1955). Until the 'doves' or 'owls' in any leadership group are in the majority (and the process of building up a coalition in support of a peace initiative, de-escalation or a negotiated compromise is usually a slow one) the position of those advocating compromise is at least uncomfortable and frequently dangerous. (Dangers do not vanish completely even when civilian doves are in the numerical ascendency within a party 'at war'.)

The existence of debate, disagreement and general lack of consensus – about whether to de-escalate the conflict or prosecute it with renewed vigour – frequently results in quite contradictory signals being sent to the adversary. This can occur either simultaneously, which, given the natural tendency of enemies to suspect the worst of each other, results in worst-case thinking and ignoring conciliatory gestures as tricks embedded in coercive signals; or sequentially, using carrots and sticks alternatively which, as I have argued previously, frequently baffles those on the receiving end of the strategy almost as much as simultaneous coercion and conciliation.

Faced with intra-party obstacles of this type and extent, the process of initially deciding to abandon all-out efforts for final victory frequently takes on a character that profoundly affects the way in which governments and other leaders of parties in conflict can begin to signal to each other at the start of any hoped-for process of mutual accommodation. What were described as intra-party or 'domestic' constraints on signalling therefore arise from a prior – often incomplete – process of a party 'making up its collective mind' that the time has come to try for a negotiated settlement, if a satisfactory one proves to be on offer from the adversary.

Finally, once the debate at the level of decison making elites emerges publicly, those arguing for an alternative approach to continuing coercion have to deal with the problem of elites and particularly constituents who have been mobilised for the struggle by methods that attempt to fix in their minds that the issues in contention are vital and non-negotiable, the adversaries essentially unamenable to constructive cooperation – or even reasoned argument – and the option of seeking any solution short of full achievement of goals simply not discussable. Hence, the very success of a previous mass mobilisation process, which prepares constituents for the conflict and sustains them through sacrifice and suffering, becomes a major intra-party obstacle to leaders even considering the possibility of launching conciliatory moves should changing circumstances make these appear a better option than continuing the struggle. As Hermann argues, the only way in which this obstacle can be avoided is if the 'attitudes or beliefs of the dominant domestic constituents undergo a profound change' (Hermann 1990, p.7) and the change has to be in favour of making an accommodation with the adversary.

All of these intra-party factors can and frequently do constitute formidable obstacles to even the thought of launching some cautious conciliatory gesture, whatever the actual circumstances of the conflict (the context) might be at that particular moment. Intra-party cleavages, exacerbated by rival interpretations of the parties' current balance of advantage and likely future fortune, together with a constituency already aroused to a high level of belligerence and equally high expectations of success for their sacrifices present major dilemmas of initiation, which deter the thought, the discussion or the implementation of accommodative moves. For leaders seeking to initiate conciliatory processes, immediate problems involve overcoming barriers to contemplating a conciliatory signal, sending such a signal, and sending one in such a form that it presents itself as an unambiguous message to the target. The nature of these intra-party barriers requires some detailed discussion before making even tentative suggestions about the 'initiator characteristics' most conducive to launching a conciliatory initiative.

One initially useful way of thinking about the effects of such barriers has been suggested in a more general context by Robert Putnam, who has pointed out that national decision-makers always operate at two levels when making policy choices, the domestic and the international; and that the kind of changes they can make in current policy depends upon the constraints and opportunities operating at both levels, and the way in which the levels interact. Putnam uses the metaphor of decision-makers playing in two simultaneous 'games' which, when protracted conflicts are involved, can be viewed as the inter-party and the intra-party 'game'. The latter is characterised by intra-party groups that 'pursue their interests by pressuring the government to adopt favourable policies', some of which will inevitably involve the continuation of the strugge; while the party's decision-makers 'seek power by constructing coalitions among those groups' (Putnam 1993, p.416). During a conciliation process, such coalitions have to involve those whose interests would be served by a negotiated solution rather than a continuation of the conflict, so that the difficulties of first discovering and then marshalling these interests becomes a major political problem for potential conciliators among a party's leadership – even for a powerful leader such as Anwar Sadat. Putnam's two game metaphor, together with his warning that 'moves that are rational for a player at one board ... may be impolitic for that same player at the other board' (ibid.), is a useful one to keep in mind when considering some of the political constraints on initiating a conciliation process, especially when these are combined with a number of related psychological obstacles created by a strong commitment to the goals in conflict, and to winning through forcing the adversaries to abandon their own goals.

2   Entrapment and constraints on signalling

One of the consistent findings about intractable conflicts is that elites and decision-makers frequently become trapped in a particular course of action and find escape therefrom very difficult. Moreover, the problems of escape, of 'quitting', of 'making a U-turn' appear to increase the longer the conflict continues and the more politically and psychologically committed leaders become to achieving an elusive 'victory'.

In some cases, decision-makers of parties in conflict see no rational need to contemplate abandoning their original course of action. In spite of early set-backs, considerable and reliable evidence will still exist to the effect that they will be successful and that the conflict will terminate with most, if not all, their goals achieved. The leaders of the USSR thus continued the war against the Finns in 1939–40 in spite of initial military disasters, secure in the knowledge that they could overwhelm the Finns by sheer force of numbers, if necessary; and that the only dangerous potential supporter of the Finns (Hitler's Reich) would not intervene. Eventually, Soviet leaders were able to achieve almost all their original goals in the conflict through a dictated settlement with no thought of conciliatory gestures or concessions, except in the sense that these formed part of their agreement to talk with a Finnish delegation in order to arrange the settlement (Upton 1979).

This example suggests that there are cases in which the chief obstacle to any de-escalation and a negotiated (as opposed to dictated) solution lies in the fact that one party is, or perceives itself to be, clearly on the verge of success, so that it can afford to continue coercion and wait for the other party to ask for minimum terms. Indeed, it is only reasonable to emphasise that, in most international and inter-communal conflicts, it is the perceived balance of advantage between the parties in the arena of coercion that provides the main obstacle to the initiation of any de-escalation process.

However, there are numerous other cases and many stages (even in conflicts that are eventually settled by the success of one party) when the conflict stalemates, drags along inconclusively or appears to offer no imme-diate – or even medium term – prospect for success for either side. Yet, in many such cases, the decision-makers involved appear to find it just as difficult to decide to try for a negotiated settlement, to signal a willingness to talk, or to begin a process of accommodation. Even in stalemated situ-ations, with an evenly poised balance of advantage, leaders often find themselves unwilling or unable to alter coercive strategies without a great deal of effort, which involves breaking a sense of commitment and a pattern of behaviour arising therefrom.

One common explanation of the difficulty experienced by decision-makers in beginning a process of conciliation can be found in the idea that leaders of parties in conflict become the victims of a process of entrapment in a particular (coercive) course of action and feel that, because they come to have 'too much invested to quit', there is no alternative but to continue a strategy to which they are personally and politically committed, irrespec-tive of its diminishing prospects for success. This entrapping process pro-gressively makes it more and more difficult for a group of leaders to consider the prospect of conciliation. It thus prevents conciliatory gestures, concessions or confidence building measures being made, so the conflict continues.

2.1   The nature of 'entrapment'

Theories of entrapment focus on a complex process that was investigated in some detail during the 1980s. (Teger 1980; Brockner and Rubin 1985). Its central feature is that, while there are a number of 'rational' reasons for continuing on an apparently failing course of action – for example, the desire to minimise eventual net losses by achieving some off-setting success – the main psychological reasons for leaders continuing an often obviously (to outsiders) failing policy are 'rationalising' rather than 'rational'. Often, these take two forms: firstly of justifying past choice of the strategy for which decision-makers are responsible (*choice justification*); and secondly of justifying previous sacrifices made and costs suffered in pursuit of those chosen goals via the chosen strategy (*investment justification*).

Entrapment has been defined as 'a decision-making process whereby indi-viduals escalate their commitment to a previously chosen, though failing, course of action in order to justify or "make good on" prior investments' (Brockner and Rubin 1985, p.5), and by Glen Whyte as 'a tendency to con-tinue an endeavour, regardless of its merits, once an investment of time, effort and resources has been made' (1993, pp.430–1). It is important to keep in mind that there are normally two targets for such justification: others and – often more importantly – oneself. Entrapment partly involves a need for decision-makers 'to prove *to themselves* and others that they are, indeed, competent and rational' (ibid. p.431 emphasis added).

The degree to which decision-makers leading a party into a salient conflict over valuable goals find themselves 'entrapped' will obviously affect their willingess to contemplate – or even be psychologically capable of contemplating – reversing course. By implication, this would mean admitting to themselves and others that (i) their initial choices were mistaken, and (ii) the investments (lives, resources, status, time, effort, honour) are lost forever, or for nothing. Hence, levels of psychological entrapment will be a key consideration in explaining the presence or absence of efforts to de-escalate a conflict, engage in conciliation and settle for negotiation. The more decision-makers have invested in the conflict, the more they are entrapped and the greater the obstacles to conflict termination by any means other than some increasingly improbable 'victory'.

The theory provides a number of suggestions about factors which increase the probability that decision-makers will become entrapped even in an increasingly obvious failed course of action, so that conciliatory alternatives become psychologically as well as politically constrained. There has been enough observation of the effects of entrapment in the worlds of organisational, domestic and international conflict to suggest factors that produce obstacles to any change of course, given that such a change will, by definition, involve an abandonment of some goals and an admission of mistaken decisions and vain sacrifices. Among important factors that create obstacles to change and accommodation, five seem to be most deterring:

1   the size of previous investment of resources;
2   the decreasing marginal value of further investments;
3   leaders' direct responsibility for existing policy;
4   prior efforts to overcome initial opposition to the existing policy;
5   the existence of an audience for a change of policy.[1]

Perhaps it is in its analysis of the effects of previous costs of a policy that entrapment theory produces the seemingly most bizarre findings. 'Rational' decision models predict that the increasing level of costs experienced by a party in attempting to achieve desired goals will lead eventually to costs outweighing potential benefits and the abandonment of efforts to achieve those goals. In contrast, entrapment theory argues that the more that has been sacrificed (invested) in pursuit of salient goals, the more difficult it will be to 'cut losses' and quit. For decision-makers, to do so will involve admitting to themselves and to others, who often possess sanctions, that wrong – perhaps disastrous – choices were made in the past and that sacrifices demanded have been in vain. Thus, the tendency is to make further investments, partly to justify the initial ones and partly to indicate continued faith in original choices. Up to some point – not yet clearly understood – the larger the previous sacrifices, the more the pressure to increase further investments in trying to achieve success, even though the indications of probable failure might be so clear that there is an obvious risk of 'throwing good money after bad'.

A second major factor in the entrapment process which reinforces the propensity to go on investing is the tendency of decision-makers subjectively to evaluate further investments (which are regarded as 'investments' rather than 'costs') as worth less than might an 'objective' observer, especially 'at the margin' – that is, when viewed as additional investments to those already made. In other words, entrapment increases the tendency for decision-makers to see sacrifices as incremental additions, often small compared with what has already been invested in the pursuit of the desired goals. To bankers who have already loaned $10 billion to some Third World government, a request for an additional $0.5 billion may appear less than to the same bankers facing an initial request from another government for precisely the same amount. A military commander who has already committed 15 divisions to a battle is likely to find it easier to add another 2 in order to justify his original decision to fight that battle, quite apart from the impact the additional 2 divisions might have on ensuring victory. In both cases, the marginal addition of investment appears less to a committed decision-maker, an observation that has led Brockner and Rubin to argue that decision-makers are much more 'rationally' cost and benefit aware at the start of any process of commitment to a course of action than they are later, once well committed – and hence 'entrapped'.

A third argument from entrapment theory that seems highly relevant for the initiation of conciliatory processes is that the more decision-makers feel personally responsible for a course of action, however unsuccesful it proves, the more the process of entrapment will make them wish to justify their choice by making further investments in continuing that policy (Staw 1976). In political terms, those identified with starting a policy are likely to be heavily committed to its continuation and hence more unwilling to think about abandoning the policy even when there is evidence that it is far from achieving its goals. In many ways, this suggestion might help to explain the anecdotally observed fact that governments that begin wars do not make peace – when the time has come to make peace, new leaders come into office who are not identified with previous policies. While this piece of conventional wisdom is usually employed to explain why an adversary will be willing to deal with new leaders, it is equally a comment on why original leaders will not face failure and reverse policies until every last effort has been exhausted.

A number of modifications should be made in this simple 'responsibility increases commitment and hence entrapment' argument, however. For example, Brockner and Rubin (1985) make the point that an individual's sense of responsibility for a policy may be less intense in its entrapping effects than a group's sense of responsibility. There is the possibility of a diffusion of individual responsibility within leadership groups, so that individual members may feel less committed to a group-decided, but failing, policy.

On the other hand, there are numerous historical examples of individual leaders becoming thoroughly committed to policies chosen through group-based processes – and, indeed, of decision-makers becoming thoroughly committed to a policy they have inherited, so that, as in the case of the US policy towards Vietnam, the failing policy continues under several 'generations' of leaders. Such examples argue that factors other than the need for individual self justification can produce strong entrapment effects, and work to make decisions emerging from groups even more entrapping than decisions made individually and privately.

Glen Whyte, for example, points to the well-documented tendency of groups to make 'more extreme' decisions than the individuals making up the group would if the choice were to be made individually (Whyte 1993). He then goes on to note the individual aversion to sure loss of previous effort represented by abandonment of an existing policy, plus the resultant willingness to invest further in an existing course of action suggested by prospect theory. Finally he argues that, groups exacerbate the effects of individual members' biases through such pressures for uniformity and consensus as 'groupthink' (Janis 1982), the pressure to maintain good relations with other group members, and Asch's (1951) 'majority effect' increasing with the level of uncertainty. Hence there will usually be a strong 'conservative' tendency among groups, encouraging a choice to carry on and invest more in an existing policy, rather than abandon it and try something new and uncertain: if a majority of group members initially advocate increasing commitment ... as prospect theory implies, uniformity pressures will facilitate conformity to the majority view and ensure that the majority preference is reflected in the group decision.' (ibid. p.435), so that an 'escalating commitment may occur more frequently in group than in individual decision-making' (ibid. p.434).

Another factor enhancing the strength of entrapment is early opposition, which may make it yet more difficult for leaders to reverse course later and attempt conciliation. Among findings about entrapment in organisational settings, Fox and Staw (1979) have discovered that early opposition experienced by decision-makers to a particular course of action is likely to increase the degree of entrapment later in that course of action. The reason for this is simply that 'if decision-makers adopt a policy in spite of initial resistance to it, then they will be even more motivated to justify the appropriateness of the plan if it produces undesirable results in the short run.' (Brockner and Rubin 1985, pp.97–8). Of course, as far as political decisions about initiating conflicts by government cabinets, committees and polit-buros are concerned, internal dissension and disagreement appear to be the rule rather than the exception! Thus, while entrapping decisions made in groups may permit a diffusion of a sense of personal responsibility among decision-makers, within-group divisions, disagreements and resistance to options are more likely to make those whose proposed policy is eventually adopted more zealous in defending it internally and justifying the original choice by further investment, even if things are going badly wrong.

Moreover, this effect is likely to be reinforced if, as in many cases involving long-drawn-out, costly conflict, opposition arises within the party in general. Overcoming opposition within a government, from a formal political opposition or in the country at large, is likely to increase the commitment of those responsible for and identified with the 'successful' choice – that is, the one that was adopted as official policy.[2] Lastly, there is a large body of experimental and anecdotal evidence to the effect that leaders become more entrapped when they are concerned about how their decision (or a reversal of a previous set of decisions) is observed by an audience. This is particularly so if that audience is either (1) esteemed in some way by the decision-maker; or (2) in a position to impose sanctions, such as loss of career prospects, or ejection from office. Partly, this constraining factor is a matter of what psychologists call 'self-presentation' or, in everyday language, the problem of 'saving face' or not looking a fool in order to avoid loss of support or reputation. Concerning experimental findings, Brockner and Rubin say that 'Time and again it was reported that decision-makers became more ... entrapped when their need to save face was high.' (1985, p.126). In the case of the political decision-making involved in starting and prosecuting a major conflict, it is hardly likely that this process will take place other than before an 'interested and affected audience'. In some conflicts, it may be possible to delude followers for a time about the nature of the decision-making process that took them into a protracted conflict – that is, about who was responsible for the selection of an option for coercion and war, or what has been the relative success or failure of the selected course of action to date. However, the fact that such an audience inevitably exists seems very likely to affect significantly the decision-makers' own sense of entrapment in the chosen course of action. The costs in 'face saving' and in the presentation of self to valued or sanctioning others seem likely to be very high in terms of lessening political support or even complete loss of office if decision-makers eventually admit earlier errors and concurrent failure. Hence, it seems likely to be the rule rather than the exception that decision-makers' psychological and behavioural reactions will be to deny failure and increase the justificatory additional investment in the original course of action. The likely effects of such a reaction on the unlikelihood of concessions and the start of conciliation need not be spelled out.

2.2   Entrapment and political costs

Viewed in a slightly different way, the idea of decision-makers entrapping themselves into a failing coercive policy from which it is difficult to escape can take the form of those decision-makers actually facing high and deterring political costs of reversal, which they evaluate as outweighing the immediate and, perhaps, even long-term costs of continuing that policy. In the longer-term case, the eventual costs of failure are being deferred, possibly to be paid by others, while decision-makers are also likely to cling to a belief that there is a good chance that the balance of advantage will turn against the adversary, so that the costs of continuing will be offset by long term success, even if the latter turns out to be more limited than complete 'victory'.

Furthermore, leaders need not necessarily be the victims of entrapping processes which are solely psychological in order to recognise that they, their faction or their entire government may face realistically heavy costs if they are forced to 'back down', reverse a policy that they have been advocating as the correct one for some time, or admit that the investment in the pursuit of their chosen policy has been in vain. Most modern societies seem, at least somewhere in their culture, to have considerable respect for the norms of both consistency and persistence, and to have lesser respect for flexibility and a willingness to learn about and from one's own errors.[3]

The punishment for 'having misled' a country's electorate or another constituency can be severe, and something that most leaders would rather put off or avoid altogether if this is possible. Decision-makers' feeling of entrapment may arise from a sensible and quite 'rational' fear of loss of influence, loss of reputation or loss of office. 'Costs of reversal' need have no connection with losses already suffered as a result of the conflict, but can take the form of feared future events which result in leaders losing rewards or office, the anticipation of which can work against abandoning the conflict.

Add to these anticipated costs (1) the sacrificed investments which have already been devoted to coercing the adversary and trying to achieve the goals in dispute; (2) the opportunity costs represented by these goals, particularly in terms of the objectives of other, rival factions within the decision-making group *not* pursued because of limited means; (3) the preparations for further efforts which would be wasted by the abandonment of the present policy; and (4) the decision-making time and effort already devoted to carrying through the strategy thus far – and one has a long list of reasons for wanting to avoid reversing course and an equally compelling reason for not abandoning the previously chosen policy. Moreover, these constraints are likely to apply equally to leaders wishing to initiate some form of conciliatory move and to leaders in a party which is the target of some gesture of conciliation designed to elicit a response that will involve at least some reversal of existing policies. Both initiation and response may be constrained by intra-party factors likely to go unrecognised by the adversary.

Costs of reversal that form major obstacles to modifying a policy which has been the subject of much internal dissension and involved high levels of sacrifice are well illustrated by the Government of North Vietnam's tenacity during the 1960s in pursuing a policy of all-out military effort to free the South (as opposed to the use of political and diplomatic means or a lower-level, protracted guerrilla war). The military strategy had been advocated within the Central Committee by Le Duan, Le Duc Tho and their 'southern' faction, in the face of apparently strong opposition by those, like General Giap, who advocated building up the economy of the North and a slower, more cautious effort in the South. Having won that debate by arguing that quick success was likely owing to the political and military chaos in the South and the improbability of direct US intervention, this faction appeared to become dominant during the mid-1960s in North Vietnamese decision-making regarding the South. It also became committed to, and entrapped by, the policy it had fought for, as the strategy of a rapid 'push' to liberate the South appears to have been adopted after facing considerable internal opposition within both Plenum and Central Committee, and had originally been endorsed officially at the 1960 Party Congress. However, it was a policy posited on the achievement of rapid success in 1964–5 and no further US involvement.

The United States, of course, did respond with increased military assistance, direct military intervention and a ferocious air war, which extended to bombing the North Vietnamese supply trails southwards, as well, eventually, as North Vietnam itself, in order to coerce Hanoi into abandoning its strategy of infiltration and increased guerrilla activity and into negotiating an 'acceptable' settlement. However, as Wallace Thies points out, the faction in the North Vietnamese Government that had initiated, argued for, and succeeded in getting the adoption of the 'forward' military policy was thoroughly entrapped by it, particularly in view of the long preparations and longer debate that had led up to the final commitment. Thies's comments about the Le Duan faction reinforce many of the points about entrapment already made, for he argues that the costs of policy reversal were, for them, far too high. Such men (and, in effect, the whole DRV leadership) had

> invested a quarter century or more in the struggle for national independence and reunification ... [and] had also engaged in a 10 year effort to promote the cause of armed struggle in the South and increase the North's role in the war. This latest effort, moreover, was one in which careers and professional reputations had been staked on the argument that a quick victory in the South was possible and that the Americans could be defeated if they intervened. To have reversed themselves in the face of the bombing would not only have constituted a tacit admission

that they had been wrong all along ... but would possibly have jeopardised their position in the Party hierarchy. (Thies 1980, p.262)

Moreover, quite aside from the status of certain individuals within the Party hierarchy, there existed other more practical obstacles to reversal, to 'calling the whole thing off'. One of these consisted of the resources poured into preparations for the struggle in the South.

> By March 1965 ... DRV preparations for a wider war had been under way for more than six years. In the process ... regimental size units had been created in the South and equipped with modern, Soviet-style weapons; an extensive and highly effective logistical system had been set up; a sizeable apparatus for training men and infiltrating them from North to South was in place; and preparation had been made in anticipation of an American invasion of the North. Even considered separately, each of these was no small undertaking; considered together, they represented an enormous investment in human and material resources ... When large organisations are created and thousands of military and civilian personnel mobilised to staff them, the momentum built up is not easily reversed. To have expected ... that elements of the DRV leadership would argue (successfully) that the fruits of six years of hard labor should be thrown away, especially when victory in the South was so near, simply because of a few air strikes ... appears, in retrospect, to have been the height of folly. (ibid. p.269)

2.3   The need to escape entrapment

The arguments and examples above indicate the nature and range of serious psychological and political obstacles to changing course during a conflict and beginning a successful conciliation process. The obstacles posed to conciliation by the phenomenon of entrapment, and by leaders' consciousness of the associated costs of reversal, are considerable.

Literature from organisation theory does offer some suggestions for overcoming entrapment in situations where a change of commercial or investment policy is indicated by lack of success – a situation probably easier to recognise in cases of injudicious economic investment, when losses are repeated and clear cut, than in protracted social conflicts. Whether remedies such as setting prior limits on effort or on total investment, building in agreed 'opt out' points, prior awareness of entrapment phenomena, or a more accurate understanding of the nature, value and costs of 'success' will also work to avoid entanglement in major social conflicts is another matter, given that such conflicts are almost always:

1   Examples of phenomena in which costs are 'front loaded' and 'benefit deferred' until the final stage of the interaction, often making further

investment a 'rational' decision in order to continue to have any chance of offsetting costs from final benefits; and

2 Examples of ambiguous situations in which, according to Simonson and Staw 'future returns depend upon innumerable uncertainties in one's organisation and economic environment.' (1992, p.120).

These last authors suggest that remedies, that might help leaders avoid entrapment are based on principles firstly of 'threat reduction', minimising the need for self- or external justification; and, secondly, of stimulating more accurate decision-making. Under the first principle, they suggest – rather unrealistically – keeping key decisions confidential and non-attributable. More interesting is their suggestion that, by recognising the existence of high uncertainty and relying less on 'accountability by outcomes' and more on 'accountability by process' – that is, having followed normally effective decision processes – in evaluating leaders' 'success', much of what they term 'evaluation apprehension' might be avoided, and more effective choices made.

Under the second principle of 'decisional vigilance', they advocate being clear and specific about the original goals of the policy; using procedures to ensure a thorough evaluation of all options, including reasons for and against selecting each alternative; outlining minimum targets which, if not achieved, will serve as an agreed threshold for considering a justifiable change of strategy; and including in the original strategic decision a planned alternative course of action as a legitimate possibility arising from agreed-upon evidence that targets were not being met and that back-up procedures should be activated. This might be termed the 'On to Plan B' rather than 'We are not interested in the possibility of defeat' principle.

There may be some occasions on which such remedies for entrapment might be usable in protracted conflicts, so that some psychological and psycho-political obstacles to altering a strategy of continued coercion can be removed. Unfortunately, however, these are not the only obstacles to initiating conciliation, for while it may be the case that escaping at least from psychological entrapment is a basic requirement for the beginning of successful conciliation, it is not enough in and of itself. Conflicts differ from many entrapping situations in that final escape and reversal of a pattern of interaction involve at least two parties, rather than the one involved in other cases of entrapment. While it may be enough for a firm to recognise that further investment in an unsuccessful but prestigious design is fruitless and wasteful, with regard to a policy of coercing another party in a dispute it requires more than such a recognition to bring that policy to an end. Conciliation and the ending of a conflict might demand that a party first escape from a process of entrapment, but also required are successful signalling of that escape to an adversary, the clear indication of a willingness to talk, and a more-or-less simultaneous agreement on the appropriateness of negotiations.

In other words, a party's recognition of its entrapment and determination to escape from it and face the costs of reversal, may be a necessary condition for the start of conflict termination through de-escalation, but it is nowhere near sufficient. Other obstacles attend further aspects of accommodation and conciliation.

3   Intra-party differences over strategy

The first part of this chapter emphasised the absence of internal consensus as one of the likely obstacles to sending any clear and unambiguous signal to an adversary to the effect that an initiator was willing to begin talking about a compromise settlement.

In any protracted conflict, internal disagreements about the course of that conflict and the relative balance of advantage at any point in time are likely to widen cleavages existing within a government or decision-making elite, and lead to bitter in- fighting over whether, when and how to signal a willingness to talk to an adversary. The intra-party 'game', to use Putnam's metaphor, is likely to become more rancorous and much more dangerous for decision-makers. The effects of this absence of consensus on the necessity for, timing of, and likely success of, clear signalling are further discussed below, in section 5. First, it is necessary to outline the kind of constraint imposed on any leadership by this lack of consensus and say something about the nature of the differences that frequently come into being as a result of confronting the choice between carrying on or quitting.

Examples of conciliatory processes usually show that differences within a leadership can be created – or, if they exist already, substantially exacerbated – over a number of issues involved in any decision to signal a willingness to compromise:

1 Differences about the *need* for conciliation, accommodation and a negotiated settlement;
2 Differences about the best *method* of beginning a successful accommodative sequence and later bringing about an acceptable settlement;
3 Differences about the *timing and tempo* of conciliatory tactics;
4 Differences, on a tactical level, about the nature and level of *appropriate response* from the target, if the initial feelers are to be extended and the process continued;
5 Differences over the *uneven distribution of sacrifices* demanded by any future compromise or accommodation.

Of these issues, it is usually the first which presents the most serious initial obstacle to achieving any consensus among decision-makers about conciliatory processes. The key question is whether decision-makers can agree that they have arrived at the optimal – or sometimes the least bad –

point for ending the conflict, after which the balance of advantage will turn irrevocably against them; or that they are already on the downward slope towards defeat and disaster – however distant this might be – so that terminating the conflict 'now' will offer unambiguous advantages over having to terminate it 'later' from an even more marked position of disadvantage.

A major part of the problem is the difficulty of arriving at a clear and certain evaluation of the two sides' relative positions of advantage in the struggle; and of extrapolating the present position to that likely to exist in the future. Even leaving aside entrapment effects discussed above, honest differences of opinion about likely future success or about changes in military, economic or diplomatic fortune, are likely to exist and exist justifiably within a group of leaders contemplating the future of the dispute in which they are engaged. Iklé talks about the 'fog of military estimates' in this connection and quotes Clausewitz to the effect that a great part of the information obtained in war is 'contradictory, a still greater part is false, and by far the greatest part is subject to considerable uncertainty' (1989, p.17). It takes time for the facts and implications of political stalemate or military reversal to sink in, particularly as leaders conducting a war have a political and psychological investment in hoping for, and seeking out, best interpretations. Stalemates have to last for a long time before it is accepted that they are unlikely to be broken and that a war of attrition might be a costly and ultimately unsuccessful way of achieving goals sought originally by rapid military victory.[4] Disasters can – for a time – be rationalised away.

Acknowledging the lack of success of coercive strategies is likely to come at different times to different leaders, so that a consensus on the need to compromise and negotiate will usually develop slowly. Recognition of this necessity is likely to come initially to those leaders who were originally sceptical of (and least committed to) a policy of coercion; and lastly to those directly responsible for the policy's adoption and execution. The latter will, indeed, have too much invested to quit in terms of both political position and professional reputation, and are likely to feel that early adherents to a negotiated end to the conflict are both personal and national traitors. Debate between 'pro-continuation' and 'pro-conciliation' factions is likely to be bitter and divisive. A strong consensus about the need to compromise frequently takes a long time to emerge, particularly in the many cultures where the value attached to persistence and unwavering commitment is very high. In some cases such a consensus never emerges. In others, the dispute is continued inconclusively, with marked disagreements among decision-makers. In still others, what Charles Hermann calls a 'regime change' occurs, and the pro-continuation faction is ejected from office and replaced by a leadership united in a commitment to end the conflict, if suitable terms can be gained. Even when the existing leadership remains in office and arrives at a – perhaps temporary – consensus to try for a negotiated end to the dispute, other differences frequently persist and present obstacles to signalling a clear willingness to talk about compromise.

Disagreements can arise about means and methods for making concilia- tory gestures. Some decision-makers will advocate a simultaneous strategy of continuing coercion – perhaps even increasing it – to show that the offer of negotiation does not arise from weakness, while indicating the possibil- ity of fruitful negotiations, provided indications are received from the target that these will take place 'under the right conditions'. Other leaders may advocate a sequential strategy of abandoning or suspending salient forms of coercion (a temporary truce, a bombing pause, a release of prison- ers) while efforts are made to reduce tension, build confidence and begin preliminaries for negotiation. Yet others may argue for a strategy of tit-for- tat, de-escalating initially and then responding appropriately to the target's response; or for making some concession provided one is first offered as a gesture of good faith by the adversary.

Whatever the situation *vis-à-vis* the adversary, achieving a continuing consensus about the strategy and tactics of conciliation is a difficult and time-consuming matter. It is one which, to the confusion of the adversary, is often subject to reversals and revisions, either because of continuing arguments about means or more fundamental disagreements about the real need to abandon a policy of winning through coercion. Moreover, debates and disagreements about means frequently involve differences over the timing and tempo of conciliatory initiatives. What is an appropriate point at which to start some programme of conciliatory moves and signals? Does one wait until some coercive tactic has succeeded to make clear that the offer of compromise does not arise from a sense of failure? If so, what are the agreed indicators of success? Does one take advantage of some symbolic incident or time – a Christmas truce which can be extended, a call for peace from some internationally recognised individual or institution? Or does one merely take a decision and press onward, on the grounds that it is better to begin early rather than wait for a temporary internal consensus to become unravelled and frustrate future moves towards a settlement?

Finally, another disagreement likely to place an obstacle in the way of beginning a successful process of de-escalation is over the eminently practi- cal issue of what constitutes a 'satisfactory reponse' from the target, indi- cating clearly that:

1   the initiative has been picked up and interpreted correctly by the target's decision-makers; and
2   the target is also willing to make conciliatory gestures and concessions in order to continue the movement towards a negotiated settlement?

For some members of the initiator's governing body, a minor gesture will often be enough to encourage them in the belief that their signal has been received, understood and answered appropriately. The same gesture will be regarded by others as either inadequate or as a trap, and demands consequently made for much more significant indications of the target's willingness to conciliate and compromise.[5] The debate on how 'satisfactory' is a target's response, and how 'serious' its leaders in their wish to compromise, is likely to have a major effect on whether the accommodative sequence accelerates, is delayed significantly or abandoned as pointless.

The list of obstacles discussed above applies equally to other key parties in the interaction. A target's leaders are equally likely to be divided internally over the existing balance of advantage at the time their opponent signals a willingness to talk or be conciliatory. Pro-continuation factions are likely to be committed to 'carrying on' and to be able to see 'light at the end of the tunnel', where pro-conciliation factions see only continuing darkness. Leaders' positions are equally likely to be tied to existing policies and expectations of success. In addition, however, significant differences are likely to arise about the interpretation of the initiators' signal, with psychological factors influencing whether individual leaders will recognise the move as a 'genuine' conciliatory gesture, and political considerations affecting whether anyone will openly acknowledge and view as significant the nature of a conciliatory move by the enemy. To that degree, the target's dilemma seems more complicated than that of the initiator, although in both cases the eventual decision to launch or respond to an initiative depends largely on the nature, extent and intensity of the intra-party divisions that already exist or are opened up by the other's move. I discuss factors affecting a target's response in Chapter 11.

4   Major intra-party divisions and constraints

While to some degree intra-party differences and disagreements about initiating a conciliatory process arise from the nature of dilemmas facing leaders, they are also much affected by the structure of elite factions, groups or institutions involved in policy making, by the expectations and aspirations of rank-and-file constituents and by relations with allies. For example, it is a very different thing to initiate peace feelers from within a single government involved in a conflict, however divided, compared with undertaking a similar initiative as one government within an alliance of other governments. Difficulties are multiplied when a potential initiating party is characterised by fundamental ideological or organisational cleavages at the elite level, rather than a unified leadership with a similar mind set.

Of course, as Margaret Hermann points out, the type of 'leadership' in a party in conflict will have a major effect on any decisions about strategy, large or small (Hermann 1995). Whether the leader is a single person, a cabal or an elected executive with a complex validation process, its involvement with the conflict will differ over time, as will its degree of accountability, sensitivity to intra-party moods and attitudes, and the general level of support from constituents which it enjoys. However, even in a situation where conciliation is clearly 'leader driven', as was the case with Sadat's visit to Israel, and the leader is able to impose his own vision of the necessary redirection of policy, divisions over the change in policy can remain profound and compensating actions be necessary. Sadat, for example, made sure that his delegation to Israel contained a representative balance of key interests in Egypt (military, technocrats, 'conservative' and 'radical' political tendencies, urban and rural notables) and, on his return from Jerusalem, made it his business to strengthen the influence of institutions and groups in Egypt that would support a peace agreement with Israel (Friedlander 1983; Stein 1993). Even so, domestic opposition in Egypt to Sadat's strategy grew after November 1977, revealing a major absence of consensus about accommodation with Israel at both elite and constituency levels.

Any lack of a consensus about the need to offer concessions and to conciliate, or about the most appropriate means of doing so, can thus afflict various types of decision-making group, ranging from a single group of leaders to a coalition of such groups. The following list is only suggestive of the different potential divisions or 'structures of cleavage' that might exist in different parties in a complex conflict to bedevil efforts to signal an adversary when starting a conciliatory initiative:

1 Divisions within top decision-makers themselves (civilian and military officials, diplomats and politicians, 'hawks and doves'), which could result in those opposing an initiative sabotaging or leaking details of a proposed gesture.
2 Divisions between decision-makers and domestic political opponents at the elite level (government ministers and parliamentary opposition, political parties in power and those out of power). Such domestic adversaries could oppose conciliatory initiatives simply as an integral part of their more general role as intra-party rivals or oppositionists, or through genuine disgreements about how to conduct the conflict.[6]
3 Divisions between decision-makers and aroused and committed constituents, whether such rank-and-file opinion consists of single issue publics, interested and influential publics in general or – more rarely but not infrequently when a major conflict is involved – the general mass public which has usually been previously mobilised in support of the struggle by the leaders.
4 Divisions between decision-makers and the leaders of other allied or aligned parties. Such allies or patrons might view possible conciliation as a surrender of their interests and, if so, would oppose any initiative.

The extent to which such divisions and resulting dissensus present obstacles to launching a conciliatory initiative depends firstly upon the development of a pro-conciliation faction somewhere within the top echelons of decision-makers; and secondly on the potential costs to pro-continuation factions threatened by pro-conciliation forces, which might, at times, include an outraged general public which feels betrayed and misled by its leaders.

However, pro-conciliation factions, even if their members occupy power-ful offices within a governing hierarchy, often feel deterred from even con-sidering launching what they perceive as necessary and too-long-delayed conciliatory moves if the costs to them are also likely to be high – wide-spread criticism, accusations of selling out, loss of support, loss of office, in some cases even loss of freedom. Naturally, the level of potential costs to pro-conciliation decision-makers will vary over time, especially if it becomes clearly the case that the balance of advantage is turning in favour of the adversary. However, the deterrent effect of any domestic lack of con-sensus will be affected by the level of political support for those leaders, including such factors as their degree of: (i) vulnerability to loss of office; (ii) inconsistency represented by their new advocacy of a conciliatory strat-egy and (iii) lost credibility likely to be suffered by their adoption of a policy involving a public U-turn.

In addition, pro-conciliation decision-makers often have to weigh poten-tial costs of launching peace feelers which arise from the reactions of allies outside the domestic arena.[7] Allies' protests, leaks, agitation or even efforts to sabotage conciliatory initiatives constitute powerful obstacles to success-ful accommodation, either through the anticipation of such reactions (and a consequent deterrent effect) or through actual behaviour to ensure that conciliatory gestures are undermined or offset by escalatory actions.

Major obstacles can also arise even from clients who are ostensibly dependent upon an initiator for their very survival, but who are worried that their particular interests are likely to be sacrificed should their patron become conciliatory in the search for a compromise solution. The United States frequently found that its efforts to de-escalate the stuggle in Vietnam as a preliminary stage in a peacemaking process were frustrated as much by the activities of the regime in Saigon, determined to wreck any compromise that did not take their minimum objectives into account, as by intransi-gence in Hanoi. Similarly, the anticipated costs to Arab leaders of any uni-lateral and 'premature' peacemaking with Israel constantly deterred most from making even minimal conciliatory gestures towards their adversary. They were undoubtedly a major negative factor in Presidents Sadat's calcu-lations about the costs and benefits of his Jerusalem initiative (Friedlander 1983). The wisdom of such a cautious weighing of gains and losses seems to have been borne out by the experience of Sadat following both his visit to Jerusalem in 1977 and the process that ended in the 1979 Egyptian/Israeli Peace Treaty, which cost Egypt and its President dearly in terms of economic support from Arab oil countries, of Egypt's position as political leader in the Arab world, and of continued overt hostility (plus specific efforts to undermine and overthrow the Egyptian government) from the Arab world in general – and the members of the Rejectionist Front in particular.

5   Intra party divisions and unsuccessful signals

This summary of the nature of the 'internal' obstacles to initiating some form of accommodative sequence next requires some consideration of the likely effects of such internal divisions, lack of consensus, in-fighting, and factional disagreement about continuing a conflict or conciliating. What, specifically, are the effects of such constraints on the process of signalling conciliation to a target, and in what manner might the existence of such obstacles interfere with the successful launching of an accommodative sequence leading towards a non-coercive solution?

At its most extreme, the obvious way in which internal divisions and disagreements can interfere with the process of launching some de-escalatory initiative is by aborting the whole process so that no conciliatory gesture is ever made. In such cases, some decision-makers, at least, consider the option of such an initiative, but are deterred from signalling by a lack of internal consensus or by the anticipated costs to themselves, their institution or their government. Lack of success is complete – no 'initiation' takes place.

Other effects might be less extreme, but almost equally detrimental to starting a process of conciliation. Internal constraints can result in:

1   *Muted*, unobtrusive or unnoticeable signals being sent to a Target.
2   *Delayed* signals being sent, so that these arrive at inappropriate times or too late to have the effect on the target anticipated by the initiator.
3   *Mixed*, *ambiguous* or *contradictory* signals, such that the target is unable to distinguish genuine conciliatory gestures from signals conveying other (often coercive) messages.

Leaving aside the case in which the anticipated costs in terms of internal unity or political fortune deters a group of decision-makers entirely, why might internal divisions and disagreements lead to these other effects on signals intended to convey conciliatory gestures?

5.1   Muted signals

In the case of muted signals, which may, because of their frequently incremental nature, pass unnoticed by the target, much evidence indicates that these arise through a compromise between: (1) those arguing for a clear indication of their party's willingness to talk; (2) those arguing that such a gesture will only be interpreted as a sign of weakness and lack of will by the target; and (3) those arguing that the shortest way of ending the conflict is by escalation, greater levels of coercion and a major effort to break the adversary's will to continue.

Frequently, the result of such differences seems to be that the leaders compromise and agree to a minor gesture of de-escalation as a means of 'testing the water', one which partially satisfies those pressing for moves towards negotiation while not thoroughly outraging those demanding increased coercion and a strategy of not 'showing weakness'.

An example of this problem of internal constraints resulting in the sending of only muted signals to a target could well be the minor decline in Viet Cong guerrilla activity recorded but regarded as insufficient by the US Government during the period of the 37-day bombing pause on North Vietnam, begun on 24 December, 1965. Given the divisions within the North Vietnamese Government at that time, between those led by Le Duan who advocated pressing on for a quick victory, and those more cautiously advocating a negotiated settlement which allowed the US an easy exit from South Vietnam, a minor de-escalation of military activity might well have been the only compromise gesture that could be agreed in Hanoi. As with many such compromise gestures, this seems to have been too muted a signal to have had any impact on US decision-makers, so that the conciliatory process aborted (Thies 1980, p.118).

5.2   Delayed and mis-timed signals

The December 1965 US bombing pause mentioned above may also provide an example of the delaying effect of internal divisions. The existence of major divisions between decision-makers is often likely to result in a long-drawn-out debate about whether, when and how to launch a conciliatory initiative – or when and how to respond. This can have the effect of fatally delaying a move, so that it occurs at an inappropriate time, often far too late to have the impact necessary to launch a conciliation process successfully. In this case, the resolution of internal debates within the North Vietnamese Government over whether to respond to US initiatives accompanying the bombing pause came too late to have any effect on US decisions to end the pause and escalate the air war still further. What might have proved a North Vietnamese offer to open substantive negotiations arrived at the US/North Vietnamese contact point in Rangoon on the evening of the day that US bombing of the North resumed. The episode might well illustrate those cases in which domestic constraints in a target result in a delay during which the 'doves' temporarily overcome the 'hawks'' reluctance to respond. The delay can result in the initiative being destroyed because it has given the initiator's 'hawks' an opportunity to overcome their own 'doves' with the argument that there has been no response from an obviously uninterested and intransigent target (Thies 1980, pp.113–20 and 312–13).

5.3 Contradictory signals

The US bombing pause in 1965 may also illustrate the third effect of internal divisions and constraints on clear signalling of concessions: the fact that internal divisions lead frequently to mixed, ambiguous and contradictory signals which may abort any move towards accommodation. While it is certainly the case that US decision-makers intended to make a clear conciliatory gesture by halting their bombing from 24 December 1965 to 31 January 1966 and that they accompanied this with several other signals to Hanoi indicating that they were seeking a reciprocal move to start substantive negotiations, it is also the case that during this same period the US government: (i) increased the level of aggressive ground activity – search and destroy operations – in South Vietnam; and (ii) introduced an additional 8500 US troops there. Moreover, a few days after the ending of the bombing pause and while the US was still trying to sustain the momentum towards negotiation, US and South Vietnamese leaders met in Honolulu and produced a Declaration, promising to continue the fight against the Vietcong and insisting that there was no question of negotiation, let alone one of forming a coalition government – Hanoi's minimum demand. Given the range of ambiguous and contradictory signals directed at them by the US Government, it is hardly surprising that decision-makers in Hanoi chose to proceed cautiously on the basis of a worst-case analysis of the initiative, to respond minimally, and to assume that the US was operating in bad faith solely to probe North Vietnamese commitment and determination.

6 Noise, mixed signals and lack of impact

The US/North Vietnamese examples seem all too typical of problems that leaders face in making conciliatory gestures against a background of other signals, many of which convey to a target contrary information about intentions and credibility, thus negating any positive impact a conciliatory signal might have. The conciliatory move 'gets lost' in the noise of other actions and signals; or is discounted as an isolated aberration among other coercive signals indicating the adversary's 'true' intent. This is particularly the case when the parties are involved in a long-term pattern of mutual coercion and violence, when both are pursuing a strategy of either coercive warfare or simultaneous 'carrots and sticks'. With both strategies, conciliation is likely to be submerged in coercion and the carrot vanishes among all the sticks.

Even at lower levels of overt conflict, during stalemates or mutual 'stand-offs', conciliatory gestures are likely to be incrementally de-escalatory at best, and hence likely to be lost in the noise of mixed signals exchanged by adversaries. Five reasons can be suggested for the almost inevitable difficulty of mixed signals being sent to a target and the consequent problem of underlining or emphasising the conciliatory gesture so that its occurrence and meaning will be unmistakable. Firstly, parties engaged in efforts to get an adversary to the negotiating table through simultaneous (or even sequential) strategies of coercion and conciliation will inevitably direct a barrage of signals towards the target which may seem perfectly differentiated to the initiator, but ambiguous and contradictory to a target that does not share the assumptions or frame of reference of the Initiator. Secondly, internal divisions within the Initiator will result in the apparently monolithic institution of, say, a national government speaking with many, often contradictory, voices. This will particularly be the case when issues of continuing the struggle or compromising are debated, so that cleavages open between 'hawks' and 'doves'; and even more so when leaders are tied to coalition partners whose pronouncements contribute to the 'noise' of contradictory signals.

Thirdly, if divisions are wide and bitter, it is often the case that those in favour of fighting on by continuing coercion will be able to sabotage conciliatory gestures by countervailing, coercive actions that easily confirm to their counterparts in the target that the gestures are merely public relations exercises, traps, probes or efforts to test out commitment and will. Such actions help to discredit 'doves' in both initiator and target. Additionally, and fourthly, even relatively united parties in a conflict face a multiple audience problem and have to communicate differently with each. Quite apart from signals to the adversary, governments – for example – have to communicate with legislatures, opinion leaders and the press; with other governments, allies, patrons or interested observers; and with their own constituents so that public opinion does not turn too massively or suddenly against present strategy. As each of these audiences has different goals and preferences, a set of leaders will have to convey different messages to each. Inevitably, much of this stream of signals will be picked up by decision-makers in the adversary and will play a part in the interpretation of signals directed at that adversary. The overall package of information available is likely to be ambiguous at least, and contradictory at worst.

For example, President Johnson's deliberate warning to the North Vietnamese regarding US commitment to South Vietnam, sent via a speech at UCLA in February 1964, was rapidly followed by three implicit and explicit denials (two by the President and one by Secretary of State Rusk) that this meant extending the war to North Vietnam. The latter were intended to calm an aroused anti-extension public in the USA, but they were undoubtedly also noted by decision-makers in Hanoi; as Wallace Thies comments, 'government leaders cannot tell an opponent to stop listening when they speak for domestic consumption only.' (Thies 1980, p.285).

Fifthly and finally, streams of ambiguous and wholly contradictory signals can result from the sheer complexity of conducting policy, and from the inability of complex parties such as governments to co-ordinate their initiatives into a coherent pattern that will carry a clear message of conciliation to an adversary. In connection with efforts by national governments to coerce an adversary, Thies refers to this as a problem of 'orchestration' but it is undoubtedly a more general problem of co-ordination of signalling for all parties in conflict, and one which affects efforts to use carrots and sticks, to implement an 'I-will-if-you-will' strategy, or to begin a process of conciliation by using unilateral initiatives as an initial tactic. Even when not engaged in a limited, or even all-out war to achieve particular goals, the implementation of a policy of compellence[8] or confrontation creates a multiplicity of problems for any leaders desiring to change that policy for a more conciliatory one.

As Graham Allison's work long ago made clear (1971), one of the major obstacles to carrying out a coherent and co-ordinated policy is the fact that the institution carrying out the policy – the national government, the union leadership, the organisation's governance structure – consists not of a rational, unitary actor but of a set of separate and usually competing leaders and agencies with interests of their own which they defend under normal circumstances, as well as under the abnormal circumstances attending stressful efforts to begin ending a conflict. Another obstacle is the disjunction between the top decision-makers, who assemble and consider a range of feasible options and then choose one or another for action, and the agencies actually charged with implementing that choice and sending the appropriate signal at the appropriate time.

The first obstacle leads to the probability, already noted and discussed, that a variety of signals may be sent in the direction of the target, simultaneously and confusingly. The second leads to the problem that, in implementing the chosen activity, the differing interests, timetables and standard operating procedures of the implementing agencies will interfere with the original intentions of those choosing the action. Hence, quite the wrong signal may be received by the target because of inappropriate execution or timing; or the right signal will be received but at such an inappropriate time that it interferes with other signals perhaps sent subsequently.

In the case of national governments, Thies has pointed out that the sheer size and complexity of their operations necessitates some division of labour and the granting of a large amount of flexibility to agencies charged with implementing policy. However, this inevitable division of labour and operational flexibility often works directly against the carrying through of any very coherent policy, especially *vis-à-vis* an adversary being coerced. It makes it likely that mistakes, delays, operational errors and communications breakdowns will result in the sending of incoherent and contradictory messages to a target. Sometimes the contradictions can occur through sheer accident or through operational conditions not taken into consideration at the decision-making levels where an initiative was chosen. As an example of such implementational errors, Theis (1980, pp.322–48) quotes the wrecking of a promising de-escalatory initiative through Warsaw by a sudden fierce increase in the bombing of Hanoi, authorised in early November 1996, delayed by subsequent bad weather, but carried out later, in mid-December, just as a peace initiative was being launched.[9]

The point about this example, and many others from that period of the Vietnam War and elsewhere, is that contradictory signals and coercive acts that undermine conciliatory moves often occur not through any conscious effort at sabotage but through the workings of complex bureaucracies which are so vast as to resist even the best efforts of top decision-makers to pursue an 'orchestrated', coherent or co-ordinated strategy, whether of escalation or conciliation.

7   Conclusion

The discussion of intra-party factors likely to affect the success of any con-ciliatory process has turned up a daunting if confusing list of potential bar-riers to the contemplation, selection and launching of any move in an accommodative sequence by an initiator, as well as to the likelihood of a positive response from a target. Some of these barriers are psychological, some political, some organisational. Some arise from the positions, expec-tations and ambitions of leaders within parties in conflict, others from the perceptions, attitudes and expectations (however overblown) of aroused constituencies within those same parties. Some affect leaders' abilities to bring up for serious discussion the possibility of launching a conciliatory signal. Still others present such high potential costs to those contemplating a conciliatory move that they are deterred from acting on their changed analysis of optimum strategies, as the move would be deemed surrender in the eyes of intra-party opponents or the mass of followers. Finally, there are similar intra-party contraints that hamper the making of any unambigu-ously conciliatory move in reaction to an adversary's attempt to initiate an accommodative sequence.

From this review of potential constraints, however, it is possible to take a more positive approach and to produce at least a tentative profile of the kind of intra-party circumstances that would be conducive to the consider-ing and launching of some conciliatory initiative, if only by noting factors which would encourage such a process through their absence! Clearly, the fewer the factions and cleavages within a party in conflict, the easier it will be for leaders to change course and implement conciliatory moves, once they themselves have concluded that some form of conciliatory strategy might be for the best. Given the inevitability of divisions between leaders and constituents in the real world, a situation of complete unity or unifor-mity is most unlikely in any party in conflict, but the degree of existing dis-unity within a party, particularly at the elite level, will clearly affect pro-conciliation leaders' ability to implement a change of course. Whether an elite is unified, divided or wholly fragmented makes a crucial difference to the ease with which conciliatory moves can be considered, discussed and implemented.

The continuing commitment of rank-and-file followers to the goals for which the struggle is being waged and to the need for continued sacrifice is another key influence on the likely success of a conciliatory initiative, at least as far as its launching is concerned. Strong grass roots opposition to continuing the conflict, as in the United States during the late 1960s regarding the Vietnam War, should usually make it easier for pro-conciliation factions within an elite to plan, propose and implement a popular conciliatory strategy. On the other hand, it is equally likely that constituents, having been convinced over a long period of time of the salience of goals, the malevolence of the adversary and the justness of the cause, will not be inclined to support a new strategy of 'appeasement' or 'abandonment'. The extent of grass-roots opposition will also provide an opportunity for rivals at the leadership level to capitalise on the likely unpopularity of leaders appearing to advocate a policy reversal, and thus create leadership divisions even in the unlikely event that none existed previously. Hence, a key consideration is likely to be the leaders' vulnerability, both to elite criticism and to rank-and-file protest.

Conceptually, this 'leadership vulnerability' aspect of conciliation processes should be thought of as leaders' internal weakness, a factor that is frequently confused with leaders' strength or weakness *vis-à-vis* their external adversary. These two characteristics need to be clearly distinguished, as weakness *vis-à-vis* an external adversary is not the same as weakness *vis-à-vis* domestic opposition, whether this consists of powerful elite rivals or massive unpopularity at the grass roots, constituency level. The point is well illustrated by the example of President Saddam Hussein of Iraq in 1992, who proved very weak in comparison with his international adversaries, but apparently invulnerable within Iraq itself – an example which emphasises that invulnerability can arise from a high level of popular support or from highly effective domestic coercion.

In certain cases, then, it may be that the leaders are relatively invulnerable as they have been in power for some time, are firmly in control and are able to nullify opposition at both elite and grass-roots levels. In others it may be that leaders' legitimacy – or even popularity – with grass-roots constituents makes them relatively insulated from elite criticism. In yet others, it may be that leaders seeking to implement a new strategy of conciliation with an external adversary can put together a coalition of individuals and factions who can see advantages in a new strategy, and who are strong enough to overcome others opposed to the change. Low vulnerability can take a variety of forms.

A third factor that may ease the task of a group of leaders seeking to initiate a conciliatory process is likely to be the degree of responsibility that group must take for the previous policy. There are two obvious aspects to this irresponsibility factor. The first is psychological and involves the degree to which the potential pro-conciliation group need to overcome their own level of commitment to, and entrapment, in the existing strategy of coercion and sacrifice. The second is political, and concerns the degree to which the group will be able to avoid accountability for a past strategy now being portrayed as fundamentally mistaken – a difficult task if all or any of the now pro-conciliation group have stridently and publicly supported the old policy in times past, and helped to convince rank-and-file constituents of the importance of the goals being pursued and the soundness of the means being used to pursue them. The lower its level of responsibility for previous strategies, the easier it is for a pro-conciliation group to initiate an alternative strategy.

To a large degree, of course, the strength of the opposition to conciliation and the ability of leaders to consider and implement a conciliatory strategy is intimately linked to the salience of the issues in conflict. It will usually be the case that protracted conflicts are not waged over issues that can be lightly abandoned, but factors that can assist in modifying a strategy in the direction of conciliation, compromise and a negotiated solution are either: (1) a relative lessening of the overall salience of the issues in conflict compared with a party's other goals and interests; or (2) a change in the balance of influence on policy between those for whom the issues in conflict are paramount, and those who give prominence to other aims and aspirations.[10]

This initial sketch of propitious intra-party circumstances for initiating a conciliatory move suggests that key factors are likely to involve a convinced and unified pro-conciliation leadership; either a unified pro-conciliation elite, or a strong faction supporting conciliation; leaders who possess the support and trust of rank-and-file constituents or who can survive public unpopularity during at least the initial stages of a conciliation process; a diminished salience for the issues in conflict, or the diminished influence of those for whom the issues do remain paramount; and an ability of the pro-conciliation faction to overcome both psychological and political entrapment, often through the factor of 'irresponsibility'.

It seems reasonable to add to this sketch the obstacle posed by the level of sacrifice already made in pursuit of 'victory', and by the investment effect. The larger the sunk costs expended by any party in conflict, the greater the psychological and political obstacles to abandoning the costly strategy and contemplating an alternative of conciliation.

Filling in further details of this profile will undoubtedly be helped by reviewing the factors also affecting likely target responses, for, as I noted earlier, many of the internal constraints on initiating a conciliatory process also affect the likelihood of a target being able (or willing) to recognise and respond to such a move by its adversary. However, the fact that a target faces some already undertaken action or statement from the other side, to which some response is anticipated – if not required – often adds further complications to the analysis of intra-party constraints on furthering a conciliatory process. These observations give rise to two further questions.

Firstly, what are the important additional effects – if any – of being the recipient of inevitably ambiguous signals on a target facing intra-party constraints on leaders' ability to respond positively, should they choose to do so?

Secondly, given a long list of intra-party factors that can – and often do – act as constraints on the successful launching of, reacting to, and continuing of a conciliatory process, what, theoretically, is the best mix of intra-party factors for the succesful conduct of an accommodative sequence? And what, practically, might be the range of strategies that could best be adopted to minimise the negative effects of intra-party obstacles to clear and effective signalling of conciliatory gestures, both by initiators and targets? These queries form major themes in the next chapters.

11
Obstacles to Prompt Reacting

'The question is whom one betrays by keeping one's promises.'
Malim Akerstrom

In Chapter 10 I discussed a number of internal obstacles, both political and psychological, to a party wishing to initiate a conciliatory process by sending a clear signal to its adversary. The signal, if actually made, could become the first move in an accommodative sequence, and the main argument of the last chapter was that a variety of intra-party factors would influence whether the signal was contemplated and undertaken, besides influencing the nature and clarity of that signal, as well as its credibility. Together with influences (previously discussed) arising from the overall circumstances of the conflict itself (the context), these factors should have a major effect on the immediate and longer-term success of the conciliatory move.

Throughout the chapter, I noted that many of the intra-party obstacles to initiating a clear signal to an adversary – a sense of entrapment, divided counsels, an aroused constituency – would also have a strong influence within the target on whether the conciliatory move was recognised as such and whether the leaders of that party felt able – and willing – to respond with a gesture of their own likely to be recognised as a positive response – and a *sufficiently* positive response – by the initiator. I also implied, however, that there were a number of additional constraining factors likely to be particularly influential on parties on the receiving end of conciliatory moves, and that these would need to be reviewed separately. This present chapter, therefore, discusses what I have termed the respondability of initiatives by considering intra-party factors influencing the nature of the response to a conciliatory move, whether it be positive, negative or wholly absent; and the characteristics of a target that will have an impact on the likely success of a conciliatory initiative (see Figure 11.1 overleaf).

Before starting these tasks, however, a preliminary question, which I raised briefly in Chapter 3, is whether it is always possible to distinguish

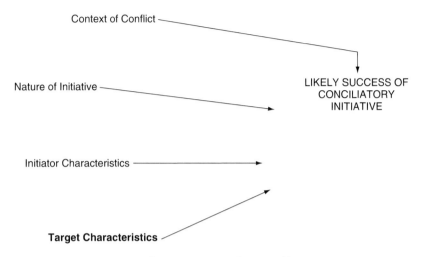

Figure 11.1   **Influences on Conciliation Effectiveness VI**

clearly between the initiating party and the target of a first conciliatory move.

1   Targets or initiators?

Although it may be easy (analytically and with hindsight) to identify sequences or stages in any conciliatory process and thus to determine what is an initiative and what a response from the target of that initiative, it is usually much less simple to those actually involved in such a complex interaction, particularly one which might already have involved a number of abortive attempts at initiating a process of conciliation.

It may seem clear, for example, that President Sadat's announcement of his willingness to go to Israel if invited by the Israeli Government constitutes an 'initiative', so that Prime Minister Begin's reply in the form of the invitation Sadat had requested was plainly a 'response'. However, this clear picture is somewhat muddied when one takes into account the previous signals that had been sent by Sadat and others, and the behind-the-scenes contacts that had taken place between Egyptians and Israelis even before Sadat's surprising statement to the Egyptian parliament. Which was the original initiative? Who was responding to whom?

The issue becomes even more complex when the parties involved in the dispute have been carrying out simultaneous strategies of coercing and offering to conciliate in a complex pattern of action and reaction over a considerable period of time, as was the case, for example, with President Johnson's Government and the Government of North Vietnam between

1964 and 1967. Over this period of time it is extremely difficult to pick out clearly delineated sequences of conciliation and accommodation, succeeded by periods dominated by coercion and violence. Both forms of interaction were going on continually – although the coercion was nearly continuous save for brief truces – and they undoubtedly affected each other, so that processes overlapped and carried on from one another with brief pauses. To participants in the complex interaction, each sequence of conciliatory moves must have seemed to build, at least to some degree, on what had gone before, further complicating the issue of who was reponding to whom.[1]

In spite of this caution, in many cases and for certain periods even during a continuous interaction, it is reasonably plain which party tries to initiate an accommodative sequence. An observer can justifiably point to a distinction between an initiator and a target (at least for the first round) and ask whether there are any key differences in the actions undertaken and the internal processes involved within the initiator, on the one hand, and the target on the other.

One starting point is to emphasise that ostensibly similar divisions, debates and disagreements about the best way of prosecuting the conflict often exist within any target of conciliatory gestures as within any initiator. Intra-party differences and divisions within the recipient of conciliatory signals form a similar constraint on the target's decision-makers. On the other hand, it could equally well be argued that, if leaders looking to start a conciliatory process suffer from **dilemmas of initiation** – for example, asking if the risk of making a move is calculable and worth it – then leaders on the receiving end of an initial conciliatory gesture suffer from somewhat different **dilemmas of response** – for example, asking if the other's move is simply a trick, or how easy it might be to respond to that particular gesture.

The latter difficulties might, indeed, arise from many of the same factors that affect leaders in an initiating party, such as those involving psychological and political commitments to pursuing victory, cultures that reward persistence (even in pursuing forlorn hopes), unreconstructed hawks levelling charges of betrayal, and aroused constituents failing to understand or sympathise with a change of course from one they have come to regard as right, proper and inescapable. On the other hand, there is at least a plausible argument to be considered that the leaders of a party targeted by an adversary wishing to start a conciliatory process have a relatively simpler task in that the first move has already been made by the initiator. However, additional problems of interpretation and credibility usually arise, presenting obstacles that precede issues of whether it would be divisive and costly to respond to what may be a trick.

At this point, the fact that communication is a two-way process becomes important, and while a target may not initiate a sequence of signals, it later may become an initiator itself, and suffer similar problems to those already experienced by its adversary. On the other side, if the target does respond, the original initiator becomes a target in its turn. The roles – and the dilemmas – are reversed.

2   Targets and dilemmas of response

For the decision-makers in any parties to a protracted conflict, the process of beginning to consider the possibility of some compromise or of changing basic strategy normally involves overcoming a series of internal obstacles, first to arriving at a decision to effect a major change in aspirations and procedures, and then to communication of this intention clearly to an adversary. For an initiator, as noted in Chapter 10, these barriers will initially be those concerned with building a decision-making consensus to initiate a conciliatory signal, with sending any such signal, and with sending a clear, unambiguous signal. For the target, on the other hand, leaders will initially need to overcome problems of detecting a signal, interpreting it accurately, persuading themselves that this represents a genuine change of course by the adversary, and lastly responding appropriately and effectively. As Charles Hermann points out, this is usually a problem on at least two levels: that of a target's middle-level bureaucrats with responsibility for monitoring and reporting on the effectiveness of strategy, and who 'may be in a better position than their superiors to receive signals that current policy is not working' (Hermann 1990, p.12); and that of decision-makers themselves, who bear the responsibility for ultimate choice. Moreover, as the cybernetic model in Chapter 3 emphasises, incoming information about an initiator's initiative has to pass through numerous filters before any range of responses is considered and one chosen.

2.1   Problems of initial recognition

Initially it appears that the internal obstacles and constraints confronted by any target are very similar, in principle, to those facing an initiator, especially those arising from major differences and divisions within the target itself over the party's goals, appropriate means, perception of concurrent balance of advantage and need for abandoning existing strategy. In the case of a target divided over the issue of continuing or conciliating, and searching for a compromise settlement, questions will always arise about those divisions and the relative readiness for a major change in policy that result from them.

1   Who, internally, has made the major commitment to the existing strategy of continued coercion, whose interests will be adversely affected by the present offer, who will put up the greatest resistance to abandoning the current strategy, and who has a vested interest in not responding to a conciliatory gesture from the adversary?

2 Are there any leaders or elite factions within the target who might, as a result of recognising the proffered initiative's advantages to them, become pro-conciliation and indicate in return a readiness for major behavioural or attitude change?
3 What is the balance of forces within the target for ignoring the gesture from the other side and continuing to fight on (pro-continuation); or for exploring the opportunity offered by the initiative and even the distant possibility of a negotiated compromise (pro-conciliation)?
4 Who, among allies and patrons, will urge the continuation of the conflict, how vigorously and for what reasons?

While these queries remain basically similar to those posed about an initiator, I would argue that they take on a slightly different form from those raised about a party initiating a conciliatory process. Moreover, there are a number of additional problems for targets in a conciliation process which are by no means trivial and which arise from the simple fact of their being 'second'. For example, the fact of being a potential respondent to an initiative launched by an adversary auomatically means that there is a tendency for initiators to 'set the agenda' or 'limit the terms of the interaction' by the very fact of going first; and for targets to respond within a framework set by the party acting first. The disadvantages of 'going second' have been noted in a variety of stages in a conflict process. Even in settings where the interaction is heavily influenced by an ostensibly impartial third party whose task it is to balance exchanges, such as in mediation or facilitated negotiation, analysts have noted that those parties initiating an exchange tend to dominate it simply by introducing topics, terms and implied limits to which the party going second usually feels called upon to respond – but in responding tacitly accepts the terms of the ensuing interaction. At the interpersonal level, Sara Cobb notes that 'the initial narrative all too often functions to dominate the session.' (Cobb 1993, p.250), while she and Janet Rivkin have gone as far as to claim that, at this level, 'the first story that is told is the one that frames the agreement.' (Cobb and Rifkin 1991). The justification for this conclusion is that those initiating an exchange 'construct the semantic and discursive space on which all subsequent speakers must stand by providing a set of coherent relations between plots, characters and themes' (Cobb 1993). While it may not be necessary to accept the postmodernist jargon, the main point remains wholly valid. Going second and responding to a conciliatory move does usually involve accepting the focus and the limitations imposed by the initiating party.

Secondly, some of the issues raised in our discussion of the problems likely to face an initiator in making an initial conciliatory gesture suggest strongly that the target is likely to face a first move that emphasises the negative and risky consequences of continuing the struggle. Initiators, all too conscious of their own intra-party opposition and the need to placate it by demonstrating resolve even while suggesting an alternative approach, are more than likely to frame their offer within a series of warnings about the costs and risks to the target of continuing, about the improbability of achieving their goals through continued coercion, and about the high level of sacrifices already made for goals that will simply not be achieved. Unfortunately, as Brockner and Rubin (1985) point out in their studies of entrapment and the reasons for decision-makers persisting in failing policies, prospect theory suggests that posing a choice within this type of negative frame is more likely to persuade a target's decision-makers to persist in the riskier course of action (that is, continuation), which at least offers a chance of recouping losses, rather than to change strategies and try something radically different (that is, conciliation), which accepts losses already incurred.

In explaining this seeming paradox, Brockner and Rubin note that 'An entrapped decision-maker typically is evaluating a losing proposition and must decide whether to accept a sure loss (i.e. not to invest further) or to try to recoup all that has been expended (i.e. to allocate further resources.' (1985, p.52–3). This is echoed by Glen Whyte, who argues that 'Project abandonment is perceived as accepting a certain loss, whereas escalation is perceived as possibly increasing losses, combined with a chance that losses may be avoided ... Escalating commitment is the natural consequence of negatively framing a decision about the entire course of action.' (Whyte 1993, p.433). Hence, if an initiator in making a conciliatory gesture clearly implies that continuation is a riskier course of action for a target but does involve some prospect of success, then the likelihood that the target's decision-makers are going to reject the move and escalate their commitment to continuing the conflict, even though that course of action seems to be failing, 'is consistent with the prediction offered by prospect theory' (Brockner and Rubin 1985, p.55).

Unfortunately, this reaction may be equally likely both for situations of self-correcting change, when the target's leaders have been in power for some time and are largely responsible for present costly strategies, and for regime change, when a new set of decision-makers, with little responsibility for previous strategies, is evaluating an initiator's gesture. While new leaders might not be as susceptible to the constraints arising from prior advocacy of a now clearly failing policy, as the self-justification hypothesis suggests, the influence of the negative framing of a conciliatory offer is likely to produce strong advocacy for continuation rather than conciliation in the target's decision-making group. Whyte (1993, pp.434–6) argues that, even in the absence of a need for individual decision-makers to justify previous advocacy of, and support for a failing strategy, group uniformity pressures (uncertainty, the need to maintain good inter-group relationships, polarisation tendencies) are then likely to push the target's leadership towards making a pro-continuation choice, which risks greater loss but also offers a chance of gain, and hence to the rejection of the initiative. Even if these obstacles are overcome and the target's leaders choose a conciliatory response, an additional dilemma, which does not exist to the same degree for the initiator, is how to go about reframing the initiative in a positive way, and then reacting in such a way that the response itself is positively framed and does not elicit negative reactions within the adversary's decision-makers.

The third type of problem for the party responding to an initiator's conciliatory move arises from the fact that, while the initiator may have been able to make the first move as a surprise and thus prepare for and possibly head off domestic opposition, protest and criticism, such a strategy is not usually open to the decision-makers in a target called upon to respond to an opening move, particularly one that is made openly and in public, possibly to gain maximum credit for flexibility and 'being reasonable'. As Robert Behn argues, many likely reactions to any conciliatory initiative are almost pre-destinedly negative; those who 'benefit from the policy and those who are ideologically committed to it will complain – immediately and loudly' (Behn 1978, pp.394–5). While it might be open to an initiator to avoid this problem simply by not giving intra-party adversaries the time – or the information – necessary to formulate and organise strong opposition (in other words, to employ a 'strategy of insulation'), the same luxury is not easily open to a respondent. One has only to compare the position of Anwar Sadat, announcing his willingness to visit Israel as a complete surprise to an astonished Egyptian Assembly, with that of Menachem Begin faced with a target's task of formulating an appropriate response in full view of an alert (and, in many cases, critically negative) Israeli public. Initiators can prepare to deal with pro-continuation factions while targets often have little opportunity to plan ways of offsetting protest and criticism.

Fourthly, in addition to the difficulties posed by internal divisions and opponents, a target's decision-makers also have the problem of first picking out the conciliatory gesture and 'validating' it from the mass of contradictory signals and noise emanating from an adversary trying to signal a willingness to be conciliatory. This preliminary problem of recognition forms an additional barrier to the carrying through of a conciliatory process beyond the first stage of tentative initiation. In communications theory it is a matter of the acuteness of a party's sensors and the ability of its screening and interpreting process to pick out genuine conciliatory signals from those which are merely probes to test out commitment, or public relations ploys designed to buy off the initiator's own doves or third parties pressing for a really unwanted compromise. In the real world, it is a matter of trying to interpret the motives for an (apparently) conciliatory gesture from a (possibly) divided adversary who is attempting to coerce or otherwise prevent one from achieving legitimate goals, and whose good faith has to be questioned.

A final set of factors likely to affect the initial recognition of a conciliatory gesture by leaders of the targeted party arise from the psychology of leaders, elites and their followers. Some take familiar forms of efforts at dissonance reduction simply by rejecting information that does not conform to one's image of an implacable and thoroughly untrustworthy adversary (Festinger 1957). An equally likely reaction, given the almost certain high salience and centrality of decision-makers' beliefs and attitudes about the conflict, the adversary and the adversary's leaders, is to trivialise the discrepancy between expectations about an adversary and information about the adversary's latest – conciliatory – move.[2] Other reactions involve variations on the entrapping processes, that prevent both psychological recognition and political willingness to respond, already discussed in the context of initiating conciliation and to which I return below, after discussing some of the problems the leaders of a target might have in responding to a conciliatory move.

2.2   Problems of responding

Aside from familar problems of recognition and acknowledgement, it is also likely that major problems of implementing and co-ordinating a conciliatory response will exist for most targets, even those able to overcome internal opposition (at least temporarily) so that a decision can be taken to send a conciliatory signal as a response to the adversary's initiative.

As I mentioned in connection with an initiator's problem of delayed signals, most conciliatory processes involve targets where there is a division between those who decide that a certain response shall be made and those charged with implementing the response clearly and on time. This is particularly likely to be the case where a clear response requires some kind of diminution of coercive activity by those agencies who have their own agenda and timetable for prosecuting such activities. Hence, one should expect strong resistance to any conciliatory offer which involves interfering with such an agenda. As I discussed in the case of the US December 1965 bombing pause during the Second Vietnam War, resistance by advocates of a rapid military victory in the South – who dominated the Politburo in Hanoi – was able to prevent, or at least mute and delay, any response to the pause and its associated diplomatic campaign so effectively that the initiative came to nothing. (Not that this was, apparently, much regretted by hawks in Washington). Moreover, later US initiatives were also frustrated by the delay in getting any response from Hanoi, and in the apparent inability (interpreted as unwillingness) of the North Vietnamese to undertake any significant slow-down of military activity in the South.

On occasions when the target of conciliatory gestures is divided at any or all of the three levels of decision-makers, elite and constituency – and often deeply divided, sometimes to the point of incoherence – obtaining a conciliatory response can be almost impossible because of the absence of any chain of command to co-ordinate a reaction. Part of the Carter Administration's problem in dealing with the crisis involving American hostages in Iran lay in the facts (1) that the internal power struggle in Iran made anyone wishing to compromise with the USA over the hostages vulnerable to charges of treachery from rival factions; but also (2) that there was a complete disjunction between those in the government who were signalling to the USA and taking the official decision to hold or release the hostages and those who actually held the hostages and were responsible for implementing that 'decision' in which they had played little or no part. In another situation of intense conflict, the US Secretary of State, Alexander Haig, has recorded how the disunity of the ruling junta in Buenos Aires – consisting of squabbling representatives of the Argentine army, navy and air force – prevented any coherent response to offers of mediation or negotiation over the Falklands/Malvinas Islands, even though there were clear options available other than British re-invasion (Haig 1984). As with initiators, differences and divisions within a target can pose major obstacles to action.

3   Targets and entrapment

I noted above that all of the aspects of entrapment previously discussed as costs of reversal applied both to leaders seeking to begin a conciliatory process as well as to leaders facing the need to respond in some manner to a conciliatory initiative launched by an adversary. All leaders, to some extent, become entrapped by their psychological – and political – commitments to a chosen course of action in which effort, material resources and personal reputation have been devoted.

However, other types of politico-psychological constraints seem particularly relevant to the leaders of target parties, although – once an accommodative process gets under way – either set of leaders can become seriously concerned about how to avoid or overcome these constraints. Two frequently encountered constraints are those involving *costs of naive delusion* and *costs of betrayal*.

3.1   The costs of 'naive delusion'

The first set of constraints arises in situations in which one party has made a conciliatory gesture or set of initial offers, thus confronting the target's leaders with the choice of responding to or ignoring the signal. One of the major dangers for the target's leadership is that of responding with some gesture of its own, or some apparently safe concession, only to have its concession taken by the other side without any further compensating move. In order to do this, of course, the target's decision-makers will have to overcome all the costs of reversal mentioned previously but an additional obstacle will be the fear of having been publicly deluded into responding with a conciliatory move, only to have this come to nothing. The perceived danger is that of being seen to be naive enough to believe in the credibility of an undoubted enemy, and having undertaken a risk that a sensible and appropriately cautious leadership should never have undertaken.

Confronted with such a scenario, the target's leaders have a major interest in playing safe, in assuming the worst and in not laying themselves open to being made to look foolish by an adversary that has previously demonstrated its fundamental lack of trustworthiness. Thus, the risk of being let down and the costs of being seen by one's followers as naively deluded, form a major barrier to a target's leaders deciding to respond to a conciliatory intitiative, even when one is unambiguously offered.

3.2   The costs of 'betrayal'

If the costs to leaders of seeming naivety can be considerable, especially in terms of domestic criticism from pro-continuation factions and loss of support from constituents, then the costs of appearing treacherous are even higher. It is clearly possible for the leaders of both targets and initiators to be seen as 'betrayers' of their parties, their promises and their followers, once they embark on any conciliatory process, and to find the threat of that accusation a major element in both their entrapment in continuing even a hopeless conflict and their decision to continue in order to avoid being seen as betrayers.[3] Moreover, this seems a particularly pertinent barrier to the decison makers of a target as, by definition, some offer will already have been made to them, so that the likelihood that they will be seen as 'selling out' is increased by the very fact that they might be thinking of taking the proffered 'bribe'.

Malim Akerstrom (1991) has discussed some of the reasons why the accusation of betrayal might act as a major obstacle to responding to any conciliatory initiative from an adversary. Although his work mainly concentrates on two types of betrayal of trust, the first being betrayals of secrets (by telling) and the second the betrayal of membership (by leaving), it also deals indirectly with a third type, namely betrayal of expectations and aspirations (by abandonment). All three are examples of 'letting down' a social group – the 'we' as Akerstrom terms it – by one of its own members, and Akerstrom argues that the betrayal by some member of an elite is always regarded as more seriously despicable than betrayal by rank-and-file members of the 'we'. The level of contempt felt by those who deem themselves betrayed and the level of shame and guilt frequently experienced by those accused of betrayal form major barriers to any leaders considering the risks of acknowledging or returning any conciliatory move by an enemy.[4]

A number of other factors often increase the sense of betrayal, the level of contempt felt for betrayers and thus the anticipated costs of being accused of the treachery (or even treason) involved in advocating an abandonment of goals in favour of a search for an alternative. The first of these is the originally high degree of trust placed in leaders and in their claimed capacity for pursuing the parties' goals through best available means; and the increased sense of betrayal resulting from that initial, misplaced trust.

The second is the fact that the greater the perceived danger to the 'we' – and it is unlikely that situations of conflict are seen by parties as anything other than dangerous – the greater the sense of outrage at any form of betrayal and the greater the number of activities likely to be so defined. It goes without saying that protracted, deep-rooted conflicts are customarily perceived as posing extreme danger to all involved in them.

Thirdly, Akerstrom argues that the perceived magnitude of the sense of betrayal on the part of the betrayed increases markedly to the degree that it is unexpected. This level of surprise is likely to be high if a 'surrender' or a 'compromise' is advocated by those initially responsible for mobilising effort, enthusiasm and commitment for the course of action they are now abandoning. Often allied to this are the multiplying impacts of perceived inconsistency which affect – and often deter – political leaders who might appear to be abandoning something they argued for only a short while before. As Akerstrom argues, 'we tend … also to demand a permanency from each other – that is, we should not change our views.' (ibid. p.96) and in most societies this norm is almost as strong as that condemning betrayal. Another factor reinforcing the tendency of decision-makers not to want to appear to abandon goals or betray their followers' expectations is the reward of consistency and fidelity. In Akerstrom's words, groups and nations safeguard against betrayal through the 'anticipated … admiration from one's own group if one has been able to withstand the pressure to betray' (ibid. p.73) – often a relatively easy course open to leaders weighing the options of responding to or rejecting a conciliatory gesture from the adversary.

The intractable nature of such barriers is emphasised by Lewis Coser in his analysis of groups under threat, their resultant search for unity, and the manner in which such groups punish any form of disloyalty by persons viewed as renegades or 'heretics'. According to Coser, renegades are inevitably seen as threats to group unity – 'a desertion of those standards of the group considered vital to its well being, if not its existence' (Coser 1956, p.69). Intra-party hostility is, therefore, likely to be focused on dissenters suggesting any major alternative to defeating the enemy or that a compromise could be sought, even after some major reverse or undoubted swing against their side in the overall balance of advantage. Coser even suggests that, following a major reverse, intra-party factors may make this exactly the wrong time for leaders to be thinking about responding to some initiative, because groups 'tend to deny that reverses in conflict can be attributed to the strength of an adversary, for this would be an admission of their own weakness. Hence, they look in their own ranks for a dissenter who hampered unity and the concerted action against the enemy.' (Coser

1956, p.106). Anticipation of such levels of hostility may, therefore, deter leaders from accepting and responding to an initiative from the adversary or even seeming to be willing to receive such an offer.

In all, then, the dynamics of a protracted conflict place all leadership groups, but especially those in receipt of an offer or a conciliatory move, in a position where the chances of being seen as betrayers are very high, should they consider deviating from the vigorous and consistent pursuit of enunciated goals; and where a number of built-in factors increase the intensity of any sense of betrayal on the part of their followers and other members of the elite. Hence also the inevitably increasing costs of 'betrayal' to those involved in any such move. Desire to avoid even the possibility of such an accusation, of such a label, becomes a major barrier to any target recognising, acknowledging and responding to an initiator's signal, and thus to the continuation of a conciliatory exchange.

Moreover, and quite apart from a target's decision-makers' desire to maintain their own self image, there is always the consideration of not providing an opportunity for intra-party adversaries to mount a major attack against existing leaders and their policies – a constant concern of leaders anywhere but especially leaders of parties in conflict contemplating a change of course and thus a constant obstacle to making such a change.

4   Intra-party differences and divisions: three levels

The existence of intra-party opponents of conciliation within both a target and an initiator of any conciliatory move is so frequent as to seem almost invariable. I noted in Chapter 10 how these might develop or intensify within a party considering the launching of some conciliatory initiative, and similar cleavages are likely to exist or develop within a party contemplating a response to such an initiative.

It is important to recognise that differences, divisions and dissensus within initiators, as well as targets, can occur at three important levels:

1 within the leadership itself;
2 at the level of elites and opinion formers where, in pluralist systems, a major role of any opposition factions is to discredit the leadership in order to achieve power for themselves; and
3 at the constituency level of rank-and-file followers.

At the level of leaders, the issue of a target making a positive response is very much affected by the extent to which continuation 'in office' is linked to the continuation of the conflict.[5] For this reason, the degree of dissensus within the actual leadership is likely to reflect constituents' attitudes towards the struggle and its continuation. This is a matter of specific support for continuation of the struggle, as opposed to generalised support for the leadership, but it is always possible for a party's rank and file to be profoundly divided about either or both, as well as being divided from its leaders over the issue of continuing the struggle. General bellicosity may continue long after decision-makers and elites have concluded that accommodation is necessary.

Thus, even if a leadership is itself united in its determination to pursue a course of action, whether this be to continue the conflict and – in a target – ignore a proffered concession, or to change course and pursue a process of conciliation, significant differences and divisions may arise at both elite and grass-roots levels. On many occasions, while leaders and elites may be divided over issues of continuation or conciliation, pro-continuation sentiments and commitments are likely to prevail among constituents, especially in the initial stages of any peace process. Unless a profound feeling of 'war-weariness' has set in after much sacrifice, struggle and time, rank-and-file followers are still likely to be committed to continuation and victory, and to view efforts at conciliation and compromise as betrayal and the occasion for leadership change. Unless such a bedrock of pro-continuation forces can be circumvented or ignored, the leaders of a target party are likely to feel internally vulnerable and to play for safety by ignoring tentative conciliatory gestures from a long-term adversary.

However, this 'standard scenario' – of leaders (or some leaders) contemplating a change of policy to search for a compromise settlement and rival elites and rank and file constituents opposing such a 'betrayal' – is by no means the only one possible. The Anti-Vietnam War Movement in the USA during the 1960s emphasises that other situations are possible, while Natalie Frensley points out, in her study of Northern Ireland and the effects of intra-party cleavages on the rejection of peace proposals, that it is not always the case that leaders, rivals and followers conform to a model in which leaders pursue conciliation and compromise over obstacles provided by politicking rivals and uninformed, but intransigent followers (Frensley 1998). In some cases leaderships may be pro-continuation while constituencies are pro-conciliation. Elites may press for a more conciliatory policy while leaders and constituents remain pro-continuation. Most likely, all three sets of actors may themselves reveal profound differences and divisions. Leaders themselves may be divided about the wisdom of continuing (and about responding to a proffered olive branch); elites may line up on different sides of the continuation issue; and major differences may exist within public opinion at the rank-and-file level. Table 11.1 illustrates the possible range of circumstances regarding intra-party divisions, and suggests some consequences of various combinations of commitment and cleavage among Targets, some of which undoubtedly apply also to parties trying to initiate accommodative sequences.

While a range of possible circumstances can exist, it seems most likely that, in the initial stages of a peace process, intra-party differences and

Table 11.1 Effects of Intra-Party Cleavages on Conciliation Process

Constituent stance	Elite Stance Mainly Pro-continuation	Mainly Pro-conciliation	Divided	Leaders' stance
Pro-continuation	Support for leaders' policy and moves for escalation	Elite criticism of leaders' policy plus efforts to 'educate' rank and file on costs of continuing	Muted criticisms of leaders by pro-conciliation elite? Cultivation of leaders' rank-and-file support by hawks	
Pro-conciliation	Efforts to convince rank and file of salience of goals and need for further effort/sacrifices	Massive elite criticism of leaders plus efforts to mobilize support for their ouster	Pro-conciliation elite factions make strong effort to build with grass roots to begin mass anti-continuation movement	Pro-continuation
Divided	Support for pro-continuation elements at grass roots	Criticism by elites of leaders' policy. Rival attempts to swing bulk of rank and file behind alternate policies	Elements of many strategies visible within party	
Pro-continuation	Elite criticism of leaders' policy plus efforts to replace leaders. Campaign to mobilize mass protest against 'surrender'	Joint efforts to persuade rank and file that goals could be better achieved via new policy of conciliation	Strong criticism of leaders by 'hawks' in elite and efforts to use mass protest to oust leaders	
Pro-conciliation	Muted criticism of leaders by elites: propaganda efforts to arouse mass support, resisted by leadership	Support for leaders' policy and moves for conciliation	Strong support for conciliation among 'dovish' elites. Criticism from pro-continuation elites, but united	Pro-conciliation
Divided	Rival efforts to obtain decisive rank-and-file support for clear policy	Efforts by leaders and elites to undermine influence of and to isolate rank and file in favour of continuing	Elements of many strategies visible within party	

divisions will usually pose formidable obstacles to a target's leadership making a positive response to a conciliatory initiative (as well, of course, to an initiator's launching one). Moreover, diminishing the obstacles posed by pro-continuation factions, then building up a coalition arguing and acting for accommodation, is likely to be a long-term business, not even begun in the early stages of a conciliatory process, when one party floats a cautious trial balloon as a conciliatory initiative. In these early stages it is likely to be particularly difficult for a target's decision-makers to overcome obstacles posed by pro-continuation forces, with the result that, at least initially, no response is forthcoming. This probability argues for persistence on the part of an initiator, but this is easier said than done. Hence, early in any accommodative process, many initiators will become convinced of the futility of continuing, unless completely empathic about the strength of internal opposition within a target (an unlikely situation).

Even in the longer term, considerable obstacles remain. In many protracted and deep-rooted conflicts, the struggle itself and winning it become the only issues, so that the provision of other, laudable goals as substitutes or alternatives is much more difficult for any leaders arguing for involvement in an accommodative sequence. In many conflicts, the issues become defined as the survival of the party itself, its way of life, its ideological foundations. Such conflicts about identity and survival frequently become 'institutionalised' within parties, in a sense that goes way beyond the normal use of this term of a party becoming committed to a policy or that agencies or institutions are established to pursue the goals in question. Rather, the goals in conflict become integrally part of the party itself, so that the conflict is seen – at least by one side – as being about 'our being' or 'our existence' – issues which appear (with good reason) to be utterly non-negotiable. Hence, any move towards some form of conciliation with those threatening such values is seen as completely undermining and those making such moves as the ultimate traitors.

This intractable situation can be illustrated by many conflicts (the Arab–Israeli conflict being one), but Lucy Nottingham's study of the Iran–Iraq conflict in the 1980's offers an interesting variant on this general principle (Nottingham 1994). In seeking to explain the resistance to de-escalation and conciliation experienced during this First Gulf War, Nottingham argues persuasively that, for the revolutionary Iranian leaders, continuation of the war came to represent the continuation of the Islamic revolution itself, which therefore became an absolute value admitting no form of compromise and hence no role for conciliation. Such wars about the existence of the revolution 'are characterised by doctrinal absolutism and ... unlimited aims.' (Nottingham 1994, p.80). The stakes in such struggles are so high as to admit no compromise. The conflict becomes a crusade 'undertaken in the name of righteousness' (ibid.), so that the pursuit of such goals tends both to justify the full mobilisation of rank-and-file constituents behind the struggle and affect all political, economic and social life within the crusading party.

In the face of such total, organised commitment to continuing to victory, the prospects for this type of target responding to conciliatory gestures seem dim. This was borne out by the steadfast refusal of any kind of accommodation by the leaders in Tehran until the whole country was overwhelmed by eight years of bloodletting and a pro-conciliation faction finally formed and gradually became more influential. However, I would argue that this particular conflict merely represents an extreme case of the kind of obstacles that present themselves to any leaders seeking to push forward a conciliatory process. In almost all cases of protracted conflict, at least in the initial stages, there is a tendency to regard the party goals as being absolute values, so that conciliation (usually defined as 'surrender' to the adversary) is a meaningless concept. In the medium term, removing intra-party obstacles to accommodation involves the interlocking tasks of reducing the influence of pro-continuation factions relative to pro-conciliation groups and individuals, and bringing about some degree of change in the intra-party psychological climate which allows for the possibility of a negotiated, non-absolute solution.[6]

5   Conclusion and potential remedies

Once again, a review of constraints on decision-makers in parties that are the target of conciliatory initiatives results in a list of problems similarly difficult to those affecting decision-makers in initiating parties. However, there are ways of overcoming these constraints in both types of party and, in spite of the many practical difficulties of diminishing the many obstacles to conciliation and helping to push forward an accommodative sequence, the principle underlying such a process seems reasonably clear: reduce the influence of those committed to continuing. This might be done through a variety of strategies, including:

1   As far as possible, insulating the conciliation process from those opposed to accommodation, thus keeping exchanges with the adversary low-key, especially in the initial stages of the process.
2   Diminishing both the influence of pro-continuation factions within the party and removing or modifying their motivation for undermining any conciliation process.
3   Taking advantage of dynamics both within the party and in the conflict system itself to strengthen pro-accommodation factors and factions so that – eventually – a solid coalition in favour of conciliation can emerge.
4   Creating an intellectual and psychological climate generally within both elites and constituents that is supportive of accommodation rather than continuation.

Thus, while major difficulties in pushing forward with a conciliatory process will aways exist for all parties concerned, there are factors which can operate as enablers, rather than obstacles, as well as tactics that might be adopted to overcome major obstacles. It is to these more positive possibilities for an initiator's or a target's decision-makers that I turn in the following chapter.

12
Conciliation and Intra-Party Conflicts

'Leaders' victories and defeats are not always victories and defeats for their underlings. There have even been cases where a defeat proved a victory for the underlings'

Bertold Brecht *Mother Courage and her Children*

One clear implication of the ideas discussed in the preceding two chapters is that there exists an inevitably close connection between the constraints existing for decision-makers at the level of intra-party politics and the opportunities available at the level of inter-party interaction. These two environments provide a clear illustration of Robert Putnam's two level game model and so the nature – and likely impact – of any conciliatory gesture will be affected by both sets of conditions rather than by a single, isolated environment. Often the interaction between these two levels will present major dilemmas to the parties involved. For example, the more focused or 'closed' a planned gesture, and the more privately it will be conveyed, the less the potential risks of elite or constituency protest for leaders of the initiating party, but the more revocable and deniable it is likely to appear to the leaders of the target. On the other hand, the more open the gesture, the greater its likely impact on the target and the less its deniability, but the more likely it is to be seen (at least initially) as a propaganda ploy to influence the initiator's pro-negotiation public opinion or to undermine the target's rank-and-file support.[1] The dilemmas of dealing with intra-party constraints in order to send precisely the right signal are constant and considerable.

However, as I indicated at the end of the last chapter, there are clearly a number of ways of overcoming some of these constraints on clear and effective signalling, whether they are created by internal divisions, co-ordination and implementation problems, a confusing initial set of signals from an initiator, or unclear responses emanating from a target.

1 Insulation as a remedial strategy

In theory, one obvious remedy for such confusion is for any pro-termination faction to try to separate and insulate the conciliatory signals. Insulation in this setting has two aspects. First it is necessary to insulate an initiator's conciliatory signals from the other stream of acts and statements directed at – or inadvertantly received by – the target, and equally when the target responds to the initiator. This implies the need to try to control other signals being sent to an adversary, either as a part of the continuing policy of coercion, (or as defence against the adversary's coercion) so that the conciliation initiative or response is not swamped by background 'noise' that it passes unnoticed by the adversary.

Secondly, it is necessary to try to insulate the overall process of conciliation from those who would try to prevent, alter or subvert it, and it is the second of these insulation tasks that is usually the most difficult to carry out successfully. For one thing, it is almost impossible to conceal even the first of a sequence of peace feelers from other decision-makers or implementers in even the most tightly knit group of leaders or the most closed system of government. Carrying through conciliatory initiatives of the most subtle kind in some unobtrusive and insulated fashion in 'leaky' and open systems must seem a hollow joke to those involved in such efforts. In any attempt to carry out such an activity, a pro-conciliation group trying to signal or respond to an adversary with as little domestic attention as possible would do well to consider four initial questions:

1 Who do we *not* want to know that this initiative is being made?
2 How powerful and dangerous might they be to the present initiative?
3 How powerful and dangerous might they be to our position or survival within or as the government?
4 What might be done to prevent them learning about the initiative until as late as possible?

Some of the practical complexities of dealing with potential obstacles and 'insulating' the conciliatory process can be seen in the US Government's efforts to defuse tensions between itself and the Government of the CPR during 1970–2, thus normalising relations between the two countries after 20 years of open hostility, isolation and occasional confrontation. The process, supervised by President Nixon and NSC Adviser Henry Kissinger, had to take place without alarming or antagonising a large number of potential obstacles, some of which were dealt with successfully, others less so. Within the United States and particularly the President's own party there were the powerful pro-Taiwan lobby and the right-wing advocates of confrontation with both China and the USSR. Within the US administration were the agencies who might approve but could leak, and the agencies who shared outside views about never abandoning the Chinese Nationalist regime on Taiwan and who would leak. Naturally, external obstacles were most clearly represented by the Nationalist Chinese regime which relied upon US support for its continued survival, and which thus had to be kept 'out of the picture' as much as possible. Within the CPR itself, there seem to have been several factions vying for control of policy, including one under Lin Piao, which was against any compromise with the USA, and one led by Chou En Lai which was prepared for a negotiated settlement if the price was right. Finally, there were the allies of China, who would be affected by any US/CPR rapprochement (North Vietnam), and China's adversaries who would be affected by US re-alignments resulting from a diminution of mistrust and hostility between Washington and Peking.

In carrying out the process of conciliation as a preparation for negotiations and *rapprochement*, if not a settlement, Dr Kissinger and President Nixon were obviously aware of the need to insulate the process from internal US interference. Quite apart from wanting to reap all the political credit for the move, as Seymour Hersh suggests (1983), Kissinger had obviously learned about the problems of clear and unhampered signalling during de-escalation from his familiarity with the ambiguities and mistakes of the Johnson era, in which he had been once directly involved and harmed.[2] One reason for Kissinger's obsessive secrecy in making this and other contacts may have been his dissatisfaction with the shortcomings of co-ordination and control of the policy of military coercion practised under President Johnson.

In this particular case, the strategy for insulation was a three-fold one of (i) centralisation, (ii) disinformation, and (iii) isolation in the channels of communication used. As an initial policy decision, the moves towards China were started from the White House and every effort made to centralise decisions and communication channels into that part of the executive branch of the government, to the exclusion of all other relevant agencies. Central control of the policy was concentrated at the very top of the executive hierarchy and all others levels, as far as possible, excluded.

In addition to centralising the conduct of the process (an action helped by the fact that, unlike most other interactions – especially that proceeding concurrently between the USA and Vietnam – there was very little noise to interfere with signals sent from the White House to Peking), the Nixon-Kissinger strategy also contained a substantial amount of disinformation, designed to head off negative reactions from pro-Taiwanese lobbies in the USA and from the Nationalist regime itself. Much of this consisted of reiterations of US commitment to Taiwan and to the idea of two Chinas, while signals of a quite different nature were sent via informal means – through other governments – to the Chinese Government in Peking. Thus communications proceeded along two quite different channels, the public and the private, the two differing less about the US desire for a new relationship than in the nature of the concessions offered to Peking for a restoration of normal relations and, implicitly, a lessening of Chinese help for the North Vietnamese struggle.[3]

Finally, the Nixon–Kissinger initiative insulated itself in terms of isolating the channels of communication used between the governments who were signalling a willingness to talk. Partly as a result of President Nixon's access to top leaders who could pass on messages to Peking, and partly because of Henry Kissinger's desire to cut out the State Department from policy making and his skill in setting up 'backchannels', the number and variety of unknown and unsuspected lines of communication set up and used between 1970 and 1972 were considerable. Beginning with French contacts through President de Gaulle as early as 1969, a series of channels were opened and used including the Rumanian Government, the Pakistani Government and private citizens such as Edgar Snow. The only time any serious exchange of views and ideas involved 'normal' diplomatic channels was the occasion when formal contacts between the USA and China were resumed in Warsaw, with some success. These were ended by the US invasion of Cambodia and not resumed, at least partly because Kissinger and the White House did not want to lose their central control and co-ordinating role in the initiative (nor the credit for the achievement, should it take place.)

The process of re-establishing normal relations with the CPR exemplifies a major effort at avoiding many of the obstacles to clear signalling and a co-ordinated process of de-escalation which were discussed in preceding chapters. To a large degree, Dr Kissinger and President Nixon succeeded in insulating their effort from internal interference and sabotage, co-ordinated their efforts to create the right perceptions and anticipations in the minds of those in the target they hoped to affect, and isolated their signals to that target by using different and distinct channels and carefully 'flagging' and emphasising messages that came through those channels. They also tried to signal to their target with a degree of subtlety which would ensure that their message would be picked up and interpreted correctly in Beijing, but pass unnoticed by adversaries within the USA and Taiwan.

2   Dealing with pro-continuation factions

As the US–Chinese case suggests, a second strategy for increasing the target's ability to respond positively to an initiator's conciliatory gesture involves attempting to lessen the usually negative influence of pro-continuation forces and thus diminishing the intra-party, political obstacles to exploring the possibility of accommodation. This can often be a complex process in itself, as the sources of resistance to conciliation can be widespread and various, as well as inevitably being powerful and well entrenched in any protracted conflict. As I noted above, the 'strategy of surprise', whereby the intra-party opposition is not given time to mobilise protest and criticism against a concilatory move, is rarely open to targets confronting some gesture already made by an initiator, unless the latter is most discreet in its signal and leaks do not reveal widely that such a move has been made. However, other strategies may be available.

2.1   A strategy of compensatory activity

One very common strategy for decision-makers contemplating even a cautiously positive response to a conciliatory move by an adversary is to accompany the response with another action calculated to reassure – and to some degree to 'buy off' – intra-party opposition that is stongly pro-continuation. In such a strategy, opposition factions are compensated in some form by an activity that they can support, or that provides benefits for them. Hence, their sense of outrage and subsequent open opposition to the decision-makers' avoidance of a policy of outright rejection of the adversary is muted and containable, in view of the clear linkage between the 'retreat' represented by the return of the adversary's olive branch, and the 'reward' or 'reassurance' represented by the compensatory move.

One common form this strategy takes is the reshuffling of important roles within a group of top decision-makers that contains pro-continuation figures or factions. If a pro-conciliation leadership can promote such figures to new and prestigious roles, or bring into positions of power external critics of a conciliatory policy, then this might prove a successful way of compensating a pro-continuation opposition, otherwise outraged by the suggestion of a conciliatory response to an initiating adversary. (It is a strategy that can work doubly well if prominent 'hawks' can be removed from positions where they might be able directly to sabotage positive reactions to alternatives where such actions are less effective.) This last strategy was clearly one used by President Sadat following the agreement at Camp David, when he reshuffled the Egyptian government and the People's Assembly leadership, with a view to removing potential opponents of the Accords – frequently by promotion – and bringing into key positions supporters of an agreement with Israel.[4]

The difficulties with such a strategy are not negligible, however. Ideally, the compensatory move should be one that does not undermine the target's acceptance of the initial conciliatory action; that is, it should be made in an intra-party arena quite separate from that concerning the inter-party conflict. (In other words, the compensatory move should not be one that imposes, or even increases, costs on the initiating adversary.) However, the easiest way of both compensating and reassuring a strong and potentially vocal pro-continuation faction or constituency, and hence the most frequently employed, is to make the compensating move one which is central to the conflict itself. Often, this takes the form of accompanying a positive response to the proffered concession with some gesture that re-emphasises commitment to the struggle, the means being used and the goals being sought, although this inevitably tends to undermine that credibility of the positive response in the eyes of the initiator's decision-makers.

The principle seems to be one of pursuing a line of (possibly domestic) policy popular with pro-continuation factions as a reward for non-interference with the pursuit of conciliation, but the practice of such a principle is not likely to be simple or straightforward, given the centrality of the conflict and the issues at the heart of the struggle.

2.2 A strategy of involvement without influence

A second method by which decision-makers in a target might be able to minimise the influence of pro-continuation factions is to involve the latter notionally in the pursuit of a policy of conciliation without providing them with the level of influence needed to damage or terminate the policy. Again, this is not a simple strategy, although it is usually easier in situations where there is a rank-and-file constituency strongly in favour of a conciliatory policy towards the adversary and mobilisable in support of such a new policy.

Inclusion of pro-continuation leaders in decisions about responding to initiatives from the other side, while ensuring that theirs remains a minority voice, is one common tactic open to leaders wishing to head off widespread criticism of a move towards a more conciliatory policy. Another is to involve prominent figures who were previously pro-continuation in decisions to respond positively to a gesture from the adversary.

A third strategy is to by-pass potential sources of opposition in the decision-making process by keeping the policy at a 'higher' level which represents – but actually cuts out – individuals and factions that might support a policy of rejection and continuation of unchanging coercion. An example of such a strategy in action – admittedly in a different stage of a conciliation process – was Prime Minister Begin's refusal to submit the 1998 Camp David Accords to his own (Herut) party's decision-makers for approval – which they were unlikely to give – arguing that this was a matter of national importance that could only be dealt with by national bodies (the Israeli Cabinet and the Knesset); and secondly that, as the Herut were represented in both bodies – indeed formed a major proportion of both – the party had, in fact, an opportunity to evaluate the agreements.

2.3 A strategy of neutralisation

A third strategy for blunting potential opposition to a conciliatory policy is one not necessarily open to all leaders wishing to reverse a coercive strategy and engage in a search for a negotiated solution, for it involves neutralising potential critics and complainants – at least on a temporary basis while the process gets under way. Furthermore, while it is sometimes relatively easy to remove any possibility of pro-continuation individuals or factions having any direct influence upon decisions to engage in a conciliatory process, it is usually less easy to silence them completely and to avoid criticism of a conciliatory policy – and, hence, the existence of or potentiality for such a policy – becoming public knowledge, with deterring or damaging effect if that public is still highly committed to continuation and victory.

This is not to imply that strategies of temporary neutralisation are not commonly used. President Sadat, for example, had no hesitation in dismissing those who opposed or argued against his proposed visit to Jerusalem, a strategy which included the dismissal of his long-serving Foreign Minister, Ismael Fahmy, who had been involved in Sadat's search for the start of a negotiated solution for a considerable time.

2.4   A strategy of substitution

Finally, a fourth common way in which decision-makers considering possible involvement in a conciliatory process attempt to minimise intra-party opposition involves the use of third parties to deflect or mute internal criticism from pro-continuation factions. The next chapter deals in greater detail with roles for third parties in the successful launching of conciliatory gestures or the forwarding of accommodative processes. At this point I am merely suggesting that third parties can be used in the very early stage of a conciliatory process, frequently in roles that help to take some of the intra-party pressures off decision-makers seeking an alternative to continued coercion, frustration and loss.

For example, third parties can reinforce the impact of conciliatory gestures by calling for a positive response from the target, thus enabling the latter's leader to argue that they are responding to a respected outsider, rather than a mistrusted and hated adversary. An alternative role for third parties at this stage of a peace process might well involve quietly adopting a scheme for a possible response from a target unwilling to run the domestic risk of advancing the possibility itself, and suggesting this as the next move in a possible sequence of moves leading towards a settlement. This latter role of 'substitute proposer' is a well-known one when adversaries reach the stage of face-to-face negotiation, and one side is wary of making a proposal that its own supporters might see as giving too much away. However, there seems to be no reason why a similar third party role cannot be enacted earlier in the process.

Finally, and even during the inital stages of a conciliatory process, third parties might well be able to help targets 'out of a corner' into which intra-party opposition has driven them by bringing pressure to bear on pro-continuation individuals and factions, in support of those seeking an alternative to 'more of the same'. The role of the United States Government in helping to re-start a peace process in Northern Ireland by convincing first itself and then other parties in Britain and Northern Ireland that Sinn Fein was serious about a possible end to violence and the search for a solution, and then legitimising the Sinn Fein leadership, is only one recent example of how third parties can assist adversaries in heading off potential opposition – in this case within Britain and within the ranks of Northern Ireland Unionists – by its actions and its involvement. The use of third parties' resources, prestige and presence takes many forms at all stages of a peace process, and I discuss some of these in greater detail in Chapter 13. Here I simply note that third parties can play a significant role in helping to remove intra-party obstacles to a conciliatory response.

3   Creating a climate for conciliation: reframing possibilities

Pro-conciliation forces within adversaries can begin to remove some of the psycho-political obstacles to a succesful search for a non-coercive solution by a variety of strategies. Some of these focus on the idea of reframing the number of possibilities and the range of alternatives facing both their own party and the adversary, although a number of such strategies are likely to be more effective once a process of conciliation has been well launched. Broadly speaking, using such strategies will both form part of an effort to make positive responses to initially proffered concessions easier, even when considerable opposition to conciliation exists internally; and to contribute to the later development of a pro-conciliation coalition that – at both elite and constituency level – will be necessary if the obstacles posed by pro-continuation factions and policy inertia are to be overcome. Efforts to begin the process of changing the way in which the conflict and the adversary are regarded and discussed are likely to be only the first steps in assembling a coalition of intra-party forces that see an advantage in conciliation processes. However, these first steps – and their continuation – are important in the long run. If they are successful, they could produce a coalition that will eventually outweigh an inevitably powerful and committed set of individuals, groups and factions in favour of continuing the struggle until 'victory' is achieved.

There is a wide variety of changes that need to be brought about in this process of building up a pro-conciliation coalition, but I would argue that the most important have to do with two psycho-political factors. Firstly, there is development of broadly shared perceptions that options other than fighting on do exist; and secondly, that it is realistically possible to treat the adversary (previously viewed as implacably hostile and destructive) as a potential partner in the search for a negotiated solution. Without such a change among at least some decision-makers, elite members and rank-and-file followers, it is doubtful whether a conciliation process will get very far, even if initial moves and responses take place successfully.

3.1   Reframing the range of possibilities

One of the key aspects of any change of strategy from one of coercing an adversary to one of seeking some alternative solutions through conciliation and negotiation involves conflicting parties' capacity to learn over time and to change their views of the adversary and the range of current and future possibilities available to end the conflict in question. Many analysts have observed that the first stages of any protracted conflict involve both adversaries' perceptions that the particular goals they seek are utterly essential; that the only acceptable solution is for them to be able to achieve their own goals, irrespective of what efforts to do so might have for the other party; and that the most effective way of doing so – indeed, the only way open to them – is through a policy of effective coercion to make the other side abandon their objectives that have brought about the goal incompatibility at the heart of the conflict. Moreover, and particularly in protracted conflicts, pursuit of the party's core goals rapidly becomes overlain with a psychological and ideological justification that de-legitimises both the adversary's objectives and behaviour as well as any suggestion that 'our side' might pursue other goals, using alternative means. What might be termed the 'zero-sum conflict frame' comes to dominate the thinking – and hence the behaviour – of the vast majority of the leaders, the elites and the constituents within the involved parties.

Before any accommodative sequence can be initiated by one side or any conciliatory response made to an initiative by the other, some change in the existing conflict frame must take place. Moreover, for the process to continue one key aspect of it must increasingly involve the development of an alternative framework in which at least the relative salience of the goals being pursued is reconsidered, so that alternative means and an alternative relationship with the adversary become possibilities.

For example, Lucy Nottingham's study of the conditions surrounding the eventual end of the Iran–Iraq War emphasises the manner in which some Iranian leaders eventually began: (1) to question the goal of exporting the Iranian revolution to neighbouring Islamic countries, especially in the light of the costs in terms of military casualties and economic damage; (2) to popularise the concept of defeats as military disasters rather than as blessings; and (3) to regard those killed at the front more as casualties than as martyrs (Nottingham 1994, pp.112–17). This alternative way of framing the conflict at the end of eight long years of apparently fruitless struggle went some way to enabling a pro-conciliation faction to develop, even within the Iranian clerical leadership itself. It also effected a change in the views of a substantial section of Iranian grass-roots opinion, even though the pro-continuation faction continued to define the conflict in absolutist terms and to argue for its vigorous prosecution. What seems to have occurred in this case is an example of what, in a vastly different setting, Eugene Bardach mentions as the 'delegitimation of the ideological matrix in which the party is embedded' which is, he argues, one of the necessary conditions for any policy termination (Bardach 1976, p.130).

The need for a 'change of frame' is clearly linked closely to the argument advanced in Chapter 4 about the way in which a change of context can contribute to the probable success of a conciliation process. Contextual changes help to bring about altered views among leadership, elite and rank and file about the centrality and salience of goals, about available means, and about possible relationships with an adversary. For example, major changes in the place of both Ireland and the United Kingdom within an increasingly integrated European Union over the last 30 years presented opportunities for cross-national co-operation, the construction of new identities, the relocation of decision-making centres and the eventual deconstruction of the conception of absolute, territorially based 'sovereignty' within both countries. For the protracted conflict in Northern Ireland, contextual change of this sort between 1969 (when neither Ireland nor the UK were even members of the then EEC) and 1998 (when issues of a common European currency were being discussed) at least called into question the salience of goals such as 'uniting Ireland' or 'restoring the North' on the one hand, and 'maintaining the union' or 'being loyal citizens of Britain' on the other. As long held goals lost some of their salience, a series of new ways of framing the conflict enabled new options and strategies to become possible, many based on the conception of national identity and loyalty focused upon people rather than territory. Finally, many modernising changes in both mainland Britain (the acceptance of devolution) and the Republic of Ireland (increasing prosperity and the diminishing infuence of the Catholic Church) over this period changed the framing of the conflict in such a way that perceptions of an implacable, unchanging adversary began to fit less and less well with constant information about major alterations of structure, interests and behaviour. As a result, the possibility of adversaries entering – warily – into a new relationship became less impossible to contemplate.

3.2   Identifying a viable negotiating partner

Many of the kinds of change of frame mentioned above take much time to bring about, and hence are less central to the issue of forwarding the initial stages of a conciliatory process. However, at least a minimally altered view of the adversary – what Kelman has described as the discovery of a 'viable negotiating partner' – is one key change needed very early in any process of conciliation, and one major consideration in an initiator's decision to make a conciliatory move and a target's decision to respond or not. At the very least, a change must occur in the image – forming part of any zero-sum conflict frame – that fixes the adversary as a unified and a uniformly malevolent entity, with no internal differences, cleavages or factions. This change is always difficult to bring about, especially at the start of any conciliation process, but it does occur. Even the most inflexible leaders with the most rigid ideological frame can begin to redefine the nature of their adversary and hence the possibility of alternative strategies and outcomes, as when British Prime Minister Margaret Thatcher decided that Soviet Premier Gorbachev was 'A man we could do business with' and passed on this conviction to President Reagan.

Bringing about even such a relatively minor change is no easy matter, however, and the question of whether the changed image needs to occur before a conciliation process can start, or whether only the start of the process itself can begin to change enemy images, is something of a conundrum. At the very least, the two interact, and the discussion of changes in context in Chapter 4 emphasises that, while systemic changes can bring about long-term shifts in the relationship between adversaries, it is the shorter-term strategic and tactical changes that are likely to have the necessary impact on frames and images which enables initial conciliatory moves to be made and responded to.

A number of analysts, most notably Herbert Kelman, have written about the changes, and especially the psychological shifts, that are necessary before one side – by starting to view the other as at least a potential member of an 'adversary partnership'[5] – will feel itself sufficiently secure to initiate or continue an accommodative sequence. One important aspect of these psychological shifts discussed by Kelman is that they should not be made by a process of completely divorcing and differentiating pro-conciliation individuals and factions on the other side from that parties' mainstream – so that the image of implacable enmity can be preserved; but through a process of image revision, so that the adversary comes to be seen as more complex in structure and aspirations, and more flexible as regards means and methods. In Kelman's own words, applied to the Israeli-Palestinian dispute, it is possible that both sides can revise their image of each other's movement, 'changing it from the view of a movement whose only purpose is to destroy one's own group to that of a movement that has some positive goals as well and with whom it may be possible, therefore, to negotiate a mutually satisfactory solution.' (Kelman 1993, p.252).

The next step in the process, according to Kelman, is the growing recognition by a number of individuals on both sides of the conflict that there are those on the other side with whom it is possible to have a meaningful dialogue and – perhaps – even some informal negotiations. The coherent perception of the other side as uniformly adversarial gives way to something more complicated, which includes a possible role for a negotiating partner. At least some of the adversaries have learned 'that there is someone to talk to on the other side and something to talk about – a discovery that may be limited, but is not insignificant in a conflict in which the abiding assumption has been that there is no one to talk to and nothing to talk about' (Kelman 1986, p.310).

Much of Kelman's analysis of the manner in which such reframing takes place has occurred through his use of interactive problem solving approaches to conciliation and conflict resolution. This work mainly focuses on meetings of small groups of key individuals from adversaries in problem solving workshops, and the establishment of fragile, cross-adversary coalitions of pro-negotiation (and, hence, pro-conciliation) members of elites from both sides. These are at least willing to explore possible solutions to their conflict and to develop options that official leaders may later consider at the policy making level (Kelman 1993). Many have argued that it is unlikely that such work can take place at the very start of any conciliation process but on the other hand others have made the argument that such unofficial, 'Second Track' activities are often the only kind of conciliatory process that can take place during stages characterised by high mistrust and continuing mutual coercion, while zero-sum conflict frames dominate the thinking of leaders and most elites within the adversaries.

Whatever the force of such arguments, two things seem clear about such informal contacts. The first is that, at least at the elite level, they are one interesting way by which new channels of communication can be opened up between adversaries; old assumptions, images and frameworks challenged; and the possibilities of new options, solutions and relationships explored. Whether they precede and assist, or follow and depend upon, the exchange of conciliatory gestures at the official level seems to depend on circumstances, and undoubtedly this will vary from case to case.

The second point is that such meetings once again re-emphasise the need to consider the range of third party roles that might assist the succesful implementation of a conciliatory strategy, whether one looks at it from the viewpoint of an initiating party, seeking to launch a successful conciliatory initiative, or a target party, contemplating the risks and rewards of a positive response. I turn to this last aspect of the process in the next chapter, following an attempt to summarise arguments regarding the constraints and opportunities of parties in receipt of conciliatory signals.

4   Conclusion

The many and varied constraints on both initiators and targets discussed in the previous two chapters constitute a long list of obstacles to initiating clearly a conciliatory process, responding to an initial move, and maintaining the usually vulnerable interaction long enough for internal constraints to be overcome and a robust accommodative sequence to develop. The untramelled effects of all the internal constraints on the target enumerated in Chapter 11 clearly lead to outcomes somewhat similar to those outlined earlier in Chapter 10 as far as the initiator is concerned, although there are differences in detail (see Table 12.1 overleaf).

Table 12.1   **Adverse Impacts of Intra-Party Divisions and Conflicts**

Internal Constraints	*Likely Ineffects*			
IN THE INITIATOR	No signal sent at all	Unobtrusive signal sent but not recognised	Delayed signal sent	Strong signal sent but undermined by internal dissent and repudiation
IN THE TARGET	Reaction to signal deterred; no response	Unobtrusive response sent but deemed insufficient	Delayed response made but post-deadline	Strong response made but negated by criticism, dissent and possible repudiation
	Level 1	Level 2	Level 3	Level 4

Both sets of effects are likely to result in the overall failure of a conciliatory process and, often, to the addition of yet another obstacle – previous failure – to the likely success of future efforts at conciliation.

However, the overall discussion has also highlighted – at least by implication – both possible remedies for intra-party constraints and some factors that might increase the likelihood of success for a conciliatory process. Summarising briefly, the most propitious set of intra-party circumstances for the successful launching of a conciliatory process seem to include the following:

1 Low leadership commitment to existing goals and coercive strategy.
2 Low leadership responsibility for present goals and strategy.
3 High leadership security in office.
4 Low leadership accountability for policy and policy changes.
5 High level of agreement within leadership circles plus low level of factional rivalry.
6 High and efficient level of leadership supervision over policy implementing agencies.
7 High degree of sophisticated ability to analyse nature of adversary's political and perceptual structure, thus ensuring appropriate choice and framing of gestures.
8 Wide degree of choice in selecting and framing conciliatory moves.
9 Survival of party not threatened by outcome of conflict, irrespective of result.

10 If outcome of conflict involves continued existence of party in its present form, ability to find other roles and purposes for continuation.
11 Declining importance of issues to elites and rank-and-file constituents.
12 Low level of factional rivalry within elite, and especially weak pro-continuation factions.
13 Unambiguous, immediate and well distributed pay-offs from policy of conciliation.
14 Absence of 'groupthink' among leaders and elites, and of a rigid 'zero-sum conflict frame' among constituents.
15 Widespread recognition that sunk costs to date are irrecoverable.
16 Low level of risk associated with sure rewards from strategy of conciliation.
17 Low level of constituency support for present goals and/or for coercive methods used in trying to achieve them.
18 High level of support for and trust in present leadership.

It is highly unlikely, of course, that all – or, indeed, many – of the above factors will be present in most situations where embattled parties wish to attempt conciliatory initiatives. However, my argument is simply that the more of these factors that are present in a particular case, and the higher the degree to which they are present, the more likely it will be that some kind of a conciliatory gesture will be considered, discussed by leaders and launched. A similar range of propitious factors will contribute to the likelihood that a target will be able to make a positive response to the initial conciliatory move by its adversary, and the reverse list of constraints make it less likely. In the case of parties enacting the role of target, it is important to add four more influential factors:

1 A high ability on the part of monitoring, advising and implementing agencies to separate conciliatory signal from accompanying coercive moves and general 'noise'.
2 Considerable flexibility among leaders regarding alternative means of pursuing goals.
3 The absence of 'spoilers' especially within implementing agencies.
4 Widely shared perceptions among leaders and elites of ability to continue struggle if found necessary and so desired by strong pro-continuation elites and constituencies.

As a final comment, however, it is important to repeat once more that the likely success of any conciliatory process will also be strongly affected by the channels through which the message is conveyed, and by the role of third parties in supporting, interpreting and amplifying the signal – or, alternatively, by their misinterpreting, de-emphasising or distorting it. The next chapter discusses this final set of influences on the likely success of gestures of conciliation and ensuing accommodative processes.

13
Channels for Conciliation

'Even if one granted ... that Egypt under Sadat was changing in the
direction of peace, how tragic then that he did so little to convince
us of his intentions. I mean directly, explicitly, publicly to us, not in
veiled messages or hidden in convoluted diplomatic notes to third
parties or in interviews to some Danish newspaper.'

Amos Elon *Between Enemies* 1974

In order to make a conciliatory gesture to an adversary and to send some
kind of recognisable signal, an appropriate channel of communication is
necessary. The nature and efficiency of this channel will have a major effect
upon whether a conciliatory gesture is successful in starting an accommodative sequence, or helping to continue the latter once successfully
begun. This chapter considers the nature and effectiveness of various communication channels which can be employed in situations of conflict, and
completes the discussion of the five sets of influences, outlined in Figure
13.1, that help to determine the relative success of individual conciliatory
gestures, accommodative sequences and overall peace processes.

The need for some analysis of the nature of the channels used to convey
conciliatory moves is based upon the observation that one common feature
of protracted conflicts is that 'normal' forms of communication between
adversaries have often broken down, or at least become so attenuated that
they no longer serve the purpose of conveying important information in a
believable fashion. In situations of intense, protracted conflict, the 'normal'
form of communication has frequently become part of the pattern of inter-
party coercion – what might be termed 'persuasion by deed'. Hence, some
new form of conveying signals about conciliation is often a practical necessity as well as having the psychological advantage of distancing a conciliatory gesture from other, coercive signals conveyed simultaneously.

Normally, given the intra-party differences over the appropriateness of
conciliation discussed previously, decision-makers in a party looking to
make conciliatory gestures will often seek some unobtrusive means of

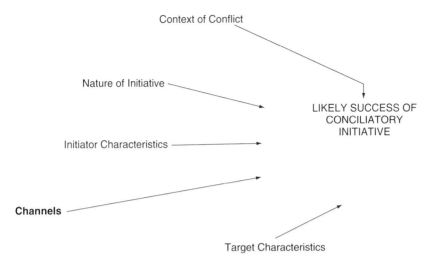

Figure 13.1 **Influences on Conciliation Effectiveness VII**

making contact and conveying signals – as I argued earlier, of 'insulating' the signal from those pro-continuation factions within the party, strongly convinced that any search for a satisfactory negotiated solution is either unrealistic or immoral. However, there are not infrequent exceptions to this general rule of the use of closed channels, one of the oddest being the occasion on which Mr Krushchev, at the height of the Cuban Missile Crisis, was forced by delays in 'normal' diplomatic channels to use an open broadcast on Radio Moscow to convey a message directly to President Kennedy. More conventionally, there are enough examples of the kind of grand, public gesture like President Sadat's visit to Israel to indicate that choices of channel do exist, even if many conciliatory gestures are conveyed as quietly and as unobtrusively as possible to 'insulate' them from the scrutiny of intra-party hawks or critics among elites, or from rank-and-file followers who might become disheartened if they knew their leaders were 'negotiating behind their backs'. On this evidence, the leaders of parties contemplating a conciliatory gesture must often weigh some of the pros and cons of using a particular open or closed channel in the belief that one or other type will have the greatest impact on their chances for success.

In many protracted conflicts, there seem to be three important choices facing parties planning to make some conciliatory move towards an adversary, the open/closed channel issue being only one of them:

1 Should a conciliatory initiative be conveyed directly to the adversary without the use of any intermediary or should third parties be utilised in an indirect approach?

2 Should the source of the initiative be clearly an official one, or should
   some kind of unofficial, private sounding be taken first?

3 Finally, should the initiative be made publicly and openly, so that
   leaders, elites and constituents in all involved parties are aware of, at
   least, the fact that the move is being made; or should things be kept
   confidential for as long as possible?

1   The debate over open or closed channels

When direct, bilateral approaches are being contemplated, the question of
whether to use open and public means of conveying a conciliatory move,
or closed and private (or even secret) channels, often revolves round issues
of commitment and credibility on the one hand, and deniability, flexibility
and innovation on the other. This is especially a problem when parties are
trying to communicate directly with one another at the start of some conciliation process and no third parties are yet being employed in the role of
contacts or go-betweens.

Obviously, gestures like that of President Sadat's journey to Israel and the
Knesset are the clearest examples of moves made publicly, directly and
through the most open of channels, including global and local news
media. Public pronouncements, such as the British lifting of the economic
embargo on trade with Argentina following the 1982 War in the South
Atlantic (Mitchell 1991), are somewhat less dramatic moves, but equally
'open', direct and subject to the scrutiny and (mis)interpretation of elite
factions and constituencies within the initiator as well as leaders, factions
and constituencies within the target – and generally throughout the
conflict system. The problem with this type of 'open channel' activity is
that it inevitably gives rise to a dilemma of credibility versus commitment,
for both initiator and target. On the one hand the public nature of the
gesture may lead to the danger that it will be perceived as playing to some
'gallery' and interpreted as something other than a genuine conciliatory
action – a move made to buy off domestic opposition, to impress third
parties urging a more flexible stance, to buy time, or to lull the target into a
false sense of security. The more public the gesture, the more likely the suspicion that there is less substance to the gesture than meets the eye.
Generally speaking, the more open the move or widely broadcast any
announcement, the more likely the target will be to view the initiative
sceptically, as being made for some purpose other than starting a genuiune
search for a solution.

On the other hand, the very fact that the move has been made publicly
helps to bind the initiator to any commitments made or implied in the
conciliatory move, and makes it difficult to back away from what has been
admitted, implied or actually promised. The whole point about a publicly
conveyed gesture is that future deniability is low if not non-existent. Like

President Sadat, the British in 1985 could hardly withdraw their commitment to ending the embargo once the 8 July announcement had been
made. Once made publicly – and, just as importantly, officially – the
gesture itself and any actual or implied commitment can only be subsequently denied with the greatest difficulty. Public channels publicly
commit the initiator, so are usually used with great caution and for not
very substantial concessions – although the extent and importance of the
latter are frequently exaggerated by those making the move, so that public
gestures can become exercises in hyperbole – hence the scepticism mentioned above.

In many other cases, parties decide not to use public pronouncements as
the channels for conveying conciliatory moves, and attempt to minimise
the risk of disbelief by using confidential channels, conveying initiatives
discreetly and directly. The great advantages of using secret, 'back' channels
are, firstly, that these avoid or at least reduce the risk that the Target of the
initiative will immediately jump to the conclusion that the moves are
being made solely for their publicity value, or to satisfy some intra-party
constituency agitating for change; and, secondly, that confidential channels offer more flexibility, providing an opportunity of conveying a great
range of possibilities, offers or suggestions – given that confidential channels can more easily be insulated from pro-continuation factions and constituencies within both initiator and target.

On the other hand, the very fact that confidential channels are being
used, while increasing the flexibility of both initiator in launching and
target in responding to the move, also decreases the perceived commitment
and increases the subsequent deniability of any initiative. Private communications can always be reinterpreted, reframed or denied outright, and the
more private and unofficial these have been, the more easily leaders of a
party in conflict can de-commmit themselves both to their target and –
should the initiatives become public property through deliberate or acci-
dental leaking – to other leaders, elites or publics in the conflict system.
The fervent denials – amounting to outright lies – of British Ministers
protesting that they had not been in secret communication with Sinn Fein
from 1990 to 1993 exemplifies the deniability factor at its most extreme,
and also the dangers of this strategy once the truth of the matter is revealed
to aroused publics, as it was when Sinn Fein published documentary
evidence of the contacts.

Moreover, bilateral channels – whether public or private – are also much
affected by the source of the signal. The initiative's credibility (and later
success) can be as much affected by who makes the move as by the manner
of its making. Clearly there is a major difference between official and
unofficial actors in enhancing or diminishing the credibility of a conciliatory move, whether an initiative or a response. Moves by top leaders, such
as President Sadat or top British Ministers, carry more commitment, less

deniability and hence much greater credibility than those undertaken by lower-level officials. Official moves by members of a decision-making hierarchy usually carry more weight than those made by rank-and-file members of a party in conflict. Again, a dilemma revolves around conceptions of deniability and commitment, with the key question asked by both target and initiator being: 'Who can genuinely commit our adversary, in what manner and through what channel?' The overall nature of the dilemma is summarised in Table 13.1.

Table 13.1   **Likely Impact of Alternative Channels**

SOURCE		CHANNELS	
	STATUS	*OPEN*	*CONFIDENTIAL*
OFFICIAL	HIGH	High credibility	High credibility
		Low deniability	Medium deniability
	LOW	Low credibility	Medium credibility
		Low deniability	High deniability
UNOFFICIAL		Low credibility	Low credibility
		Medium deniability	High deniability

This is also a question that is usually asked about third parties who act as channels in initially indirect conciliation processes. Being a channel is an often-neglected role for third parties whose 'important' tasks are usually seen as those arising from being a formal mediator, a role which can only, however, exist if the equally important role of channel, or 'go-between' has been successfully carried out in the earliest stages of any process of conciliation. The next section considers the nature of such third party 'channels' and their likely impact on the success of conciliatory moves.

2   The use of third parties as channels

The use of public and open means of signalling conciliatory gestures usually makes the process a bilateral one and places responsibility for its success or failure on the decision-makers of the parties conducting the exchange and their selected representatives. If ambiguous signals are sent, clearer signals misinterpreted, responses deemed inadequate or delays involve missed deadlines, then only the parties themselves can be held directly responsible.

There are occasions, of course, when third parties do become publicly and obviously involved in protracted conflicts as channels or intermediaries. It is, after all, part of the mission of the UN or the Organisation of American States or even NATO to act as a peacemaker in major international conflicts, while missions from both large and smaller powers such as the USA or Sweden can frequently be observed undertaking intermediary functions in conflicts that threaten international peace and security. Equally, however, these and many other institutions frequently act as confidential channels, away from public scrutiny, and particularly in the initial stages of any conciliatory process, when trust is low and risk and uncertainty high. Thus, the use of confidential channels frequently involves one or more third parties, making the process a more complex and – some would say – more problematic one. Not least is this because the third parties will have considerable influence on the relative effectiveness of the process.

In many types of conflict there are a variety of circumstances in which third parties can become involved as channels. Even in protracted and intense conflicts, some residual contact points often remain, waiting to be used, so that signals about concessions or other conciliatory moves can be exchanged directly and, at a later stage in the process, bilateral meetings take place. For example, in the early stages of the search for a *rapprochement* between President Nixon's administration and the government of the CPR there were initial and important contacts on the 'neutral' ground of Warsaw between the US Ambassador there and the *chargé* in the CPR Embassy (Hersh 1983, pp.360–1). Similar fora were available in Paris and in Rangoon during the prolonged efforts to bring the war in Vietnam to an end under both Presidents Johnson and Nixon. Even in intense civil strife some possible points of contact often exist, although in such conflicts it is frequently difficult to use formal diplomatic networks.

Equally often, however, contacts between the adversaries have broken down to such an extent that it is necessary to involve third parties anew as channels and contacts, and this process can involve the use of a wide variety of third party intermediaries, private and official, conventional and unconventional, in order to make the first contact and either convey the first gesture, emphasise it or even warn of its imminent transmission. These third party channels form the focus of the remainder of this chapter.

Three important limitations on the following discussion of third parties should be noted, however. The first is that the discussion focuses on the role of third parties at the very beginning of any conciliation or peacemaking process – the stage at which initial contacts are being established and preliminary signals about conciliation tentatively made. The nature and functions of third parties in a full-blown intermediary role – that is, as an official mediator or conciliator – will not be reviewed.[1] Instead, attention is concentrated upon the much more limited role in the very early stages of conciliation processes from which, frequently, the initial contact withdraws for others to take over full intermediary functions.

Secondly, the discussion will concern itself more with situations which involve one or other of the parties in conflict actively seeking an intermediary channel once someone among relevant decision-makers have come to the conclusion that a negotiated settlement is feasible and, indeed, preferable to a continuation of coercion. In such cases, one of the adversaries usually searches for an appropriate channel and then uses it. This contrasts with cases in which the initiative comes from – often strongly from – the intermediary itself, so that an approach is made to the parties in conflict, rather than on behalf of one of them. In many historical cases, the distinction is by no means as clear-cut as suggested, and a kind of 'courting' process between potential intermediary and potential conciliators takes place, making it difficult to determine who, precisely, is the 'initiator' of this particular move. In others, it is plainly a party initiative or an intermediary initiative. What follows merely excludes the latter from consideration, thus omitting from consideration UN engendered peace missions, 'Great Power' initiatives to be 'honest brokers', and self-generated initiatives by non-aligned or neutralist governments, such as Sweden or Algeria.

The third limitation involves the discussion concentrating upon third party activities which are mainly undertaken at the level of leaders and decision-makers, to the exclusion of a great deal of other intermediary 'channeling' activity that involves elites, factions and constituencies. This is not to deny either the existence or the importance of an activity that opens channels at other, non-decision-making levels, and conveys information, ideas or aspirations between opinion makers and opinion takers within rival parties – and between decision-makers and these other levels. Many analysts, particularly Lederach (1996) and Diamond and McDonald (1996), have emphasised the importance of the role of third parties in establishing contacts and communication at a wide variety of different levels – ranging from leaders to grass roots – within adversaries.[2] It also seems unarguable that such activity, if it is undertaken tactfully and skillfully, can make a major contribution to constructing a full resolution of the conflict in the long run, not the least by convincing elites and rank-and-file constituents that there exists a range of alternative ways of achieving their aspirations, but also in conveying the wide variety of different types of information between leadership, elite and constituency levels outlined in Figure 13.2 opposite. However, for the purposes of the rest of this present study, attention will be concentrated on leader to leader channels, and on the role of third parties in conveying conciliatory gestures at this, decision-making level, as it is at this level that key decisions regarding the initiation or continuation of conciliation and accommodation must first take place.

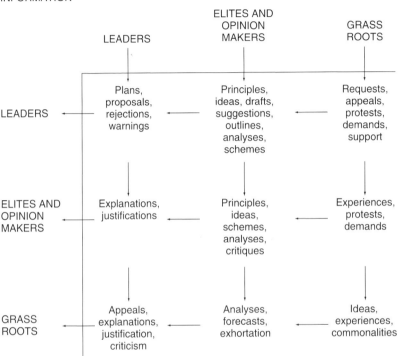

Figure 13.2 **Levels of Information Exchange Via Intermediaries**

3 The variety of third party channels

Determining the profile of the 'ideal' third party channel for initiating a de-escalatory process is extremely difficult, as empirical evidence seems to show clearly that the exigencies of conflicts force parties to use channels that are available to them, not those they would select under some mythical, ideal conditions. For example, in the initial stages of negotiating a release of the hostages taken from the US embassy in Iran, the Carter administration seemed to have little choice but to use as intermediaries a French and an Argentinian lawyer, both living in Paris, who had worked as legal advisors for the new Iranian regime and who were being used as unobtrusive contacts by those in the government of Abolhassan Bani-Sadr wishing to negotiate an end to the hostage crisis (Jordan 1982). Later, the Algerian Government took over the role of intermediary, but the initial contacts had, in this case, been made by private citizens acting confidentially as unofficial emissaries. Similarly, a wide variety of third party intermediaries was used by both Washington and Hanoi during the various stages of their attempts to begin face to face negotiations in the period 1964–9. During that period, the list of intermediaries conveying signals and messages included the Canadian representative on the International Control Commission (ICC), the Italian and Swedish Governments, the Polish ambassador in Saigon, British Prime Minister Wilson together with Soviet Premier Kosygin, the Rumanian Government, the Norwegian ambassador in Peking, and two private French citizens (Raymond Aubrac and Herbert Marcovich) who set up contacts between Hanoi, Washington and Paris which involved, at one stage, Henry Kissinger as an informal US contact (Thies 1980).

3.1   Necessary qualities of third party 'channels'?

Amid this enormous variety of intermediary channels, a number of shared qualities do emerge in rather tenuous form. These might be summarised by saying that intermediaries conveying signals of de-escalation in the early stages of the process usually (1) possess physical access to the target and initiator; (2) have pre-existing and mutually valued linkages – of some sort – to both sides; (3) are relatively independent of both; and (4) are relatively neutral towards the conflict itself. All of these qualities appear to lead to the potential intermediary being invested with a limited degree of trust and some minimum credibility as an effective channel.

The most obvious quality enjoyed by intermediary 'channels' is the fact that they have relatively easy physical access to both sides in the dispute which is (of course) usually the reason they are asked to act as channel in the first place. Ambassador Lewandowski in Saigon had access to Hanoi through Polish membership of the ICC; Messrs Villalon and Bourguet had access to Iranian leaders through their previous legal work and through contacts they had developed with those leaders while the latter were in exile in France; Pakistani leaders had contacts both with Washington and Peking through their alignments with both governments on a variety of issues. In a very basic sense, intermediaries that convey conciliatory gestures have a 'foot in both camps' and can move with relative – if only relative – ease between either.

However, in a more important sense, intermediaries that are useful in this task of conveying conciliatory signals frequently have pre-existing linkages that tie them to both sides of a dispute, and these linkages help to give them not merely access but attention and some credibility. The linkages do not tie them completely to one party or the other, so that the attributes of linkage and independence appear to run together for successful third parties, at least at this stage of the conflict. For example, a government that frequently acted as a third party channel for adversaries in the Middle East during the 1970s and early 1980s was that of President Ceausescu in Bucharest. The Rumanians were linked to the Arab world through East European ties established during the 1950s and 1960s, and they had provided political support and material aid to many Arab countries, including Egypt and Syria. However, they also recognised and maintained good relations with Israel, so that Bucharest frequently became the site of sequences of meetings between Rumanian and Israeli leaders and subsequently between Rumanian leaders and leaders from Arab governments. At times, King Hassan of Morocco played a parallel third party role. In this case, the King had excellent credentials in most of the Arab world (although being the frequent brunt of antagonistic policies by various 'radical' Arab leaders), but he also had a less hostile attitude towards Israel, partly because of the large community of Moroccan Jews who emigrated voluntarily to the latter country in the 1950's, and who still retained close contacts back in Morocco.

Moreover, in both cases, the respective governments retained a large degree of independence from the main adversaries in the Middle East conflict. Morocco was not a confrontation state although Moroccan military units had been sent on occasions to countries around Israel. Similarly, Rumania remained independent from the anti-Israeli stance espoused by the Soviet Union while managing to retain the respect of many leaders in Arab countries. Neither was dependent upon any of the major adversaries in the conflict, while the reverse was also true. Both, then, provided good examples of third parties that have good access and linkages to adversaries in a conflict, are relatively independent of them and manage to retain a considerable degree of neutrality as far as the dispute itself is concerned. In many ways, they illustrate necessary qualities for third parties acting as channels, qualities which one can also find in: (1) non-governmental and unofficial bodies that have acted as channels in other disputes – the World Council of Churches in the first Sudanese civil war, for example; the International Committee of the Red Cross in Nigeria from 1966 to 1969; or the San Egidio Community in Mozambique – and (2) private individuals who frequently act as message carriers or channels for signals between antagonists – Elmore Jackson making contact betwen President Nasser and the Israeli Government in 1955 (Jackson 1983), or Aubrac and Marcovich (Theis 1980) acting as 'go-betweens' for Hanoi and Washington in 1967.[3]

3.2 Credibility v deniability

While some of the desirable qualities for third party channels are obvious and unarguable, this is not to say that intermediaries with such qualities are always handily available, or that such qualities exhaust the range of desirable attributes. It is equally obvious that decision-makers looking to signal a quiet, conciliatory gesture would wish to utilise a channel that is simultaneously both unobtrusive to internal critics and credible to the target. Unfortunately, these two qualities are often at odds or, at least, difficult to combine in one channel. On the one hand, the use of private and unofficial intermediaries is frequently the best strategy for avoiding domestic disputes and crises over 'selling out' or 'surrendering', should the initiative come to light. Such emissaries can be easily denied or rebuked for exceeding their brief. It would have been easy to claim that private and unofficial intermediaries – Dean Gullion, or M. Aubrac and M. Marcovich, for example – were acting largely on their own initiative in holding talks with Mai Van Bo in Paris. It is less easy to do this with the ambassador of a friendly government, who will obviously have cleared his initiative with decision-makers in at least one capital before embarking on the exchange of signals.

On the other hand, this very deniability works against such a channel being highly credible to a target and, to some degree, the reverse argument holds good as regards credibility. The more official (and, to some extent, the less unobtrusive and deniable) the intermediary, the more credible the channel is likely to be in the target's eyes. The more an initiator utilises unobtrusive emissaries, the more effort has to be made to get the target to take serious notice of the signals conveyed through that channel. It is easy to envisage a continuum of credibility and visibility, running at one end from official emissaries who have to conceal the very fact that they are in contact with an adversary – or with a third party who could be in contact with an adversary – (Dr Kissinger as National Security adviser 'falling ill' to go to Pakistan and Peking; Foreign Minister Dayan disguising himself to fly secretly from Paris to visit King Hassan in Morocco in 1977); to relatively invisible but much less credible private emissaries travelling between capitals and having to overcome obstacles to access, let alone disbelief, when they arrive at their destination.[4]

One obvious answer to this problem is for decision-makers wishing to use a private and unobtrusive channel to try to ensure that channel's credibility (at least as far as it is perceived to represent a party's signal in some official manner) by some form of symbolic or practical indication of official endorsement that will be obvious to the target but less noticeable to domestic critics. A clear and direct channel of communication back to top decision-makers in an initiator is one way of using such a tactic. Hamilton Jordan has reported how the informal and unofficial emissaries from the Iranian Government during the hostage crisis established their credibility simply by picking up a telephone and talking directly to the Iranian Foreign Minister in Teheran – something the US Government had, up to that time, been unable to do (Jordan 1982, p.118). Some similar means of unobtrusively establishing credibility with the Target would seem to be necessary for any informal channel conveying a signal. At least this would deal with problems of access and noticeability, if not with Jervis's point about the final stage of credibility – belief that the source of the signal can be trusted to carry it through (Jervis 1970, p.24).

Even if a party wishing to begin a process of conciliation is in the fortunate position of being able to select as a channel a relatively neutral intermediary with, linkages, easy access to and some credibility with all parties – and decision-makers more often have to take what they can get – this by no means guarantees success. The manner in which a third party carries out the task of channelling a conciliatory move must affect the impact of the signal and the chances of reciprocation. This is our next topic.

4   Success in functioning as a 'channel'

In communications theory, a channel is generally regarded as a more or less efficient way of transferring information between sender and receiver. It is also regarded as 'stable' (in the sense that any distortions of information will form a pattern or – at least – be in the form of a regular deterioration) rather than 'erratic', meaning that distortions and addition or suppression of information can occur in a relatively random fashion to affect the message eventually reaching the receiver.

Unfortunately, in the case of the channels used in political communication, it is perfectly possible to discover that a chosen channel has behaved in a quite different way from another previously employed channel, or from the same channel used at a previous point in time. 'Erratic' transmission of information might well be regarded as the rule rather than the exception. Political 'channels' often have goals of their own which can be forwarded by acting as a third party intermediary (Mitchell 1989). They often have perceptual and evaluative barriers of their own that affect their interpretation of the signal they carry and the manner in which they deliver it. Finally, such 'channels' are often subject to crucial delays, so that signals that might have an optimum impact if delivered in a particular form and at a particular time often have a lesser effect quite simply because of the time and the manner of their delivery.

All of these general problems apply with just as much force to conciliatory gestures and processes as to other forms of signalling during conflicts. This section, therefore, discusses a number of positive effects that a third party channel might have upon a conciliatory signal that a party in conflict is seeking to make to its adversary. These include third party functions of *conveying, amplifying, endorsing, enhancing credibility* and *creating minimal trust*. It then considers some potentially negative effects which include *manipulating* or *distorting* the signal being conveyed. It should also be emphasised that both beneficial and negative effects can occur throughout an accommodative sequence, when adversaries take turns in becoming targets for one another's signals. It might be, for example, that distortions mar or wholly undermine an initial gesture of conciliation from initiator to target. It might equally well be the case that a third party channel has a similar negative effect at this and all subsequent stages during what is likely to turn out to be an abortive effort to move towards a solution.

4.1 Beneficial channel effects

The experience of individuals and organisations that have fulfilled the role of initial channel for conciliatory gestures in the very earliest stages of a peace process suggests that the set of functions listed above are not completely inaccurate, even if they are not exhaustive. For example, the Society of Friends has often acted as an initial point of contact for, and channel between, parties in protracted conflicts, and has frequently helped to start conciliation processes leading towards a solution. In reviewing the Quaker experience, Mike Yarrow has argued that Quaker third parties typically carry out a variety of tasks in circumstances in which adversaries have no other regular means of communication:

1 Personal visitation and contact between antagonists;
2 Providing a medium of exchange for adversaries that may have no other direct contact;
3 Assessing realities on both sides of this communications 'gap';
4 Identifying conditions that may permit partial solutions or steps towards a final settlement;
5 Listening to each side's perceptions, aspirations and proposals; and
6 Proposing small steps away from unswerving confrontation and coercion (Yarrow 1978).

The list suggests that, besides conveying a message together with a clear and accurate assessment of the background to an initiator's signal to the target and the meaning of the signal itself, a third party can perform as a channel in a variety of ways that increase the probability that the conciliatory initiative will be a success. For example, the Quaker intermediary, Adam Curle, lists a number of things to be done by informal intermediaries acting as a channel between adversaries whose normal form of communication consists of harmful acts and vilifying statements:

'This includes such tasks as taking messages from one side to the other, usually enlarging on the implications and meanings behind the message; they do a tremendous amount of explaining the motives and intentions of the one side to the other; they interpret the statements or the cryptic 'smoke signals' sent up by either combatant; they correct wrong impressions and mistaken impressions obtained from statements and speeches by leaders of the others side … they make suggestions about how to improve communications between the protagonists.' (Curle 1986, pp.11–12).

Echoing Curle, I have noted elsewhere that a party carrying out such a variety of functions could be characterised as fulfilling an Explorer's role, the first of 13 possible roles for third parties seeking to assist in the search for a solution (Mitchell 1993, p.147). Within this role, an intermediary can suggest the utility of exploratory contacts to one or both parties or act as a sounding board for an initiator's initial message, by pointing out counter-productive content or format. At a slightly later stage, apart from simply conveying the message, the role expands to include other core functions:

1 clarifying;
2 interpreting;
3 amplifying;
4 endorsing;
5 reassuring;
6 trust building.

The first two of these involve firstly clarifying the nature of the concilia-tory move and then interpreting the intra-party context within which the signal has been made. Allied to this is the third party's task of emphasising, 'pointing up' or amplifying positive aspects of the signal to the target's decision-makers, so that the initiator's intentions become clear (assuming, again, that it is a genuinely conciliatory intention). Almost inevitably in a protracted conflict, the parties involved come to have a negative and over-simple view of the adversary, particularly as regards its internal unity and unchangeable malevolence. Third parties can help to make one side's view of its adversary at once more complex and more realistic, and thus provide a more accurate context against which to view the actual initiative being conveyed to the target. The task is to increase not merely the accuracy of information conveyed but also its richness. As Adam Curle describes the task:

'There is obviously more to being a messenger than just carrying a message and delivering it like a postman. For one thing, it will often not be written down, but even if so there is always much to say about the circumstances in which it was sent, and the mood of the senders. In addition, it will probably need to be amplifed and explained, ambigui-ties elucidated and so on. The first necessity, therefore, is that mediators should be accepted in this fairly active role ... and can communicate with the leaders concerned ... in the sense of presenting material they will listen to and understand.' (Curle 1986, p.21)

There are two particularly important aspects of the interpreting role. The first involves the third party helping to break down a common assumption that the uniform intransigence of an adversary means that there is no hope of any jointly negotiated solution to the dispute. This task of changing a perception of unbroken and unbreakable malevolence and intransigence is an inevitable and important preliminary task for a go-between. Secondly, and in contrast, third parties will need to deal carefully with what might be termed the 'willingness–weakness dilemma', which is the likely result of their conveying a conciliatory move by one side, but the other immediately interpreting the motives for this as arising from the increasing weakness of their adversary. Any third party will need to clarify the intra-party situation within the initiator that has led to the transmission of the signal, at least to the extent of emphasising that this should not be taken as a sign of weakness, either materially nor as regards a readiness to continue if the gesture is rejected in an intransigent manner. Again, this will require altering a common perception in protracted conflicts that the only language the adversary's leaders understand is force, and the only factor motivating them to learn is loss. The go-between can also amplify the seriousness of the move and the risks being run by the adversary's decision-makers, the existence of a more intransigent pro-continuation faction, and the fact that this is likely to be merely the first of a series of conciliatory gestures provided it is responded to appropriately.

To a large degree, the success of the clarifying, interpreting and amplifying functions depends upon the channel's own knowledge, contacts and credibility, especially with regard to his or her direct knowledge of views and objectives among the initiator's decision-makers. It would be fatal to overclaim more knowledge than could reasonably be expected from that particular third party; the channel always has its own credibility problem. Moreover, the openness with which a channel discusses conditions within the initiator is something to be viewed with caution as the target will assume all too easily that a similar openness – or garrulousness – might characterise that channel's interaction with the initiator regarding the target. Nonetheless, a channel's successful emphasis of positive aspects of one party's signal and amplification of new and less coercive intentions can help considerably in increasing the credibility of the signal and of a wish to conciliate and to talk.

If amplification is the most obvious benefit that an efficient and competent third party channel can provide to a signalling party, almost equally important is the service of providing an endorsement of the signal by agreeing to transmit it. In a sense, and particularly when the signal is sent through another government, an international agency or organisation with a reputation for hard-headedness and absence of gullibility to preserve, the very fact of agreeing to act as channel for the message adds a degree of credibility to the signal. In a sense, the message has to go through a process of double vetting, first by the channel and then by the target. By the time it is delivered to the target the latter can at least be sure that it, and some of the background to the making of the gesture, have already been scrutinised by decision-makers in the channel. Given that no government, NGO or individual relishes looking a fool or being seen as the gullible carrier of meaningless, false or deceptive messages, the act of transmitting or delivering the message (particularly by a – relatively – neutral third party) has some effect by reassuring the target that this is something a little more than a propaganda exercise – indeed, in an earlier article I refered to this task as one of reassuring a target (Mitchell 1993). No party to a conflict will want to antagonise a friendly channel by playing false too often – or even at all – and recognition of this principle can provide a target with some minimal guarantee of the fact that the other side is, indeed, committed to exploring a process of conciliation.

However, seriousness of general intent is not the only guarantee of authenticity that an effective channel can provide to a target on behalf of a party making a conciliatory gesture. In many ways, a third party channel with a reputation for disinterest – and with that reputation to lose – can also authenticate the circumstances in which the initiative was launched; can inform the target about the relative seriousness with which the other side views the move; can add information about possible follow-up moves from the initiator should the process successfully get under way; and – in all these things – can add its own endorsement of that process through an implicit guarantee of its own commitment to the process. In this sense, a channel can increase the level of guarantee to the target by adding its own commitment (using the term in its 'everyday' meaning) to that of the initiator, and occasionally being able to offset the target's inevitable perception of a lack of seriousness of the adversary, or the target's concern about vulnerability. Again, the element of authenticity comes in here, because the fact that the third party – if possessing appropriate qualities – has agreed to risk its own status and reputation in acting as channel could help to reassure the target about the credibility of the initial move. If the channel's commitment to the initiative is added to that of its originator, the combination may help to offset the inevitable suspicion and uncertainty of a target.

This argument has a bearing on another major benefit that the use of appropriate channels can confer upon an initiator, and this concerns the huge difficulty of developing in the target (and, indeed, later in the initiator) the minimum level of trust for the de-escalation process to start and then continue without faltering. As I argued in Chapter 9, there is absolutely no reason why, in a protracted conflict, one party should trust the other, even to the minimal level necessary to begin serious negotiations. Even with the most appropriate and convincing conciliatory initiative, the chances of a target being willing to run the risks inevitably associated with responding to such a move, and being ready to trust the adversary even that far, are slim indeed.

However, to the extent that the target trusts the channel *not* to bring a signal which is merely a probe or a publicity gimmick, the conciliatory gesture might be responded to. In a sense, what is proposed here might be seen as the third party substituting its own reliability for the unreliability of the source of the signal. A suitable third party might therefore find itself as a focus of transferred trust from the target who, still regarding the other party as basically untrustworthy, is nonetheless willing to proceed on the grounds that it trusts the channel not to allow the process to result in unacceptable harm before calling a halt or warning of likely adverse consequences.[5] Moreover, as well as using its own 'trustworthiness' as a guarantee on behalf of an initiator while a target still mistrusts the latter, the third party can also reinforce the initiator's efforts to demonstrate trustworthy behaviour so that, gradually and if the accommodative sequence continues successfully, some of the target's trust in, and reliance on, the good faith of the channel can transfer to its erstwhile adversary. A similar process of trust-transfer can also affect the initiator as regards the target so that a 'working trust' can be built up.[6]

It may be possible, then, for an appropriate and effective third party acting as a channel to have a very positive effect on the progress of the initial stages of a de-escalation process, either because that party can explain and persuade the target to take the gesture seriously or because the 'channel' can add its own commitment, reputation and trustworthiness to the interaction and thus authenticate it enough to keep it going. Unfortunately, it is also the case that a third party acting as a channel, even when possessing other appropriate qualities – such as neutrality or discretion – can have an adverse effect on the move by distorting the signal in a negative manner.

4.2   Negative channel effects

Negative third party effects on conciliatory processes can take three basic forms: *suppressing*, *distorting* and *manipulating*. At the most extreme, a third party asked to perform as a channel for a conciliatory gesture can, for its own reasons, simply suppress the signal so that it is not received by the target. Stalin, for example, simply failed to pass on to the United States the peace feelers sent to Moscow by the Japanese Government during the last few months of the Second World War. Other third parties have failed to recognise more subtle hints that parties in conflict were hoping could be passed on to their adversaries as a form of kite flying without any overt commitment.

More usually, the alteration of the signal takes the form either of distortion, which involves the inadvertent changing of some aspects of the signal in transit by the channel, or the more deliberate manipulation, in which the nature of the signal is deliberately altered by the channel either for its own purposes or because it believes that a 'better' outcome – usually a greater flexibility or willingness to reciprocate on the part of the target – will result.

Distortion inevitably occurs – to some degree – in any transfer of messages involving a third party, if only because, as outlined in the previous section, the latter will usually go well beyond the mere text of the message to provide a context for its genesis and manufacture. As long as the additional information is not too inaccurate or subjectively interpreted, little harm and some good may be done. However, it is often the case that third parties do not confine their role to acting as simple channels, or as sources of further (accurate) information only on request from the target. Just as often, third parties will add their own messages to the signal, provide subjectively biased interpretations, or exaggerate particular aspects of the signal over and beyond what might have been intended by the party making the conciliatory move.

A common form of distortion, partly caused by the need of many third parties to be seen as successful in their mission, is to exaggerate the willingness of the other side to make further concessions and conciliatory moves in the future, thus raising unrealistic expectations on the part of target parties. This is a natural temptation for third parties, who see it as part of their technique to emphasise the positive aspects of messages and intra-party contexts. It can often backfire. One instance of such distortion, on this occasion certainly brought about through over-enthusiasm, is the case of the 'very specific peace offer' which Ambassador Lewandowski, the Polish representative on the ICC, brought from Hanoi in June 1966, which – it was claimed – included a northern demand for a suspension (not cessation) of US bombing and an insistence that the NLF be represented at future talks but not necessarily as the sole representative from South Vietnam (Thies 1980, pp.138–9). However, a month later, Lewandowski speaking under instructions in Warsaw rather than in Saigon, as had previously been the case, restated the North Vietnamese position in harsher terms which reflected Hanoi's previous public bargaining position and which contained no mention of the new flexibility which, he had said, was evident in June. This seems to be a clear case of a third party enthusiastically distorting a signal from one adversary to another in such a way as to imply greater conciliation than actually existed, a strategy that always possesses its own in-built time bomb, as both the Ambassador himself and the US Government discovered.

It is in this sense that such distortions usually turn out to be costly. For one thing, targets usually find it hard to disentangle the reality of their adversary's signal from the additional information included by the third party and to evaluate the precise degree of conciliation displayed by the adversary (even if not actually felt). Secondly, the effects of disillusionment experienced if the positively slanted signal is believed by the target but then denounced or 'reneged on' by a party convinced that it had offered less than the target perceived, will inevitably lead to more firmly established cognitions of one another's untrustworthiness and real commitment to continuation and coercion, as well as discrediting the third party and producing a greater wariness of future gestures. The conciliation task will become that much harder.

While distortions of signals are usually the result of genuine mistakes in interpretation or perception, or of over-enthusiasm and efforts to 'get the process moving' by third parties, other occasions have seen the deliberate manipulation of signals by the party transmitting them. Manipulation can take place because the third party feels that additional information, exaggeration, slanted emphasis, suppression or playing down of unpalatable aspects of the signal could all contribute to a faster or more effective *rapprochement.*

It can also take place because of a third party's own interest in the relationship between the adversaries, or some seeking for advantage by a third party with objectives of its own – other than a reputation for being an 'honest broker' – to achieve. The procedures involved in manipulation are much the same as those in distortion and produce the same result of an altered signal or series of signals. However, manipulation differs from distortion in terms of (i) the degree to which the signals in question are altered; (ii) the underlying intentions of the third party; (iii) the calculation and self-awareness with which the process is carried out; and (iv) the likelihood that particular signals are made at the deliberate suggestion of the third party and as part of a manipulative pattern.

Like distortion, manipulation has its own inherent drawback in that it is likely to be discovered and the whole conciliation process wrecked once parties obtain their own independent means of checking on information. On occasions, it can be kept up for a considerable length of time and develop its own dynamic, which may have beneficial effects in the long run, and even lead to successful de-escalation and agreement in spite of the deceit and deliberate distortions of the information exchange. Many writers have observed that Dr Kissinger, while Secretary of State, brought manipulative intervention to a fine art and it could be argued that his form of third party *realpolitik* was, in a limited sense, successful in the Middle East. On the other hand, it seems to have wrecked his attempts to achieve a settlement in the Rhodesian conflict during 1976. At that time, as part of his efforts to conclude an agreement based upon the white minority's acceptance of the principle of black majority rule in the country, he deliberately misled the whites' leader, Ian Smith, into believing that a draft plan for an interim government into which the white regime would 'invite' black nationalist leaders had already been reviewed and accepted by those leaders as well as by the Presidents of the 'Front Line States' (Zambia,

Mozambique, Botswana and Tanzania). Such deliberate use of what one of Kissinger's staff called 'tactical ambiguity' backfired when Kissinger's plan, together with additional conditions for acceptance advanced by Smith himself, was rejected by both groups of African leaders on the grounds that Kissinger had no brief to negotiate anything other than Smith's acceptance of majority rule.[7] Kissinger again manipulated communications, omitting to inform Smith of these significant (and unacceptable) African objections in order to try to get him publicly to accept the principle of African majority rule (Meredith 1979, pp.256–60). When the deceptions and distortions were discovered, the whole conciliation process broke down, illustrating only too well the dangers of a third party engaging in wholesale manipulation of communication between adversaries.

There are a number of explanations for a third party seeking to manipulate or distort a communication process between adversaries in which it is engaged, in order to achieve rapid success or a particular outcome. For one thing, it should never be forgotten that many third parties themselves have intra-party divisions, disputes and critics, and that the role of intermediary – and sucess in that role – can often be used to divert attention from such divisions or undermine domestic critics. Using external success as a third party can be an effective way of reducing domestic vulnerability for that party's leaders, a point well illustrated by President Clinton's role in both Middle East and Northern Irish peace processes in the 1990s and by President Ceausescu's role in Israeli–Egyptian relations two decades earlier.

More frequently, the key factor explaining the tendency of many third parties to use the power involved in acting as a channel of communication to distort signals and manipulate both initiator and target is that party's own degee of interest in the conflict and the eventual settlement (or lack of a settlement). Stalin, for example, was hardly enthusiastic about the Japanese Government concluding a cease-fire and a negotiated settlement with the Western Allies, at least until the USSR had involved itself militarily in the final defeat of Japan and thus also in the negotiations about the post-war settlement on the Soviet Union's far eastern borders. Kissinger and the US Government had major and continuing interests in the Middle East, and in developing a solution that maintained US long-term support for Israel without damaging relations with the conservative, oil-exporting Arab regimes. In the case of Rhodesia, a peaceful transition to a 'moderate' African government in Zimbabwe was closely connected with US support for South Africa as a bulwark against 'communist penetration' of southern Africa.

In all these cases, the channel had a strong interest not only in achieving a solution through a process of peaceful conciliation, but also in achieving a particular type of solution – one which maintained their own vital interests in the conflict system. The risks of pursuing such a strategy of deliberate distortion and manipulation are clear, and in most cases distortions and

272 Gestures of Conciliation

manipulations become obvious with the passage of time and increased communication between the adversaries. However, the damage – not merely to the on-going conciliation process but also to future processes – in terms of increased mistrust of one another, of other third parties and of conciliation processes in general, is not often taken into account. The lack of success of one conciliation process is frequently not the only price to be paid for a third party's playing its role through distortion and manipulation. Future initiatives also bear the costs of mistrust, lack of credibility, cynicism and demoralisation.

5   Conclusion: third parties as indirect channels

I began this Chapter by making a distinction between direct and indirect channels for making conciliatory gestures, between open and public versus closed and confidential channels, between official and unofficial sources of the conciliatory information and among the various inter- and intra-party levels at which intermediaries could operate in conveying conciliatory initiatives. Thus President Sadat's initiative in going to Jerusalem in 1977 was an example of a direct, open and official conciliatory gesture, carried out at the level of top leadership. The British initiative of opening talks with leaders of Sinn Fein in 1990 was an example of a direct but closed, official, top level initiative. The opening of the Oslo talks between PLO officials and Israeli academics – with informal contacts to the Israeli government – and brokered by Norwegian officials was an example of an indirect, unofficial, closed, elite-level process which evolved into indirect, official, top-level exchanges that remained closed until a draft agreement had been worked out. Other conciliatory initiatives can be fitted into the categories formed by these four dichotomies, as illustrated in Figure 13.3 opposite.

Preliminary consideration of these various types of channel that have been used in launching conciliatory initiatives provides no really unambiguous indication of which type is most likely to be successful in initiating an accommodative sequence and ultimately arriving at a solution to protracted conflicts. President Sadat's 1977 initiative argues the case for direct, open, official, top-level channels being most likely to initiate an on-going conciliation process. The public and official nature of such moves minimise the possibility of their later being denied, while their leadership-to-leadership quality provides them with a degree of seriousness and commitment lacking in initiatives taking place at other levels. On the other hand, there is always a danger of such initiatives being perceived as playing to some gallery or other, and the relative lack of success of Sadat's initiative over the Suez Canal and the complete failure of the British move in lifting economic sanctions on Argentina show that other factors, particularly the nature of the gesture itself, can cancel out the effects of using even this type of channel.

CHANNEL

	Official	Unofficial	
	Leaders or formal officials instructed by leaders	Informal, private individuals with some links to leaders	
Direct Bilateral	President Sadat's visit to Israel, 1977	Former President Carter's mission to N. Korea, 1996	**Open and Public**
	British Government opening contacts with Sinn Fein, 1990 Dayan–Tuhamy meetings, in Marrakesh, 1977	Lord Derby's visit to leaders of Dail Eirean in Dublin, 1921	**Closed and Confidential**
Indirect Multilateral (via third parties)	OAU Presidents's mission to Mid-East, 1971	San Egidio Order meetings between FRELIMO government and RUF in Mozambique, 1990–92	**Open and Public**
	World Council of Churches/AACC mission to SPLM and Khartoum government in Sudan, 1971	Quaker Elmore Jackson's mission from President Nasser to Prime Minister Eshkol, 1955	**Closed and Confidential**

Figure 13.3   **Types of Channel in Leadership Level Conciliation**

Moreover, even if it is the case that the use of this type of channel enhances the likely success of the conciliatory initiative to a considerable degree, it is likely that the use of such channels will remain a comparative rarity, an argument supported by the uniqueness of Sadat's daring move. The risks to an initiator, particularly from intra-party pro-continuation factions, are inevitably considerable. Success is highly dependent on a sufficiently precedent-breaking response from a target who, given the dynamics of protracted conflicts, is likely to be highly suspicious, prone to cling to worst-case analyses and thus unwilling to respond in other than a non-committal fashion.

Empirically, then, it seems most likely that conciliatory gestures, particularly those initiating what their users hope will be a successful sequence of such moves, will use channels that are closed, indirect and usually unofficial, even if the level at which these are undertaken involves leaders or decision-makers, rather than opinion makers or grass roots constituents. This being the case, the crucial question becomes what characteristics of this type of channel will help or hinder their likely success or, in the case of indirect channels using an intermediary as agent, what it is about particular third parties that assists in launching a successful conciliation process.

Given the argument that the nature and activity of third parties who channel signals about conciliation and de-escalation from one party to another do, indeed, play a considerable part in determining the likely success of those initial signals, the selection of an appropriate third party as channel (if a selection is realistically available) can materially enhance the chances of signals being accepted and believed. Broadly speaking, two factors are involved in this: firstly, involving the third party's reputation and trustworthiness in the process of signalling; and secondly the third party's adroitness in acting as a means of communication between mistrusting adversaries.

5.1   Third party qualities

Third party qualities likely to enhance the success of any conciliatory move in terms of accurate recognition, unambiguous acknowledgement and positive reaction by a target include:

1. Direct but unobtrusive physical access to decision-makers in both parties, so that time and effort do not have to be expended by the third party in obtaining entry to key leaders. In this regard, the Quaker strategy of establishing a long-term physical presence on both sides of a conflict 'divide' seems fruitful, while it seems also to be the case that relief and humanitarian NGOs with presence on 'both sides of the lines' may also be in a position to act as key channels in this early stage of a conciliation process.

2. Minimal credibility with key decision-makers in both parties. The problem with 'credibility' is that it is an elusive concept – credible to do or be what? – and its sources can be many and varied. Some third parties achieve credibility by establishing a reputation for being trustworthy, in the sense of not leaking information; others for previous discretion; still others for their long-term, stable contacts with the party seeking to initiate dialogue, or with those on 'the other side'. Still other third parties achieve credibility through bilateral linkages that have little to do with the on-going conflict. There is also the possibility of credibility through a reputation for hard-headedness, or for not being gullible. Whatever the source of such credibility, of course, it is always a fragile commodity and can be lost rapidly and for factors often beyond the third party's control.

3. Low or no stake in the outcome of the conflict itself, especially in the nature, credit for, or timing of the settlement. This is a very rare

quality, as most third parties have at least some stake in the reputational rewards accruing from success in achieving a settlement (See Mitchell 1988, pp.21–45). That apart, many examples support the hypothesis that, at least in the very early stages of a conciliation process, the likely success of that process will be aided by using a disinterested go-between, even though other types of third party may be more useful in later stages. This quality is also associated with the fourth and fifth characteristics.

4. Low visibility and high deniability, which are both characteristics that seem important in opening up channels and starting a process, as opposed to those of mobilising support and enhancing credibility once the process is under way. It is quite true that the example of President Sadat and many other public and dramatic conciliatory gestures seem to cast doubt on this proposition, but even with this example one should never forget the cautious use of quiet and private channels that took place as a preliminary to Sadat's dramatic move, or the fact that Sadat had tried many low-key approaches before frustration finally led him to the use of a grand gesture and to Jerusalem.

5. Low accountability to outside parties. Again, this factor is linked to the ideas of credibility for third parties (as well as to that of disinterest) as it can be argued that third parties that are 'free agents' – that is, have no constituency to whom they must report and justify their work, have no mandate that can be revoked, have no additional interests that must be satisfied by their activity – are likely to command lower levels of mistrust from their contacts and greater confidence in their ability to put the interests of the adversaries first (and even the most extreme adversaries are likely to share interests in confidentiality, receiving accurate information about the other and the chances for a less costly solution).

If the argument for a low-key, disinterested, unencumbered and barely noticeable party, with existing contacts, and hence easy access to both parties in conflict, is accurate, then it leads to the conclusion that, at least in this initial stage of a conciliation process, the most appropriate go-between and most effective channel for conveying conciliatory gestures might well be non-governmental organisations working on both sides of the conflicting divide. Development agencies, humanitarian organisations, business concerns, academic research centres, religious organisations, and relief agencies can all possess these requisite qualities and opportunities, provided they are not already involved in some activity that leads them to be perceived as committed one way or the other in the conflict. Furthermore, even though most such organisations do have a direct stake in the conflict, this usually consists of an interest in achieving a stable situation which will enable them to pursue their own activities, and predisposes them in favour of a peaceful solution. Whether playing the role of go-between is inimical to successfully fulfilling their other role is a matter for careful analysis by each individual organisation.

Whatever the role for such organisations might be in particular cases, the general argument about the need for channels with access, deniability, low visibility, high disinterest and some level of demonstrable credibility with both sides seems clearly to preclude the use of highly visible, and politically interested third parties, no matter how prestigious, powerful or persuasive, at least in this delicate initial stage of a conciliatory process.

5.2 Third party performance

Apart from the characteristics of the third party, the effective performance of a role as believable channel can also be a major contribution to re-assuring a target and to obtaining a positive – if still cautious – reaction that moves a de-escalation process one notch further towards an eventual solution. Maintenance of the following tasks seem most likely to increase the probability of successfully initiating and mantaining a conciliatory process, and of moving an adversarial relationship in the direction of one less conflictful and more co-operative, at least as far as the parties being able to indulge in a joint search for a solution are concerned:

1 Keeping a low level of distortion in the information provided to both sides, and not overclaiming about an adversary's eagerness for a settlement or willingness to make compromises (*Accuracy*).
2 Providing an accurate and realistic picture of the background assumptions of the other side's decision-makers and of the obstacles that would need to be overcome in any process leading towards a settlement (*Reality*).
3 Interpreting the reactions of the adversary to moves initiated by one side – a task which requires accurate and realistic knowledge about the intra-party processes of all sides (*Sophistication*).
4 Keeping both sides informed about the limits of information about the other that the third party has promised to observe (*Clarity*).
5 Avoiding a natural tendency to over-eagerness which leads to the 'over-selling' of possibilities, intentions and proposals and may lead into the weakness/willingness dilemma if unchecked (*Restraint*).
6 Providing useful and timely information regarding the opening of a conciliation process, about the background to signals sent by the adversary, and about likelihood of further progress towards settlement should offers or options be taken up (*Richness*).

To summarise, a third party carrying out its communication function with accuracy, clarity, sophistication, reality, restraint and richness will have a positive influence on the process. The last quality is, of course, the most difficult thing for any go-between to control and if a genuinely conciliatory signal sent by one party is summarily rejected by the other, in spite of the persuasiveness of the third party, there is little positive that can be carried back to the initiator, save an interpretation of reasons for rejection. However, if there is any willingness to contemplate conciliation on the part of decision-makers on either side, then other factors will help to determine whether this can be exploited successfully or not.

In other words, the channels involved in communicating conciliatory moves between mistrustful adversaries, the nature and behaviour of third parties fulfilling key communications functions, can and will contribute much to the success of initial conciliatory gestures and subsequent accommodative sequences. Hence there appears to be much justification in the original decision to include these factors in the list of key influences discussed in previous chapters.

However, the overall process of starting and maintaining conciliation and accommodative sequences remains a highly complex one. This chapter has merely added a number of further elements to an already long and complicated list of 'influences' grouped under our five main headings, together with a number of tentative but not, one hopes, too implausible hypotheses about connections between some of these influences and the likely success of efforts at conciliation.

In the final summary chapter, I bring together the arguments of previous chapters, review them briefly and put them into a framework that can provide a basis for a set of testable hypotheses that might form part of a tentative theory of conciliation. Others can then proceed with the work of refutation, improvement or total replacement.

14
Hypotheses on Conciliation

'The concessions of the weak are the concessions of fear.'

Edmund Burke

This study began with two observations. The first of these was that President Anwar Sadat's conciliatory initiative of visiting Israel and addressing the Knesset had clearly 'succeeded', in at least two senses. Firstly it had altered the perceptions, behaviour and perceived options of Israeli leaders, elites and constituents, as well as many others in and outside the Middle East; and secondly it initiated an accommodative process leading towards a solution of at least the Egyptian–Israeli component of the protracted, intractable conflict between Arabs and Israelis.

The second observation was that this was not the first of Sadat's attempts to initiate a conciliatory process between Israel and Egypt, but that the others could hardly be said to have had a similar impact to Sadat's Jerusalem visit. Like so many conciliatory gestures made on all sides in the Arab–Israeli conflict, most were signal failures. From this latter observation arose the question that became the central theme of the study: what qualities, in general, contribute to the success or the failure of conciliatory initiatives?

Gestures of Conciliation has sought answers to that question in a variety of ways and from a variety of sources. Conceptually, the enquiry has led in a number of directions, ranging from an examination of theories of system change to those concerned with entrapment or commitment, and to ideas about concessions, trust creation and the interplay of inter-party and intra-party processes. Empirically, it has touched upon efforts to launch conciliatory processes between the USA and North Vietnam in the 1960s, between the British and Argentine governments in the mid-1980s, between Iranian and Iraqi leaders during the First Gulf War, and between Northern Irish unionists, nationalists and the British Government in the 1990s. A framework for the enquiry has been provided by ideas from communications theory, the initial assumption being that successful conciliation – like so many human activities – depends largely upon the construction, transmission, reception and interpretation of accurate, clear and convincing signals, persuasive enough to elicit a positive response from the signal's target.

However, bearing in mind that the major focus of the book's enquiry was on the question of circumstances and situations that brought about a successful rather than a failed conciliation initiative, an approach was needed that tried to clarify any regular associations between pre-determining factors that enhanced or decreased the likelihood of success for conciliatory gestures, defining 'success' firstly as the launching of a conciliatory move, then as its recognition and sympathetic evaluation, next as the eliciting of a conciliatory response and finally as the development of a sequence of conciliatory interactions between adversaries, termed an 'accommodative sequence'. The enquiry discussed the possible nature of such pre-determining factors by focusing on five broad topics: contextual factors, characteristics of the initiative, conditions within both initiator and target, and the nature of the channels through which the conciliatory gesture was conveyed. A large number of ideas about factors making for success or failure were discussed under each of these five headings, together with various theories and hypotheses drawn from disciplines that seemed relevant to the enquiry. A number of tentative ideas were advanced about factors affecting the likely success of conciliatory gestures.

In this final chapter I bring these ideas together systematically, to order and clarify them, and to present them as tentative hypotheses, based either on what seem to be relevant formulations from existing theories or from empirical examples of conciliatory initiatives, starting with Sadat's efforts in the 1970s. I start with ideas about propitious contexts for launching conciliatory moves.

1   Contextual factors

One theme that emerges clearly from the previous review of contextual variables affecting likely success of conciliation in protracted conflicts is the core need for prior change, at least of a structural or strategical nature. Such change provides the occasion for the leaders of parties locked in a protracted conflict to consider the possibilities offered by major systemic change and to review the basic choice they have between continuing with the coercively violent strategies and tactics or changing to a more conciliatory pattern of behaviour, at some stage involving a joint search for solutions.

The key role played by structural and strategical change clearly emerges from a consideration of Sadat's early initiatives in 1970–1 and his moves in 1975 and 1977. Particularly in the latter case, the whole structure of patron–client relationships in the Middle East political system had undergone major changes since 1973, so that an entirely new context existed for the protracted conflict between Israel and Egypt. The latter had ceased to be closely associated with the USSR, thanks to Sadat's expulsion of Soviet personnel and rejection of Soviet influence in 1973. The USSR had ceased to be a patron of the Egyptians, who were, by 1977, seeking a new relationship with the USA, Israel's major ally. Thus, at a systemic level, the pattern of relevant alignments had changed markedly, so that – quite apart from the results of the 1973 October War – both Egypt and Israel were facing a very different situation, one in which, for example, an Israeli Government no longer saw the menacing shape of the Soviet Union looming behind any Egyptian President making a conciliatory move. The political changes that took place in 1973 clearly qualify for the description system transformation and, once the immediate effects of the October War had worn off, these opened up opportunities for new thinking and new policies. Once major political changes occurred within Israel – as they did with the coming to power of the Likud government – systemic, structural changes combined to provide an opportune context for some major tactical move by one of the adversaries. Sadat made that move in October 1977.

   The ejection of Soviet advisers from Egypt and the ending of the patron–client relationship between Egypt and the USSR, the *rapprochement* between London and Dublin in the early 1990s, and the involvement of Iraq in a second major conflict, quite a part from that continuing between Baghdad and Tehran, are all examples of major structural change that is, I have argued, conducive to reconsideration of options and opportunities and the likely launching of conciliatory gestures. In Chapter 4 I reviewed changes at three levels – structural, strategical and tactical – that seemed likely to lead towards leaders trying out a conciliatory strategy. Summarising that review now, its main argument held that various forms of change had an influence on the likelihood that decision-makers might consider a change of policy from coercive to conciliatory, and major, testable hypotheses arising from this basic premise take the following form:

Hypotheses I   Successful conciliation is more likely to occur when:

A. the number of core actors in the system decreases;
B. the pattern of ally, or patron–client relationships in the conflict system changes;
C. adversaries become involved in another salient conflict;
D. future inter-adversary relationships become salient considerations for leaders;
E. other, unrelated issues become salient to adversaries;
F. goals in conflict come to be viewed as unrealistic;
G. resources for prosecuting the conflict become scarce;
H. resource equalisation and a stable balance of coercive capability occurs between adversaries;

I. mutually shared definitions of the nature of the problem replace differing views of nature/causes of conflict;
J. long-term stalemate confronts adversaries;
K. intensity of conflict diminishes;
L. adversaries have experienced a major shock, connected or unconnected with the on-going conflict;
M. an important symbolic threshold has been passed;
N. a change in leadership has taken place in one or other adversary;

As I emphasised in Chapter 4, many of these hypotheses are advanced very tentatively, partly because some are derived from – at most – one or two empirical examples; partly because some have been deduced from theories developed in other fields or disciplines where structures and processes seem analogous (and, hopefully, homologous) to those observed in protracted social conflicts, but may not be; and partly because, for precisely the same variables, perfectly plausible but opposite hypotheses can be advanced. For example, whether a change of leadership in one party encourages thoughts in the other about possible conciliatory moves will depend very much on the nature of the new leadership and its perceived commitment to the continuation of the conflict. The simple fact of there being new leaders will hardly be conducive to conciliation if they are regarded as more hawkish than their predecessors – although the example of the new Likud government in 1977 should warn against an easy assumption that hawks newly in office either deter an adversary seeking to use change to initiate accommodation or ensure a wholly negative reaction.

Similarly, a plausible case can be made that an equalisation of coercive capability will make successful conciliation less rather than more likely, as the party achieving equality will continue to strive for coercive advantage and the side losing dominance will seek to regain it.

Even with this caveat in mind, however, the above list will serve as a starting point for examining contexts propitious for conciliation. Similar hypotheses can be advanced about propitious conditions within parties contemplating the possibility of some conciliatory initiative; the nature of the initiative itself and qualities that make some initiatives more conducive to success than others; propitious conditions within the target of the initiative; and the nature and qualities of helpful channels.

2   Conducive intra-party conditions

If appropriate contextual conditions can 'set the stage' for conciliation – that is, provide the occasion and opportunity for decision-makers to engage in some re-evaluation of policies – they by no means determine whether this opportunity will be used. Nor do they necessarily control whether any such reconsideration will result in leaders seriously discussing the possibility of some – usually tentative – conciliatory move. Finally, contextual factors probably play only a minor role in leaders deciding whether they can safely go ahead with the launching of some conciliatory move, the long-term benefits of which must remain uncertain while immediate costs are likely to seem less problematic. In this regard, conditions within the leaders' own party are likely to have the most significant influence on this particular aspect of success or failure, and the cluster of factors I have termed Initiator Characteristics will be closely associated with the likely success of conciliatory moves.

Again this can clearly be seen in the case of Anwar Sadat's changed situation with regard to domestic conditions within Egypt. By 1977, although under pressure from a failing Egyptian economy, Sadat was in a politically powerful position within his own country. He was clearly no longer in the shadow of his predecessor, Gamal Abdul Nasser, while his fighting of the October War, whatever its military outcome, had equally clearly been a political success, domestically and internationally, apart from its effect in further distancing Sadat from responsibility for the disasters of 1967. Internally, he had reduced the influence of the left wing group within the old 'Free Officers' movement even before the ejection of the Soviet Union, and had subsequently balanced the influence of military, technocratic and urban elites, as well as traditional, rural and religious factions within Egypt, so that none presented a major challenge to his own position.[1] Thus, while not having a totally free hand, Sadat and his regime had, by 1977, achieved a level of coherence, credibility and flexibility that enabled Sadat to consider the benefits of a major conciliatory move internationally against the likely costs of such a move domestically, and come to the conclusion that – given adroit domestic tactics on his part – the former far outweighed the latter. The only major negative factor of some major conciliatory move lay in the likely reaction of Egypt's Middle East allies, especially Saudi Arabia, and Sadat appears to have convinced himself that costs imposed by Riyadh could well be offset by benefits originating in Washington.

Quite apart from the example of Anwar Sadat, the other examples and the theoretical ideas discussed in Chapters 10 and 12 provide some initial indications of what types of domestic political, social and psychological conditions are conducive to the successful launching of a conciliatory initiative, and what conditions militate against a potential initiator carrying through with an amended strategy. This review of cases and ideas gives rise to the following tentative list of hypotheses that concern domestic factors that are more or less conducive to the initiating of a conciliatory process:

Hypotheses II   Successful conciliation is more likely to occur when:

A.   current leaders are not responsible for original involvement and heavy investment in the conflict;

B. current leaders have a low or lessening commitment to success through coercion – or to 'victory';
C. there is a high level of agreement within leadership circles;
D. leaders are secure in their retention of office and face no significant internal opposition;
E. there is a low level of factional rivalry within elites and no strong, pro-continuation faction;
F. leaders possess a wide range of choice in selecting alternative strategies and of instruments for implementation;
G   the survival of the party and its members is not threatened by the outcome of the conflict;
H. rank and file constituents have not been aroused in support of the goals in conflict and committed by major long term sacrifices;
I. there is a high level of rank and file trust in, or support for, the leadership; or rank and file are (kept) quiescent and unlikely to attempt to influence policy;
J. alternative roles and rewards are readily available for those currently involved in planning and implementing strategies of coercion *vis-à-vis* the adversary;
K. leaders have a high degree of control over pro-continuation factions, especially within coercion implementing agencies;
L. cultural factors promote approval of flexibility and adaptability, rather than perseverance and commitment.

Again, the list needs to be followed by words of warning about the tentative nature of these propositions. It may, indeed, be that a new leadership, with little direct or personal responsibility for originating the policy that led to overt conflict and costly coercion, will have less commitment to the goals set by predecessors – and hence have greater flexibility. On the other hand, there are enough examples of several 'generations' of leaders becoming leaders because they were thoroughly committed to traditional goals and enmities; or of the transmission of goals, values and hatreds across generations, so that young Serbs in the 1990s recall with venom Croat Ustashe actions against their grandparents in the 1940s; and generations of nationalists in Northern Ireland can recite a litany of British wrongs against the Irish reaching back to the sixteenth century and before.

A second obvious problem with the list of hypotheses is the empirical one that it seems highly unlikely that this set of 'conducive conditions' will ever exist complete and intact – always assuming that the list is a theoretically valid one. More likely some of the conducive conditions will exist but be accompanied by others that militate against the successful launching of a conciliatory move. Most historical situations seem likely to offer a mix of conditions, some of which are positive and some negative influences – leaders not responsible for the choice of policy or the costs of involvement and wishing to explore conciliation facing a factionalised elite and an aroused, pro-continuation rank and file in a culture that anathamatises lack of persistence and 'inconstancy'. At our present state of knowledge it is difficult to weigh the strength of such opposing influences and even to rank them according to the impact they are likely to have on the probability of a conciliatory process being started. All one can suggest is that the more conducive factors are present, the more likely conciliation will proceed. Unfortunately, similar limitations of knowledge affect other sets of factors likely to influence the probable success of conciliation, and this is especially true of those characterising the conciliatory initiative itself.

3   Appropriate conciliatory gestures

The third set of factors that influence the likely success of a conciliatory initiative involves the nature of the conciliatory move or moves themselves, and the characteristics that make such a move easily discernible by a target's decision-makers, as well as making that move credible as an 'olive branch' and something that can be simply and positively responded to. Once again, Sadat's October 1977 initiative illustrates these broad principles in operation. A public offer to visit Israel by a previously adamant Arab leader was hardly something that would go unnoticed by an adversary whose main attention was constantly focused on the nuances of Arab leaders' policies and statements, nor by anyone remotely interested in Middle East politics. A major change from a long-term strategy of refusing to have any relations save coercive ones with Israel, and of resolutely declining to acknowledge that a member of the international community of states called 'Israel' even existed, would achieve at least a minimum level of credibility as a conciliatory move, even if only on the grounds that the public offer of a visit to Israel could hardly be followed by a subsequent return to a posture that the country did not exist. Finally, the offer to go to Israel and speak to the Knesset *if invited* gave the decision-makers in the adversary a relatively straightforward, low-risk and low-cost way of responding positively by simply issuing an invitation. Sadat had attached no conditions to the offer of a visit, and the presence of the Egyptian president plus a small delegation of hand-picked advisors hardly constituted a major danger to Israeli political life or national security. To respond by saying 'Yes' to Sadat was much easier than saying 'No', so that in retrospect Egypt's President seems to have fulfilled all of the theoretical conditions for making what Roger Fisher terms a 'Yes-able Proposition'.[2] Not surprisingly, after some little debate, the Israeli Cabinet responded to Sadat's gesture with one of its own that was (relatively) easy to make.

At least some similar characteristics are identifiable in other conciliatory gestures discussed or mentioned in previous chapters. The Irish Republican Army ceasefire in August 1994 was a clearly discernible action – in both the sense that it was publicly announced and immediately testable[3] – which carried considerable credibility because it was the first such move for almost 20 years and followed a crescendo of inter-communal violence in Northern Ireland which began in 1990. Moreover, a response was relatively easy: a cessation of anti-terrorist activities on the part of the security forces and an equivalent ceasefire by Protestant para-military organisations. The collapse of the truce 18 months later should remind one that however successful an opening conciliatory move, there is no guarantee that the process will succeed in preparing for a settlement nor that the conflict will not cycle back to renewed coercion and violence.

The overall list of characteristics that seem likely to affect a conciliatory move's discernability, credibility and respondability were originally set out in Chapter 6, and the following chapters discussed some theoretical reasons for supposing that these were, indeed, key variables determining the success or failure of conciliatory moves. Whatever the theoretical backing for such a list of suggested influences, it is still necessary for these initial propositions to be set out in some testable form so that empirical investigation of the suggested relationships can be undertaken and the hypotheses validated, amended or disproved. The arguments in *Gestures of Conciliation* therefore suggest the following hypotheses about those characterictics of conciliatory gestures that maximise the effect on a target, and therefore contribute to the overall success of a conciliation process:

Hypotheses III   Successful conciliation is likely to occur when:

A. the gesture represents a major change from a previous position or strategy;

B. the gesture is something wholly unfamiliar that has not been employed before in that conflict;

C. the gesture fits into and 'resonates' with the culture, historical memory and values of the target, either practically or symbolically;

D. the gesture is undertaken in an open manner so that its enactment and importance cannot subsequently be denied by the initiator;

E. the gesture involves considerable, irrecoverable costs to the initiator;

F. the gesture involves some elements of risk and uncertainty to the initiator;

G. the gesture commits the initiator firmly to a new course of action, and in such a manner that reversion to a previous strategy will be very difficult;

H. the gesture is undertaken in a voluntary manner and without any special pressure from others.

I. the gesture is made without any conditions being attached, at least as far as the initial moves are concerned;

J. the gesture is made in such a way that it is non-reversible

K. the gesture is structured so as to offer the target's decision-makers an
    easy way of responding positively, either by leaving the response up to
    them, or by specifying a number of precise but straightforward and
    low risk reactions.

I suggest this list of important characteristics somewhat less tentatively
than the others in this work, largely because it seems clear that the absence
– often inevitably and for very good reasons – of many of these qualities
have doomed many well-intentioned conciliatory moves to failure, as in
the case of the British Government's lifting of sanctions on Argentina in
1985. However, once again a great deal of investigation is needed before it
is possible to say which of these qualities carry the most weight in determining a target's evaluation of a particular move, and which play a role in
determining whether the target will respond or not.

4   Readiness for conciliation

As I noted in Chapter 11, many of the arguments about intra-party
factors affecting the likelihood of an initiative being launched are also
important in determining whether decision-makers in a target are willing
to respond to even the most carefully crafted initiative. Menachim Begin
had to overcome significant opposition to the idea of issuing an invitation to Anwar Sadat. However, his position as head of a Likud-dominated
government elected to power for the first time and therefore in a relatively strong position *vis-à-vis* its Labour Party predecessor – especially in
the sense of not being responsible for Israeli failures at the start of the
October War – gave the cabinet a great deal of flexibility in determining
its reaction to Sadat's move. Moreover, given Likud's previous attitudes
towards retention of Israel's 1967 conquests and the generally expansion-
ist bent of its overall philosophy, it was unlikely that Begin and his fellow
ministers would be suspected of any dovish 'sell out' to the Egyptians.
Finally, even though it was not the case that Begin faced a quiescent
Israeli public (no Israeli government ever has, especially where issues of
national security are concerned), it was difficult for the Labour opposition
to criticise any decision to respond positively to Sadat, as much of their
own anti-Likud rhetoric had painted their rivals as dangerously more
'hawkish' than themselves.

All of these factors were as conducive to the target making a positive
response in this case as they were for the initiator launching the original
move. However, as I argued in Chapter 12, other factors can come into play
in determining a target's response or lack of a response, and to some degree
these also played a role in affecting the Israeli response to Sadat. It was, of
course, true of Begin's government that, like all Israeli governments since
1948, their main means of pursuing their goals of security from attack and

defence of whatever was defined as 'national territory' was through coercive military means so that their ability to adjust their overall strategy (that is, their adjustability) was limited, at least in the sense of basic means. However, this particular conciliatory gesture came from an adversary where, at least as far as some goals were concerned, there was more flexibility than with others. Whatever Likud's attitudes towards Judea and Samaria (the West Bank), on the matter of Sinai they were more flexible, and the return of Sinai was perceived as being Egypt and Sadat's main interest. Given Israel's over-arching goal of national security, at least as far as Sinai was concerned, there might be a number of ways in which a solution could be sought with Egypt that maximised Israel's security needs. Hence, the Israeli leaders were more flexible with regard to conciliatory moves from a Soviet-less Sadat than they would or could be with any from Syria's President Assad or any militant Palestinian leader.

Bearing in mind that the list of hypotheses about conducive conditions affecting initiators is also applicable to understanding the success of conciliatory efforts in facilitating a positive reaction from targets, a number of additional suggestions can be advanced about factors within responding parties that assist or hinder the likelihood of them responding and carrying a conciliatory process a stage further:

Hypotheses IV   Successful conciliation is likely to occur when:

A. target's monitoring agencies are highly sensitive to the nuances of an adversary's communication patterns and are able to discriminate between types of signal;
B. target's decision-makers have a range of alternative and acceptable means for pursuing key goals, or can adjust strategies and stances in order to achieve underlying basic interests;
C. target's decision-makers are able to control or negate the behaviour of potential 'spoilers' within monitoring or implementing agencies and elsewhere;
D. ample residual capability remains for reverting to previous strategies should the conciliatory process prove dangerous or break down at an early stage.

It should be apparent that a number of the above 'conducive conditions' which I propose mainly as affecting targets can also, on occasions, play a role in influencing the behaviour of potential initiators. As with the list of hypotheses outlined in section 2 of this chapter, this is a matter of emphasis and all that is being argued at this point is that the factors discussed above seem more likely to be relevant to targets than to initators, while those in section 2 seem more relevant to parties seeking to begin rather than respond to a conciliatory process. Hopefully, empirical analysis will provide some indications of what factors have the greatest impact in what circumstances.

5   Conducive channels

The final set of hypotheses arise from the discussion of the nature of appropriate channels or carriers of the conciliatory moves and counter-moves that might go to make up a successful process. As outlined in Chapter 13, the focus on 'channels' inevitably gives rise to two rather different sets of hypotheses, depending upon whether direct – adversary-to-adversary – channels are used, or whether the conciliatory initiative takes place through third party intermediaries, at least in its early stages.

Again, it is possible to use President Sadat's 1977 initiative as an illustration of both approaches, given the fact that, even though this might appear an example *par excellence* of a direct, adversary-to-adversary initiative, there had, in fact, been previous preparatory meetings under the auspices of King Hassan and a more indirect exchange of messages via President Ceasescu in Bucharest. Similarly, the British move in lifting the embargo on Argentina did not come completely without prior confidential contacts, both officially, if unsuccessfully, under the auspices of Swiss and Brazilian intermediaries in Bern and unofficially through inter-parliamentary contacts at the University of Maryland (See Little and Mitchell, 1988).

Analytically, however, it assists clarity to keep the two types of channel separate, even though the same question, 'what are the features of inter-adversary channels that increase the likely success of conciliatory gestures?', can be asked of both. In the case of direct, bilateral channels, I would suggest the following as starting hypotheses for investigation:

Hypotheses V   Successful conciliation is likely to occur when:

A.   open and public communication channels are used, so that it is difficult to deny the fact or details of the offer, even if the conciliatory process subsequently breaks down;
B.   the initiative is made by top leaders who might be accused of 'playing to the gallery' but whose seniority adds credibility to the move;
C.   the initiative is made through channels which clearly connect the initiating leadership to the target's leaders, but also to rank-and-file constituents in the adversary;
D.   the initiative is made from an arena which is both official, in the sense that it adds to the credibility of the move, and appropriate, in that it is one that adds to the transparency, commitment and undeniability of the gesture.

Again, it needs to be emphasised that using this overall method of conveying conciliatory gestures may be the ideal way of ensuring success, but historically it is likely to be most difficult for embattled leaders seeking to send a conciliatory signal to a long-time adversary. Far more caution and 'covering' is usually perceived as necessary, so that it is more likely that, in most cases, low-level and sacrificable officials, employing confidential 'back' channels that provide high deniability and low commitment, will be used in the initial stages in any peace process. However, what such means gain in terms of risk reduction and security is often lost in terms of the move's credibility to a target, and the latter's willingness to respond.

The customary way around this dilemma is, of course, to employ a trusted intermediary, in the hope that some of this trust will 'rub off' on the initiator and that the endorsement of the chosen third party will convey the appropriate level of commitment – and hence credibility – to the target. This alternative then directs attention to the question of the qualities of indirect intermediary 'channels' that help to increase the likely success of conciliatory moves, especially those which are low key and sensitive to various forms of 'derailment'.

Hypotheses VI   Successful conciliation is likely to occur when:

A. the initial stages are conducted using low-key, unofficial and confidential channels to convey and endorse signals;
B. there are demonstrable if deniable connections between unoffical intermediaries and decision-making circles in the initiating party, so that signals are sure to reach key leaders on both sides;
C. the third parties involved have a high degree of credibility with the leaders on both sides of the conflict, and some considerable degree of trust which can be transferred to each adversary at an early stage of the process;
D. the third parties involved have an established reputation for discretion and for not seeking public credit for fulfilling an intermediary role;
E. the third parties have themselves no stake in the nature of any outcome from the conflict, nor any hope of gain from their role in helping to achieve a solution;
F. the third parties have already established valued linkages with one or (better still) both adversaries;
G. the third parties have low visibility both within the adversaries and generally, which will clearly assist in their maintaining high levels of confidentiality;
H. the third parties are not accountable to any outside party, particularly those with some stake in the outcome of the conflict or in seeing a solution achieved.

If one adds to this list a high degree of skill, competence and sensitivity in carrying out the various roles involved in this early stage of a conciliatory process, then one has arrived at what might be termed the 'Archangel

Gabriel' theory of third party conciliation, a point which stresses the unlikelihood of ever finding this remarkable combination of qualities in any earthly intermediary. However, all that I am suggesting here is that theoretically, all these third party qualities should make it more likely that adversaries who are serious about seeking to start or continue some conciliatory process by using such channels will succeed in their objective; and that empirically, intermediaries that have at least some of these qualities are more likely to fulfil their roles successfully than those who lack many or most of them. Once again, which are the most important qualities and which are the least important, and whether there are others omitted from the list, are matters for empirical investigation and testing.

6   Conclusion

Anyone who has worked his or her way through *Gestures of Conciliation* to this point will be in no doubt about the complexity of any conciliation process, even in its earliest stages, or about the many obstacles to its successful completion in some solution to a protracted and intractable conflict, such as that in Northern Ireland, in Cyprus, in Bosnia, in Israel/Palestine. These obstacles are political, psychological, military, cultural and economic, and provide both analysts and decision-makers with a wide variety of reasons that explain the difficulty of getting conciliatory processes started and then of maintaining them in the face of the multiple forces making for their probable breakdown. The dynamics of protracted conflicts are such that reversing – or even diverting – them usually proves to be more difficult tasks than initiating, maintaining or accelerating them. As the distinguished peace activist, economist and conflict researcher Kenneth Boulding once said, 'It is far easier to do harm than to do good,' and while I hope that this is not always true, it certainly seems to be the case that the forces working towards conflict maintenance are very powerful, perhaps more powerful than those working towards conflict resolution.

But the example of Anwar Sadat in 1977 provides us with evidence that even the most protracted and intractable conflicts are never hopeless, and that some conciliatory gestures do begin processes that can reverse malign spirals, escalations and processes of violent compellence. So do events such as the successful peace process in South Africa, the ending of the civil war in Mozambique, the slow, faltering yet on-going search for agreement in Northern Ireland, the fragile but holding settlement of the multi-party, externally generated civil war in Lebanon. Quite apart from these historical examples of successful conciliation processes, there are signs that some serious intellectual effort is being made to understand not only the circumstances that lead to protracted conflicts and their maintenance over prolonged periods of time, but also the factors – political, psychological cultural – that constitute serious obstacles to their ending and, more importantly, what might be done about these. As an academic I am, of course, committed to the proposition that knowledge about the political and social world – and particularly the world of human conflict – is a necessary preliminary to 'doing something about it'. The more we know about the obstacles to conciliation and conflict resolution – entrapment, the dynamics of mistrust, the sometimes malign connections between intra-party politics and inter-party conflict – the more ways of coping with these we will be able to envisage, devise and increasingly implement. This present work is a preliminary contribution to increasing such knowledge and providing some tools to remove these obstacles.

Epilogue: Nearing Camp David

'The contradiction between wanting an agreement and fearing its outcome is ... ever-present.'
Ambassador L.N.Rangarajan *The Limitation of Conflict* 1985

If Anwar Sadat's main purpose in the autumn of 1977 had been to re-start a faltering peace process and to begin a new accommodative sequence between Egypt and Israel, there can be little doubt of the success of his initiative. Following an initial exploratory meeting between Tuhamy and Dayan under the auspices of King Hassan, he had made the offer to go to Jerusalem if invited. The Israelis had responded with an invitation and the visit had taken place. It was true that Sadat's speech to the Knesset had contained little more than a restatement of the existing Arab conditions for negotiation, while Begin's own speech in reply had been cautious in the extreme, especially when compared with that of Shimon Peres, the Labour Party leader. However the important thing was not particularly what was said but the fact that it was said at all and, above all, where it was said and by whom. Through Sadat's surprising initiative, the Israelis and Egyptians now had an opportunity for direct negotiations, something Israeli Governments had been calling for over a twenty year period; for talks unencumbered by the proxy struggles of the super-Powers for influence in the region; and for developing a deeper understanding of the factors underlying one another's fears, concerns and aspirations for the future.

However, subsequent events were to show that it is one thing to start a conciliatory process successfully, even one that opens the door to direct negotiations, and quite another to maintain it without breakdown. Sadat appears to have come away from Jerusalem convinced that his visit had fundamentally changed the relationship between Israel and Egypt and to a large extent it had, in the sense that each side knew that the other was determined not to go to war again. However, this did not mean that a new co-operative era was about to dawn or that the road to even a minimally satisfactory agreement was going to be easy. First signs that enormous differences still remained in both side's actual bargaining positions appeared during a second meeting between Tuhamy and Dayan, held secretly in Marrakech on 2 and 3 December, during which profoundly different positions on the military aspects of an agreement about Sinai and on the nature of an overall political settlement were revealed. On the latter issue, Dayan's position was that a bilateral Egyptian–Israeli settlement should be quickly concluded, while Tuhamy indicated a strong preference for a broader settlement bringing in other parties. The Cairo Preparatory Conference held on 14 December also made little progress on political issues, although military officials there made some progress in drawing up tentative plans for Israeli withdrawal from Sinai[1] and this did something to overcome Sadat's concern that the appointment of Eliahu Ben-Elissar, the Director General of the Prime Minister's Office, to lead the Israeli delegation signalled a downgrading of the meetings, and a lack of concern for, or urgency about, the peace process on the part of the Israelis.

However, the real extent of the gap between Israeli and Egyptian aspirations was revealed at the later high-level conference held at Ismailia in December. In spite of the initial success of both sides agreeing to establish permanent Political and Military Committees to forward the process, the substantive proposals which Prime Minister Begin brought to the meetings fell far short of the expectations of the Egyptians and especially of Sadat himself, who pressed Begin throughout the conference to agree to a declaration of general principles, rather than to engage in a discussion of precise details for a settlement. The meeting broke up without anything having been achieved, but having revealed considerable disarray and disagreement within the Egyptian delegation, particularly between Sadat and his foreign ministry advisers.

Even less was achieved at the first meeting of the Political Committee held in Jerusalem on 17 January 1978, a meeting which almost failed to take place because of disputes over the agenda. Sadat abruptly withdrew the Egyptian delegation on the second day of the meeting, although analysts differ as to whether this was because of injudicious public comments made over dinner by Begin, in violation of a prior agreement not to make such pronouncements, or because domestic pressures were mounting on Sadat. Whatever the reason, and in spite of the continuation of Military Committee meetings in Cairo until the end of January (and subsequent contacts between Sadat and Ezer Weizman, the Israeli Minister of Defence until the summer), by early Spring of 1978 the bilateral process initiated with high hopes in the previous November had reached an impasse, and the United States government was once again about to assume the role of key mediator.

The ending of the bilateral accommodative sequence involving Egypt and Israel following Sadat's Jerusalem initiative illustrates all too well the difficulties of maintaining a conciliatory process and converting one into successful negotiations. In the case of Sadat's Egypt and Begin's Israel, at least five basic reasons can be suggested for the breakdown of the process and its reversion to a revised process involving the adversaries and a formal mediator.

Firstly, many observers of and participants in the meetings and discussions of that post-Jerusalem period have commented on the markedly different negotiating styles of Anwar Sadat and Menachim Begin, although at this early stage of their long-drawn-out interaction it seems evident that they did develop some wary respect for one another and were less antagonistic than later. One commentator (Friedlander 1983, p.127) argues that in the Jerusalem and Ismailia meetings there was less antagonism between the two leaders than between them and their advisers! However, throughout this period it is clear that Sadat was happier with a broad consideration of general principles on which a settlement might be based, and made agreement on these and their enunciation his major goal. In contrast, Begin's view of negotiation was of a slow, careful bargaining, dealing with detail by detail so that both sides were clearly committed and tied down to thoroughly considered specifics fully protecting Israel's interests. While this latter process seems to have worked for both Israelis and Egyptians in discussing the military aspects of possible agreement, the clash between Israeli presentation of detailed political proposals – especially on the future of the West Bank and Gaza – and Sadat's wish for a broad agreement on the principle of full Israeli withdrawal therefrom and a commitment to principles of self-determination for those dwelling in the captured territories – provided they agreed to live alongside Israel in peace – proved impossible to resolve.

An important aspect of this was the second reason advanced by observers for the process coming to a frustrated halt. Sadat clearly anticipated and wished for a grand gesture from the Israelis similar to his in going to Jerusalem. On several occasions he made clear that he felt that a reciprocal move from Begin's government was needed to confirm that they were seriously committed to a peace process. One that was clearly indicated from Cairo was an Israeli declaration that the government fully accepted the provisions of UN Resolution 242 regarding Israeli withdrawal from the territories captured in 1967, although privately Sadat made it plain that he anticipated that in any solution there would need to be border adjustments, on the West Bank or possibly in Gaza, although he could not afford to be seen sacrificing historically Egyptian territory. It was, of course, unlikely that such 'adjustments' would go anywhere near fulfilling Menachim Begin and Likud's historical commitment to reclaiming Eretz Israel, but at this time nobody was yet quite sure about how absolute this commitment was.

When no reciprocal gesture was forthcoming from Israel, Sadat was seriously disappointed and this contributed to his growing conviction that

Begin and his government were not serious about the search for peace.[2] Even as late as July 1978, when the bilateral process had clearly reached an impasse and the US Government was taking over the initiative in the peace process, Sadat was still suggesting to Ezer Weizman that Israel should make a unilateral gesture to indicate good faith. On this occasion he suggested that the Israelis could hand over Al Arish and Mount Sinai to Egypt who would supply these enclaves by air, or could even withdraw to a line running from Al Arish to Ras Muhammad at the tip of the Sinai Penisula (Weizman 1981, pp.316–17). When the idea was suggested to Moshe Dayan on a visit to Washington, the foreign minister said that this could not be done as a unilateral gesture but only as a result of negotiation (Quandt 1986, p.200). No Israeli gesture equivalent to Sadat's would be forthcoming.

The third set of factors held as contributing to the ending of the bilateral conciliation process centred around the curious reluctance of the adversaries to abandon their reliance on the United States, which could have been effectively sidelined as a result of Sadat's move, and in November–December 1977 was searching for a role in this new process. I use the term 'curious' here because, publicly at least, both Egypt and Israel had reasons for wishing to by-pass Super-Power involvement in any search for a solution to their regional problems. Clearly, neither wished to have the Soviet Union involved in any peace process, which was one reason for Israel's willingness to deal directly with Sadat, as this would exclude parties closely aligned with the USSR, such as Assad's Syria. Even in the case of the USA, both had reasons at least to say that they preferred direct contacts with one another. Sadat was anxious to avoid a Geneva conference that would involve a wide range of other Arab parties, radicals and conservatives alike, and such a meeting had been one of the main objectives of US strategy since President Carter took office and revised US policy towards the region. The Israeli Government, like all its predecessors, had called constantly for direct, formal negotiations with Arab governments, partly as a way of obtaining official recognition of the state of Israel, but also because of confidence in its ability to turn formal negotiations to Israeli advantage.

With Sadat's opening of direct contacts, all this now seemed possible, but both sides proved reluctant to abandon ties to the USA and to undertake bilateral conciliation and negotiation processes. Even allowing for the strong ties between Israel and the USA, for example, it was strange that Menachim Begin chose first to reveal the Israeli plan for West Bank autonomy to President Carter and his Middle East team, rather than directly to their new Egyptian negotiating partner – unless the main goal was to obtain prior US endorsement of the plan.[3] Equally, even allowing for Sadat's strong desire to obtain US help and backing for Egypt, especially to maintain key ties with Saudi Arabia, his call for the US to be represented at the Cairo Preparatory Conference showed that, in spite of his having undertaken his Jerusalem initiative without consulting or informing the USA, he was still interested in having the USA fully involved in any peace process that might result from his move.

Almost inevitably, as the bilateral talks in Ismailia and Jerusalem produced no result, and the level of acrimony in public and private exchanges between Cairo and Jersalem grew, the US government began to assume a greater and greater role in the peace process once again. It is interesting to speculate the extent to which this consciousness of always having the USA to fall back on encouraged both sides, but particularly the Israelis, to be cautious and to take tough stances on a variety of issues. Whatever the effects of this factor, it is clear that by the spring of 1978 the bilateral process was running its course, and responsibility for continuing the process initiated by Sadat's breakthrough had returned to Washington.

The fourth set of factors that helped to undermine the accommodative sequence started in November was the resurgence of intra-party opposition to, and criticism of, both Sadat and Begin that occurred once the euphoria of Sadat's visit had worn off and the price of peace was becoming clear. In the case of Egypt, there had always been serious doubts among many of Sadat's advisors and bureaucrats, as well as other top leaders, about the initiative, and although he may have outmanoeuvred them temporarily in November, once the visit was over the organised growth of opposition and criticism was inevitable. Within the country at large, elements of the religious right were strongly opposed to dialogue with Israel and the remnants of the Moslem Brotherhood were implicated in several plots against Sadat in the period immediately following his visit. In decision-making circles, members of the military were becoming wary of a process that seemed not unlikely to lead to the retention of some Israeli military presence in Sinai and a demilitarised area on sovereign Egyptian territory. A powerful group in the national security council led by Air Force General Hosni Mubarak were concerned about Egypt's loss of influence in the Arab world and particularly about the possibility of deteriorating relations with Saudi Arabia. Finally, many of Sadat's advisors, having experienced the tough Israeli bargaining position at the Ismailia meetings, were beginning to raise serious objections to the President's continued commitment to the bilateral process he had initiated. From his return to Cairo in November, Sadat knew he needed some rapid progress in negotiations preferably including some major concession from the Israelis that he could use to head off his domestic critics. The fact that the Israelis seemed impervious to this need for speedy progress only served to intensify Sadat's doubts.

However, a similar problem faced Menachim Begin, in charge of a government that was, like all Israeli governments, a coalition, and confronting an Israeli public that was itself divided on the issue of seizing what some of its members saw as a unique chance for peace, while others – now that Likud had come to power – pressed for an expanded settlement programme, partly for security reasons but mainly in order to confirm Israel's hold on Judea and Samaria. Thus, Begin's government faced increasing criticism from both the Israeli 'left' and its own supporters on the 'right' (including the NRP and Gush Emunim). The ultra-right possessed strong representation both within the Knesset and – more importantly – a government now including Ariel Sharon as Minister for Agriculture. Moreover, the commitment to an expanded Israel was thoroughly in tune with Begin's own desire to hold on to the West Bank territories and to fulfil the dream of Eretz Israel.

Both Sadat and Begin, therefore, were in a position where they confronted a growing opposition to further conciliatory moves that hamstrung their strategy *vis-à-vis* each other. Unfortunately, as is often the case with domestically confined leaders, they assumed that the other side had far greater understanding of, and would make far greater allowance for, their own domestic constraints than they ever had or would make for the other. This common phenomenon led, as usual, to major misunderstandings, disappointments and a perception of the other's lack of sensitivity to 'our' problems on the part of both Israeli and Egyptian leaders. This impression was reinforced, especially on the Egyptian side, by a recognition that the peace process was moving at a snail's pace when rapid, obvious and positive results were needed to answer domestic critics.

The slow pace at which even minor progress was achieved exacerbated the fifth, final and most inevitable set of influences operating to undermine the Egyptian–Israeli conciliation process. These were the mutual suspicions, misperceptions and mistrust that made both sides immediately suspect bad faith on the part of the other as an explanation of events not unfolding smoothly or in the anticipated manner. Sadat himself later referred to these obstacles as 'the other walls' which prevent adversaries from making any progress towards peace, and which constantly undermine the inevitably tenuous belief that the other was genuinely committed to the search for a peaceful solution.

As I have argued throughout this book, during even the most successful conciliation process it is almost inevitable that those involved will make statements or undertake actions that are misguided, or so ambiguous as to be easily open to immediate misinterpretation. This is particularly the case when the leaders are trying to forward the process while intra-party criticism and doubt rise, and opposition to 'further concessions' or 'appearing weak' grows apace. Such factors inevitably played a role with Sadat and Begin in the months following Sadat's Jerusalem trip, when both leaders felt that the other should be capable of great sensitivity and sympathy with his own domestic constraints.[4]

One major misguided move made early on by the Israelis was to begin work on new 'settlements' in Sinai, and to strengthen those settlements already existing in the so-called 'Rafa Salient'. The former were seen as a particular provocation by Sadat – and by the US Government, then becoming increasingly re-engaged in the process. Subsequent accounts by Israelis involved in the decision to start work on these four settlements indicate that Ariel Sharon, who first suggested the move and then argued strongly for it, felt that the settlements in question would test out Sadat's commitment to the removal of other settlements in Sinai or could be used as a bargaining chip in later negotiations (Weizman 1981, pp.142–4).[5] Others have argued that the settlements were also intended to placate forces on Begin's right who were pressing for increased settlement in the territories captured in 1967 (Friedlander 1983, p.152). Whatever the reasons, Sadat's not unreasonable reaction was one of outrage, a sense of betrayal and a perception that Israel was playing a double game and could not be trusted at all, an impression that was reinforced by the promise that Begin had earlier given President Carter that no new settlements would be begun 'during the year', of which Sadat was undoubtedly aware.[6]

On the Israeli side, suspicion and mistrust of the Egyptians was also endemic, so that moves by Sadat such as the breaking of formal relations with the five Arab states of the 'Rejectionist Front' – intended by Sadat to make more credible his own commitment to the process – went almost unnoticed.[7] Although it appears that Sadat and Begin got on well during the initial meetings at Ismailia, Sadat's increasing estrangement from the Israeli Prime Minister pushed him in the direction of establishing contacts with other Israeli leaders, including Ezer Weizman, which did little harm, and Shimon Peres the opposition leader, which did a great deal. The tacit arrangement involving the US Government and the Egyptians, whereby the former put pressure on Begin also did little to diminish mistrust between Cairo and Jerusalem – to say nothing of Jerusalem and Washington. This gradual and well-documented spiralling of suspicion and recrimination was a major factor in bringing the bilateral process to a final halt by the late spring of 1978.[8]

However, although the process engendered by Sadat's dramatic gesture the previous November appeared stalled at this point, it was to be reinvigorated by President Carter and his Middle East team of advisers who had been impressed by Sadat's initiative and his obvious commitment to finding a solution, and by the initial Israeli response. The adversaries in this protracted conflict had attempted briefly to seek a settlement on a bilateral basis, but this process had foundered on the numerous political and psychological rocks awaiting any conciliatory process attempting to end a conflict that had produced four wars in 25 years. Both the Egyptians and the Israeli leaders had become convinced that the assistance of the United States was a necessary condition for any progress towards a peace settlement, if they had ever really felt otherwise, so that the stage had been set for a new third party move. Following an abortive foreign minister's conference chaired by Secretary of State Cyrus Vance and held in mid-July at Leeds Castle in

England, some major move was clearly needed to 'unstick' the parties from what had become their entrenched positions and to regenerate the process. On 30th July 1978 President Carter told his top Middle East advisers that he intended to hold a summit meeting with President Sadat and Prime Minister Begin at Camp David in Maryland, and that Secretary Vance would travel to Cairo and Jerusalem to issue the invitations.

The Camp David talks opened on 5 September 1978, just under a year after Sadat's visit to Jerusalem. The ensuing ten months had been frustrating ones for all concerned with Sadat's initiative, and the process by which that initiative had gradually undermined and finally stalled had been a painful one. However, a great deal had been learned and, by the time the Camp David meetings began, both the adversaries and the intermediaries were under no illusions about the difficult problems they faced. The period between November 1977 and September 1978 had been one filled with learning for all concerned, but one of the most important lessons for the leaders assembling in Maryland that September was that neither adversary wanted another war and both sets of leaders were willing to make some concessions for peace. Moreover, both knew that there were leaders on the other side who would run risks to obtain a settlement. In that sense, Sadat's initiative and the process that followed, whatever its own outcome, were important precursors to the Maryland meetings. Melvin Friedlander is quite correct in his assessment that 'Sadat's journey to Jerusalem ... began the dialogue that would eventually culminate in a peace treaty between Egypt and Israel' (1983, p.94).

Notes

Prologue: The Sadat Initiatives

1. Tripoli Radio. Report of meeting of the Libyan Congress, 15 November 1977.
2. As noted in Chapter 2, it can reasonably be argued that Sadat's visit to Jerusalem arose initially in response to an Israeli signal sent via President Ceasescu of Rumania.
3. Shlomo Aronson, an inside observer of Israeli diplomacy during this period, comments that, after the ending of the 1969–71 War of Attrition, many Israelis fell victim to a 'status quo' syndrome, which involved 'psychological satisfaction with the situation along the existing border' (Aronson, 1978 p.136).

1 Frustration and War: 1970–1973

1. At the very end of 1970, Sadat had publicly indicated his willingness to 'recognise the right of Israel as an independent state as defined by the Security Council of the UN', but this had been preceded by an uncompromising demand that 'Israel must give up every inch of territory she captured from the UAR in the Six Day War' (28 December 1970. Interview in the *New York Times*; quoted in Israeli 1978 Vol.1 p.14).
2. The details of this enquiry involved suggestions of an Israeli withdrawal to the Mitla Pass, a distance of some 40 kilometres, an Egyptian 'thinning out' of its troops for an equivalent distance west of the Canal (leaving its air defences intact) and an exchange of prisoners of war. In addition, a longer cease fire was to be negotiated through Ambassador Jarring, which would involve a 10-mile prohibited zone for aircraft on both sides of the Canal, the latter being opened for the free passage of all ships (Rafael 1981 p.258).
3. Eban reports the decision thus: 'On March 22 the Israeli Government, at the initiative of Moshe Dayan, took another important decision. It virtually renounced the principle (to which American adherence had been obtained) that not a single Israeli soldier would be withdrawn from cease-fire lines except in the context of a contractual peace settlement' (Eban 1977 p.474). It seems unlikely that this decision would have been taken without Sadat's private probes and public utterances.
4. Henry Kissinger, again with hindsight, argues strenuously that, quite apart from the confusion over the linkage between a partial and a comprehensive agreement, the initiative was doomed to failure because the adversaries had radically different purposes in trying to achieve a partial settlement. While Egypt wanted an interim agreement as the first stage of a total Israeli withdrawal, Dayan saw it as a means of forestalling this (Kissinger 1979 p.1280).
5. This memorandum was drafted in May 1971 (apparently unofficially) by Donald Bergus, the US representative in Cairo, and on the basis of an official Egyptian document outlining the latter's formal position on an interim agreement. The amended draft was taken to be an official communication by President Sadat. It was leaked to the Israelis and created a major crisis between Israel and the USA.
6. There is evidence that Sadat continued to try to establish contacts with his adversaries in Israel almost up to the start of the October 1973 War. Mrs Meir recalls in her memoirs that in early 1972 Sadat sent a message through President

Ceausescu of Romania that he was willing to agree to a high level meeting, perhaps involving himself and the Israeli Prime Minister.

Informal contacts, which must have had Sadat's tacit approval, took place at the 'level of officials' in January 1973 using the Quaker intermediary, Sydney Bailey, as a channel. Nothing came of the 1972 initative, but Bailey speculates that the 1973 contacts may have contributed to the a major Israeli policy shift in the summer of 1973, when Mrs Meir accepted the principle of 'security for sovereignty' – an earlier version of 'land for peace' (Bailey 1990).

7. Gideon Rafael, reflecting upon the Israeli mood after the war notes that 'both sides came out of the war thoroughly sobered ... Egypt had regained its self esteem while Israel was deeply shaken in its self-confidence. It had lost not only the aura of invincibility of its army but also the trust in the competence of its leaders'. The shock of the Yom Kippur War was, however, 'not a downfall, but rather a climb down from the clouds to solid ground' (Rafael 1981 pp.314–15).

8. Other scholars have noted this concession, even if its practical importance was lost in the frantic scramble to end the fighting and to end it in an advantageous position. 'On 27 October, bowing to American pressure, Israel allowed non-military supplies to cross its lines and reach the beleaguered Third Army, in return for which Sadat accepted a proposal that he had previously rejected regarding direct negotiations with the Israelis. Sadat had repeatedly pledged in the past not to negotiate with Israel; he sought an honorable way out of this bind by dubbing the talks as "technical" and emphasising that they dealt with "the military aspects of implementing Security Council Resolutions 338 and 339"' (Israeli 1978 Vol.1 p.142).

9. Sadat's actions over the exchange of prisoners can be contrasted with Syrian President Assad's. The latter refused steadfastly to discuss the issue in the period following the ending of hostilities, even to the extent of refusing to exchange lists of prisoners held through the International Red Cross.

10. The unexpected nature of Sadat's concession on this point obviously struck Kissinger strongly at that time. He recalls that, on that very first occasion, Sadat astonished him. 'He did not haggle or argue. He did not dispute my analysis. He did not offer an alternative. Violating the normal method of diplomacy – which is to see what one can extract for a concession – he said simply that he agreed with my analysis and my proposed procedure ... to give the diplomacy I had outlined a chance, he would defer the issue of the October 22 line. Anything less was too trivial to justify the suffering and the risk of war' (Kissinger 1982 p.640).

11. Mrs Meir made this offer publicly on 16 November, but it was rejected the following day by the Egyptian government, a spokesman claiming that the suggestion was 'for internal consumption in Israel, as general elections are approaching' (Account in *Facts on File* Vol.33 No. 1725 p.961).

12. In a subsequent interview with Michael Brecher, General Yariv claimed that there were two reasons for moving the talks to Geneva. The first was that Israel wanted to put a political stamp on what were talks between officers on a military agreement. The second was Kissinger's interest in 'making the Kilometre 101 talks part of a process towards a disengagement agreement' (Brecher 1980 p.306).

13. Abba Eban recalls that, as early as 15 November, Kissinger tried to abort the Kilometre 101 discussions, warning Eban in Washington that the decisions to be made at the talks 'required political authority, not merely military understanding'. Moreover, 'this applied especially to the Israeli proposal under which we would withdraw from positions west of Suez in return for the liquidation of the Egyptian bridgehead east of the Canal. The United States did not believe that Sadat would ever agree to remove Egyptian troops from their cherished gains in

western Sinai, but some compromise by way of reduction of forces might be feasible. Beyond this, however, it was useless for General Yariv to ask General Gamasi to give answers. Things were not run in Egypt at that level. Kissinger therefore advocated that the issues not resolved at Kilometre 101 be transferred to the opening session of the Geneva Conference' (Eban 1977 p.541).

In addition, however, it seems clear that members of the Israeli government were also worried about the rapid progress of these talks. Dayan recalls that the 'progress in the Yariv–Gamasi talks at Kilometre 101 had not been to my liking. It seemed to me that we were about to make vital concessions without receiving anything appropriate in exchange and without a suitable settlement and I was unable to prevent it' (Dayan 1976 p.524).

2   Suez and Jerusalem: 1974–1977

1. Plans for the clearing of the Canal and the reconstruction of the three main canal zone towns had been announced by the Egyptian Government in November 1973, when a new Ministry of Reconstruction had also been set up.
2. Interview in *Time*, 5 April 1975.
3. Interview in *Al-Siyassah* (Kuwait), 11 April 1975 (Israeli Vol.2 1979 p.831).
4. Interview on NBC Network news from Salzburg, 2 June 1975 (Israeli Vol.2 1979 p.898).
5. Sadat recalled in his own memoirs that he took this decision fully conscious of the risks involved: 'I knew only too well as I reopened the Canal that the entire region – the Canal itself and the three Canal towns – was within range of Israeli, American-supplied artillery. And that was why I declared that the region was now part of the mainland and any attack on it would be regarded as an attack on the Egyptian mainland towns' (Sadat 1978 p.274).
6. Israeli, with hindsight, makes the nature of Sadat's move very clear. 'Reopening the Canal was an implicit concession to Israel's claim for non-belligerency; the reopening of the Canal and the rebuilding and repopulating of the Canal cities constituted *de facto* non-belligerency, because Sadat would not want to jeopardise these "gains" of the October War' (Israeli 1985 pp.154–5).
7. Ismail Fahmy recalls that 'members of the Assembly and the Egyptian people did not think that Sadat's statement should be interpreted literally: the applause greeting the announcement did not mean that the members of the Assembly approved Sadat's idea of going to Jerusalem or even that they believed he intended to go. They were simply carried away when the President declared his readiness to go anywhere in the world to save the blood of his sons' (Fahmy 1983 p.266).
8. Begin's speech included a declaration that his government's prime concern would be 'to avoid another war in the Middle East. I am calling on King Hussein, President Sadat and President Assad to meet me, whether in our own capitals, or on neutral territory, either in public or out of the limelight, to discuss the establishment of real peace between them and Israel … If this call is rejected, we shall take note of Arab intransigence, which will be nothing new. Five prime ministers that have preceded me … repeatedly called for such a meeting, but the other side has either avoided a response or answered in the negative' (Handel 1981 p.302).
9. Two alleged outcomes of this contact were the brief 'border war' that flared between Egypt and Libya from 1 to 25 July (in which case the Mossad information would have had to have been delivered before 23 July; one version of this story has the information being passed directly to Egyptian intelligence in Rabat in mid-July); and further contacts between Israeli and Egyptian intelligence officers in Morocco later in 1977 (see Israeli 1985 p.226; and Handel 1981

p.346). Whether this story is in any way true or not, the fact remains that Prime Minister Begin did take the unusual step of reassuring Egypt in the Knesset that Israel would not take advantage of the border war – possibly a signal of goodwill towards Sadat.

10. Shimon Shamir states that Begin's message about a meeting was routine and not important, but that Sadat's subsequent questions to Ceausecu were – by revealing a serious Egyptian interest in meetings – as were Ceausescu's answers, which indicated that Begin was equally serious and could make any agreement stick – but said nothing about his ideological intransigence (Shamir, personal communication).

11. Dayan subsequently claimed a major preparatory role for the Moroccan meeting at the time of the Jerusalem visit – he released his notes on those meetings to journalists immediately after that event – but Shimon Shamir subsequently talked with both Sadat and Begin, both of whom denied that the Moroccan talks were in any way connected with Sadat's Jerusalem initiative (Shamir, personal communication).

12. According to Dayan, Sadat told him that he had been searching for an initiative that would produce 'shock waves, positive ones' and had considered a Big Five meeting in Jerusalem but, returning from Riyadh to Cairo following his talks with the Saudis, he decided that the Big Five might fail so, therefore, 'I ... decided that I would go myself to Israel' (Dayan 1981 p.88).

13. *Time* 2 January 1978 p.31.

3 Conciliation: Concepts, Frameworks and Models

1. Both Frank Edmead (personal communication) and Dean Pruitt (1997) have argued that, on occasions, parties in conflict find themselves in circumstances in which they are ready to seize upon almost any move by an adversary as a conciliatory gesture, perhaps only if their situation is desperate enough. This idea raises the question first of what are the circumstances in which one party will adopt this high level of 'readiness to recognise' a gesture as conciliatory; and second, whether opportunities to undertake conciliatory gestures are, as are occasions for escalation, regularly occurring, 'like tramcars'.

2. Karl Deutsch (1963), for example, proposes a sequence which involves the need to analyse: (1) the *source* of the signal; (2) the *channel* for the signal; (3) the *nature* and *content* of the signal; (4) the *intention* underlying the signal; (5) the *noise* accompanying the signal; (6) the *reception* and *interpretation* of the signal by the target.

3. This last question emphasises that all communication processes involve aspects of *perception* (and possible *misperception*) of signals and of underlying intentions. Even individuals who are quite close to one another can wholly misinterpret signals one to the other, while enemies' propensity to misinterpret the meaning of signals is enhanced by the level of hostility and mistrust each feels for the other. Hence, in all conflicts (and particularly during their height) leaders trying to signal a willingness to talk or to make conciliatory gestures face constantly a problem of *perceptual congruence* and of ensuring that the content of the message sent by the initiating party (the 'Initiator') is the same as that received by the adversary (the 'Target'). Given the prevalance of perceptual distortions during conflicts, this is no easy matter.

For discussions of the basic dynamics of perception and misperception in conflicts, particularly international conflicts, see Holsti (1962) and Jervis (1970 and 1976).

4   Contexts for Conciliation

1. In discussing the nature of change in the international system, for example, Holsti *et al.* argue that such change can be differentiated according to its direction, magnitude, pace and reversibility, while another means of distinguishing types of change is by the source (Holsti *et al.* 1980 pp xvii–xviii).

2. The role of anticipated costs is clearly an important one in the version of a hurting stalemate that involves the imminence of a major (usually mutual) catastrophe – what Zartman refers to as an approaching 'precipice' (Zartman 1985 Final Chapter).

3. All of these characteristics can be regarded as 'emergent properties' of conflict systems.

4. Bercovitch *et al.* (1991) use a slightly different term in arguing that the greater the 'dispute intensity', then the 'more polarised the parties' positions will become and the more determined will each party be to reject any mediation attempts and "win" at all costs' (ibid. p.13). They then operationalise 'intensity' by the number of fatalities experienced by the adversaries and find confirmation of this relationship, at least as far as international conflicts are concerned.

5. Randle, for example, argues strongly that 'should a dispute affect vital security interests of the parties, no amount of mediation by third parties is likely to prevent the outbreak of hostilities' (Randle 1973 p.49). Others (e.g. Wall and Lynn 1993 p.175) have associated 'salience of issues' with ideological – as opposed to material – concerns, or issues that involve principles, intangible interests or indivisibles, arguing that these conflicts are inherently more intractable than other types.

6. The literature on conflict often makes an unfortunately ambiguous distinction between conflicts of 'interest' and conflicts of 'value', while John Burton proposes a similar dichotomy distinguishing intractable 'conflicts' (over needs or values) and bargainable 'disputes' (over interests and goals) (Burton 1988).

7. Debates about the effects of structural symmetry or asymmetry within a conflict system are more general versions of the debate in International Relations about whether the existence of a preponderance or a balance of power within the international system leads to a greater or lesser likelihood of conflict being pursued through violence or coercion. The evidence here is inconclusive. For example, one study of international conflicts between 1816 and 1965 finds clearly that 'conflicts were more likely to escalate when power was unequal' (Siverson and Tennefoss 1984 p.1061). Another study of international conflicts between 1815 and 1939 shows, on the other hand, that 'conflicts between equal ... great power opponents were much more likely to escalate to war than were conflicts between unequals' (Moul 1988 p.242). Where that leaves the issue of deescalation and conciliation is difficult to say.

8. However, a study of seven cases of efforts to end warfare through the application of arms embargoes seems to show that, at least on their own, such strategies are not effective. Brzoska and Pearson argue that, while continuing arms deliveries during a war 'generally prolonged and intensified the fighting', an arms embargo, whether partial or total 'has little chance of compelling warring parties to stop wars or come to the negotiation table when it was not in their perceived interest to do so' (1994 p.216).

9. It may be that particular triggers are strongly connected with longer term, strategical changes but serve to bring the extent of this latter change to the attention of decision-makers in some symbolic way that can no longer be ignored.

10. Disaster, on the other hand, may have quite the opposite effect, of redoubling efforts to succeed through existing policies of coercion. Dunkirk, coupled with the loss of France as an ally, did not appear to have led to the British Government's making conciliatory moves towards Germany in 1940, nor did the military disaster at Stalingrad persuade Hitler that the time had come to send an olive branch to Stalin.

11. Obviously, how and why the new leaders come to power will have a major impact on whether a policy reconsideration takes place and in which direction policy might change. Some leaders come to power pledged to change, others to redoubled efforts.

5   Varieties of Olive Branch

1. Ambassador Dobrynin contacted the White House on the morning following the speech to ask about the implication of using the title, but was told it had no special significance! (Hersh 1983 p.365).

2. Jervis comments that, while both systems 'are established by convention, the former permits the users to send an infinite variety of messages, whereas the latter lacks this flexibility and can only communicate a much narrower set of messages' (Jervis 1970 p.21).

3. One of the major differences in the context for concessions is that, during a continuing negotiating process, the parties have a relatively clear picture of their adversary's stance on the issues being bargained and thus are usually able to recognise quickly the nature and extent of any concession being offered.

4. A classic example of this might be that of one leader drinking from the cup to be used by a rival to demonstrate that the drink was not poisoned. A more modern instance would be the moving of a mobile weapons system well out of range of its target.

5. The best exposition of the basic TFT strategy is to be found in Axelrod's classic studies of the best means of eliciting co-operative behaviour between adversaries in an inescapably continuing relationship (Axelrod 1984; Axelrod and Dion 1988). However, there exist many variations on the basic TFT model. Most of these are well decribed by Stoll and McAndrew (1986) and particularly by Druckman and Harris (1990).

6. In the case of Osgood's GRIT strategy, a fair degree of tolerance for non-reciprocity is deliberately built into the early stages of the initiative (Osgood 1962).

7. In March 1964 when the members of the Johnson Administration were considering three strategies against the DRV leaders in Hanoi (covert war in the North, overt pressure through a bombing campaign, or a combination of threats and promises), Ambassador Lodge argued strongly (but relatively unsuccessfully) for a strategy of C&S, the threat of air strikes if the Viet Cong did not withdraw from the South being the 'stick', and the promise of the withdrawal of some US forces plus some economic assistance being the 'carrot'. However, Lodge himself admitted at the time that such a move 'would not be a real *concession* on our part', even though he hoped this would be a 'saleable package' to the leaders in Hanoi (Thies 1980 pp.33 & 294–5).

8. There are quite frequent examples of one party to a conflict deliberately setting up a potential concession as a 'bargaining chip' by starting some activity (possibly violent or coercive) which can be abandoned later 'as a concession'. For example, immediately following Sadat's visit to Israel, Ariel Sharon suggested the rapid establishment of some new Israeli 'settlements' in Sinai, that could be

'given up' as an Israeli 'concession' in subsequent negotiations. Empirically, targets seem to treat such actions as anything other than conciliatory and this move did much to anger Sadat and undermine the conciliation process. Such common tactics prompt a definitional question about whether such negative benefits can be classified as 'conciliatory gestures'. Stopping loss, pain and hurt is hardly the same thing as offering a positive benefit.

9. Historical examples do seem to show that initiating parties occasionally seem to feel quite genuinely that stopping damage and pain are the equivalent of offering some positive benefit. Why this should be so is not at all clear.

10. I outline the main features of GRIT below in Chapter 7. For a full discussion of the strategy, see Osgood (1962); Lindskold (1978); Mitchell (1986); and Ramberg (1993).

6 The Nature of the Initiative: Characteristics and Impact

1. For a more detailed discussion of this episode, see Mitchell (1991)

2. This would argue very strongly for a gesture that was characterised by maximum visibility and concession, but – given intra-party obstacles and divisions, – the so-called 2-audience problem – the obvious need is for a signal that conveys maximum conciliation to the target, but minimises this for domestic hawks or rivals.

3. A number of observers have argued that changing an adversary's basic attitudes is not essential for the start of any accommodative process or even for the achievement of a solution. See especially Burton (1969)

4. Kelman (1985 p.225) links this idea to the first stage of attitude change (in Lewin's terms the 'unfreezing' stage), without going on to argue that the initiative – or even the overall accommodative sequence – will achieve the later Lewinian stages of 'changing' and 'refreezing'. For the original conceptions see Lewin (1951).

5. As I argue in a later chapter, high-cost moves are more likely to be attributed to genuine 'changes of heart' on the part of an adversary than are moves which cost little and can be attributed to change of circumstances. See Kelley (1971) and Mogy and Pruitt (1974) for expanded versions of this argument.

7 Increasing Recognisability

1. After several different students have done this on the same book, one often finds that 90 per cent of the text has been highlighted with yellow pen. This illustrates only too well the ease with which different parts of a given set of information can appear important to people with different views about the content, and with differing objectives, attitudes and belief systems.

2. Jervis emphasises that 'a person is less apt to reorganise evidence into a new theory or image if he is deeply committed to the established view. Commitment means not only the degree to which a person's power and prestige are involved but also ... the degree to which this way of seeing the world has proved satisfactory and become internalised.' (1976 p.196).

3. The 1990's bumper sticker advising readers to 'practice random acts of kindness and goodwill' was clearly based on the theory that the very randomness of these actions would ensure that they stood out and were noticed and appreciated.

4. It is also the case that the distinctiveness of the source does not necessarily make a conciliatory gesture visible or noticeable. Sadat used exactly the same arena to make a de-escalatory initiative in February 1971, following the termination of the

Rogers Initiative, but this was ignored by both Israel and the USA (see Sadat, 1978 p.280).

5. In many protracted conflicts, parties appear to 'anchor' their evaluations of current situations, choices, offers and options in some historical or even mythical past, with the result that concessions, conciliatory moves or compromise suggestions are almost inevitably framed as 'losses' compared with a golden age that serves both as a past and a future aspirational metric. Thus Irish nationalists use a mythical 'United Ireland' as a reference point; Israelis employ the historical standard of a Biblical 'Greater Israel' and Serbs of a 'Greater Serbia'; Karabakses compare today's achievement of an Azeri-free Ngorno Karabak with the historic boundaries of the Kingdom of Armenia, ally of Rome in the time of Marcus Aurelius.

6. The conflict between such pro-change and pro-continuation factions can be viewed at one level as a conflict over whose choice of anchoring point will be used to measure the outcome of the conflict.

7. Dean Pruitt (1965 p.406) goes much further than this 'notice-ability' argument, stating that multiple channels of communication 'can be used to transmit information about capabilities and intentions ... there is less guesswork for the other side.'

8   Enhancing Credibility

1. Ross and Stillinger also suggests that similar mechanisms to devalue an offer or proposal will operate, possibly less strongly, once it is known that an adversary has agreed to *accept* a plan, even one suggested by a third party (1991 p.395).

2. More recent work on *attribution theory* has focused on dimensions of causality other than *locus*. One such is *consistency* of cause, which – not surprisingly – involves continual demonstrations of a specific form of behaviour arising consistently from one source. Others are *stability* and *generality*.

3. Inevitably if paradoxically, the same processes will operate on a target's decision-makers to make them resistant to accepting the genuineness of the change.

4. For a discussion of the various meanings of 'commitment' in sociology, international politics and decision theory, see Weinstein (1969); Robey (1960); and Becker (1960).

5. This finding is thoroughly consistent with the predictions of theories of cognitive balance. An adversary suddenly framing an initiative positively as a promise, where threats and coercion had been the norm, would find – in spite of any 'positive' frame – that the target's estimate of the move's credibility would inevitably be low, if only to restore the latter's cognitive consistency. This is quite in line with Heider's theories about the need to maintain balance (Heider 1958).

   On the other hand, one other interesting finding is that a reputation for keeping promises enhanced the credibility of a subsequent threat ('Good people sometimes do bad things'), while a reputation for not keeping promises also enhanced credibility if a subsequent threat is made ('Welshers are bad people and bad people usually carry out threats') (Heilman 1974 pp.323–4).

6. Fisher suggests an interesting way of demonstrating commitment by placing what is promised in a situation which is beyond the future control of the initiator. Thus mortgage payments are placed 'in escrow' and beyond the reach of the purchaser should he or she change their minds and be tempted to renege on an agreement for sale. Fisher also suggests that one way in which President Johnson's 1967 offer of $1 billion in aid to North Vietnam could have been made

more credible through an irevocable commitment was to have placed the sum at the Asian Development Bank for automatic release to Hanoi once peace was achieved in Vietnam. Under such an arrangement, the USA could not have prevented implementation of the offer, even if the government had changed – as it did in 1968 (Fisher 1969 pp.118–19).

9 Reducing Mistrust

1. 'Mutual trust' indicates that all parties in a relationship hold similar expectations, although not necessarily to the same degree.
2. Zand gives the case of trusting a babysitter with one's children while one goes off to see a film as an example (1972 p.230).
3. Trust does enter into the situation in another way which provides an obstacle to peacemaking. Unless great care is taken in launching a conciliatory initiative, intra-party trust can also become an important negative element in the process. Any peacemaking efforts are likely to begin an erosion of such leaders–followers trust, which could lead finally to a sense of betrayal of trust on the part of a substantial section of the followers of the peacemaking leaders. Leaders of parties in conflict make many efforts to maintain a high level of trust in their competence and commitment to the cause of victory. Efforts to generate even minimal trust in an adversary can seriously undermine that level of intra-party trust. The situation almost appears to involve a limited amount of available 'trust': the more it grows between erstwhile adversaries, the more it is likely to diminish between the adversaries' leaders and the led.

   For any conciliatory initiative, the dilemma therefore comes to involve how it might be possible to increase trust between parties while not diminishing it within parties. The command 'Trust me – I am about to explore the possibilities of peace with our hated enemy, whom we *can* really trust after all' does not have a convincing ring to it.
4. Rotter defines interpersonal trust as 'an expectancy held by an individual or group that the word, promise, verbal or written statement of another individual or group can be relied on' (Rotter 1971 p.441).
5. Other writers, mainly from a background in sociology, have argued that trust may be based upon a strong positive emotion for the object of the trust ('emotional trust') or rational reasons why the object of the trust merits it ('cognitive trust'). Presumably, the same distinction can be made about mistrust.

   The argument continues to the effect that everyday (mis)trust is a mixture of both, but that the stronger the emotional content the less likely contrary evidence will weaken the (mis)trusting relationship, culminating in a situation of 'blind faith' ('Love and hate make one blind' Luhmann 1979 p.81)

   Lewis and Weigert (1985 pp.972–3) also hypothesise that trust relationships will have a preponderance of emotional motivation in small systems (families, groups) and of cognitive-rational in larger communities, but this seems open to question with regard to mistrust – witness the feelings of widespread mistrust of the enemy in time of war.
6. Haas and Deseran give the example of giving a platter as a wedding gift rather than its equivalent in cash, and make the point that, although the newly married couple might well be able to use the cash, the platter also represents the time and trouble the giver has taken to select the gift, and this symbolic 'good' adds to the value of the gift (1981 p.7).

7. In many cultures, the final action in any resolution or reconciliation process takes the form of a shared meal involving the parties until then in a relationship of conflict of feud.
8. Complete and diffuse trust might be one feature of 'being in love'.
9. In one problem solving workshop I attended involving Iraelis and Palestinians, a great deal of trust was evinced by Palestinian participants in one particular Israeli who made no secret of his exclusive devotion to the security of Israeli, his basic indifference to the fortunes of the Palestinians but his recognition that the two were inter-connected. Palestinian participants grew to understand his predictable responses, and to respect his honesty and openness about his motives (even if they didn't agree with his viewpoint or conclusions). In some sense, this individual had achieved a minimum level of trust from his adversaries at least as far as the predictability and malevolence–indifference–benevolence dimensions were concerned.
10. To attempt the latter, argues Herb Kelman, would exacerbate participants' re-entry problems should they try 'to persuade their compatriots that – on the basis of their peculiar experiences – the enemy can be trusted' (Kelman 1991 p.153).
11. Parks and his colleagues do, however, produce the interesting findings that individuals prone to trust easily generally need a longer series of non-cooperative moves from another before changing their own behaviour towards conflict than do 'low trusters' faced with unexpected co-operative behaviour. However, lest one should be carried away with this finding, low trusters' also tend to exploit very rapidly the other party's continuing series of co-operative moves (Parks *et al.* 1996).

10   Obstacles to Clear Signalling

1. Other factors on the list include a desire not to waste already committed resources, personal preferences for 'consistency', the availability of cultural models for consistency, the nature of the adversary, interpersonal competition and political vulnerability.
2. Lord Milner once dismissed the growing public clamour in Britain against the continuation of the war against the Boer Republics as 'Disregarding the screamers.'
3. Staw and Ross discuss the prevalance in certain cultures of what they call 'turn-around scripts' (that is, historical models of apparently hopeless situations being turned around into triumphs through further efforts and endeavour); of successful models of persistence; and of the existence of norms 'such that persistence is interpreted as strong leadership, whereas withdrawal is viewed as a sign of weakness' (Staw and Ross 1987 p.59).

   Of course, this whole phenomenon may not be entirely unconnected with the tendency for political leaders to claim singular infallibility for their own predictions and policies but – again – this may itself be a function of having to operate in a competitive political system that places a high premium on 'being right' as a price of re-election or re-selection for office.
4. The sparseness and superficiality of the debates among the Allies over a negotiated peace during 1916 and 1917 is an illustration of this point. See Iklé (1989).
5. With the latter group, the argument that a target might also be subject to internal divisions that only permit incremental concessions will tend to be dismissed as irrelevant, or merely as a sign of the continued predominance of the target's hawks.

6. The existence of pro-continuation factions within a target, criticising, opposing or sabotaging a conciliatory initiative simply as part of their on-going political conflict with a pro-conciliation group is often a seriously neglected aspect of many conciliation processes. Initiating parties frequently exhibit a tendency to perceive targets as unitary actors and to treat them as undifferentiated wholes.

7. On occasions, anti-conciliation factions can establish an alliance with external governments whose interests would be damaged by a 'premature' effort to negotiate a compromise peace or even the launching of a conciliatory process.

8. Strategists commonly make a distruction between strategies designed to prevent undesired actions (deterrence) and those designed to bring about desired actions (compellence). See Schelling (1966) for a discussion of these concepts.

9. Paradoxically, the initiative had been helped by a bombing pause while the Polish intermediary, Janusz Lewandowski of the International Control Commission, was in Hanoi, but it was effectively destroyed by two spasms of increased air attack on 2/3 December and later on 13/14 December. In all cases, however, the air strikes had occurred completely independently of the diplomatic efforts at de-escalation. In fact, the raids had been authorised on 10 November, but bad weather had prevented them being carried out until the start of December and then again (after a further week of bad weather) in mid-December. Lewandowski's first visit to Hanoi had coincided with bad weather and hence a bombing lull. Thereafter, the US Air force continued with its 'normal and authorised' escalation of the bombing. The effect of such contradictory signals on a divided North Vietnamese government, with hawks arguing that to show signs of interest in negotiations would only encourage the USA to increase pressure, needs little imagination.

10. Limiting cases in which goal salience is unlikely to change are those where the sole *raison d'être* for the existence of the party is the pursuit of the goals in question – where the 'party' has come into being in order to achieve a particular outcome. Single-issue struggle groups, such as secessionist guerrillas like the IRA or ETA, are unlikely to change the salience of the only goals that they have, as these justify their existence, so that conciliation is only likely to work if the process also involves the transformation of these groups into something else with a different future.

11 Obstacles to Prompt Reacting

1. This points out that during the 16-month period from November 1966 to March 1968, the parties exchanged diplomatic signals about negotiation through 8 major channels simultaneously, frequently using several at once, as well as continuing with the parallel strategy of mutual coercion, thus further increasing the confusion (Thies 1980 p.144).

2. The process of 'trivialisation' – reducing the discrepancy between an attitude, value or opinion and contrary information about either another's or one's own behaviour by reducing the importance of one of these – could be a positive factor in encouraging conciliatory initiatives or responses.

   Such conciliatory behaviours – or even the mental action of contemplating them – are likely to be highly discrepant with existing attitudes or values (i.e. they involve actually treating with the enemy) but uncomfortable psychological tension within and among decision-makers might be diminished by 'reducing the importance of one or more of the dissonant elements' (Simon, Greenberg and Brehm 1995 p.247), that is, by diminishing the importance of negative attitudes towards the adversary or – more likely – the importance of the conciliatory action being proposed or undertaken.

'It's only a small step,' might be a common way of defensively trivialising a conciliatory initiative or response.

3. Betrayal can be defined as a 'breach of trust' in the sense of broken expectations from those within the group or collectivity. The intensity of the sense of betrayal on the part of those betrayed (and the concomitant punishment of those betraying) will vary depending on circumstances, some factors intensifying it, others mitigating it.

4. Akerstrom notes the way in which betrayers' names tend to become notorious landmarks in the folk memories of particular groups or nations – Judas, Vidkun Quisling, Brutus, Phillipe Petain, Benedict Arnold. Recall also the story of Ian Smith (the Rhodesian Prime Minister who had led the white minority's struggle for independence and continued white dominance in what later became Zimbabwe) returning to his capital from London after agreeing to negotiate with his African nationalist adversaries, only to have 30 pieces of silver flung on to the tarmac in front of him by a group of whites who, shortly before, would have welcomed the return of 'Good Old Smithy'.

5. A wartime coalition will almost certainly split apart once its *raison d'être* – the war itself – looks like coming to an end.

6. The biggest obstacle to participating in a conciliatory process, however, remains the centrality of the issues in conflict to party members, and the way in which the struggle becomes institutionalised within the parties involved. Ways of justifying accommodation and a negotiated solution frequently take the form of arguing (1) that goals may be achieved by other means; (2) that achieving the goals by coercive means is proving too costly; (3) that alternatives might be found to substitute for what would be gained by the achievement of those goals; or (4) that other important goals are being sacrificed in the pursuit of those in dispute.

In this way, convincing arguments can be made to the legitimacy of at least exploring the possibility of conciliation, discussion and negotiation, as when some Indonesian leaders began to argue in the mid-1960's that the diversionary strategy of Confrontation with Malaysia was simply diverting attention from other important issues for the country, such as stagnant economic development.

12   Conciliation and Intra-Party Conflicts

1. In the latter case, the 'public' gesture also raises questions about who is really the target, and why the gesture was made in such a manner as to ensure that it would be recognised by the target's internal opposition, opinion leaders, mass public opinion and other third parties as well as the target's decision-makers.

2. See Thies (1980) for an account of Kissinger's role in informal talks held in Paris during 1967.

3. The US-Chinese initiative was aided in this respect by the fact that both elite and public attention was focused upon the wars in Vietnam, Laos and Cambodia, and not upon what seemed to be peripheral issues.

4. Sadat actually reshuffled his Cabinet, bringing in the popular Mustapha Kamil (former president of the Arab Socialist Union and a member of the technocratic elite) as Prime Minister; replacing General Gamassy as Minister for War with a close friend of Vice President Mubarak, Air Force General Kamal Hassan Ali, but offering Gamassy the post of Special Presidential Advisor; and appointing a 1973 war hero, Major General Ahmad Badawi, as Chief of Staff.

5. I believe that this term was first used by President Kennedy in the early 1960s during the early days of the Cold War 'thaw' to describe the changing relationship between the USA and the USSR.

13   Channels for Conciliation

1. For a review of traditional intermediary functions see Mitchell (1981); Pincen (1992); and Bercovitch and Rubin (1992).
2. Diamond and McDonald (1996) argue that at least nine 'tracks' or types of intermediary channel can be distinguished in patterns of intermediary activity in protracted conflicts. These range from official diplomacy ('Track 1') through 8 other tracks, such as the media, business exchanges and citizen diplomacy.
3. There seems to be a 'decomposition' factor at work with regard to appropriate third party channels and mediators, in that successful use undermines their unobtrusiveness. If particular third parties have suitable qualities and are used, then this often becomes generally known and observers begin to expect that they will be used as channels on a regular basis. This happens to governments (for a time, King Hassan of Morocco was expected to be a regular contact point between Israel and the Arab world) and to some individuals.
4. A good example was the problem of credibility experienced by Sydney Bailey, the Quaker intermediary, in January 1973, being unable to say to Israelis that his mission, an early initiative by President Sadat, had the President's direct approval (Bailey, 1985 and 1990).
5. The phenonemon of 'transferred trust' is a common one, involving actions such as accepting letters of introduction from a trusted friend and accepting a total stranger on that basis; endorsing a product in advertising or a candidate in politics; being vouched for by an existing member of a club; listening to a character witness; or writing a reference.
6. Much of this argument depends upon the third party acting as channel being authentically neutral and relatively independent. No target is likely to trust an ally, friend, client or associate of the adversary – or even another party with a similar ideology or parallel position on similar issues. In such circumstances few positive functions are likely to be carried out by the third party; even amplification will be seen as arguing a friend's – or master's – case.
7. The draft 'Pretoria Agreement' involved Smith accepting black majority rule within two years and an interim government, 'invited' by Smith, consisting of a Council of State with half white and half black members, and a Council of Ministers with a black prime minister and a majority of black ministers. However, Smith's required amendments involved a white chairman for the Council of State and the reserving of the portfolios of Defence and Law and Order. None of this was acceptable to the nationalist leaders or the presidents of the Front Line States (Meredith 1979).

14   Hypotheses on Conciliation

1. It is true that Sadat had needed to head off (with Israeli assistance) at least one major assassination plot, but failed assassination plots (and even successful ones) are as often a sign of political weakness – even impotence – as they are of strength.
2. Fisher (1969) argues that a key task for any party in a conflict undertaking any kind of a de-escalatory initiative *vis-à-vis* an opponent is to frame the proposal so as to make it easy for the adversary to answer 'Yes' by (1) thinking about the

latter's options; (2) being precise about the details of the proposal; and (3) making clear to the target that the advantages accruing from accepting far outweigh those gained from rejecting.

3. A similar move by the Basque nationalist guerrilla organisation, ETA, in 1997 had very little effect as the truce was a temporary – one week – one, and thus due to last such a short time that it was impossible to test whether ETA had, in fact, suspended its relatively rare operations.

Epilogue: Nearing Camp David

1. The relative success of the military discussions paralleled failures at the political level. Weizman, Shapir and Shlomo Gazit had tough but useful talks with General Gamassy and his aides in Cairo just before the Ismailia Conference. Two further meetings in January discussed a wide range of detailed security concerns associated with the handing back of the Sinai territory, but came to no consensus. Weizman again met with Sadat in late March in Cairo and in mid-July in Austria.

2. Ezer Weizman records that at the time of Sadat's Jerusalem visit, Arial Sharon had suggested that Al Arish should be unilaterally returned to Egypt in recognition of Sadat's move, but that this proposal had been rejected. It is interesting to speculate what such a gesture might have done to improve both Sadat's position in Egypt and elsewhere in the Arab world, and to the development of some working trust on the part of unconvinced Egyptians (Weizman 1981 p.317).

3. There is controversy over the US reaction to Begin's autonomy plan for the West Bank. What seems clear is that Begin believed that President Carter gave the scheme a far warmer reception than Carter intended – another case of the common error of hearing what one wishes to hear – and had concluded that the plan was a fair basis for negotiation. This perception was to bedevil future discussions, as Begin frequently tried to get a public US endorsement of the plan. US refusal would lead Begin to the conclusion that Carter had deliberately misled him.

4. Of Begin, Friedlander writes that he 'was too confident that the Egyptian elites would be far more solicitous over his domestic situation and historical commitments than he himself would be over Sadat's internal constraints' (Friedlander 1983 p.127).

5. In Weizman's account, the 'settlements' were clearly only meant as dummies. Sharon arranged for water towers to be erected, buses and trailers to be put in place and the land surrounding the four settlements to be ploughed, but there is no record of anyone ever occupying the sites (Weizman 1981 p.144–5).

6. This impression was reinforced by the fact that the Israeli cabinet simultaneously gave the go-ahead to the establishment of 20 new settlements on the West Bank.

7. In March, Sadat also tried to underline his commitment to the peace process by condemning the PLO attack on an Israeli bus that resulted in 30 dead; and shortly afterwards refused to join in the condemnation of Israel's assault into Lebanon.

8. See Friedlander (1983); Quandt (1986); Weizman (1981).

Bibliography

Abelson, R.P. and A. Levi 'Decision-making and Decision Theory' in G. Lindzey and E. Aaronson (eds) *A Handbook of Social Psychology* 3rd edn. Vol.1. (New York; Random House; 1985) pp.231–309.

Aguilar, J.L. 'Trust and Exchange: Expressive and Instrumental Dimensions of Reciprocity in a Peasant Community' *Ethos* 12 (1) Spring 1984 pp.3–29.

Akerstrom, M. *Betrayal and Betrayers; The Sociology of Treachery* (New Brunswick, NJ; Transaction Publishers; 1991).

Allison, G.T. *Essence of Decision* (Boston; Little, Brown; 1971).

Aronson, S. *Conflict and Bargaining in the Middle East* (Baltimore; Johns Hopkins Press; 1978).

Asch, S.E. 'Effects of Group Pressure on the Modification and Distortion of Judgements' in H. Guetzkow (ed.) *Groups, Leadership and Men* (Pittsburgh, PA; Carnegie Press; 1951).

Ashworth, A. *Trench Warfare 1914–18; The Live and Let Live System* (New York; Holmes and Meier; 1980).

Axelrod. R. *The Evolution of Cooperation* (New York; Basic Books; 1984).

Axelrod, R. and D. Dion 'The Further Evolution of Cooperation' *Science* 242 9 December 1988 pp.1385–90.

Azar, E.E. *The Management of Protracted Social Conflict; Theory and Cases* (Aldershot; Dartmouth Publishing; 1990).

Bailey, S.D. 'Quaker Experiences in International Conciliation' *International Affairs* Spring 1985 61 (2) pp.205–22.

Bailey, S.D. 'A Case Study in Quaker Mediation' *The Friends Quarterly* April 1990 26 (2) pp.88–95.

Barber, B. *The Logic and Limits of Trust* (New Brunswick, NJ; Rutgers University Press; 1983).

Bardach, E. 'Policy Termination as a Political Process' *Policy Sciences* 7 (2) Sept. 1976 pp.123–31.

Bazerman, M.H. 'Negotiator Judgement; A Critical Look at Rationality Assumptions' *American Behavioural Scientist* 22 (2) November 1983 pp.211–28.

Becker, H.S. 'Notes on the Concept of Commitment' *American Journal of Sociology* LXVI (1) July 1960 pp.32–40.

Beggan, J.K. and L. Manelli 'Estimating the Credibility of Social Influence Contingencies Framed as Threats and Promises' *Journal of Social Behaviour and Personality* 9 (1) March 1994 pp.163–70.

Behn, R.D. 'How to Terminate a Public Policy; A Dozen Hints for the Would Be Terminator' *Journal of Policy Analysis* 4 (3) Summer 1978 pp.393–413.

Bennis, W.G. *et al. Interpersonal Dynamics; Essays and Readings on Human Interaction* (Homewood, IL: Dorsey Press; 1964).

Bercovitch, J. (ed.) *Resolving International Conflicts; The Theory and Practice of International Mediation* (Boulder, CO; Lynne Rienner; 1996).

Bercovitch, J., J.T. Anagnoson and D.L. Wille 'Some Conceptual Issues and Empirical Trends in the Study of Successful Mediation in International Relations' *Journal of Peace Research* 28 (1) February 1991 pp.7–17.

Bercovitch, J., and J. Langley 'The Nature of the Dispute and the Effectiveness of International Mediation' *Journal of Conflict Resolution* 37 (4) December 1993 pp.670–91.

Bercovitch, J. and J.Z. Rubin (eds.) *Mediation in International Relations; Multiple Approaches to Conflict Management* (New York; St Martins Press; 1992).

Blau, P.M. *Exchange and Power in Social Life* (New York; John Wiley; 1964).

Bomsdorf, F. 'The Third World, Europe and Confidence Building Measures' in Hugh Hanning (ed.) *Peacekeeping and Confidence Building Measures in the Third World.* (New York; International Peace Academy; 1985).

Bonoma, T.V. *Conflict; Escalation and De-escalation* (Beverly Hills; Sage; 1976).

Boulding, K.E. *The Image* (Ann Arbor, MI; University of Michigan Press; 1956).

Brecher, M. *Decisions in Crisis; Israel 1967 and 1973* (Berkeley, CA; University of California Press; 1980).

Brockner, J. and J.Z. Rubin *Entrapment in Escalating Conflicts* (New York; Springer Verlag; 1985).

Brown, B. and J.Z. Rubin *The Social Psychology of Bargaining and Negotiation* (New York; Academic Press; 1975).

Brzezinski, Z. *Power and Principle* (New York; Farrar, Straus and Giroux; 1983).

Brzoska, M and F.S.Pearson *Arms and Warfare; Escalation, De-escalation and Warfare* (Columbia, SC; University of South Carolina Press; 1994).

Bueno de Mesquita, B. 'An Expected Utility Theory of International Conflict' *American Political Science Review* December 1980 74 (4) pp.917–31.

Bueno de Mesquita, B. 'The War Trap Revisited; A Revised Expected Utility Model' *American Political Science Review* March 1985 79 (1) pp.156–77.

Bueno de Mesquita, B. and D. Lalman 'Reason and War' *American Political Science Review* 80 (4) December 1986 pp.1131–50.

Burton, J.W. *Conflict and Communication* (London; Macmillan;.1969).

Burton, J.W. *Conflict Resolution as a Political System* (Fairfax, VA; Center for Conflict Analysis and Resolution; 1988) Working Paper No. 1.

Cobb, S. 'Empowerment and Mediation; A Narrative Perspective' *Negotiation Journal* 9 (3) July 1993 pp.245–59.

Cobb, S. and J. Rifkin 'Practice and Paradox: Deconstructing Neutrality in Mediation' *Law and Social Inquiry* 16 (1) Winter 1991 pp.35–62.

Coser, L.A. *The Functions of Social Conflict* (London; Routledge and Kegan Paul; 1956).

Coser, L.A. 'The Termination of Conflict' *Journal of Conflict Resolution* V (4) Dec. 1961 pp.347–53.

Curle, A. *In the Middle; Non-Official Mediation in Violent Situations* (New York; Berg Publishers; 1986).

Dayan, M. *Story of My Life* (New York; William Morrow; 1976).

Dayan, M. *Breakthrough; A Personal Account of the Egypt-Israeli. Peace Negotiations* (New York; Alfred Knopf; 1981).

Deutsch, K.W. *The Nerves of Government* (New York; Free Press; 1963).

Deutsch, M. 'Trust and Suspicion' *Journal of Conflict Resolution* II (1) March 1958 pp.265–79.

Deutsch, M. *The Resolution of Conflict* (New Haven; Yale University Press; 1973).

Diamond, L. and J.W. McDonald *Multi-Track Diplomacy; A Systems Approach to Peace* 3rd edn (Westport, CT; Kumarian Press; 1996).

Druckman, D. 'The Social Psychology of Arms Control and Reciprocation' *Political Psychology* 11 (3) Sept. 1990 pp.553–81.

Druckman, D. 'Negotiating in the International Context' in I.W.Zartman and L.Rasmussen (eds.) *Peacemaking in International Conflict* (Washington; USIP Press; 1996).

Druckman, D. and T.V. Bonoma 'Determinants of Bargaining Behaviour in a Bilateral Monopoly Situation; Opponent's Concession Rate and Similarity' *Behavioural Science* 21 (4) July 1976 pp.252–62.

Druckman, D., K. Zechmeister and D. Solomon 'Determinants of Bargaining Behaviour in a Monopoly Situation: Opponent's Concession Rate and Relative Defensibility' *Behavioural Science* 17 (6) November 1972 pp.514–31.

Druckman, D. and R. Harris 'Alternative Models of Responsiveness in International Negotiation' *Journal of Conflict Resolution* 34 (2) June 1990 pp.234–51.

Eban, A. *Abba Eban; An Autobiography* (New York; Random House; 1977).

Elon, A. and S. Hassan *Between Enemies; A Compassionate Dialogue between an Israeli and an Arab* (New York; Random House; 1974).

Evans, P.B., H.K. Jacobson and R.D. Putnam (eds.) *Double Edged Diplomacy; International Bargaining and Domestic Politics* (Berkeley, CA; University of California Press; 1993).

Fahmy, I. *Negotiating for Peace in the Middle East* (Baltimore; John Hopkins Press; 1983).

Festinger, L. *A Theory of Cognitive Dissonance* (Stanforn, CA; Stanford University Press; 1957).

Fisher, R. *International Conflict For Beginners* (New York; Harper and Row; 1969).

Fox, F.V. and B.M. Staw 'The Trapped Administrator' *Administrative Science Quarterly* 24 (3) September 1979 pp.449–71.

Frensley, N.J. 'Ratification Processes and Conflict Termination'. *Journal of Peace Research* 35 (2) May 1998 pp.167–91.

Friedlander, M.A. *Sadat and Begin; The Domestic Politics of Peacemaking* (Boulder, CO; Westview Press; 1983).

Gazit, M. *The Peace Process 1969–1973; Efforts and Contacts* (The Magnes Press; 1983) Jerusalem Papers on Peace Problems No. 35.

Genco, S.J. 'Integration Theory and System Change' in Holsti, O.R. *et al.* (eds) *Change in the International System* (Boulder, CO; Westview Press; 1980).

Gibb, J. 'Defense Level and Influence Potential in Small Groups' in L. Petrillo and B.M. Bass (eds) *Leadership and Interpersonal Behaviour* (New York; Holt, Rhinehart and Winston; 1961) pp.66–81.

Giffin, K. 'The Contribution of Studies of Source Credibility to a Theory of Interpersonal Trust' *Psychological Bulletin* 68 (2) 1967 pp.104–20.

Gochman, C. and R. Leng 'Realpolitik and the Road to War; An Analysis of Attributes and Behaviour' *International Studies Quarterly* 27 (1) March 1983 pp.97–120.

Goffman, E. 'On Face Work' in *Interaction Ritual; Essays in Face to Face Behaviour* (New York; Pantheon; 1967).

Govier, T. 'Trust, Distrust and Feminist Theory' *Hypatia* 7 (1) Winter 1992 pp.16–33.

Haas, D.F. and F.A. Deseran 'Trust and Symbolic Exchange' *Social Psychology Quarterly* 44 (1) March 1981 pp.3–13.

Haber, E., Z. Schiff and E. Yaari *The Year of the Dove* (New York; Bantam Books; 1979).

Haig, A.M. *Caveat; Realism, Reagan and Foreign Policy* (New York; Macmillan; 1984).

Handel, M.I. *The Diplomacy of Surprise; Hitler, Nixon, Sadat* (Cambridge; Harvard Centre for International Affairs; 1981).

Heider, F. *The Psychology of Interpersonal Relations* (New York; John Wiley; 1958).

Heilman, M.E. 'Threats and Promises: Reputational Consequences and Transfer of Credibility' *Journal of Experimental Social Psychology* 10 (4) July 1974 pp.310–24.

Held, V. 'On the Meaning of Trust' *Ethics* 78 (2) January 1968 pp.156–9.

Hermann, C.F. (ed.) *International Crises; Insights from Behavioural Research* (New York; Free Press; 1972).

Hermann, C.F. 'Changing Course; When Governments Choose to Redirect Foreign Policy' *International Studies Quarterly* 34 (1) March 1990 pp.3–21.

Hermann, M.G. 'Leadership and Foreign Policy Change: When do Leaders Choose to Change Course?' in D. Druckman and C. Mitchell (eds.) *Flexibility in International Negotiation and Mediation* Annals of the American Academy of Political and Social Sciences Vol. 542 Nov. 1995 pp.148–167.

Hersh, S.M. *The Price of Power; Kissinger in the Nixon White House* (New York; Simon and Schuster; 1983).

Hewitt, J.P. *Self and Society; A Symbolic Interactionist Social Psychology* (Boston; Allyn and Bacon; 1976).

Holst, J.J. and K.Merlander 'European Security and Confidence Building Measures' *Survival* 19 (4) July/August 1977.

Holsti, O.R. 'The Belief System and National Images; A Case Study' *Journal of Conflict Resolution* VI (3) September 1962 pp.244–252.

Holsti, O.R., R.M.Siverson and A.L. George (eds) *Change in the International System* (Boulder, CO; Westview Press; 1980).

Horsburgh, H.J.N. 'The Ethics of Trust' *Philosophical Quarterly* 10 (4) October 1960 pp.343–54.

Iklé, F.C. *How Nations Negotiate* (New York; Harper and Row; 1964).

Iklé, F.C. *Every War Must End* 2nd ed. (New York; Columbia University Press; 1989).

Isaacs, K.S., J.M. Alexander and E.A. Haggard 'Faith, Trust and Gullibility' *International Journal of Psycho-Analysis* 44 (4) 1963 pp.461–69.

Israeli, R. (ed.) *The Public Diary of President Sadat.* 3 Vols. (Leiden; E.J. Brill; Vol.1 1978, Vols. 2 and 3 1979).

Israeli, R. *Man of Defiance; A Political Biography of Anwar Sadat* (Totowa, N.J.; Barnes and Noble; 1985).

Jackson, E. *Middle East Mission* (New York; W.W. Norton; 1983).

Janis, I.L. *Groupthink* (Boston; Houghton Mifflin; 1982).

Jervis, R. 'Hypotheses on Misperception' *World Politics* 20 (3) April 1968 pp.454–79.

Jervis, R. *The Logic of Images in International Relations* (Princeton, NJ; Princeton University Press; 1970).

Jervis, R. *Perception and Misperception in International Politics* (Princeton, NJ; Princeton University Press; 1976).

Jervis, R. 'Political Implications of Loss Aversion' *Political Psychology* 13 (2) June 1992 pp.187–204.

Jones, E.E. 'The Rocky Road from Acts to Dispositions' *American Psychologist* February 1979 34 (2) pp.107–117.

Jones, E.E. and R.E. Nisbett *The Actor and the Observer; Divergent Perceptions of the Causes of Behaviour* (New York; General Learning Press; 1971).

Jordan, H. *Crisis; The Last Year of the Carter Presidency* (New York; G.P.Putnam; 1982).

Kahn, H. *On Escalation; Metaphors and Scenarios* (New York; Praeger; 1965).

Kahneman, D., J.L. Knetsch and R.H. Thaler 'Experimental Tests of the Endowment Effect and the Coase Theorem' *Journal of Political Economy* 98 (6) December 1990 pp.1325–48.

Kahneman, D. and A. Tversky 'Prospect Theory; An Analysis of Decision Under Risk' *Econometrica* 47 (2) March 1979 pp.263–91.

Kahneman, D., and A. Tversky 'The Simulation Heuristic' in D. Kahneman. P.Slovic and A. Tversky (eds.) *Judgement Under Uncertainty; Heuristics and Biases* (Cambridge; Cambridge University Press; 1982.

Katzev, R. and T. Wang 'Can Commitment Change Behaviour? A Case Study of Environmental Actions' *Journal of Social Behaviour and Personality* 9 (1) 1994 pp.13–26 To be completed.

Kelley, H.H. *Attribution to Social Interaction* (Morristown, NJ; General Learning Press; 1971).

Kelley, H.H. 'The Process of Causal Attribution' *American Psychologist* 28 (2) February 1973 pp.107–128.

Kelley, H.H. and J.L. Michaela 'Attribution Theory and Research' in M.R. Rosenzweig and L.W. Porter (eds) *Annual Review of Psychology* Vol.31 (Palo Alto, CA; Annual Review Inc.; 1980) pp.457–503.

Kelley, H.H. *et al. Close Relationships* (New York; W.H. Freeman; 1983).

Kelman, H.C. 'Overcoming the Psychological Barrier; An Analysis of the Egyptian–Israeli Peace Process' *Negotiation Journal* July 1985 1 (3) pp.213–34.

Kelman, H.C. 'Interactive Problem Solving; a Social-Psychological Approach to Conflict Resolution' in W. Klassen (ed.) *Dialogue Towards Inter-Faith Understanding* (Jerusalem; Tantur Ecuminical Institute for Theological Research; 1986).

Kelman, H.C. 'Interactive Problem Solving: The Uses and Limits of a Therapeutic Model for the Resolution of International Conflicts' in Volkan, V. *et al. The Psychodynamics of International Relations* Vol.II (Lexington MA; Lexington Books; 1991).

Kelman, H.C. 'Coalitions Across Conflict Lines; The Interplay of Conflicts Within and Between the Israeli and Palestinian Communities' Chap 14. in S. Worschel and J. Simpson (eds.) *Conflicts Between People and Groups* (Chicago; Nelson Hall;1993).

Kiesler, C.A. *The Psychology of Commitment* (New York; Academic Press; 1971).

Kissinger, H.A. *White House Years* (Boston; Little, Brown; 1979).

Kissinger, H.A. *Years of Upheaval* (Boston; Little, Brown; 1982).

Kleiboer, M. 'Ripeness of Conflict; A Fruitful Notion?' *Journal of Peace Research* 31 (1) February 1994 pp.109–16.

Kriesberg, L. 'Interlocking Conflicts in the Middle East' in L. Kriesberg (ed.) *Research in Social Movements, Conflicts and Change* Vol.3 (Westport, CT; JAI Press; 1980) pp.99–119.

Kriesberg, L. 'Non-Coercive Inducements in US-Soviet Conflict' *Journal of Political and Military Sociology* 9 Spring 1981 pp.1–16.

Kriesberg, L. 'Social Theory and the De-escalation of International Conflict' *Sociological Review* 32 (3) Aug 1984 pp.471–91.

LaPorte, T.R. 'Organised Social Complexity; Explication of a Concept' in T.R. LaPorte (ed) *Organised Social Complexity* (Princeton, NJ; Princeton University Press; 1975).

LaTour, S. *et al.* 'Some Determinants of Preference for Modes of Conflict Resolution' *Journal of Conflict Resolution* 20(2) June 1976 pp.319–356.

Lederach, J.P. *Preparing for Peace: Conflict Transformation Across Cultures* (Syracuse, NY; Syracuse University Press; 1996).

Levi, A.S. and J.B. Pryor 'The Use of the Avaliability Heuristic in Probability Estimates of Future Events; The Effects of Imagining Outcomes versus Imagining Reasons' *Organisational Behaviour and Human Decision Processes* 40 (2) October 1987 pp.219–34.

Levy, J.S. 'An Introduction to Prospect Theory' *Political Psychology* 13 (2) June 1992 pp.171–86.

Lewicki, R.J. and B.B. Bunker 'Trust in Relationships: A Model of Development and Decline' in B.B. Bunker and J.Z. Rubin (eds.) *Conflict cooperation and Justice: Essays Inspired by the Worth of Morton Dentsch* (San Francisco: Jossey Bass 1995).

Lewin, K. *Field Theory in Social Sciences* (New York; Harper; 1951).

Lewis, J.D. and A. Weigert 'Trust as a Social Reality' *Social Forces* 63 (4) June 1985 pp.967–85.

Liddell Hart, B.H. *The Revolution in Warfare* (New Haven; Yale University Press; 1947).

Lindskold, S.J. 'Trust Development, the GRIT Proposals and the Effect of Conciliatory Acts on Conflict and Co-operation' *Psychological Bulletin* 85 (4) July 1978 pp.772–793.

Little, W. and C.R. Mitchell *In the Aftermath; Anglo-Argentine Relations After the 1982 War* (College Park, MD; CIDCM Press; 1988).

Lomnitz, I.. *Networks and Marginality; Life in a Mexican Shantytown* (New York; Academic Press; 1977).

Luhmann, N. *Trust and Power* (New York; John Wiley; 1979).

Mallie, E. and D. McKittrick *The Fight for Peace; The Secret Story Behind the Irish Peace Process* (London; Heinemann; 1996).

McClelland, C.A. 'The Beginning, Duration and Abatement of International Crises' Chap. 5 in C.F. Hermann (ed.) *International Crises* (New York; Free Press; 1972).

Meadows, A.J. *et al.* 'Influence of Brainstorming Instructions and Problem Sequence on Creative Problem Solving Tests' *Journal of Applied Psychology* 43 December 1959 pp.413–6.

Meredith, M. *The Past is Another Country; Rhodesia, UDI to Zimbabwe* (London; Andre Deutsch; 1979).

Mitchell, C.R. *The Structure of International Conflict* (London; Macmillan; 1981).

Mitchell, C.R. 'GRIT and Gradualism – 25 Years On' *International Interactions* 13 (1) 1986 pp.59–90.

Mitchell, C.R. 'Motives for Mediation' in C.R. Mitchell and K. Webb (eds.) *New Approaches to International Mediation* (Westport, CT; Greenwood Press; 1988).

Mitchell, C.R. 'A Willingness to Talk' CCAR Working Papers No. 5 (Fairfax, VA.; George Mason University; 1990).

Mitchell, C.R. 'Ending Conflicts and Wars; Judgement, Rationality and Entrapment' *International Social Science Journal* Vol.127 February 1991a pp.35–55.

Mitchell, C.R. 'A Willingness to Talk' *Negotiation Journal* 7 (4) October 1991b pp.405–430.

Mitchell, C.R. 'The Process and Stages of Mediation; Two Sudanese Cases' in D.Smock (ed.) *Making War and Waging Peace* (Washington, DC; US Institute of Peace Press; 1993).

Mitchell, C.R. 'The Right Moment; Notes on Four Models of "Ripeness"' *Paradigms; The Kent Journal of International Relations* 9 (2) Winter 1995 pp.38–52.

Mogy, R.B. and D.G. Pruitt 'Effects of a Threatener's Enforcement Costs on Threat Credibility and Compliance' *Journal of Personality and Social Psychology* 29 (2) 1974 pp.173–180.

Morrow, J.D. 'A Twist of Truth; A Re-examination of the Effects of Arms Races on the Occurrence of War' *Journal of Conflict Resolution* 33 (3) Sept. 1989 pp.500–529.

Moul, W. 'Balances of Power and the Escalation to War of Disputes Among the European Great Powers, 1815–1939; Some Evidence' *American Journal of Political Science* 32 (3) Sept. 1988 pp.241–75.

Muromcew, C. 'Soviet Negotiating Behaviour' (Washington, DC; State Department Bulletin; 1977) pp.6–14.

Newcombe, A.G. and B. Stolfi 'Unusual Patterns in International Interactions' in A.G. Newcombe (ed.) 'GRIT 2' *Canadian Peace Research Reviews* VIII (2) February 1979.

Nottingham, L. *Resistance to Conflict De-Escalation; The Impact of the Revolution on Iranian Behaviour in the Iran–Iraq War* Unpublished M.A. Dissertation (Department of International Affairs; Carleton University; Ottawa; 1994).

Organski, A.F.K. *World Politics* 2nd ed. (New York; Alfred Knopf; 1968).

Osgood, C. *An Alternative to War or Surrender* (Urbana, Ill.; University of Illinois Press; 1962).

Osgood, C. 'GRIT for MBFR' in A.G. Newcombe (ed.) 'GRIT 1 and 2' *Canadian Peace Research Reviews* VIII (2) February 1979.

Osgood, C. 'The GRIT Strategy' *Bulletin of the Atomic Scientists* May 1980 pp.58–60.

Ott, M. 'Mediation as a Method of Conflict Resolution: Two cases' *International Organisation* 26(4) Autumn 1972 pp.595–618.

Parks, C.D., R.F. Henager and S.D. Scamahorn 'Trust and Reactions to Messages of Intent in Social Dilemmas' *Journal of Conflict Resolution* 40 (1) March 1996 pp.134–51.

Parloff, M.B. and J.H. Handlon 'The Influence of Criticalness on Problem Solving in Dyads' *Psychiatry* 27 (1) 1964 pp.17–27.

Pincen, T. *Intermediaries in International Conflict* (Princeton, NJ; Princeton University Press; 1992).

Pruitt, D.G. 'Definition of the Situation as a Determinant of International Action' in H.C.Kelman (ed.) *International Behaviour* (New York; Holt, Rhinehart and Winston; 1965).

Pruitt, D.G. *Negotiation Behaviour* (New York; Academic Press; 1981).

Pruitt, D.G. 'Determinants of Short-Term and Long-term Success on Mediation' in S.Worchel and J.A. Simpson (eds.) *Conflict Between Peoples and Groups; Causes, Proceses and Resolutions* (Chicago; Nelson Hall; 1993).

Pruitt, D.G. 'Ripeness Theory and the Oslo Talks' *International Negotiation* 2 (2) 1997 pp.237–50.

Pruitt, D.G and J.Z. Rubin *Social Conflict: Escalation Stalemate and Settlement* 1st edn. (New York; Random House; 1985).

Putnam, R.D. 'Diplomacy and Domestic Politics; The Logic of Two Level Games' in P.B. Evans *et al.* (eds.) *Double-Edged Diplomacy; International Bargaining and Domestic Politics* (Berkeley, CA; University of California Press; 1993).

Quandt, W.B. *Decade of Decisions* (Berkeley, CA.; University of California Press; 1977).

Quandt, W.B. *Camp David; Peacemaking and Politics* (Washington DC; The Brookings Institute; 1986).

Rabin, Y. *The Rabin Memoirs*. (Boston; Little, Brown; 1979).

Rafael, G. *Destination Peace* (New York; Stein and Day; 1981).

Ramberg, B. (ed.) *Arms Control Without Negotiation* (Boulder, Co, Lynne Reinner; 1993).

Randle, R. *The Origins of Peace* (New York; Free Press; 1973).

Rangarajan, L.N. *The Limitations of Conflict; A Theory of Bargaining and Negotiation* (New York; St Martins Press; 1985).

Riker, W.H. 'The Nature of Trust' in J.T. Tedeschi (ed.) *Perspectives of Social Power* (Chicago; Aldine Press; 1974).

Roby, T.B. 'Commitment' *Behavioural Science* 5 (3) July 1960 pp.253–64.

Rokeach, M. *The Open and Closed Mind* (New York; Basic Books; 1960).

Rosenau, J.N. *Turbulence in World Politics* (Princeton, NJ; Princeton University Press; 1990).

Ross, L. 'The Intuitive Psychologist and his Shortcomings; Distortions in the Attribution Process' in L. Berkowitz (ed.) *Advances in Experimental Social Psychology* Vol.10 (New York; Academic Press; 1977) pp.174–77.

Ross, L. and C. Stillinger 'Barriers to Conflict Resolution' *Negotiation Journal* 7 (4) October 1991 pp.389–404.

Rotter, J.B. 'Generalised Expectancies for Interpersonal Trust' *American Psychologist* 26 (5) May 1971 pp.443–52.

Rubin, J.Z. and B.R. Brown *The Social Psychology of Bargaining and Negotiation* (New York; Academic Press; 1975).

Rubin, J.Z., D.G. Pruitt and S.H.Kim *Social Conflict; Escalation, Stalemate and Settlement* 2nd ed. (New York; McGraw Hill; 1994).

Sadat, Anwar al *In Search of Identity.* (New York; Harper and Row; 1978).

Schelling, T.C. *The Strategy of Conflict* (New York; Oxford University Press; 1960).

Schelling, T.C. *Arms and Influence* (New Haven, Yale University Press; 1966).

Sigal, L. *Fighting to a Finish; The Politics of War Termination in the United States and Japan, 1945* (Ithaca; Cornell University Press; 1988).

Simon, L., J. Greenberg and J. Brehm 'Trivialisation; The Forgotten Mode of Dissonance Reduction' *Journal of Personality and Social Psychology* 68 (2) February 1995 pp.247–60.

Simonson, I. and B.M. Staw 'Deescalation Strategies; A Comparison of Techniques for Reducing Commitment to Losing Courses of Action' *Journal of Applied Psychology* August 1992 77 (4) pp.419–26.

Sivard, R.L. *World Military and Social Expenditures* (Leesburg, VA; WMSE Publications; 1978).

Siverson, R.M. and R.A. Miller 'The Escalation of Disputes to War' *International Interactions* 19 (1–2) 1993 pp.77–97.

Siverson, R.M. and M. Tennefoss 'Power, Alliance and the Escalation of International Conflict 1815–1965' *American Political Science Review* 78 (4) December 1984 pp.1057–69.

Snyder, Glenn H. 'Crisis Bargaining' Chap. 10 in C.F. Hermann (ed.) *International Crises; Insights from Behavioural Research* (New York; Free Press;1972).

Sobel, Lester A.(ed.) *Peace-Making in the Middle East* (New York; Facts on File Inc.; 1980).

Staw, B.M. 'Knee Deep in the Big Muddy' *Organisational Behaviour and Human Performance* 16 (1) August 1976 pp.27–44.

Staw, B.M. and J. Ross 'Behaviour in Escalation Situations' *Research in Organisational Behaviour* Vol.9 (Greenwich, CT; JAI Press; 1987) pp.39–78.

Stein, J.G. 'The Political Economy of Security Agreements; The Linked Costs of Failure at Camp David' in P.B. Evans *et al.* (eds.) *Double Edged Diplomacy* (Berkeley, CA; University of California Press; 1993) pp.77–101.

Stoll, R.J. and W. McAndrew 'Negotiating Strategic Arms Control, 1969–79' *Journal of Conflict Resolution* 30 (2) June 1986 pp.315–26.

Strickland, L.H. 'Surveillance and Trust' *Journal of Personality* 28 (2) 1958 pp.200–15.

Swinth, R.L. 'The Establishment of a Trust Relationship' *Journal of Conflict Resolution* XI (3) Sept.1967 pp.335–44.

Taylor, S.E. 'The Availability Bias in Social Perception and Interaction' in D. Kahneman, P. Slovic and A. Tversky (eds.) *Judgement Under Uncertainty; Heuristics and Biases* (Cambridge; Cambridge University Press; 1982).

Teger, A. *Too Much Invested to Quit* (New York; Pergamon Press; 1980).

Thaler, R.H. 'Towards a Positive Theory of Consumer Choice' *Journal of Economic Behaviour and Organisation* I (1) 1980 pp.39–60.

Thies, W.J. *When Governments Collide; Coercion and Diplomacy in the Vietnam Conflict 1964–68* (Berkeley, CA; University of California Press; 1980).

Tomlin, B.W. 'The Stages of Pre-Negotiation; The Decision to Negotiate North American Free Trade' Chap. 2 in J.G. Stein (ed.) *Getting to the Table* (Baltimore, Johns Hopkins Press; 1989) pp.18–43.

Tuchman, B.W. *The March of Folly; From Troy to Vietnam* (London; Michael Joseph; 1984).

Tullock, G. 'The Prisoners Dilemma and Mutual Trust' *Ethics* 77 (3) April 1967 pp.229–30.

Upton, A. *Finland; 1939–40* (Newark; University of Delaware Press; 1979).

Vance, Cyrus *Hard Choices* (New York; Simon and Schuster; 1983).

Wall, J.A. and A. Lynn 'Mediation; A Current Review' *Journal of Conflict Resolution* 37 (1) March 1993 pp.160–94.

Weiner, B. '"Spontaneous" Causal Thinking' *Psychological Bulletin* 97 (1) January 1985 pp.74–84.

Weinstein, E. and P. Deutschberger 'Some Dimensions of Altercasting' *Sociometry* 26 (4) 1963 pp.254–66.

Weinstein, F.B. 'The Concept of Commitment in International Relations' *Journal of Conflict Resolution* XIII (1) March 1969 pp.39–56.

Weizman, E. *The Battle For Peace* (Toronto; Bantam Books; 1981).

White, R.K. *Nobody Wanted War* (New York; Doubleday; 1970).

Whyte, G. 'Escalating Commitment in Individual and Group Decision-making; A Prospect Theory Approach' *Organisational Behaviour and Human Decision Processes* 54 (3) April 1993 pp.430–55.

Worchel, P. 'Trust and Distrust' in W.G. Austin and S. Worchel (eds.) *The Social Psychology of Intergroup Relations* (San Francisco; Wadsworth/Brooks-Cole; 1979) pp.174–87.

Yarrow, C.H. *Quaker Experiences in International Conciliation* (New Haven; Yale University Press; 1978).

Yourcenar, M. *Memoirs of Hadrian* (London; Secker and Warburg; 1955).

Zand, D.E. 'Trust and Managerial Problem Solving' *Administrative Science Quarterly* 17 (2) June 1972 pp.229–39.

Zartman, I.W. *Ripe for Resolution; Conflict and Intervention in Africa* (New York; Oxford University Press; 1985).

Index